AI Integration Into Andragogical Education

Viktor Wang
California State University, San Bernardino, USA

IGI Global
Scientific Publishing
Publishing Tomorrow's Research Today

Vice President of Editorial Melissa Wagner
Managing Editor of Acquisitions Mikaela Felty
Managing Editor of Book Development Jocelynn Hessler
Production Manager Mike Brehm
Cover Design Phillip Shickler

Published in the United States of America by
IGI Global Scientific Publishing
701 East Chocolate Avenue
Hershey, PA, 17033, USA
Tel: 717-533-8845
Fax: 717-533-8661
Website: https://www.igi-global.com E-mail: cust@igi-global.com

Library of Congress Cataloging-in-Publication Data

Names: Wang, Viktor editor
Title: AI integration into andragogical education / Edited by Viktor Wang.
Description: Hershey, PA : IGI Global, [2025] | Includes bibliographical references and index. | Summary: "This anthology sheds light on how AI is redefining educational philosophies, practices, and policies, specifically tailored to adult learners. As the educational landscape continues to evolve, understanding AI's role becomes imperative for educators, administrators, and policymakers alike"-- Provided by publisher.
Identifiers: LCCN 2024053042 (print) | LCCN 2024053043 (ebook) | ISBN 9798337305028 hardcover | ISBN 9798337305035 paperback | ISBN 9798337305042 ebook
Subjects: LCSH: Adult learning. | Artificial intelligence--Educational applications. | Education, Higher--Effect of technological innovations on.
Classification: LCC LC5225.L42 .A42 2025 (print) | LCC LC5225.L42 (ebook) | DDC 374/.133463--dc23/eng/20250310
LC record available at https://lccn.loc.gov/2024053042
LC ebook record available at https://lccn.loc.gov/2024053043

British Cataloguing in Publication Data
A Cataloguing in Publication record for this book is available from the British Library.

Table of Contents

Detailed Table of Contents

AI's role in higher education is multifaceted, influencing how teachers perceive and implement their teaching philosophies. Teachers who embrace AI tools may develop dispositions that value data-driven decision-making, continuous assessment, and the customization of instruction to meet diverse student needs. Furthermore, AI can reinforce a philosophy of lifelong learning among educators as they continually adapt to new technologies and methodologies. This ongoing professional development shapes teaching dispositions open to innovation, reflective practice, and a collaborative learning community. The authors assert that as AI becomes more embedded in educational practices, it transforms teaching philosophies and reshapes educators' fundamental dispositions, aligning them more closely with modern, technology-enhanced teaching philosophies.

This chapter explores the transformative impact of Artificial Intelligence (AI) on adult education, drawing on the foundational work of Malcolm Knowles, who emphasized the necessity for adaptive and self-directed learning practices. It examines the rapid technological advancements since Knowles' time, highlighting how modern AI technologies, particularly Generative AI, are reshaping the landscape of adult education. By aligning AI with andragogical principles, educators can enhance the learning experience while addressing potential challenges such as algorithmic bias and inequity. The chapter is structured into three sections: the first explores AI-based learning science and its congruence with Knowles' principles; the second assesses the evolving nature of andragogy in the digital era; and the third projects future pathways for integrating AI in adult learning, emphasizing the implications for education delivery and knowledge production

This chapter draws from the analysis of the body of research and literature already in existence that offers an overview of artificial intelligence (AI) applications in higher education, focusing on its integration in reshaping teaching and learning dynamics by facilitating personalized and compelling learning experiences. Applying the literature review, the chapter explores AI's role with intelligent learning tools proving crucial in improving user intent to use. The chapter looks at how AI has developed in educational contexts, looks at different ways that AI is used in teaching and learning, and discusses the advantages and disadvantages of integrating AI. The chapter provides ideas on AI's influence on educational paradigms and highlights its potential to revolutionize learning and teaching processes.

This chapter examines the integration of artificial intelligence (AI) and andragogy in higher education, focusing on how adult learning principles can guide the ethical use of AI technologies. It provides an overview of andragogical principles, discusses AI's impact on adult learning, and presents strategies for aligning AI with andragogical approaches. Key areas include enhancing self-directed learning, supporting experiential and problem-centered learning, and fostering critical thinking with AI. The chapter explores practical implementation strategies, educator training, and ethical considerations such as data privacy and algorithmic bias. It also examines emerging AI technologies and their potential impact on andragogy, identifies areas for further research, and discusses preparing adult education for an AI-enhanced future. Throughout, the importance of balancing technological innovation with sound andragogical practices is emphasized, providing insights for educators, administrators, and policymakers in higher education.

This chapter focuses on the impact artificial intelligence is having on higher education, specifically in academic research and writing, and explores an array of AI tools tailored to enhance academic endeavors, providing insights into their significance, purpose, and impact within higher education settings. AI tools can greatly speed up the process for academic researchers in gathering, analyzing and presenting research data. In addition, the chapter reviews the use of AI tools for writing, editing, paraphrasing, and summarizing literature and recommends numerous tools for use. The potential organizational challenges are also addressed such as faculty resistance, the impact to technology support, and the ethics related to academic integrity associated with the use of artificial intelligence for both students and faculty. Recommendations for future research and a call to educators for next steps are included.

This chapter examines the transformative impact of Artificial Intelligence (AI) on education and workforce preparation. It delves into how AI technologies are redefining teaching methods, learning experiences, and the skillsets necessary in today's job market. The chapter explores AI's potential to personalize learning, boost student engagement, and develop critical thinking and problem-solving skills. It also addresses the challenges and opportunities of integrating AI into education, including the need for comprehensive educator training, AI literacy programs, and adaptive regulatory frameworks. Ethical considerations related to AI use in educational settings are discussed. Emphasizing the importance of balancing technological advancement with core educational values, the chapter advocates for approaches that nurture essential workforce skills while leveraging AI's capabilities. It concludes by underscoring the need for continued research and adaptation to ensure that AI integration prepares students for an AI-driven future while preserving the fundamental objectives of education.

Higher education and workplaces have expressed an increased need and priority for intercultural training to facilitate collaboration in a global workforce (World Economic Forum, 2023). This chapter proposes an andragogical approach to intercultural exploration using large language models (LLMs), specifically a generative AI (Gen AI) tool. This approach takes advantage of the inherent bias in these models to create customized case studies which are relatable for rich learner discussions. Researchers will discuss the supporting theory and provide examples on how educators can best use LLMs to support inclusive learning environments. The Researchers offer both a tested Gen AI case study template for learning activities and a LEAP (Launch, Experiment, Assess, and Ponder) workshop format available for execution.

This chapter explores the integration of Artificial Intelligence (AI) in higher education with an emphasis on pedagogy, instruction, and administration for student learning and achievement. The paradigm shift moved the focus from teacher-centered to learner-centered systems involving AI-powered tools for personalized learning systems such as intelligent tutoring, adaptive learning systems, natural language processing (NLP), machine learning (ML), robotics, automated grading, and feedback to offer enhanced learning opportunities for teaching and learning. However, the AI technological transformation presented challenges in the form of ethical considerations, algorithm biases, curriculum development, lack of infrastructure, and accessibility issues. The chapter discusses the history and evolution of AI, AI technologies in higher education, enhancing pedagogy with AI in higher education, faculty support, and administrative efficiency. Additionally, it addresses the ethical considerations and future trends for AI adoption in higher education.

Foreword 1

Integrating AI into Pedagogical and Andragogical Education, edited by Viktor Wang, is a groundbreaking anthology that delves into one of the most transformative developments in modern education: the integration of Artificial Intelligence (AI) into teaching and learning practices. The contributors of this book have masterfully compiled a comprehensive exploration that spans the breadth of education, from K-12 to higher education and adult learning, offering a nuanced understanding of how AI is reshaping educational philosophies, practices, and policies.

Each chapter in this anthology is a testament to the critical role AI plays in the evolution of education. Viktor Wang and Linda Ellington's examination of AI's influence on teaching philosophies in higher education sets a profound tone, emphasizing the alignment of AI with lifelong learning principles and the continuous evolution of educators. Geraldine Torrisi-Steele's focus on the transformative role of AI for students highlights the revolutionary impact of AI-driven tools on learning experiences and student outcomes.

The anthology's strength lies in its balanced perspective, addressing both the opportunities and challenges that come with AI integration. Seema Yadav's exploration of AI's potential to transform education for diverse learners, coupled with insights into the necessity of addressing bias and ensuring equity, is particularly timely and crucial. Similarly, Praveen K. Dubey's discussion on personalized learning provides a theoretical framework that is invaluable for educators and researchers striving to maximize student engagement and achievement in AI-enabled classrooms.

As the book progresses into the realm of adult education, Valerie A. Storey and Amiee Wagner's analysis of AI's alignment with andragogical principles offers a forward-looking perspective that is both insightful and practical. The cultural considerations presented by Andrew Schenck, particularly in Confucian contexts, add a critical layer of understanding, reminding us that AI integration is not a one-size-fits-all approach.

The concluding chapters, particularly the comprehensive reflections by Greg Kaiser and Sue Kaiser, bring the anthology full circle by synthesizing the collective insights into a cohesive vision for the future of education. The inclusion of case studies and success stories serves not only as an inspiration but also as a practical guide for educators, policymakers, and researchers.

This anthology is an essential resource for anyone committed to advancing education through the thoughtful integration of AI. The contributors have offered a diverse and thorough examination of the opportunities and challenges that accompany this technological revolution, emphasizing the need for ethical and culturally responsive approaches. As we navigate the complexities of AI in education, *Integrating AI into Pedagogical and Andragogical Education* stands out as a critical guide for enhancing educational practices in the 21st century.

Viktor Wang and the Editorial Advisory Board deserve commendation for their dedication to this important work. This book is not just a collection of essays; it is a beacon of insight and innovation, guiding us towards a future where AI and education intersect to create more effective, inclusive, and dynamic learning environments.

William Rothwell
Penn State University, USA

Foreword 2

In the Call for Chapters for this latest collaboration with educationists and researchers in the field of education, *Integrating AI into Pedagogical and Andragogical Education*, Dr. Wang echoes the enthusiasm of many about Artificial Intelligence (AI). AI is described as a revolutionary field of computer science that focuses on creating machines and systems that can mimic human-like thinking, learning, and problem-solving. AI is, indeed, breaking ground in the field of Adult Education in which we toil. AI is sure to have an impact on our praxis as we now seek to enrich the foundations of our profession by planting these AI seedlings into our education terrain. AI certainly has the potential to revolutionize our traditional teaching and learning methods. Equally certain is a solemn concern about what a transformation of our teaching and learning approaches should look like. AI's function in the education landscape is generally understood as a technology that allows machines to execute tasks that have traditionally required human cognition. Hence, it is a matter of great concern that ought to be seriously vetted *by and with* the very human stakeholders who will nurture and harvest what exactly will grow from this new AI plant in our midst, given its promise to improve our praxis. Will we purposefully cultivate this AI plant *or* allow it to become an invasive species in our field? The collection of chapters in this book brings us myriad thoughts to analyze; and it gives us a robust opportunity to clarify our assumptions, hopes, and fears about this new plant taking root in our field.

In the words of Kenneth Gergen (2009), "As we confront the future of our professional endeavors, we tend to rely with confidence on longstanding and widely honored assumptions about the world and ourselves" (p. x). Yet, in the 19 chapters, patterns of themes emerge from the presented perspectives, which nudge us rather serendipitously to also find intersections among the authors' standpoints. Within the context of values and principles of instructional approaches, applied by the authors to the utilization of AI, we can uncover and question the prevailing fundamental *paradigmatic assumptions* (Brookfield, 1995, 2017) about *andragogy v. pedagogy* --- perhaps our own as much as those of our author colleagues here. Consequently, in addition to providing us solid insights into instructional practices to enhance our repertoire of learning activities, we may clarify the essential differences and intended purposes of these two *...gogies*. Typically, we simply drew the line at teaching adults versus teaching children to define the two theories. Yet, within the chapters of this collection, we also uncover that, by clarifying the appropriate use of instructional methods and that of tools like AI, we can more succinctly tailor the teaching to the learning tasks at hand. With that I mean, we can select and apply instructional methods that align to the readiness level of learners by moving back and forth along a metagogical spectrum of pedagogic *and* andragogic approaches (Strohschen 2011; 2014; Strohschen & Elazier, 2019; 2020). This refocuses our practices from an *either-or* approach toward (perhaps a truly) transforming praxis suitable for a 21st Century paradigm of lifelong and life wide learning (Römer, 2021).

Integrating AI into Pedagogical and Andragogical Education offers more than useful considerations about AI-based strategies, methods, and techniques. Showing us how to embrace AI in our teaching, the chapter themes center on principles of the *...gogies*, specific tools, students' skillset needs and personalized learning, contemporary socio-environmental changes and their influences on teaching methods, competence in curriculum design, and teacher training and development needs. And, remarkably, critical questions about the impact of AI on our education mission are included. Given this era of The Fourth Industrial Revolution (Wigmore, 2020), as educationists we *are* called upon to examine and spearhead appropriate changes for educating adults. We need to be prepared with the requisite knowledge, skills, and attitude to achieve our vision of improving the quality of life *for and with* students by means of education. *Integrating AI into Pedagogical and Andragogical Education* aids us in "...stretching our imaginations and dreams of possibility" (Gergen, 2009, p. x). This book is an essential resource for critical reflection on and development of our profession.

Gabriele Strohschen
DePaul University, USA

REFERENCES

Brookfield, S. (1995, 2017). *Becoming a critically reflective teacher*. John Wiley & Sons.

Gergen, K. (2009). Foreword. In G. Strohschen *The handbook of Blended Shore education: Adult Education Program Development and Delivery*. Springer Verlag International.

Römer, K. (2021, February 9). *It's time to embrace not just the lifelong but the life-wide dimension of learning*. [Blog]. https://thelifelonglearningblog.uil.unesco.org/2021/02/09/its-time-to-embrace-not-just-the-lifelong-but-the-life-wide-dimension-of-learning/

Strohschen, G. (2011). Teaching Adults across Cultures, Distance, and Learning Preferences: Universal Tools for the 21st Century. In Wang, V. X. (Ed.), *Encyclopedia of Information Communication and Adult Education Integration* (pp. 469–484). IGI Global. DOI: 10.4018/978-1-61692-906-0.ch028

Strohschen, G. (2014). Education Collaboration Development: A Blended Shore Education Approach to Sustainable Development. In Wang, V. X. (Ed.), *Handbook of Research on Transnational Higher Education* (pp. 512–525). IGI Global. DOI: 10.4018/978-1-4666-4458-8.ch026

Strohschen, G., & Elazier, K. (2019, November 25-26). The Metagogy Theorem: A Framework for Educating Adults. *International Forum of Teaching and Studies, 15*(1), 3-15.American Scholars Press.

Strohschen, G., & Elazier, K. (2020). Metagogy: Toward a Contemporary Adult Education Praxis. In Pushpanadham, K. (Ed.), *Teacher Education in the Global Era, Perspectives and Practices* (pp. C1–C2). Springer. DOI: 10.1007/978-981-15-4008-0_19

Wigmore, I. (2020). *Fourth Industrial Revolution. TechTarget.* https://www.techtarget.com/whatis/definition/fourth-industrial-revolution

Preface

Integrating Artificial Intelligence (AI) into education is far from a fleeting trend; it marks a significant shift reshaping teaching and learning as we know it. *AI Integration Into Andragogical Education* offers an in-depth exploration of this transformative era, focusing on higher education and lifelong learning. This anthology sheds light on how AI is redefining educational philosophies, practices, and policies, specifically tailored to adult learners. As the educational landscape continues to evolve, understanding AI's role becomes imperative for educators, administrators, and policymakers alike.

THE PARADIGM SHIFT IN EDUCATION

As we navigate this new educational paradigm, it is crucial to understand the profound impact AI has on teaching philosophies and educator dispositions, especially within higher education. The infusion of AI technologies challenges traditional pedagogical approaches and calls for a reevaluation of how we view teaching and learning. In Chapter 1, "Integrating AI into One's Teaching Philosophies and Dispositions in Higher Education," we delve into how AI fosters a shift toward data-driven decision-making, continuous assessment, and personalized instruction to meet diverse student needs. This foundational chapter underscores the necessity for educators to adapt their philosophies to align with the evolving demands of AI-enhanced education. It emphasizes the need for a growth mindset among educators, encouraging them to embrace technological advancements as tools for enriching the learning experience.

ALIGNING ANDRAGOGY WITH AI TECHNOLOGIES

Chapter 2, "Andragogy in the Age of AI: Transformative Pathways for Adult Education," examines how AI technologies align with andragogical principles. The chapter emphasizes the importance of a forward-thinking approach to AI integration while addressing pressing challenges such as algorithmic bias and equity in adult education. By reflecting on these challenges, we can ensure that AI serves to enhance accessibility and inclusivity, rather than perpetuating existing inequalities. This chapter advocates for the application of andragogical principles to facilitate adult learners' engagement with AI, ultimately leading to more personalized and relevant educational experiences.

EXPLORING THE POTENTIAL AND CHALLENGES OF AI

In Chapter 3, "Unleash AI into Higher Education: Why Not?", the advantages and disadvantages of AI integration are explored through a balanced review of the literature. This chapter assesses AI's transformative potential and its implications for teaching and learning dynamics in higher education. By critically examining the benefits of AI—such as improved efficiency and enhanced learning outcomes—alongside the risks—such as privacy concerns and over-reliance on technology—this chapter fosters a nuanced understanding of AI's role in education.

THEORETICAL FRAMEWORKS FOR ETHICAL INTEGRATION

Chapter 4, "Andragogy as a Theoretical Framework for AI Integration in Higher Education," provides a deep dive into how adult learning principles can inform the ethical and effective use of AI technologies. It offers a roadmap for educators and policymakers to balance innovation with sound pedagogical practices. The integration of andragogy and AI invites a rethinking of how educational experiences are designed, ensuring that they cater to the unique needs and preferences of adult learners. This chapter advocates for a collaborative approach, where educators and learners work together to co-create meaningful learning experiences that leverage AI capabilities.

RETHINKING SKILLS FOR THE MODERN WORKFORCE

The evolving role of AI in cultivating critical thinking and problem-solving skills is the focus of Chapter 5, "Are Critical Thinking and Problem-Solving Skills Enough to Help Prepare Students to Meet the Modern Workforce Demands with Artificial Intelligence?" This chapter challenges traditional skill sets in light of the growing influence of AI in the workforce, urging educators to rethink their approaches. As AI continues to transform various industries, educators must prioritize teaching adaptable skills that empower learners to thrive in an AI-driven job market.

ENHANCING RESEARCH AND WRITING THROUGH AI

In Chapter 6, "The AI Scholar: AI in Higher Education Research and Writing," the potential of AI to enhance students' research capabilities and writing skills is explored, opening up new avenues for academic inquiry and creative expression. This chapter highlights innovative tools that assist students in conducting research, organizing information, and improving their writing processes. By embracing these technologies, educators can foster a more collaborative and dynamic academic environment that encourages students to engage deeply with their subjects.

PROMOTING INTERCULTURAL UNDERSTANDING

Chapter 7, "Co-creating Intercultural Scenes with Gen AI Using a Case Study Framework," presents innovative methodologies for leveraging AI to promote intercultural understanding and collaboration within educational contexts. This chapter emphasizes the potential of AI to facilitate cross-cultural communication and foster global perspectives among learners. By exploring real-world case studies, the chapter illustrates how AI can serve as a bridge, connecting diverse cultures and facilitating meaningful exchanges that enrich the learning experience.

ENHANCING PEDAGOGY AND ADMINISTRATION

Chapter 8, "Integrating Artificial Intelligence in Higher Education: Enhancing Pedagogy, Instruction, and Administration," discusses the multifaceted roles AI can play in enriching pedagogical strategies, streamlining administrative tasks, and enhancing student engagement. This chapter provides practical insights on how educators can leverage AI tools to create more efficient and effective learning environments. From personalized learning experiences to data-driven decision-making in administrative processes, AI's potential to transform higher education is significant.

ADDRESSING ETHICAL CONCERNS

The ethical implications of AI integration take center stage in Chapter 9, "AI and the Humans in Higher Education," which calls for a conscientious approach to deploying AI in education. This chapter urges educators to consider the risks and benefits involved in AI implementation, highlighting the need for ethical guidelines and policies to govern AI use in educational settings. By fostering a culture of ethical awareness, educators can navigate the complexities of AI integration while safeguarding the interests of their students.

ETHICS AND EQUITY IN AI-DRIVEN EDUCATION

Chapter 10, "Ethics and Equity in AI-Driven Education," explores the critical ethical considerations and challenges that arise as artificial intelligence becomes increasingly integrated into educational systems. This chapter examines issues such as data privacy, bias in AI algorithms, and the transparency of AI decision-making processes, emphasizing the need for ethical frameworks to guide the use of AI in education. It also addresses the importance of ensuring equity in access to AI tools and resources, particularly for underserved and marginalized student populations. By highlighting the ethical implications of AI in education, this chapter underscores the responsibility of educators, developers, and policymakers to ensure that AI technologies are used in ways that promote fairness, inclusivity, and student well-being.

FOSTERING SOCIAL JUSTICE THROUGH AI

In Chapter 11, "Revolutionizing CTE: AI-Driven Andragogical Practices for Social Justice in Urban Education," the discussion focuses on how AI can be harnessed to promote social justice in Career and Technical Education (CTE), particularly within underserved urban communities. This chapter highlights the transformative potential of AI to address systemic inequalities in education and provide equitable opportunities for all learners. By emphasizing social justice, educators can leverage AI to create pathways for marginalized populations, empowering them to succeed in an increasingly competitive landscape.

FUTURE DIRECTIONS FOR AI IN EDUCATION

Finally, Chapter 12, "AI in Education: Reflections and Future Directions for Pedagogical and Andragogical Integration," synthesizes key insights from the anthology and offers a forward-looking perspective on the future of AI in education. This chapter encourages stakeholders to embrace AI's transformative potential while remaining vigilant about the ethical considerations that accompany its integration. By fostering a culture of continuous reflection and adaptation, educators can ensure that AI serves as a catalyst for positive change in education.

ACKNOWLEDGMENTS

I extend my deepest gratitude to all the contributors for their invaluable insights and to the Editorial Advisory Board for their unwavering support. Together, we hope this book serves as an essential resource for educators, administrators, and policymakers dedicated to advancing education through the thoughtful integration of AI.

EDITORIAL ADVISORY BOARD

CONCLUSION

This collection presents a comprehensive examination of AI's integration into education, illuminating both the opportunities and challenges of this technological revolution. Each chapter provides unique insights into the critical importance of thoughtful, ethical, and culturally responsive approaches to AI adoption in educational contexts. Through this exploration, we aim to inspire educators, administrators, and policymakers to harness the immense potential of AI to enhance educational practices. As we embark on this journey into the future of education, let us commit to leveraging AI not only as a tool for improvement but as a means of creating inclusive, equitable, and transformative learning experiences for all.

Viktor Wang
California State University, San Bernardino, USA
October 18, 2024

Chapter 1
Integrating AI Into One's Teaching Philosophies and Dispositions in Higher Education

Viktor Wang
https://orcid.org/0000-0001-9557-0054
California State University, San Bernardino, USA

Linda Ellington
https://orcid.org/0000-0002-7697-056X
Southern New Hampshire University, USA

ABSTRACT

AI's role in higher education is multifaceted, influencing how teachers perceive and implement their teaching philosophies. Teachers who embrace AI tools may develop dispositions that value data-driven decision-making, continuous assessment, and the customization of instruction to meet diverse student needs. Furthermore, AI can reinforce a philosophy of lifelong learning among educators as they continually adapt to new technologies and methodologies. This ongoing professional development shapes teaching dispositions open to innovation, reflective practice, and a collaborative learning community. The authors assert that as AI becomes more embedded in educational practices, it transforms teaching philosophies and reshapes educators' fundamental dispositions, aligning them more closely with modern, technology-enhanced teaching philosophies.

DOI: 10.4018/979-8-3373-0502-8.ch001

INTRODUCTION

As the integration of AI in higher education continues to evolve, andragogical approaches are fundamentally altering. Educators face the challenge of learning to use AI technologies and effectively incorporating AI into their curricula. Understanding the advantages of AI is pivotal for teachers to fully embrace and utilize AI tools in their instructional strategies (Kim & Kim, 2022). Shared values of personalization, adaptability, ethical responsibility, enhancement of human capabilities, and a commitment to innovative educational practices characterize the intersection of AI philosophy and teaching philosophy. Educators can integrate AI philosophies into the teaching philosophies by finding common ground in these areas, leading to more effective and enriching student educational experiences.

Within higher education, the integration of AI in learning is circumscribed by adult learning and the frame of andragogical approaches. Adults bring a store of prior experiences to the learning situation and hold expectations and motivations different from those of young learners. Adult learners have developed a mature view of self-responsibility for their learning; they expect meaningful, practical, and rewarding learning in their life situations. They bring with them 'habitual' ways of thinking developed through their interactions with others and social norms (Mezirow, 1991). Subsequently, transformative and emancipatory learning is at the heart of adult education. Andragogy and transformative learning principles are synergistic, guiding adult learners to solve problems with applicable learning resources and supporting self-directedness and problem-solving (Torrisi-Steele & Carim, 2019). Hence, to effectively implement transformative learning, adult educators require more than knowledge of the principles of adult learning and transformative learning. Embedded in context, education practice results from the interplay of situational factors intrinsic to learners and teachers. Factors intrinsic to learners include learner needs, preferences, and expectations. Factors intrinsic to the teacher include teacher philosophy, beliefs, expectations, and preferences. Situational factors may include the nature of the discipline and even the attributes of the physical environment (e.g., availability of resources, institutional factors). In this chapter, the authors argue that it is important for educators to be consciously aware of the factors that shape their practice. The authors also say these factors necessitate a contextual philosophy upon which practice is realized. Notably, the contextual philosophy must be dynamic and should change in consonance with variations as learning situations change. The changes now include the integration of AI into adult educators' teaching philosophy, which is a complex process that requires careful consideration of its potential benefits and challenges. The discussion begins with considering adult learners, adult education, teaching philosophies, and the connection to artificial intelligence ideology.

LEARNING THEORIES AND AI

Efficiently and effectively using artificial intelligence tools within the educational process will create a favorable AI intelligence-based learning landscape at higher education institutions characterized by efficiency, interactivity, inclusivity, innovation, and accessibility (Zadorina et al., 2024). A study by Zadorina et al. (2024) showed that artificial intelligence integrated into the educational process is used to design simulation-based activities, organize personalized learning, form specific skills among students, and automate the administrative process. AI enhances learning outcomes among students, increases efficiency, and provides greater accessibility to education during world chaos, such as the global pandemic, when the educational process can be disrupted. Some theories may seem quite ancient, yet we can connect them to AI during times of change.

Transformative Learning Theory

Adult education practice is framed by the principles of Mezirow's transformative learning (2000). However, adult educators must also incorporate two other dimensions into their practice: recognition of the complexity and dynamism of adult learning and the role of education philosophy, all at the intersection of AI.

Transformational learning theory becomes especially pertinent during world chaos, such as the global pandemic, when traditional educational processes are disrupted. Transformational learning is a profound process where individuals change their frames of reference by critically reflecting on their experiences, leading to new perspectives and behaviors. AI can play a significant role in this type of learning by providing personalized, adaptive, and interactive experiences that foster deep reflection and change. There are several ways AI can be integrated into transformational learning:

Intelligent Tutoring Systems: AI-powered tutors can provide personalized feedback, answer questions, and offer support anytime, helping learners explore concepts more deeply and from different perspectives.

Example: Virtual tutors that use natural language processing to converse with learners, guiding them through complex problem-solving processes.

Simulations and Virtual Reality: AI cameras enhance simulations and VR environments to create immersive learning experiences that allow learners to experiment with new behaviors and perspectives in a safe and controlled setting.

Example: VR simulations that use AI to adapt scenarios based on the learner's actions, providing real-time feedback and opportunities for reflection.

Collaborative Learning Platforms: AI can facilitate collaborative learning by connecting learners with peers and mentors, suggesting collaborative projects, and monitoring group dynamics to ensure productive interactions.

Example: AI-drive platforms that match learners with similar interests and goals, facilitating meaningful discussions and joint projects.

Content Curation and Recommendation: AI can curate and recommend content tailored to individual learning needs, interests, and goals. This helps learners discover new perspectives and resources they might not have found independently.

Example: AI-powered recommendation systems that suggest articles, videos, and courses based on the learner's current knowledge and learning objectives.

Emotional and Cognitive Support: AI can monitor learners' emotional and cognitive states, providing support and interventions when needed. This helps maintain motivation and engagement, which are crucial for transformational learning.

Example: AI-based systems that detect frustration or confusion and offer encouragement, additional resources, or breaks to help learners stay on track.

Facilitating Critical Thinking: AI can present scenarios and questions that challenge learners' beliefs and assumptions, encouraging them to think critically and consider alternative viewpoints.

Example: AI-driven debate platforms that simulate discussions with diverse perspectives, prompting learners to evaluate and defend their positions critically.

Lifelong Learning Companions: AI can act as lifelong learning companions, helping individuals continuously reflect on their experiences, set new learning goals, and stay updated with relevant knowledge.

Example: Personal AI assistants that track learning progress over time, suggest new learning opportunities, and help set and achieve long-term learning goals.

AI benefits a teaching philosophy about transformative learning theory by providing tools that enhance the core principles of this educational approach.

Adult education practice is framed by the principles of Mezirow's transformative learning and Knowles' adult learning theory (1975). However, adult educators must also incorporate two other dimensions into their practice: recognition of the complexity and dynamism of adult learning and the role of education philosophy, all at the intersection of AI. The AI competencies that learners should possess, mainly those without a computer science background ("non-experts), are solving problems, reasoning, making decisions, perceiving, and acting. They can achieve this learning in association with teachers who deliver the content to students using AI-based technologies, such as cloud computing to students in a format and form suitable for various student needs (Kabudi et al., 2021). In other words, the AI and teachers can work together to create the best delivery method for students with maximum positive outcomes. The benefits of using AI or delivering educational content include providing individualized and customized learning and universal access for all students who speak different languages or have some disability, such as visual or hearing impairment. Thus, it can be argued that AI-based education delivery is more learner-centric than the traditional educational delivery method.

Complexity And Dynamism of Adult Learning

Human learning at any age is a complex process. However, because of life experiences and often demanding personal situations and responsibilities, learning as an adult is much more complicated than learning at a young age. Many more social and economic factors come into play when teaching adults than children. There is much greater variability among adult learners than there is among child learners. Furthermore, adult educators must be agile, constantly anticipating, and responsive to changing circumstances, including AI-based teaching in all aspects of educating learners. The adult learner is caught up in *liquid modernity*, "the complex sociocultural-economic-political-technological change in a global environment, and is "the center of new societal demands" (Nicolaides & Marsick, 2016, pp. 9-11). Understanding and considering this complexity is foundational to successful adult education practices (Nicolaides & Marsick, 2016). Adult educators' understanding of the complexity of the adult learner's profile is as important as their knowledge of the subject matter they teach (Wang, 2003).

Equipped with an understanding of andragogy and sensitivity to the complexity and dynamism of adult learning, andragogical educators will have a solid basis for reflecting on and designing learning practices suited to adult education. However, as is well documented, teaching practices acquire much of their form because of the teacher's beliefs or philosophy about learners, the purpose of education, and the role of the teacher. Although a teacher's philosophy is personal, it likely embodies recognizable elements of the established philosophical perspectives in education and adult education frameworks. In addition to an understanding of andragogy and sensitivity and awareness of the complexity of adult learning, it is equally important for adult educators to be aware of the philosophical perspectives in their practice.

PHILOSOPHICAL PERSPECTIVES IN ADULT EDUCATION

Despite some variation in adult education frameworks, the philosophical perspectives guiding adult education (see, for example, Elias & Merriam, 1995; Tisdell & Taylor, 2000) can be categorized as liberalism, progressivism, behaviorism, humanism, and critical philosophy. Different aims of adult education are implicit in each philosophical perspective, including AI ideology.

From a liberal perspective, adult education aims to acquire knowledge but from a rational perspective. Critical thinking and the development of moral citizens are goals of education. *Liberalism* has its roots in the Greek philosophers and the Enlightenment philosophers such as Locke and Kant. The product of a liberal education is a well-rounded person. Until recently, liberalism informed higher education, and it still does in countries where universities are not seen as job-training institutions. In the U.S., when people refer to a "liberal arts college," they talk about the institution where students receive a broad humanities, social sciences, and arts background.

While a broad background in humanities, social sciences, and the arts is essential in a liberal education, the demand for education that prepares people for work in an industrial society spawned *progressivism.* Progressivism is founded on pragmatism, which values practical experience over abstract and theoretical concepts. Dewey (1938) popularized this philosophical perspective, and his influence remains strong today. When Dewey proposed that students (children and adults) learn best by doing things, this was a radical notion in a world where educational methods favored rote recall. Progressivism is the philosophical framework for adult vocational education, apprenticeship programs, skills-based training, and technical education, among other fields. Progressivism incorporates problem-solving and experiential learning; the teacher becomes a facilitator and mentor rather than an authority figure. Lindeman, who wrote *The Meaning of Adult Education* (1926), was strongly influenced by Dewey, and he applied the concepts to adult education. Much later, Knowles (1980) also drew on progressivism as he developed his andragogy model.

In an attempt to understand learning more objectively, an approach to understanding learning as stimulus-response was articulated in the *behaviorist* perspective. Skinner (1974) popularized and made a lasting contribution to behaviorism with his conceptualization of operant conditioning. Reinforced responses persist, even though the reinforcement may not be continuous. Responses that are ignored tend to fade away. Stimulus-response chains can be created to explain complicated learning sets (Kidd, 1973). Thorndike was one of the earliest behaviorists and co-author of Adult Learning (Thorndike et al., 1928). Skinner's work provided the foundation for programmed instruction, computer-assisted instruction, modularized instruction, competency-based education, and many strategies still used today in training and acquiring technical knowledge. However, as work evolves from skill-based routine tasks to AI-based jobs, practical behaviorism cannot be considered adequate in adult education and training (Torrisi-Steele & Carim, 2019). Kidd (1973) points out that the simplistic, mechanical nature of behaviorist learning theories was a "rebellion against sophisticated explanations of learning based on religious or philosophical interpretations and upon an assumption that an individual was possessed of certain properties and faculties" (p. 160).

Behaviorist learning theories are significantly influenced by the advancements in AI, such as:

Enhanced Data Collection and Analysis: AI technologies enable collecting and analyzing vast amounts of behavioral data. This aligns with behaviorist principles by providing detailed insights into how individuals respond to various stimuli, allowing for more precise shaping of desired behaviors.
Simulation and Gamification: AI-driven simulations and gamified learning environments provide immersive and interactive experiences that engage learners. These environments use behaviorist principles by offering rewards, challenges, and immediate feedback to reinforce learning behaviors.
Behavioral Analytics: AI provides sophisticated tools for behavioral analytics, allowing for the detailed examination of learning patterns. These analytics can identify which stimuli are most effective in promoting learning, helping to refine behaviorist strategies.
Scalable Behavior Modification: AI enables scaling behavior modification techniques to large groups of learners. This scalability ensures that behaviorist strategies can be applied consistently and effectively across diverse educational settings.
Continuous Improvement: AI systems can learn and improve over time by analyzing the effectiveness of different instructional strategies. This constant improvement aligns with behaviorist principles by refining reinforcement techniques based on empirical evidence of what works best.

Humanism, in stark contrast to the simplistic stimulus-response mechanism of behaviorism, is founded on the assumption that people can control their destiny, are inherently good, and have the potential for growth and development. The individual learner and the value of that person's experiences are central to humanism. This focus on the self does not mean that humanism highlights self-centeredness; individual development contributes to the good of all humanity. Maslow (1970) is generally considered the first to use humanistic psychology to understand learning. Maslow's widely recognized hierarchy of human needs posits that basic physical needs and the need for safety must precede further learning. Self-actualization—becoming all that an individual can become—is the goal of learning. Rogers (1969), a humanist psychologist who developed client-centered therapy as a model for working with clients, also influenced how adult learning is understood. Knowles (1975) applied Rogers' humanist philosophy to his conceptualization of self-directed learning and, more generally, andragogy. Humanist philosophy, centered on human values, dignity, and the potential for individual growth, is increasingly influenced by advancements in AI, such as:

Augmented Human Capabilities: AI enhances human potential by providing tools that improve decision-making, creativity, and productivity. This augmentation aligns with the humanist emphasis on personal development and achievement.

Redefining Human Identity: AI challenges traditional notions of what it means to be human. With machines performing tasks that once required human intelligence, humanists re-examine humans' unique societal qualities and roles.

Education and Learning: AI-powered tools personalize learning experiences, catering to individual needs and fostering lifelong learning, a core humanist principle. This technology democratizes access to knowledge and promotes intellectual growth.

Social Justice and Equality: AI has the potential to address social inequalities by providing solutions in healthcare, education, and economic opportunities. Humanist philosophy now includes advocating for the equitable distribution of AI benefits.

Future of Work: The rise of AI automation affects employment and the nature of work. Humanists are concerned with ensuring that technological progress benefits all, supporting policies that protect workers and promote meaningful employment.

Human-AI Collaboration: The interaction between humans and AI systems promotes a collaborative approach to problem-solving. This partnership underscores humanist values of cooperation, mutual respect, and collective progress.

By including various aspects of society and individual lives, AI is prompting a re-evaluation of humanist principles to ensure that technological advancements contribute positively to human flourishing.

Critical philosophy's tenets extend beyond the individual's confines to bring change to the broader social and political domains. Social change has long been a goal of adult education, from the founding of the Antigonish movement in Canada in the late 1920s to the founding of the Highland Folk School in the United States in 1932. Selman (1989) takes this back much further to the Corresponding Societies in Britain in the late 1700s, which were interested in political change, and the Adult Schools, which were dedicated to promoting literacy. At that time, adult educators interested in social reform were seen by many as agitators (promoting literacy empowered people in a time when the empowerment of the "masses" was seen as a threat). Freire's (1970) educational philosophy is based on the belief that the oppressed are unaware of their oppression and are, therefore, unable to overcome it. Freire's work has had a significant impact on adult education, one that continues to this day. Brookfield (2005) applied some of the central tenets of critical philosophy to adult education. He identified seven adult learning tasks drawn from critical theory. Critical theory is based on three core assumptions1) that Western democracies are unequal societies, 2) the inequities are reproduced in such a way as to seem normal and inevitable, and 3) the state of affairs can be understood and changed (Brookfield, 2005, p. viii). The latter is the goal of education from the critical philosophy perspective.

Critical philosophy, which involves the rigorous examination of assumptions, power, and structures in society, is impacted in several ways:

> *Epistemological Questions*: AI challenges traditional notions of knowledge and truth. Critical philosophers explore how AI systems generate and validate knowledge, questioning the reliability and biases inherent in algorithmic decision-making processes.
> *Ethical and Moral Issues*: AI raises significant ethical questions about autonomy, responsibility, and potential harm. Critical philosophers engage with these issues, debating the moral implications of AI deployment in various contexts and advocating for ethical frameworks that prioritize human well-being and justice.
> *Ideological Influence*: AI shapes the cultural and ideological landscape through algorithms that influence what content people see and engage with. Critical philosophy examines how these algorithms reinforce dominant ideologies, manipulate public opinion, and potentially undermine democratic processes.
> *Resistance and Empowerment*: While AI can be a tool of oppression, it also has the potential to empower individuals. Critical philosophy argues that AI can resist domination, promote social justice, and elevate marginalized voices while critically examining the implications and risks of such technologies.

Achieving understanding and change of the 'state of affairs' is achieved by seven learning tasks. Firstly, *challenging ideologies*—the ideologies embedded in language, social habits, and cultural forms. By "ideology," we mean those values and beliefs that are seen to be self-evident and true. Ideologies are hard to articulate or detect; they are deeply embedded and assumed to be beyond questioning. The second learning task is *contesting hegemony* (Brookfield, 2005). Hegemony occurs when people embrace conditions (and see them as usual) that serve those in power but work against their own best interests. For example, we value "hard work" to the point where individuals experience considerable stress, but we believe we are doing the right thing. Alternatively, people genuinely believe that possessing the products and using the services provided by corporations leads them to a happy and fulfilled life. The third learning task is *unmasking power*, which is how power plays a role in the relationships between teacher and learner or among learners. Power structures are often seen as a given; unmasking power involves recognizing how power is exercised in our own lives in everyday actions.

AI's connection to challenging ideologies in critical thinking theory is multifaceted. Mickunas (2023) emphasized the need for a critical understanding of AI, particularly its impact on vulnerable populations. This is echoed by Zhou (2022), who discussed the integration of AI into ideological and political education. However, Leung (2019) critiqued AI's reductionist approach to human thinking and highlighted the debate between human-centered and machine-centered approaches. It is necessary to strengthen mainstream ideology and to find effective ways to study the integration of information technology into the new age of philosophy of education, which can significantly improve the quality of teaching. This can potentially create new ideas confronting specific problems of thought (Zhou, 2022). Ideological teachers and policymakers must keep up with the all-around trend of the times, make full use of the benefits of intelligent new technologies and platforms, and further increase the attractiveness, attraction, persuasion, and contagion of ideological education (Zhou, 2022, p.1).

In the AI age, characterized by technology's pervasive influence, the intersection of critical thinking and artificial intelligence has become a topic of paramount importance (Moustaghfir & Brigui, 2024). In education, the pivotal question of our time is how to transform artificial intelligence from a perceived adversary to a valued ally, harnessing its strengths rather than viewing it as a threat to human thought. It is essential to navigate this into teaching philosophy. Instead of fearing the unknown, we invite students to become AI evaluators, decision-makers, and contributors. This aligns with the requirements of our digitally driven future and positions students as active participants in shaping the narrative of human-AI collaboration (Moustaghfir & Brigui, 2024).

Overcoming alienation is the fourth learning task of critical theory. We are alienated when we cannot be ourselves or be authentic in our lives and work. For example, a work context that is repetitive, structured, and bound tightly by policies and procedures that go against our values is alienating. A relationship (including a relationship between teacher and learner) in which we must hide our beliefs and assumptions to maintain the relationship is alienating. The adult learning task is to develop a sense of free agency and realize how social contexts shape our lives.

The impact of AI on students' feelings of alienation is complex and multifaceted. Li et al. (2023) found that while AI has increased learning opportunities and enthusiasm, it has also led to anxiety and a conflict between natural and intelligent feelings. This is consistent with Holian (1971), who found a close correspondence between alienation from university and society. Mahoney (2000) further identified neuroticism and low conscientiousness as corrections of alienation. Xu (2024) suggested that AI can positively impact academic achievement, potentially mitigating alienation. The authors collectively suggested that various individual and social factors influence AI's impact on alienation.

Learning liberation is the fifth adult learning task. One-dimensional thought focuses on improving current social systems rather than breaking away from them or replacing them with new ways of thinking. To do this, individuals need to separate themselves from the current social systems, such as the norms about what education can and should do, and see that system in a new way.

Reclaiming reason is the sixth task in a critical theory approach to adult learning. We consider reason appropriate for making technical decisions and working with instrumental knowledge but not for moral issues, values, and interpersonal relations. Our values and beliefs have become reified; they are not open to questioning. For example, we may believe that a person with more gadgets, a bigger house, or a higher income is happier than someone without those things. "Quality of life" indices are based on the possession of dishwashers and microwaves. Alternatively, we may assume that working-class people want to "improve themselves" by moving into a middle-class lifestyle. Reclaiming reason involves applying reason to examining how our lives have been shaped.

AI can enhance reasoning skills in adult learning, particularly in the context of critical theory. Susanto, et al. (2023) highlighted the role of AI in improving critical thinking and reasoning skills. Mickunas (2023) emphasized the importance of critically understanding AI and developing a reasoning framework. Using AI in learning environments can improve problem-solving and information analysis skills. According to Susanto et al. (2023), AI has a significant influence on the level of student's ability to argue, i.e., reason, which includes tools to gain knowledge, increase curiosity, own attention, own observation, and apply what is learned.

Finally, *practicing democracy* is the seventh learning task that Brookfield (2005) lists. Brookfield argues that the ideal of democracy is taken for granted. The word "democracy" is used in many ways and with so many agendas that it has no real meaning. What we need to do is to practice democracy through rational discourse, paying attention to ideal speech conditions, increasing our awareness of the contradictions inherent in the ideal of democracy, and paying attention to power structures related to diversity (for example, race, class, gender, ethnicity, and sexual orientation).

The use of AI in higher education can potentially enhance the practice of democracy in learning and teaching at the college level. Democratic principles in teaching can be supported by AI tools that provide personalized learning experiences (Bulathwela et al., 2021). AI systems can promote an open, transparent, and collaborative learning environment. Conversations are going on about how AI can empower access to education beyond political, cultural, language, geographical, and learning ability barriers. If correctly designed and deployed, AI tools could deliver in the long run on their potential of providing access to education beyond the political, cultural, geographical, and learning ability barriers and help create equitable lifelong learning schools of the future. The challenge is to design them to be a driver of equity and inclusion rather than a source of greater inequality of opportunity (Bulathwela et al., 2021, p. 6). Designing AI systems must provide equal opportunities for all, avoiding biases that could disadvantage certain groups. By focusing on fairness and inclusivity, AI can be a tool for positive social change instead of reinforcing disparities.

Depending on their beliefs and perspectives, adult educators may adopt different conceptions of adult learners. Educators prefer a humanistic approach to view adult learners as highly motivated and self-directed. From a humanistic perspective, adult learners assume responsibility for learning and self-development. In contrast, from a progressive philosophical perspective, educators may view adult learners as having unlimited potential for development through education. These progressive educators consider learner needs, interests, and experiences as key learning elements. On the other hand, educators who have adopted a behaviorist philosophy seek to provide an intense learning environment where learners take an active role in learning, practicing new behavior, and receiving feedback. Educators influenced by liberal philosophies of education may maintain that adult learners seek knowledge rather than information. In contrast, those with a radical perspective emphasize students' equality with their teacher in learning. In contemporary adult education, understanding the diversity and variability of adult learners may help adult educators identify the philosophies they need to adopt and adapt. An inappropriate philosophy, without question, will fail to serve the needs of tr. Ultimately, teachers can create a more supportive and effective learning environment that fosters personal and professional growth for all students by understanding and embracing the variability among adult learners.

CONTEXTUAL PHILOSOPHY

For any teacher, "acquiring a philosophy is powerful, in that it directs and influences a teacher's teaching practices in the classroom as well as how they perceive teaching and learning and the students around them" (Soccorsi, 2013, p. 21). Acquiring a philosophy is a reflective process in which the teacher considers their practices and the impact of those practices to become explicitly aware of their beliefs and values about learners, learning, the role of the teacher, and the purpose of education. Forming a philosophy is complicated as teachers reflect on their practices, ideally through their experiences and understanding of theoretical frameworks. While literature is rife with discussion of the importance of teaching philosophy and guidance on developing a teaching philosophy, the importance of contextual philosophy is neglected. It is acknowledged that philosophy should evolve (Soccorsi, 2013) but the importance of aligning philosophy to context is understated. Teachers are encouraged to develop a philosophy, and though it may incrementally evolve, they may cling to it, like a 'personal brand' or mantra, often partly decontextualized, and only requires refinement over time. The interaction of their philosophy with context is only 'hinted at' as part of any reflection on practices.

Teaching philosophy must fully embody the relationship between theory and practice if it is to be valid; philosophy must be inseparable from practice (Papadima, 2021). In adult education, where the learners are caught up in 'fluid modernity' (Nicolaides & Marsick, 2016) and highly diverse, the link between theory and practice means that a contextually adaptive, agile philosophy is imperative.

A contextually adapted philosophy means that adult educators must adjust their underlying belief systems in response to different contexts to assume the most appropriate roles for helping adult learners achieve transformation and emancipation. A contextually adapted philosophy will influence curriculum content, delivery methods, and communication with adult learners with different learning styles and personalities (for example, see Cranton, 2006). A contextually adapted philosophy may guide decisions and policy-setting (Merriam & Brockett, 1997). Above all, a contextually adapted philosophy helps define the role of adult educators by providing a conceptual framework for incorporation into their teaching methodologies. Understanding this complex, interactive process, educators often consistently embrace one philosophy or belief system without regard for the context of their practice or the characteristics of their learners. This is encouraged by leading adult educators (Knowles et al., 1998, 2011; Rogers, 1969), who argue that adult learning professionals should be humanistic and progressive. To conform to this approach, adult educators must assume the role of learning facilitators. However, what adult educators do in practice or what they must do in a specific context may conflict with these ideologies. Conflict between what adult educators do or must do in practice and the ideologies of humanism and progressivism arises because adult educators may fail to understand the relationship between a teacher's contextually adapted philosophy and a student's transformation and emancipation. Learning does not take place in isolation. Instead, it relates to adult educators' contextually adapted philosophy, situational roles, learners' preferences, and other factors. A contextual philosophy aligns adult educators' practice with the contemporary societal demands experienced by adult learners and enables practices adaptive to adult learners' diverse characteristics and needs. If it is now considered that transformative and emancipatory learning is possible only in context, then it is evident that education practice must be appropriate to the context. Philosophies must, therefore, also be contextual. Contextualized philosophies connect to teacher dispositions (the values, beliefs, attitudes, and other habits of mind). Dispositions translate into action, i.e., the teaching methods and teacher roles in education practice (Figure 1.0). As also depicted in Figure 1.0, the teaching method used by the adult educator is the result of the interaction between learner and teacher, which occurs within a situational context. The nature of the interactions is determined by how the learner's experiences, needs, motivations, and learning styles (influenced by the situational context, which is dynamic) interact with the teacher's philosophies. Aligning philosophies with the learner and situational contexts, teaching methods that effectively facilitate critical reflection will support transformative learning.

Figure 1. Disposition connected to philosophies and contextually adapted

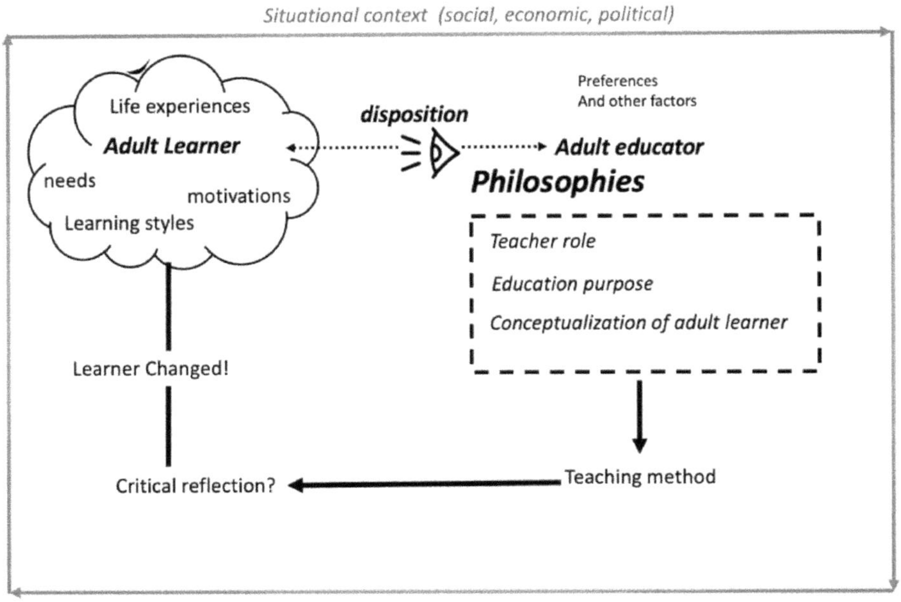

Philosophies the teacher holds influence how the teacher sees their role and what they see as the purpose of education. The beliefs or philosophies held by the teacher (along with preferences and other factors) shape understanding the learner's experiences, needs, motivations, and learning styles within the situational context (that includes broader society, institutional factors, etc.), and together with other factors, contribute to disposition, which in turn dictates action. Note the cyclic arrows around the model. The intent here is to show the dynamic nature of situational context (which influences learner, teacher, interactions, and what is required to create critical reflection appropriate for transformative learning.

The intersection of AI and contextualized educational philosophies offers transformative potential for creating more responsive, adaptive, and inclusive educational practices. When combined with AI, these philosophies can be operationalized in innovative ways to meet diverse educational needs:

Responsiveness: AI Systems can analyze vast amounts of data to identify individual learning patterns and needs. Educators can respond more effectively to students' circumstances by integrating this analysis with contextualized philosophies. For instance, AI can help detect early signs of academic struggle or disengagement, allowing teachers to intervene promptly with tailored support strategies that consider the student's background and personal challenges.

Adaptiveness: AI-powered educational tools can offer adaptive learning experiences that adjust to students' performance and learning pace in real-time. This adaptiveness is enhanced when infused with contextual understanding. For example, an AI system that understands a student's cultural context can provide more relevant and relatable examples and scenarios, making learning more meaningful and effective. This dynamic adjustment ensures that each student receives a personalized learning journey that evolves with their progress and needs.

Inclusivity: Inclusion in education ensures that all students have equal access to learning opportunities regardless of their backgrounds or abilities. AI can play a critical role by providing differentiated instruction and resources. When AI tools are designed with contextualized philosophies, they can offer multilingual support, culturally sensitive content, and accessible formats for students with disabilities. This ensures that educational practices are not just universally designed but also tailored to meet the diverse needs of all students, promoting a more inclusive learning environment.

The synergy between AI and contextualized philosophies paves the way for educational practices that are more attuned to students' varied and dynamic needs. This approach enables teachers to create learning environments that are more effective, engaging, equitable, and inclusive.

The question arises as to what philosophies are congruent with transformative learning. Humanistic, progressive, and critical philosophies usually apply to transformative learning. Because transformative learning is concerned with individual growth and perspective change, it is humanistic. It is also progressive because it involves learning through experience. It is critical because it draws from Freire's interpretation of Marxist socialism based on the critique of power structures and its emphasis on transformation and emancipation.

The *purpose of education* as defined by the teacher is influenced by the theoretical perspectives held by the teacher, whether that is to build students' intellectual powers of the mind (liberal education), develop behaviors for the preservation of the human species (behaviorist perspectives), promote social change (progressive perspective), or achieve self-actualization (humanist perspective).

Together with the contextually adapted philosophy adult educators may hold, these situational roles affect the teaching methods adult educators may use to help adult learners promote individual transformation and emancipation.

ADULT EDUCATORS AS FACILITATORS

Adult educators' roles in fostering transformative learning vary depending on the educators' philosophical perspectives and their conceptions of adult learners. For example, humanistic adult education teachers see themselves as facilitators, helpers, and partners in the learning process. They establish a context for learning and serve as a flexible resource for adult learners.

Humanistic teachers trust students to assume responsibility for their learning (Elias & Merriam, 1995, 2004). Progressive adult educators tend to regard themselves as organizers. They guide learning through educative experiences, present stimuli, and instigate and evaluate learning. In doing so, progressive teachers also become learners because the relationships between teachers and learners are reciprocal. Both should plan and learn from each other (Elias & Merriam, 1995, 2004).

Humanistic philosophy, which emphasizes the development of the whole person and values personal growth, individuality, and human potential, connects to AI in several meaningful ways:

Connection: AI can tailor educational experiences to individual learning styles and needs, aligning with the humanistic focus on personalizing education to foster each student's unique growth.

Example: AI-driven platforms like Coursera or Khan Academy adapt course recommendations based on learners' progress and interests.

Connection: Humanistic philosophy aims for self-actualization, where individuals realize their full potential. AI can support this by providing tools and resources that help individuals explore their interests deeply and develop talents.

Example: AI-based career guidance systems like Pymetrics use neuroscience-based assessment and AI to help individuals find career paths that align with their strengths and interests.

Connection: Humanistic education values inclusivity and equal opportunities for all learners. AI can democratize access to high-quality education by providing resources and support to students regardless of their geographical or socio-economic background.

Example: AI-powered language translation tools, such as Google Translate, help non-native speakers access educational content in their preferred language.

Connection: Humanistic philosophy emphasizes the importance of the emotional and social aspects of learning. AI can help monitor and support students' emotional well-being.

Example: AI-driven applications like Woebot offer mental health support and can help students manage stress and anxiety through conversational AI.

Connection: Humanistic teaching values deep, meaningful interactions between teachers and students. AI can handle administrative and repetitive tasks, giving teachers more time to focus on these interactions.

Example: AI tools like TeacherAssist automate grading and administrative work, allowing teachers to spend more time on personalized instruction and mentoring.

Connection: Humanistic philosophy encourages active participation and engagement in learning. AI can create immersive and interactive educational experiences that engage students more profoundly.

Example: Virtual and augmented reality tools, such as those developed by companies like zSpace and Nearpod, use AI To create interactive learning environments that make subjects like science and history come alive.

Behaviorist teachers predict, direct learning outcomes, and design a learning environment that elicits desired behavior. According to Elias and Merriam (1995, 2004), teachers influenced by a behavioral philosophy become contingency managers, environmental controllers, or behavioral engineers who plan in detail the conditions necessary to bring about desired behavior. Liberal teachers of adults consider themselves experts, transmitters of knowledge, and authoritative, and they direct the learning process. Liberal teachers develop intellect through reading, reflection, and production (Elias & Merriam, 1995, 2004).

AI's influence on behavioral philosophy lies in its ability to provide deeper insights, create personalized experiences, and raise new ethical challenges that must be addressed to ensure the responsible use of technology. New tools and methods exist to understand, predict, and modify behavior. Several ways AI contributes to this field are:

Behavior Analysis: AI can analyze vast amounts of data to identify patterns in human behavior. Machine learning algorithms can process information from various sources, such as social media, wearable devices, and online activities, to offer insight into behavioral trends and individual habits.

Predictive Modeling: AI systems can create models forecasting future behaviors based on historical data. These models are used in diverse fields, including psychology, marketing, and healthcare, to anticipate actions and outcomes, allowing for proactive interventions.

Ethical Considerations: Integrating AI into behavioral philosophy raised critical ethical questions about autonomy, privacy, and behavior manipulation. Philosophers and ethicists must address these concerns to ensure that AI applications respect individual rights and promote well-being.

Adaptive Learning Systems: AI creates adaptive learning environments that respond to students' needs and learning styles in education. These systems adjust the content and pace of instruction, enhancing engagement and effectiveness.

Both preferences and philosophical perspectives influence teaching methods. Preferences influence strategies to promote and evaluate learning (Cranton & Hoggan, 2012). For those who espouse a liberal philosophy of adult education, dialectic lectures and critical reading may be the preferred approaches for teaching adult learners. Under a liberal philosophy of education, learning is most often evaluated through essays, research papers, book reviews, etc. Educators working within a behaviorist framework will subscribe to teaching methods that are structured and linear, emphasizing student response rather than the process of learning. Programmed instruction, modularized instruction, and online teaching are often preferred by those who have adopted a behaviorist philosophy of adult education. Learning is evaluated primarily through objectively scored measurements (multiple choice, short answer) or performance observation.

Proponents of a progressive philosophy practice problem-solving and the scientific method when teaching adult learners; they use group work, case studies, problem-based learning, and experiential learning activities in settings appropriate to the discipline (shops, hospitals, schools, farms, and the like). Learning is evaluated through observing performance in a field setting or examining products students produced while engaging in experiential activities.

For those educators who base their practice on a critical philosophy, methods are created to present the learners with perspectives that are at odds with their current perspectives. This may include using movies and videos that portray an alternative perspective on an issue, reading fiction, holding critical debates, and using role plays in which participants take on different roles in different contexts. Learning is best evaluated through learner self-evaluation, as it is usually only the learner who can say whether their perspectives have changed.

Kinney (1953), who defined six teacher roles, suggested that adapting one's methods in teaching adult learners is necessary. They define six roles of the teacher: a director of learning, a counselor and guidance worker, a mediator of the culture, an influential member of the school community, a liaison between school and community, and a member of the profession. (p. 8) In his description of andragogy, Knowles strongly emphasized the helping role of adult educators based on his humanistic philosophy of adult education. Knowles, in *The Adult Learner* (Knowles et al., 1998, 2011), expressed the following view:

Finally, I found myself performing a different set of functions that required a different set of skills. Instead of performing the function of content planner and transmitter, which required primarily presentation skills, I was performing the function of process designer and manager, which required relationship building, needs assessment, involvement of students in planning, linking students to learning resources, and encouraging student initiative. (p. 201)

Because Knowles is considered one of the most influential figures in adult education, his humanistic philosophy has generated a wide following in the field. Inherently, followers of Knowles view themselves as learning facilitators instead of information disseminators to show that their practice is driven by their deeply held humanistic philosophy.

Knowles would likely see AI as a powerful enabler of personalized, self-directed, and practical learning experiences for adults, enhancing the overall effectiveness of adult education. Here are a few ways he might interpret AI's role:

Just-in-Time Learning: AI could provide immediate access to information and resources, aligning with Knowles' principle that adult learners learn best when they perceive the need to know something. This on-demand access to knowledge would support professionals needing quick solutions to specific problems.

Learner Autonomy: AI tools could enhance self-directed learning, a core concept in Knowles' andragogy. Intelligent tutoring systems, virtual assistants, and AI-driven feedback mechanisms would empower learners to take control of their education, offering guidance and support tailored to their pace and learning style.

Collaborative Learning: Knowles valued the social aspects of learning. AI could support this through virtual collaboration platforms, where learners can interact, share experiences, and solve problems collectively, regardless of geographical boundaries.

Lifelong Learning and Skill Development: AI could facilitate continuous learning opportunities, providing adults with ongoing access to skill development programs. This aligns with Knowles' belief that adult education should be lifelong.

CONCLUSION

Liberalism, progressivism, humanism, behaviorism, and critical philosophy are philosophies identified within the various frameworks of adult education. Implicit in each of these philosophies are beliefs about the nature of adult learners, the role of education, and the teacher. Teacher dispositions manifest as actions or, more specifically, as teaching practice. The authors believe connecting teacher dispositions to philosophies is essential to facilitate a more holistic and contextualized exploration of teaching practices. Discussing the teacher roles, educational purpose, and methods from the viewpoint of each of the philosophies provides a valuable framework for understanding dispositions and elements of teaching practices characteristic of those dispositions. More than multidisciplinary, students need to be transdisciplinary – to be proficient in various intellectual frameworks beyond the disciplinary perspectives.

AI is not a pure STEM discipline. It requires a spectrum of capabilities not covered by current teaching dispositions and philosophies across academic fields.

Dignum (2021) identified skills needed for building the AI ecosystem that is central in education curricula across the world:

Collaborate: The AI ecosystem makes collaboration possible and assumes collaboration across distance, time, cultures, and contexts.

Question: AI systems are great at finding answers and will do this increasingly well; however, it is up to us to ask the right questions, critically evaluate results, and contribute to responsible implementations within the educational ecosystem.

Imagine Skills for creative problem-solving, using empathy, logic, and novel thinking are needed. Nurturing humanities education and including humanities subjects in all technology curricula is imperative.

Learn to learn: Quickly adapting and picking up new skills is vital for success. It requires us to learn, grow, and adapt to change continuously. Understanding what is necessary to know, knowing when to apply a particular concept, and knowing how to do it are keys to continuous success.

From this perspective, adult educators must skillfully contextually adapt both their philosophies and dispositions such that their practices are appropriate to the complex, variable needs of adult learners. Notwithstanding AI's tremendous promise to improve educational systems, full integration of AI into education requires strong leadership support. Leadership in education needs moral and financial support to concentrate on creating learners who can thrive in the AI society. Governments are finding it challenging to keep up with the rapid advancements in AI for education by private organizations such as LightSide, Coursera, McGraw-Hill, Pearson, and IBM (Nagar, 2024). Addressing issues through state legislation can help set standards, provide solutions, and foster the growth of innovative ecosystems that can integrate AI into educational settings involving several vital strategies, such as allocating funding and resources toward R&D to explore cutting-edge AI applications in education. Encouraging innovative research can lead to discovering new methods to enhance learning and teaching processes, establishing partnerships among educational institutions, technology companies, and government agencies to create a robust support network, and developing scalable and flexible AI infrastructure that educational institutions of all sizes can quickly adapt. This includes cloud-based platforms and tools that support various educational applications.

REFERENCES

Brookfield, S. D. (2005). *The power of critical theory*. Jossey-Bass.

Bulathwela, S., Perez-Ortiz, M., Holloway, C., & Shawe-Taylor, J. (2021). Could AI democratize education? *Socio-Technical Imaginaries of an EdTech Revolution.*

Cranton, P. (2006). *Understanding and promoting transformative learning: A guide for educators of adults*. Jossey-Bass.

Cranton, P., & Hoggan, C. (2012). We are evaluating transformative learning. In Taylor, E. W., & Cranton, P. (Eds.), *Handbook of transformative learning: Theory, research, and practice*. Jossey-Bass.

Dewey, J. (1938). *Education and experience*. Collier Books.

Dignum, V. (2021). The role and challenges of education for responsible AI. *London Review of Education*, 19(1), 1–11. DOI: 10.14324/LRE.19.1.01

Elias, J. L., & Merriam, S. B. (1995). *Philosophical foundations of adult education*. Krieger Publishing Company.

Elias, J. L., & Merriam, S. B. (2004). *Philosophical foundations of adult education* (3rd ed.). Krieger Publishing Company.

Freire, P. (1970). *Pedagogy of the oppressed*. Seabury Press.

Habermas, J. (1971). *Knowledge and human interests*. Beacon Press.

Holian, J. (1971). Alienation and social awareness among college students. *The Sociological Quarterly*, 13(1), 114–125. DOI: 10.1111/j.1533-8525.1971.tb01835.x

Kabudi, T., Pappas, I., & Olsen, D. H. (2021). AI-enabled adaptive learning systems: A systematic mapping of the literature. *Computers and Education: Artificial Intelligence*, 2, 100017.

Kidd, J. R. (1973). *How adults learn* (revised). Association Press.

Kim, N. J., & Kim, M. K. (2022). Teacher's perceptions of using an artificial intelligence-based educational tool for scientific writing. *Frontiers in Education*, 7, 7. DOI: 10.3389/feduc.2022.755914

Kinney, L. B. (1953). *The measure of a good teacher*. Teachers Association.

Knowles, M. S. (1975). *Self-directed learning*. Association Press.

Knowles, M. S. (1980). *The modern practice of adult education: From pedagogy to andragogy*. Association Press.

Knowles, M. S., Holton, E., & Swanson, A. (1998). *The adult learner: The definitive classic in adult education and human resource development*. Gulf Publishing Company.

Knowles, M. S., Holton, E., & Swanson, A. (2011). *The adult learner: The definitive classic in adult education and human resource development* (7thed.). Taylor & Francis.

Leung, K.-H. (2019). *The picture of artificial intelligence and the secularization of thought*. Political Theology. DOI: 10.1080/1462317X.2019.1605725

Li, J., Peng, Y., & Su, J. (2023). Analysis of the impact of artificial intelligence on college students and countermeasures based on the perspective of comprehensive development. The *Frontiers of Society. Science, and Technology*, 5(9), 24–33.

Lindeman, E. C. (1926). *The meaning of adult education*. Research Center for Continuing Professional and Higher Education.

Mahoney, J. M., & Quick, B. G. (2000). Personality correlates of alienation in a university sample. *Psychological Reports*, 87(3_suppl), 1094–1100. DOI: 10.2466/pr0.2000.87.3f.1094 PMID: 11272749

Maslow, A. H. (1970). *Motivation and personality* (2nd ed.). Harper Collins.

Merriam, S. B., & Brockett, R. G. (1997). *The profession and practice of adult education: An introduction*. Jossey-Bass.

Mezirow, J. (1975). *Education for perspective transformation: Women's reentry programs in community colleges*. Center for Adult Education, Teachers College, Columbia University.

Mezirow, J. (1991). *Transformative dimension of adult learning*. Jossey-Bass.

Mezirow, J. (2000). Learning to think like an adult. In Mezirow, J. (Eds.), *Learning as transformation: Critical perspectives on a theory in progress* (pp. 3–31). Jossey-Bass.

Mickunas, A., & Pilotta, J. (2023). *A critical understanding of artificial intelligence: A phenomenological foundation*. Bentham Books. DOI: 10.2174/97898151234011230101

Moustaghfir, S., & Brigui, H. (2023). Exploring Moroccan English teacher's perception towards the use of interactive tools in teaching English as a foreign language on the development of critical thinking skills in young students. *International Journal of Linguistics, Literature, and Translation*, 6(8), 236–249. DOI: 10.32996/ijllt.2023.6.8.24

Nagar, N. (2024). Importance of artificial intelligence in education. [IJSREM]. *International Journal of Scientific Research in Engineering and Management*, 8(4).

Nicolaides, A., & Marsick, V. (2016). Understanding adult learning in the midst of complex social "liquid modernity.". *New Directions for Adult and Continuing Education*, 149(Spring), 9–20. DOI: 10.1002/ace.20172

Papadima, G. (2021, July). Is there a split between adult educator's educational philosophy in learning and teaching process? *International Journal of Instruction*, 14(3), 583–596. DOI: 10.29333/iji.2021.14334a

Rogers, C. R. (1969). *Freedom to learn*. Merrill.

Selman, G. (1989). The enemies of adult education. *Canadian Journal of University Continuing Education*, 15, 68–81.

Skinner, B. F. (1974). *About behaviorism*. Knopf.

Soccorsi, L. (2013). Instilling a personal teaching philosophy in preservice teachers: Vitally important but not always easy to achieve. *Journal of Student Engagement: Education Matters*, 3(1), 21–28.

Susanto, S., Andrianingsih, A., Sutawan, K., Marwintaria, V. A., & Astika, R. (2023). Transformation of learner learning: Improving reasoning skills through artificial intelligence (AI). [JoERI]. *Journal of Education, Religious, and Instructions*, 1(2), 37–46. DOI: 10.60046/joeri.v1i2.74

Thorndike, E. L., Bregman, E. O., Tilton, J. W., & Woodyard, E. (1928). *Adult learning*. Macmillan.

Tisdell, E. J., & Taylor, E. W. (2000). Adult education philosophy informs practice. *Adult Learning*, 11(2), 6–10. DOI: 10.1177/104515959901100203

Torrisi-Steele, G., & Carim, G.Jr. (2019). An adult-learner approach to the learning design of safety management system training in aviation. *International Journal of Adult Vocational Education and Technology*, 10(3), 39–53. DOI: 10.4018/IJAVET.2019070103

Wang, V. (2003). *Principles of adult education*. Pearson.

Xu, W. (2024). The correction strategy of artificial intelligence embedding into the negative social mentality of the marginal group of college students in the new era. *Journal of Electrical Systems*, 20(2). https://journal.esrgroups.org/jes/article/view/1222

Zadorina, O., Kurskaya, V., Sobolyeva, S., Grekova, L., & Vasylyuk-Zaitseva, S. (2024). The role of artificial intelligence in the creation of future education: Possibilities and challenges. *Futurity Education*, 4(2), 163–185.

Zhou, Y. (2022). Beliefs and practice evaluation based on artificial intelligence models under the IP environment. *Journal of Environmental and Public Health*, 2022(1), 1415142. DOI: 10.1155/2022/1415142 PMID: 36203503

Chapter 2
Andragogy in the Age of AI: Transformative Pathways for Adult Education

Valerie A. Storey
https://orcid.org/0000-0001-8868-0802
Franklin University, USA

Amiee Wagner
https://orcid.org/0009-0003-5050-0468
Franklin University, USA

ABSTRACT

This chapter explores the transformative impact of Artificial Intelligence (AI) on adult education, drawing on the foundational work of Malcolm Knowles, who emphasized the necessity for adaptive and self-directed learning practices. It examines the rapid technological advancements since Knowles' time, highlighting how modern AI technologies, particularly Generative AI, are reshaping the landscape of adult education. By aligning AI with andragogical principles, educators can enhance the learning experience while addressing potential challenges such as algorithmic bias and inequity. The chapter is structured into three sections: the first explores AI-based learning science and its congruence with Knowles' principles; the second assesses the evolving nature of andragogy in the digital era; and the third projects future pathways for integrating AI in adult learning, emphasizing the implications for education delivery and knowledge production

DOI: 10.4018/979-8-3373-0502-8.ch002

INTRODUCTION

This chapter is grounded on the work of Malcolm Knowles, who in the 1980s asked the question, "What is modern practice?" (Knowles, 1980, p.18), pointing out that modern is a temporary state and that andragogical practices must change regularly as most practices have a shelf life of less than a decade. Knowles argued that adult education must provide the resources and support for a self-directed inquiry. He suggested that thinking should focus on how and where learning should occur now that education was no longer the monopoly of educational institutions and their teachers. According to Knowles, the new mission of education is to "develop a total environment conducive to human growth and self-actualization to create an educative society" (p.38). Knowles recognized that "the notion that there is a distinct and different technology for adult learning was in its beginning stages of development" (p.14). Four decades later, the technology of andragogy has matured, and we are once again entering a "transformational" stage.

The U.S. Department of Education (U.S. DoE, 2023) states that educational technology (edtech) includes technologies specifically designed for educational use as well as general technologies that are widely used in educational settings. Artificial Intelligence (AI) is defined as "automation based on associations" (p.1). When computers automate reasoning deduced from expert knowledge, two shifts fundamental to AI occur, transitioning computing beyond conventional edtech: (1) from capturing data to detecting patterns in data and (2) from providing access to instructional resources to automating decisions about instruction and other educational processes. A more comprehensive definition of AI comes from Lu (2019), who defines AI as any theory, methodology, or technique that facilitates the analysis, simulation, exploitation, and exploration of human thinking processes and behaviors by machines.

Technological advances have influenced the field of adult learning in many ways, including improved effectiveness, customization, and learning outcomes. As technology evolves unprecedentedly, adult learning practitioners must adapt and embrace new methods to enhance educational experiences. Generative AI (GenAI) can potentially transform the field of adult learning significantly (Chan & Zary, 2019; Chen et al., 2023). Concerning adult learning, AI models typically lack awareness of andragogical strategies. For example, algorithmic discrimination can occur when adaptive GenAI speeds the curricular pace for some students and slows the pace for other students (based on incomplete data, poor theories, or biased assumptions about learning), thereby increasing student inequity (Chen et al., 2023). Therefore, educators are responsible for ensuring that AI integration into educational technology is guided by robust andragogical principles, minimizing future challenges.

This chapter explores "modern practice," validating Knowles' statement referring to the brevity of specific andragogical practices due to the rapid evolvement of AI systems in the 21st century. The subsequent sections are organized into three distinct parts. Section 1 explores the advancement of AI-based learning science and the alignment of andragogical principles articulated by Knowles with successful current AI programs grounded on learning science research. Section 2 examines the evolving landscape of andragogy in the digital age through the eyes of Knowles grounded on andragogical principles. Section 3 is focused on charting the future of andragogy and AI in adult learning and explores the impact this may have on education delivery and knowledge production.

SECTION ONE: ADVANCING LEARNING SCIENCES WITH AI ANALYTICS

The foundational principles of adult learning include andragogy, a theory emphasizing the importance of self-direction, drawing from past experiences, relevance to real-life situations, and a problem-solving approach (Jeffries & Ahn, 2024). Grounded on the work of Knowles, andragogy emphasizes the importance of understanding adult learners' characteristics and motivations, advocating for self-directed learning, and facilitating meaningful learning experiences. Also influential to adult learning is "Learning Science," which resonates with key andragogical principles. Adult learning through active participation, subject relevance to working lives, and building upon existing knowledge and experiences are andragogical principles advocated by Knowles and align with learning science principles, such as constructivism, cognitive load theory, and the importance of meaningful context in learning (Wang et al., 2023). Table 1 illustrates the alignment between learning science and andragogy.

Table 1. Characteristics of The Most Effective Learning Environments: A Comparison Between Learning Science and Andragogy

Characteristics	Learning Science (Sawyer, 2008)	Andragogy (Knowles, 1980)
Target Audience	Encompasses the study of how individuals of all ages, acquire knowledge and skills.	Specifically focuses on the education and learning of adults.
Theory and Principles	Draws on various theories and principles from fields such as cognitive psychology, neuroscience, educational psychology, and behavioral science to understand how learning occurs in individuals.	Developed by Malcolm Knowles; emphasizes self-directed learning, the importance of learners' prior experiences, and the relevance of learning to adults' lives.
Effective Learning	Occurs if each learner receives a customized learning experience; students learn better through application which allows them to think and solve problems with the content that they are learning.	Occurs when it is tailored to the unique characteristics and motivations of adult learners, fostering an environment where they can take an active role in their own learning journey; subject matter must be relevant and applicable in their life.
Instructors Role in Knowledge Acquisition	Instructors facilitate coherent knowledge rather than subject-compartmentalized knowledge; contextualized authentic knowledge rather than decontextualized course exercises; and student learning in collaboration rather than in isolation.	Instructors encourage learners to uncover knowledge independently and receive guidance and support when errors occur; irrespective of the means used to acquire information, it should undergo review, analysis, evaluation, classification, and interpretation.
Assessment	Focuses on the students' deeper conceptual understanding; extent to which their knowledge is integrated, coherent, and contextualized.	Task-oriented (e.g. skills assessments) rather than dependent on memory.
Educational Practice	Guides the development of curriculum, instructional materials, and assessment tools based on evidence-based principles of learning.	Informs the design and delivery of adult education programs; advocates for learner-centered approaches that empower adults to take an active role in their own learning process.

1.1 The Evolution of AI-Based Learning Science

While academics (in psychology, sociology, computer science, education, and cognitive science) have studied learning science for over four decades, it has not been deeply integrated with AI technology. In the twenty-first century, AI evolved first into a separate system and then into a separate branch, and ultimately AI-based learning science (Wang et al., 2023); specifically, exploring how andragogy can be enhanced with AI technology to support and scaffold individual and group learning (Sommerhoff, 2018). The empirical foundations of the learning sciences are concerned with data and its analysis and the related fields of learning analytics (LA) and educational data mining (EDM), all of which now come under the AI umbrella (Luckin & Cukurova, 2019).

The roots of AI-based learning science lie in the first generation of cognitive science. In the early nineteenth century, Herbart, a German philosopher, psychologist, and educationalist, suggested the study of education based on psychology, emphasizing the use of psychological knowledge to explain the laws of education and instruction. In the 1960s, Gagné drew on psychological ideas to build a theory of information processing that illustrated the differences and connections between human learning, the processing of external stimuli by the human brain, and the processing of information by computers. In the late 1980s, cognitive scientists established a new research community called the "learning sciences." They aimed to understand the cognitive and social processes that result in the most effective learning and then incorporate these into learning environments. This shifted the focus of learning sciences from teaching to learning (Kelkar, 2022).

At the beginning of the twenty-first century, AI became a separate system in its own right, gradually evolving into a separate learning sciences branch known as AI-based learning science. Using AI technology to analyze and process a wide range of data, combining the disciplinary expertise of educational data scientists, learning engineers, and precision education specialists in psychology, biology, and neuroscience, a new field of AI-based learning science is being established (Kelkar, 2022; Wang et al., 2023).

1.2 AI and Learning Sciences Alignment

Progress in integrating AI within education trails behind advancements in fields like applied sciences, finance, and medicine (Storey, 2023). There is far too little understanding of AI among educational practitioners, and conversely, there is too little understanding of teaching and learning among those who develop AI. However, a growing number of researchers are now publishing robust evidence demonstrating the effectiveness of well-designed AI in education (AIED). Several AI systems used in education in the last decade have demonstrated statistically significant positive impacts on student learning:

The OLI (Open Learning Initiative) learning course was developed by Carnegie Mellon University based on research in the learning sciences to promote effective learning strategies and engagement. OLI offers a range of online courses across various subjects, utilizing interactive learning materials and adaptive technologies to personalize the learning experience for students (Luckin & Cukurova, 2019).

ALEKS (Assessment and Learning in Knowledge Spaces) is an adaptive learning platform developed by ALEKS Corporation. ALEKS uses AI and adaptive questioning to assess a student's subject knowledge. Based on the assessment results, ALEKS adjusts the learning path for each student, providing personalized instruction and practice to fill in knowledge gaps and advance their understanding of the subject matter (Craig et al., 2013).

Cognitive Tutor is an intelligent tutoring system developed by Carnegie Learning that utilizes AI to adapt to individual student's learning needs and abilities, providing tailored feedback and guidance as students work through problems. It employs a step-by-step approach, scaffolding concepts and gradually increasing difficulty to support learning progression (Pane et al., 2014).

CENTURY Tech is an AI-powered learning platform designed to enhance education by personalizing student learning experiences. It employs machine learning algorithms to adapt to individual learning styles and needs, providing tailored content and feedback. The platform also provides detailed analytics to educators, allowing them to track student progress and identify areas for improvement to optimize learning outcomes. The algorithms within CENTURY Tech are informed by findings from cognitive science and neuroscience: both part of the learning sciences family.

The empirical findings supporting the effectiveness of OLI, ALEKS, Cognitive Tutor, and CENTURY Tech are important because it is generally challenging to achieve statistical significance in studies investigating educational interventions' positive impact (Luckin & Cukurova, 2019). The relative success of these four AIED-based systems can be attributed, at least in part, to their alignment with research evidence from learning sciences and learning theories that guide instructional design and technological advancement (Bower, 2019). However, these AIED systems only give feedback for foundational knowledge components and may be less effective in delivering more complex instructions like collaboration or self-explanation (Luckin & Cukurova, 2019).

More recent AIED systems can collect data that can be analyzed in a manner informed by learning sciences research. AIED technologies, learning content, and andragogical approaches should be integrated to optimize learning efficiency and effectiveness. When designing learning activities supported by AI, adult educators should consider six crucial elements to achieve the expected learning objectives: learners, context, tasks, andragogical approaches, interaction methods, and the application of AI technologies (Zheng et al., 2021).

1.3 Advancements in AI and Learning Sciences

By integrating insights from learning sciences with emerging technologies like immersive virtual and augmented reality, intelligent tutoring systems, automated essay scoring systems, high sampling resolution devices, adaptive learning technologies, and advanced language models such as chatbots, we gain a deeper understanding of various aspects of learning, including reasoning, problem-solving, and performance across diverse domains. The following are examples of current and developing AI models.

1.3a Immersive Technologies

Augmented Reality (AR) and Virtual Reality (VR) use AI to provide users with intuitive sensations while simulating mechanisms in a physical or imaginary world. Both can integrate multimedia, sensors, displays, human-machine interaction, ergonomics, simulation, and computer graphics to expand human perception and allow users to have an immersive experience by interacting with generated virtual environments (Oliveira et al., 2023). However, they operate in different ways. While VR creates a fully immersive digital environment, AR enhances the real world with digital elements.

Virtual Reality (VR)

VR replaces the real world with a simulated one. Users wear VR headsets that completely block out the physical environment and immerse them in a digital world. VR often involves interactions with this virtual environment through specialized glasses or gloves. In VR, the observing participant is fully immersed. VR can be used to solve problems in the real world (Ribeiro de Oliveira et al., 2023).

An example of VR in adult education is "Engage" by Immersive VR Education.

In Engage, users can attend virtual classes, seminars, workshops, and conferences from anywhere. Students can interact with instructors and other participants in real-time, engage with 3D models, simulations, and multimedia content, and collaborate on projects within the virtual environment. Engage is an example of how VR technology transforms adult education by providing new opportunities for remote learning, experiential learning, and collaboration in virtual environments (EngageVR n.d.). Learners can speak directly to important people throughout history (e.g. Presidents, inventors, activists). (https://engagevr.io/school-of-ai/)

Second Life is not an example of VR. Rather, it is categorized as a virtual world or a virtual environment rather than VR. In Second Life, users navigate through a digital landscape, interact with each other, attend events, visit art galleries and museums, and engage in various activities designed by the educator. While it offers an immersive experience, it does not involve using VR headsets or provide the same level of immersive, three-dimensional experience that VR technology offers.

Augmented Reality (AR)

AR overlays digital information onto the real world. Users see both the physical environment and digital elements superimposed on it. "Live View" in the Google Maps app is an example of AR. This feature uses AR to overlay digital directions onto the real-world view captured by the device's camera. It can show arrows and directions overlaid onto the streets and buildings seen through the smartphone's camera, helping users navigate more intuitively. AR is typically experienced through smartphones, tablets, or AR glasses (Ribeiro de Oliveira et al., 2023).

1.3b Intelligent Tutoring Systems (ITS)

One long-standing type of AI-enabled technology is an intelligent tutoring system (ITS), which provides feedback on specific steps of a solution process. Researchers have examined all the available high-quality studies in a meta-analysis and concluded that ITS approaches are effective (U.S. DoE, 2023).

1.3c Automated Essay Scoring (AES) systems

AES systems are designed to evaluate, score, and provide feedback on a student's writing using AI and natural language processing techniques feedback (Ramesh & Sanampudi, 2022).

E-rater: Developed by the Educational Testing Service (ETS), the E-rater is one of the earliest and most widely used AES systems to assess analytical writing skills in the Graduate Record Examinations (GRE).

Criterion: Also developed by ETS, this writing evaluation service provides instant scoring and feedback on essays based on multiple criteria, such as organization, development, and language use.

LightSIDE: LightSIDE, developed by researchers at Carnegie Mellon University, is a machine-learning tool for text analysis tasks, including essay scoring. It allows customization and training of models based on specific criteria and data.

SAGrader: SAGrader, developed by Idea Works, uses machine learning algorithms to assess and score essays, particularly when grading student assignments in online courses.

PEG Writing: PEG Writing, developed by Measurement Incorporated (MI), is an online platform that provides students with automated essay scoring and instant feedback.

Turnitin: Turnitin, developed by Turnitin (formerly iParadigms, LLC), is primarily known as a plagiarism detection tool; however, it also offers features for grading and providing feedback on student essays, including automated scoring capabilities.

Grammarly, InstaText and QuillBot: aid writing similar to AES systems, but their focus is primarily on language correctness and clarity rather than assigning a score or evaluating content comprehensively.

1.3d High-Sampling Resolution Devices (HSRD)

HSRD can capture multimodal data, such as eye movements, facial expressions, learner-system interactions, and physiological responses. Integrating advanced data capture mechanisms into the learning sciences framework enriches our comprehension of the intricate processes underlying learning (Azevedo & Gašević, 2019; Noroozi et al., 2019).

1.3e Adaptive Learning Technologies (ALT)

ALT (sometimes called personalization) has laid a solid foundation for personalized teaching and learning. Adjusting the difficulty and the order of lesson materials are among the two most common ways that edtech products adapt. The challenge is that an algorithm may only present material the learner has expressed interest in, thereby limiting the student's exposure to new topics (U.S. DoE, 2023). Of concern is that AI programs tend to be grounded on a deficit-based model, unlike a human tutor who orients to students' strengths to develop subject knowledge.

1.3f Advanced Language Models-Chatbot

A chatbot is a dialogue system that emulates and interprets human communication, allowing individuals to engage with digital devices as though conversing with an actual human being (Ciechanowski, 2019). The creation of a Chatbot involves the use of Natural Language Processing (NLP). NLP is a technology that enables a machine to comprehend, analyze, and interpret natural human languages (e.g., Apple Siri, Amazon Alexa, ChatGTP, Google Assistant IBM Watson, Microsoft Cortana, and Smarter Child).

ChatGPt, launched in 2022, can respond to prompts in a conversational manner (Health, 2023) and accomplish a wide range of tasks such as language translation, text summarization, question answering, creative writing (such as poetry or fiction), generation of high-quality long or short-form content (such as blog posts), responding to prompts in conversation, explaining complex subjects, concepts, or themes, and fixing errors in existing code or generating new codes (Eke, 2023).

OpenAI's Generative Pre-Trained Transformer (GPT-4), the most recent 2023 version of the deep-learning large-scale language model on which ChatGPT is based, claims to be more powerful and capable of performing more complex functions. ChatGPT-4 has been trained on a larger and more diverse dataset. The increased size of the model allows for more advanced natural language processing capabilities. Its capacity for reasoning and understanding prompts across multiple domains makes it more adaptable and able to handle challenging tasks. For example, if a user submits an image and requests a description, it describes it in detail. It even responds to the handwritten queries presented as graphics (OpenAI, 2023).

It is worth noting that a version of ChatGPT, Microsoft 365 Copilot, was added to Office apps, including Word, Excel, PowerPoint, and Outlook, by using machine learning to analyze data from a variety of sources, including telemetry data, user feedback, and Microsoft's expertise to provide proactive recommendations, automated issue resolution, and personalized guidance (Stallbaumer, 2023).

1.3g Advanced Multimodal Data Capture Technologies

This emerging technology is focused on a high-sampling resolution capable of capturing rich streams of multimodal data across multiple channels and modalities while students are engaged in learning activities. This includes data gathered on eye movements from an eye tracker, facial expressions of emotions using facial recognition software, learner-system interactions via timestamped log files, and physiological responses via wearable bracelets across learning tasks.

Table 2 summarizes some of the AIED learning technologies explored in this section. By applying the principles of AI to those of learning science and andragogy, AI is poised to revolutionize the delivery of adult education. The next section will explore the need for both students and adult educators to adapt to and embrace the rapidly evolving educational landscape.

Table 2. Summary: Definitions for and Examples of AIED Learning Technologies

Generative AI Technologies	**Brief Definition**	**Examples/ Applications**
Immersive Technologies VR AR	Immersive learning experiences to promote skills development and deep learning of complex concepts (Oliveira et al., 2023).	Engage Oculus Rift
Intelligent Tutoring Systems (ITS)	ITS provides feedback on specific steps of a solution process (U.S. DoE, 2023).	Duolingo ALEKS
Automated Essay Scoring Systems (AES)	AES systems are designed to evaluate, score, and provide feedback (Ramesh & Sanampudi, 2022).	LightSIDE Criterion
Advanced Language Models Chatbots	Dialogue system that emulates and interprets human communication, allowing individuals to engage with digital devices as though conversing with an actual human being (Ciechanowski, 2019).	ChatGPT Copilot

SECTION TWO: THE EVOLVING LANDSCAPE OF ANDRAGOGY IN THE DIGITAL AGE

Gen AI has already changed and will continue to change how students are taught and approach their studies, thus ultimately impacting the future workforce – regardless of industry or context. To deal with the fundamental changes accompanying the widespread use of generative AI, adult educators must aim to broaden students' perspectives on the possibilities and the fundamental limitations of these technologies (Dianova & Schultz, 2023).

Knowles' Perspective

Knowles would likely acknowledge the significant impact of digital technologies on adult learning. He would emphasize that educators should embrace these technologies to enhance and facilitate adult learning experiences. When used effectively, digital tools can support adults' preferences for self-directed, active, and relevant learning experiences.

Shift Towards Self-Directed Learning: Knowles' andragogical principles would likely emphasize the growing autonomy of adult learners in directing their educational trajectories. AI driven digital tools have the potential to offer individualized, real-time feedback as learners engage in project work, problem-solving activities, or assignment completion (Atlas, 2023). This technological augmentation of the learning process empowers adult learners to seek guidance as necessary while maintaining a significant degree of autonomy. Integrating such tools aligns with Knowles' emphasis on self-directed learning and the utilization of life experiences in adult education, potentially enhancing the efficacy of andragogical approaches in contemporary learning environments.

Additionally, Knowles would advocate for incorporating digital literacy skills into adult education curricula. Educating learners on the responsible use of GenAI could allow busy adults to work more efficiently without the need for help from the instructor. Not only can GenAI be used to offload tedious, time-consuming tasks, such as editing a paper or creating images, but also to "kickstart" assignments through the generation of project ideas or inspiration for a paper (Kalota, 2024). However, Knowles would likely caution against digital divides and advocate for ensuring that technology is accessible to all learners.

Incorporation of Active, Relevant Learning Experiences: Knowles identified that adults learn more effectively when knowledge is actively acquired through experiences that are relevant to their world. While there are mixed feelings about using GenAI in education, all agree that it is vital for educators to prepare students for the workforce (Chan, 2023). The rapid integration of AI into various industries has created an urgent need for universities to adopt teaching strategies that incorporate the use of AI. For graduates to be successful in their field, learners will need a strong grasp of AI principles and will need to be competent and responsible users of AI (Chan, 2023; Slimi & Carbillido, 2023).

Guidance on the proper use of AI is becoming increasingly important, given the possible risks and advantages involved with using AIED (Chan, 2023). Responsible use begins with responsible design by adult educators. A moral compass grounded on AI knowledge and training will support adult educators who employ AIED technologies to ensure that they do not violate users' privacy, safety, or security and will likely also enable them to recognize potential algorithmic biases.

While there is not a consensus regarding the responsible (or ethical) use of AI in the curriculum, policies regarding the implementation of AIED are largely influenced by the 2021 United Nations Educational, Scientific, and Cultural Organization (UNESCO) Education and AI Report (Chan, 2023; Nguyen et al., 2023). Figure 1 depicts a summary of the UNESCO Education and AI (2021) principles that align with concerns for adult learners (Knowles, 1980).

Figure 1. Responsible Design and Implementation of AIED (UNESCO, 2021)

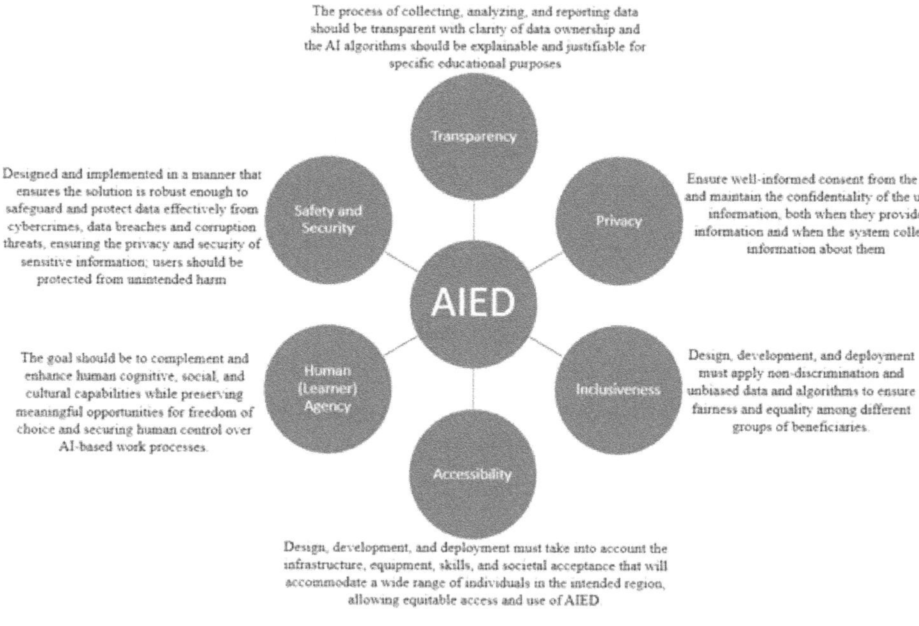

It is becoming increasingly urgent for universities to develop AI education and training for students and educators (Chan, 2023). However, due to the time it takes to develop and schedule training (in the face of the rapid rate of change in AIED technologies), the materials are obsolete when the training is deployed. Additionally, many universities are struggling to develop educational policies regarding students'

responsible (and ethical) use of AI. As the training should be aligned with university policy, this adds another challenge to developing and deploying AI training. This is discussed further in the next section.

In summary, Knowles would likely first emphasize the dual focus on leveraging digital technologies while upholding core andragogical principles. Second, advocate for including digital literacy education in all programs. Third, recommend adult educators modify their programs to align with the evolving educational landscape influenced by emerging technologies. These are fundamental to preparing students and professionals to use GenAI responsibly and to develop a critical view of advanced technologies' role in society (Dianova & Schultz, 2023).

Shifting Andragogy

Shifting andragogy from human-centered to machine-driven processes will undoubtedly shape the landscape of adult education in profound ways. This transition raises concerns about the potential loss of intergenerational wisdom, casting doubts on the sustainability of our current educational paradigms. Human andragogy, which emphasizes engaging adult learners and fostering the exchange of ideas, knowledge, skills, and values, plays a crucial role locally and globally. Adult learners' professional and personal experiences make the person who they are as learners, and a human instructor understands this. However, questions emerge about whether machine learning will uphold human teaching and learning principles.

GenAI enables learners to access and assemble abundant knowledge. Learning processes and desired outcomes change profoundly, known as "lookability" (Cope et al., 2021, p.1234). One of the key challenges ahead lies in scholarly communities' ability to discern between andragogical methods that aim to perpetuate the current unsustainable system and those that aspire to achieve different, potentially more progressive goals. This distinction will be vital in shaping the future of adult education in the digital age. Certainly, an active dialogue, indeed partnerships between GenAI designers and educators, must be developed to ensure that innovative AI technology is grounded on effective andragogical principles and AI-based learning science. There is a valid concern that machine-driven approaches might deliver material to the learner rather than working with the learner to encourage critical thinking and innovation.

SECTION THREE: CHARTING THE FUTURE: ANDRAGOGY AND AI IN ADULT LEARNING

The chapter's third section will discuss a future trajectory for andragogy and AI in adult education and its potential long-term implications for education systems. Emerging trends and technologies that potentially revolutionize the educational landscape will be explored, emphasizing their impact on adult education practices. The current discourse surrounding AI and its impact on adult learning is broad, as some educators view AI as a threat to traditional educational structures. In contrast, others perceive it as a catalyst for change, ushering in an era of accessible information and automation poised to enrich the educational landscape's scope and quality.

Knowles (1980) would likely see the integration of andragogy and AI in adult learning as a promising development that can enhance the effectiveness and accessibility of adult education while still honoring the principles of self-directed learning, experiential learning, and collaboration.

Emphasis on Self-Directed Learning: Knowles believed that adults learn best when actively involved in learning and have control over their learning experiences. With AI in adult learning, there could be opportunities to personalize learning experiences even more, allowing adults to direct their learning paths according to their needs and preferences.

Facilitation of Learning: Knowles highlighted the role of the facilitator in adult education, who acts as a guide rather than a traditional teacher. With AI, facilitators could utilize intelligent systems to support learners, providing resources, feedback, and guidance tailored to their learning goals and styles.

Experiential Learning: Knowles valued experiential learning as an effective approach for adult learners. AI technologies could facilitate experiential learning by simulating real-world scenarios, allowing learners to apply their knowledge and skills in practical contexts.

Collaborative Learning: Knowles emphasized individualized learning and recognized the importance of collaborative learning experiences for adults. Both of which AI can support.

Continuous Learning and Adaptation: Knowles advocated for lifelong learning, which AI technologies can support by providing access to a vast array of learning resources, adapting to learners' evolving needs, and offering recommendations for further learning based on their progress and interests.

AI already has a profound impact on research, knowledge development, knowledge control, and knowledge dissemination. AI-powered algorithms can sift through large datasets, scientific literature, patents, and other sources of information to discover new insights and knowledge. This shift of power dynamics combined with AI's increasing capability can lead to the discovery of new scientific theories, technologies, and innovations that drive progress and fuel further research. Natural Language Processing (NLP) and machine translation further facilitate collaboration among researchers from different linguistic and cultural backgrounds due to the elimination of language barriers.

AI techniques such as knowledge graphs and semantic reasoning enable computers to represent, organize, and reason about knowledge in a structured manner. This capability enhances data interoperability and facilitates knowledge integration across disparate sources, providing more comprehensive and holistic insights. But in the process, AI and not humans will control the knowledge kernel, bias, and all. Research has shown that AI algorithms are not immune to biases inherent in the data they are trained on or the assumptions embedded in their design.

As AI systems increasingly influence decision-making processes in research, there is a risk that biases could be perpetuated or amplified, leading to skewed outcomes or reinforcing existing inequalities. AI empirically validated research may be accepted by society while grounded on falsehood and bias. Control of AI-powered platforms such as search engines, recommendation systems, and content curation tools plays a significant role in disseminating knowledge to a global audience. The concentration of power among a few large HEI institutions and technology companies that control these platforms has the potential for algorithmic manipulation or censorship. Balancing the need for open access to information with concerns about misinformation and privacy will be a key challenge.

The challenge is that Gen AI tools such as Gemini and ChatGPT (narrative), and DALL-E (images) are opening up new frontiers that will affect how adults learn, interact, and work with each other. Our experience working with Generative AI tools suggests that it is important for educators to have the tools to ascertain whether the knowledge presented by students is new. Educators must be cognizant that GenAI depends on the prompts it receives, both in quantity and quality. Currently (ChatGTP, April 2024) cannot (i) cite and (ii) provide references to support its answers.

This is concerning as ChatGPT was initially made freely accessible to its users upon launch to support the democratization of knowledge (Pavlik, 2023), but this open access was limited. Introducing subscriptions widens socio-economic gaps by reducing access for those who cannot afford the premium fee. The response of adult educators to GenAI has varied from direct bans (e.g., the Department of Education in the Australian states of New South Wales and Queensland and New York City public schools using a firewall)(Lim et al., 2023) to cautious acceptance with institutional guidance while policies and regulations are developed or revised (Franklin University, 2024). Generally, experience suggests that more positive outcomes are generated when educators seek to utilize and integrate these technologies rather than banning them.

Passing the Turing Test is a significant milestone in AI research, but it remains elusive. The Turing Test is a concept proposed by British mathematician and computer scientist Alan Turing in 1950 to evaluate a machine's intelligence. The test assesses a machine's ability to exhibit intelligent behavior indistinguishable from a human (Johnson, 2022). It can be argued that the Turing Test sets too low a bar for intelligence since it focuses primarily on conversation rather than deeper understanding or reasoning abilities. Others argue it relies on deception and superficial behaviors rather than genuine intelligence.

There have been instances where certain AI programs have been claimed to have passed variations of the test in limited contexts or for short durations. Still, there is no consensus in the scientific community that any AI has definitively passed it. Nevertheless, the concern is not if but when AI can pass the test as this suggests machines will be conscious, adaptable, and learners in the same way as humans and that human power and control will become secondary to the AI.

CONCLUSION

Returning to Knowles and his thoughts in the 1980s, we are reminded that he believed lifelong learning should be the organizational principle for all education. "In a world of accelerating change, learning must be a lifelong process" (p.19), and adult education must be primarily concerned with providing the resources and support for a self-directed inquiry. AI has the potential to transform traditional teaching and learning methods. Going forward, we must build on AI capabilities that align and are grounded on principles of andragogy and learning sciences. AIEd can enhance the andragogical model advocated by Knowles by providing accessible resources, personalized lifelong learning experiences, adaptive support, data-driven insights, and collaborative environments for adult learners. However, it is essential that the principles of learner autonomy, relevance, and self-directed learning inherent in the andragogical model are sustained and that concerns relating to the production and control of knowledge and sustainability are well understood.

REFERENCES

Atlas, S. (2023). *ChatGPT for higher education and professional development: A guide to conversational AI.* https://digitalcommons.uri.edu/cgi/viewcontent.cgi?article=1547&context=cba_facpubs

Bower, M. (2019). Technology-mediated learning theory. *British Journal of Educational Technology*, 50(3), 1035–1048. DOI: 10.1111/bjet.12771

Chan, C. K. Y. (2023). A comprehensive AI policy education framework for university teaching and learning. *International Journal of Educational Technology in Higher Education*, 20(1), 38. DOI: 10.1186/s41239-023-00408-3

Chan, K. S., & Zary, N. (2019). Applications and challenges of implementing artificial intelligence in medical education: Integrative review. *JMIR Medical Education*, 5(1), e13930. DOI: 10.2196/13930 PMID: 31199295

Chen, Y., Jensen, S., Albert, L. J., Gupta, S., & Lee, T. (2023). Artificial intelligence (AI) student assistants in the classroom: Designing chatbots to support student success. *Information Systems Frontiers*, 25(1), 161–182. DOI: 10.1007/s10796-022-10291-4

Ciechanowski, L., Przegalinska, A., Magnuski, M., & Gloor, P. (2019). In the shades of the uncanny valley: An experimental study of human–chatbot interaction. *Future Generation Computer Systems*, 92, 539–548. DOI: 10.1016/j.future.2018.01.055

Cope, B., Kalantzis, M., & Searsmith, D. (2021) Artificial intelligence for education: Knowledge and its assessment in AI-enabled learning ecologies, *Educational Philosophy and Theory, 53*(12), 1229-1245. DOI: https://doi.org/DOI: 10.1080/00131857.2020.1728732

Craig, S. D., Hu, X., Graesser, A. C., Bargagliotti, A. E., Sterbinsky, A., Cheney, K. R., & Okwumabua, T. (2013). The impact of a technology-based mathematics after-school program using ALEKS on student's knowledge and behaviors. *Computers & Education*, 68, 495–504. DOI: 10.1016/j.compedu.2013.06.010

Dianova, V. G., & Shultz, M. D. (2023). Discussing ChatGPT's implications for industry and higher education: The case for transdisciplinarity and digital humanities. *Industry and Higher Education*, 37(5), 593–600. DOI: 10.1177/09504222231199989

Eke, O. D. (2023). ChatGPT and the rise of generative AI: Threat to academic integrity? *Journal of Responsible Technology*, 13, 100060. DOI: 10.1016/j.jrt.2023.100060

Engage (2024). *The future of learning*. https://engagevr.io/school-of-ai/

Franklin University. (2024). Office of Community Standards Academic Misconduct Process._https://www.franklin.edu/sites/default/files/fr/documents/Academic-Misconduct-Process-rev-Sep2023.pdf

Health, T. L. D.The Lancet Digital Health. (2023). ChatGPT: Friend or foe? *The Lancet. Digital Health*, 5(3), e102. DOI: 10.1016/S2589-7500(23)00023-7 PMID: 36754723

Johnson, S. (2022). *The Turing test: AI still hasn't passed the "imitation game."*https://bigthink.com/the-future/turing-test-imitation-game/

Kalota, F. (2024). A primer on artificial intelligence. *Education Sciences*, 172(14), 172. DOI: 10.3390/educsci14020172

Kelkar, S. (2022). Between AI and learning science: The evolution and commercialization of intelligent tutoring systems. *IEEE Annals of the History of Computing*, 44(1), 20–30. DOI: 10.1109/MAHC.2022.3143816

Knowles, M. S. (1980). *The modern practice of adult education: from pedagogy to andragogy*. Prentice Hall., https://bigthink.com/the-future/turing-test-imitation-game/

Lim, W. M., Gunasekara, A., Pallant, J. L., Pallant, J. I., & Pechenkina, E. (2023). Generative AI and the future of education: Ragnarök or reformation? A paradoxical perspective from management educators. *International Journal of Management Education*, 21(2), 100790. Advance online publication. DOI: 10.1016/j.ijme.2023.100790

Lu, Y. (2019). Artificial intelligence: A survey on evolution, models, applications and future trends. *Journal of Management Analytics*, 6(1), 1–29. DOI: 10.1080/23270012.2019.1570365

Luckin, R., & Cukurova, M. (2019). Designing educational technologies in the age of AI: A learning sciences-driven approach. *British Journal of Educational Technology*, 50(6), 2824–2838. DOI: 10.1111/bjet.12861

Nguyen, A., Ngo, H. N., Hong, Y., Dang, B., & Nguyen, B. P. T. (2023). Ethical principles for artificial intelligence in education. *Education and Information Technologies*, 28(4), 4221–4241. DOI: 10.1007/s10639-022-11316-w PMID: 36254344

Open, A. I. (2023, March). *GPT-4 Developer livestream* [Video]. YouTube. https://www.youtube.com/watch?v=outcGtbnMuQ

Pane, J. F., Griffin, B. A., McCaffrey, D. F., & Karam, R. (2014). Effectiveness of cognitive tutor algebra I at scale. *Educational Evaluation and Policy Analysis*, 36(2), 127–144. DOI: 10.3102/0162373713507480

Pavlik, J. V. (2023). Collaborating with ChatGPT: Considering the implications of generative artificial intelligence for journalism and media education. *Journalism and Mass Communication Educator*, 8(1), 84–93. DOI: 10.1177/10776958221149577

Ramesh, D., & Sanampudi, S. K. (2022). An automated essay scoring systems: A systematic literature review. *Artificial Intelligence Review*, 55(3), 2495–2527. DOI: 10.1007/s10462-021-10068-2 PMID: 34584325

Ribeiro de Oliveira, T., Biancardi Rodrigues, B., Moura da Silva, M., Spinassé, R. A. N., Ludke, G. G., Gaudio, M. R. S., Rocha Gomes, I. R., Guio Cotini, L., da Silva Vargens, D., Queiroz Schimidt, M., Varejão Andreão, R., & Mestria, M. (2023). Virtual reality solutions employing artificial intelligence methods: A systematic literature review. *Association for Computing Machinery*, 55(10), 1–29. DOI: 10.1145/3565020

Sawyer, K. (2008). Optimising learning: Implications of learning sciences research. OECD/CERI International Conference “Learning in the 21st Century: Research, Innovation and Policy”. OECD Publishing.

Slimi, Z., & Carballido, B. V. (2023). Navigating the ethical challenges of artificial intelligence in higher education: An analysis of seven global AI ethics policies. *TEM Journal, 12*(2). https://doi.org/DOI: 10.18421/TEM122-02

Sommerhoff, D., Szameitat, A., Vogel, F., Loderer, O., & Fischer, F. (2018). What do we teach when we teach the learning sciences? A document analysis of 75 graduate programs. *Journal of the Learning Sciences*, 27(2), 319–351. DOI: 10.1080/10508406.2018.1440353

Stallbaumer, C. (2023, March 16). *Introducing Microsoft 365 Copilot – _A whole new way to work. Microsoft* 365. https://www.microsoft.com/en-us/microsoft-365/blog/2023/03/16/introducing-microsoft-365-copilot-a-whole-new-way-to-work/

Storey, V. A. (2023). AI technology and academic writing: Knowing and mastering the “craft skills.”. *International Journal of Adult Education and Technology*, 14(1), 1–15. DOI: 10.4018/IJAET.325795

United Nations Educational, Scientific and Cultural Organization, & Organization, C. (2021). *Recommendation on the Ethics of Artificial Intelligence*. United Nations Educational._https://unesdoc.unesco.org/ark:/48223/pf0000379920.page=14

U.S. Department of Education, Office of Educational Technology. (2023). *Artificial intelligence and future of teaching and learning: insights and recommendations*. Washington._https://tech.ed.gov

Wang, C., Cai, J., Gao, C., & Ye, X. (2023). History, status, and development of AI-based learning science. *SN Computer Science*, 4(3), 316. DOI: 10.1007/s42979-023-01778-1

Zheng, L., Niu, J., Zhong, L., & Gyasi, J. F. (2021). The effectiveness of artificial intelligence on learning achievement and learning perception: A meta-analysis. *Interactive Learning Environments*. Advance online publication. DOI: 10.1080/10494820.2021.2015693

Chapter 3
Unleash AI Into Higher Education: Why Not?

Linda Marie Ellington
https://orcid.org/0000-0002-7697-056X
Southern New Hampshire University, USA

ABSTRACT

This chapter draws from the analysis of the body of research and literature already in existence that offers an overview of artificial intelligence (AI) applications in higher education, focusing on its integration in reshaping teaching and learning dynamics by facilitating personalized and compelling learning experiences. Applying the literature review, the chapter explores AI's role with intelligent learning tools proving crucial in improving user intent to use. The chapter looks at how AI has developed in educational contexts, looks at different ways that AI is used in teaching and learning, and discusses the advantages and disadvantages of integrating AI. The chapter provides ideas on AI's influence on educational paradigms and highlights its potential to revolutionize learning and teaching processes.

INTRODUCTION

Artificial intelligence (AI) integration has yet to emerge as a way of reshaping traditional paradigms. As we navigate this transformative journey in higher education, it is crucial for educators, researchers, and policymakers to actively engage with and

DOI: 10.4018/979-8-3373-0502-8.ch003

comprehend the intricate interplay between AI and education. This understanding is not just beneficial, but it is critical to unlocking the full potential of AI in learning.

AI is impacting all sectors of society, and it is therefore highly likely that higher education is also affected. Its implementation in education has brought about advancements, notably in areas such as teaching methodologies and learning processes. AI integration can bolster teaching and learning in collaboration with educators and create a critical paradigm shift in higher education (Cope et al., 2021; Jianzheng & Xuwei, 2022). The urgency of continuous curriculum changes is underscored by the fact that higher education institutions need to adapt quickly and continuously to stay relevant and afloat in the job market upheavals caused by AI (Ma & Siau, 2019).

In today's technology era, AI refers to computers' ability to perform skills generally associated with human intelligence, such as thinking, correcting, self-improvement, and learning via experience (Richards & Schmidt, 2013, p. 34). AI is powerful, can permeate, and significantly impact various sectors of society, with education being most likely affected (Shiohira, 2021). AI has been embraced and deployed in multiple methods to help students learn. One way AI has improved student learning is to customize and personalize curriculum and information based on the learners' needs, abilities, and capabilities. AI has also removed some obstacles to learning opportunities, such as national and international borders, allowing for global access to learning (Chen et al., 2020). To fully realize the benefits of AI in higher education, a balance must be struck between AI integration and the preservation of the human aspect in education while encouraging AI implementation (Nurjanah et al., 2024).

However, educators still need to clarify how to take an andragogical advantage of it on a broader scale and how it can meaningfully impact teaching and learning in higher education (Zawacki-Richter, 2019). Slimi states that "AI should be more extensively integrated into higher education curricula and that institutions need to consider the implication of AI in the development and implementation of their programs. By doing so, they can better prepare graduates for the future workforce demands" (2023, p. 17).

Integrating AI in higher education will revolutionize learning experiences by promoting accessibility, data-driven insights, lifelong learning, collaborative learning, and the globalization of education. A significant advantage of integrating AI into education is the potential to enhance accessibility for diverse learners. AI-powered tools can provide tailored support for students with varying learning styles, abilities, and needs. For example, students with disabilities can benefit from AI-driven text-to-speech and speech-to-text applications, making educational content more accessible (Zuman, 2023). Zuman states that AI can break down language barriers by offering real-time translation and language learning assistance and fostering inclusivity in multicultural classes (p.10). However, it is essential to tread carefully when implementing AI into higher education. While the benefits are evident, we must remain vigilant about potential risks and ethical concerns.

TECHNOLOGY FRAMEWORK

Artificial Intelligence in Education (AIED) has been widely applied in educational practices, such as intelligent tutoring systems, teaching robots, learning analytics dashboards, adaptive learning systems, and human-computer interactions (Chen et al., 2020). AI has been considered a powerful tool to facilitate new paradigms for instruction design and educational research that are otherwise impossible to develop in traditional education modes (Holmes et al., 2019; Hwang et al., 2023). Specifically, AIED has provided new opportunities, potentials, and challenges for educational innovations, such as the change to personalized learning, the challenge of the instructor's role, and the development of a complex educational system (Holmes et al., 2018; Starcic, 2019). According to Ouyang & Jiao (2021), AIED has undergone several paradigmatic shifts characterized by three paradigms:

- Paradigm One: Learner-as-recipient.
- Paradigm Two: Learner-as-collaborator.
- Paradigm Three: Learner-as-leader.

Paradigm One is characterized as AI-direct, learner-as-recipient. AI represents the domain knowledge and directs the learning processes while the learner acts as the recipient of AI service to follow the specific learning pathways. The theoretical underpinning of paradigm one is behaviorism, which emphasizes constructing carefully arranged content sequences that lead to the learner's correct performance. The learner receives pre-specified knowledge sequences, follows learning procedures, and executes learning activities set by AI to achieve predefined goals (Holmes et al., 2019).

Paradigm Two is characterized as an AI-supported, learner-as-collaborator. The AI system relinquishes its controlling power to serve as a supporting tool while the learner works as a collaborator to focus on the individual learner's learning process. This paradigm is grounded upon a cognitive and social constructivist view of learning. Compared to paradigm one, paradigm two is when the AI system and the learner build mutual interaction, which moves toward more learner-centered learning (Baker et al., 2019; du Boulay, 2019; Rose et al., 2019).

Paradigm Three is characterized as AI-empowered, learner-as-leader, which holds learner agency as the core of AIED (Bandura, 2006) and views AI as a tool to augment human intelligence (Law, 2019). This paradigm reflects a perspective from the complexity theory that views education as a complex adaptive system (Mason, 2008) where a synergetic collaboration between multiple entities (e.g., the learner, the instructor, information, and technology) in the system is essential to ensure the learner's augmented intelligence. In this system, AI techniques need to be designed and applied with the awareness that AI techniques are part of a more extensive system, considering learners, instructors, and human cooperation (Hoc, 2000; Riedl, 2019). This paradigm aims to optimize AI techniques to provide real-time insights about emergent learning and rethink learning changes brought by AI complex, interconnected learning systems (Ouyang & Pengcheng, 2021).

Using AI in higher education has created new opportunities for designing productive learning activities and developing better technology-enhanced learning applications. However, it remains a challenge for most researchers and practitioners from both computers and education to implement relevant systems (Kay, 2012). The challenges of developing adaptive learning systems are not only computer programming skills but also techniques of simulating the intelligence of human experts, which include the knowledge of human experience for making judgments and decisions based on the best available evidence to help solve individual learners' programs and help them learn better. These challenges occur because AIED is a highly technology-dependent and cross-disciplinary field. Without knowing the roles of AI in education and the functioning of AI technologies, practitioners might fail to implement AIED applications and activities effectively (Hwang et al., 2020).

For example, an AI application might play the role of a tutor who observes students' learning processes, analyzes their learning performance, and provides instant assistance based on their needs. Based on the potential needs of students, an interdisciplinary team can develop an intelligent tutoring system that enables students to learn, practice, and interact with peers or teachers but also provides hints, guidance, and support to individuals based on needs (Hwang et al., 2020, p. 2).

Several researchers, such as (Ma et al., 2014 Steenbergen-Hu & Cooper; 2014; Wolf et al., 2017; Gasser & Almeida 2017; Tsai et al., 2019), have reported that AIED can be categorized into four roles:

Intelligent tutor: This could be the largest category of AIED applications, including intelligent tutoring systems, adaptive/personalized learning systems, and recommendations. Cognitive Tutors are an example.

Intelligent tutee: This approach engages learners in helping others understand complex concepts, promoting their higher-order thinking competencies and knowledge level. A chatbot could be an example of an intelligent tutee.

Intelligent learning tool or partner: From the perspective of constructivism and student-centered learning, this application can help learners collect and analyze data efficiently and effectively, enabling them to focus on critical points rather than low-level tasks. For example, a concept mapping tool helps learners organize knowledge by passively connecting the relationships between concepts.

Policy-making advisor: It is possible and feasible to develop a policy-making advisor for policy building in education. With the help of AI technologies, policymakers can more precisely understand the trends and problems in educational settings from both macro and micro perspectives, which can help them build and evaluate effective educational policies.

Figure 1 depicts the roles as follows:

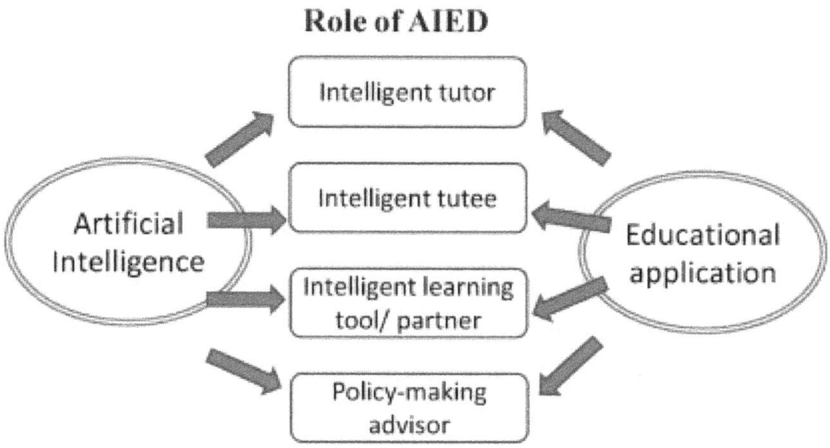

Hwang et al., 2020, p. 2

AIED has been widely applied in educational practices, such as intelligent tutoring systems, teaching robots, learning analytics dashboards, adaptive learning systems, and human-computer interactions (Chen & Hwang, 2020). AI has been considered a powerful tool to facilitate new paradigms for instruction design and educational research that are otherwise impossible to develop in traditional education modes (Holmes et al., 2019; Hwang et al., 2020). Specifically, AIED has provided new opportunities, potentials, and challenges for educational innovations, such as the change to personalized learning, the challenge of the instructor's role, and the development of a complex educational system (Holmes et al., 2018; Starcic, 2019).

AI APPLICATIONS WITHIN HIGHER EDUCATION

Generative AI and adaptive AI systems, such as ChatGPT, intelligent agents, intelligent e-learning systems, and intelligent teaching systems, suggest or provide learning materials based on what they have learned from the student as they gather information on the behaviors. This could be a level of questioning based on prior answers or suggested reading material based on what the student has searched for before.

ChatGPT: Performs several specific actions that benefit learners and teachers in higher education:

- Tutoring and homework assistance can include explaining, clarifying doubts, and helping students understand complex concepts. It can also offer step-by-step solutions to problems.
- Writing and editing support assists students in drafting, structuring, and refining their written work. It offers grammar, style, and coherence guidance, helping students improve written assignments.
- Research and study aids help by suggesting relevant literature, providing summaries of academic papers, and offering insights into research methodologies. They can also assist in data analysis and interpretation, making the research process more efficient.
- Language practice and translation help students practice new languages through conversational exercises, vocabulary building, and grammar correction. Additionally, it can assist with translating texts between languages, aiding multilingual students or those learning a new language.
- Administrative task automation can handle routine administrative tasks such as scheduling, managing course materials, and sending reminders. This automation helps reduce educators' workloads, allowing them to concentrate more on teaching and student engagement.

*Intelligent Tutoring Systems:*Huang and Chen (2016) described the different aspects of intelligent tutoring systems in higher education as:

Student Model: Information on the student's knowledge, cognitive level, learning motivation, and style.

Teacher Model: Analysis of students, strategies, and methods.

Domain Model: The knowledge representation of teachers and students collectively

Diagnosis Model: When the AI system evaluates mistakes and defects of the intelligent model.

Adaptive Learning Systems

Artificial intelligence shapes adaptive learning systems and leverages advanced technology and capabilities. Machine learning algorithms serve to scrutinize extensive datasets encompassing learner profiles, performance metrics, and educational resources. AI algorithms intelligently forecast learner needs, preferences, and future performance by discerning patterns, trends, and correlations within the data. This, in turn, empowers adaptive learning systems to dynamically tailor content, pacing, and instructional approaches according to the distinct requirements of individual learners, fostering personalized and efficient learning.

AI-driven adaptive learning systems comprise multiple interconnected components synergistically working together to deliver a personalized educational encounter. Learner modeling entails creating and keeping individual learner profiles, encompassing data such as assessment scores, learning preferences, progress tracking, and socio-emotional factors. Content customization relies on AI algorithms to dynamically adapt the complexity, format, sequence, and delivery of learning materials, guided by learner profiles and real-time feedback. Feedback mechanisms integrated into adaptive learning systems furnish timely and individualized feedback to learners, enabling them to monitor progress, pinpoint improvement opportunities, and make necessary adjustments to enhance learning strategies. Addressing challenges in platforms like OpenStax and ASSISSTments, well-known OER platforms necessitate instructors to verify their identity before accessing materials. This AI-fueled feedback loop establishes a continuous cycle of assessment, refinement, and feedback, enhancing the learning experience's effectiveness and personalization.

Personalized Learning

With AI's capability to analyze vast amounts of data, educational platforms can now tailor learning resources and recommendations based on individual student habits, capabilities, and progress. This ensures that each student receives instruction best suited to their learning style and pace—thus, gone are the days of the one-size-fits-all teaching model.

The integration of AI aims to bolster student outcomes, engagement, and overall educational ambiance by intertwining teaching with AI algorithms to recommend resources based on students' learning levels and curriculum requisites (Liang et al., 2022). Applications such as adaptive testing, predictive analytics, chatbots for learning and research, and large language models are instrumental in creating supportive learning environments (Ting et al., 2023).

Virtual Labs

Virtual labs can simulate a wide range of experimental environments. This offers students a safe and cost-effective platform for experimentation and is valuable in distance education, where access to physical labs might be limited. Integrating AI with virtual labs is poised to accelerate scientific processes and address global challenges.

These virtual labs aim to offer a standard software layer across different scientific domains, facilitating a broad spectrum of disciplines with AI assistance. Implementing virtual reality technology in conjunction with AI not only virtualizes laboratory practices but also enhances academic programs in higher education, creating immersive learning experiences and aiding the teaching-learning process (Rojas-Contreras & Ruiz-Bautista, 2020).

Intelligent Teaching Assistants

AI-driven teaching assistance can automatically grade assignments, answer common student queries, and provide feedback. This ensures consistent and unbiased grading and allows educators to focus on more complex student interactions. The augmentation of teaching and learning practices through AI presents productive affordances, enabling educators to create supportive learning environments (Bronwyn, Eager, 2023). AI technology like chatbots has demonstrated efficacy in improving English learning outcomes, thereby heightening interest in learning the language (AI-Aided Teaching Model in Education 5.0, 2023). Additionally, AI frameworks in higher education are pivotal in reshaping the educational system, with enhancements in virtual reality and AI tutors showcasing the potential to bridge the educational outcome-industry need gap (Rawan et al., 2022). The overarching narrative suggests a promising trajectory for AI integration in higher education, transforming teaching and learning processes to meet contemporary educational and industry demands.

NAVIGATING OPPORTUNITIES

While many in higher education welcome and embrace the opportunities presented by AI, there are also warnings that academic integrity and contemporary understanding of disciplinary knowledge are under attack (Stokel-Walker, 2023). There appears to be saber-rattling by those who claim that AI is yet another existential threat to the institution of higher education and that this threat will irreparably damage the academic enterprise (Farrelly & Baker, 2023). One issue identified by von Krogh et al. (2023) is that AI is not a neutral and objective entity; it depends on the quality of the data used in training and the method of refining or tuning the model, which can be subject to the human biases of their creators. Moreover, while these biases can be at least partially accounted for, the process uses human intervention and exposure to the worst elements of the internet (Halaweh, 2023; Perrigo, 2023).

Notwithstanding AI's tremendous promise to improve educational systems, full integration of AI into education requires solid legislative support. Educational leadership needs more support to concentrate on creating students who can thrive in an AI society. The government is finding it challenging to keep up with the rapid advancements in AI for education by private organizations, such as Coursera, McGraw-Hill, Pearson, and IBM (Nagar, 2024). Addressing issues through state legislation can help set standards, provide solutions, and foster the growth of innovative ecosystems that can integrate AI into educational settings. Scholars and practitioners acknowledge the disruptive potential of AI in higher education and call for a balanced approach that addresses both the challenges and opportunities it presents by emphasizing the importance of AI literacy and ethical consideration in adopting AI technologies to ensure equitable access and positive outcomes for all students (Farrelly & Baker, 2023). One idea Farrelly and Baker (2023) expressed is to revise Bloom's Taxonomy to support educators in using AI tools equitably in their teaching and leadership.

Educators are central in effectively using AI to enhance learning experiences while addressing associated challenges. It is essential to equip them with the necessary skills focused on digital literacy, data literacy, and ethical considerations (AlAli & Wardat, 2023). Educators must be empowered to assess AI tools critically, interpret data, and mitigate biases to foster fair and inclusive learning environments (AlAli & Wardat, 2023, p. 784).

Successful integration of AI in education necessitates collaborative efforts among diverse stakeholders, such as educators, policymakers, technologists, and students. The ethical, social, and andragogical implications of AI adoption can be collectively addressed through interdisciplinary partnerships. This takes transparent communication, shared governance, and participatory design to promote trust, accountability, and alignment with human-centric values (AlAli & Wardat, 2023, p. 785).

AI applications provide numerous opportunities for individuals to interact in an augmented environment in real time, creating an engaging and exciting learning environment for students (Akcayir & Akcayir, 2017). AI apps introduce educational content in a way that encourages students to take the initiative for their applications (Jerry & Aaron, 2010); the international academic literature highlights several uses of AI, which have been designed and implemented in the teaching of various subjects, including math, natural sciences, astronomy, language skills, and biology (Wang & Wang, 2021). Bower et al. (2014) expands this into a virtual perspective of poetry.

AI-integrated educational technologies are revolutionizing education by demonstrating tremendous potential for increasing access to learning opportunities for marginalized communities. These communities often encounter various obstacles, such as cost, location, infrastructure, disabilities, and social biases. Scholars like Devedzic et al. (2021) and Vinuesa et al. (2022) have emphasized the transformative impact of AI in this context. One significant way AI enhances accessibility to education is through the availability of massive open online courses and digital content. These resources are now accessible either free or at affordable prices, ensuring that students from economically disadvantaged backgrounds can access high-quality curricula (Chen et al., 2020). This equalization of education is a game-changer for individuals who previously faced limited opportunities. Moreover, AI-powered adaptive learning systems dismantle barriers for people with visual impairments or other disabilities. Technologies like text-to-speech enable these individuals to actively engage in educational activities (Nandigam et al., 2022). AI removes the stigma associated with needing additional support. This not only enhances the learning experience for individuals with disabilities but also promotes inclusivity in higher education.

NAVIGATING CHALLENGES

Integrating AI in higher education holds immense promise for altering the learning experience. However, it also presents various challenges that must be thoughtfully addressed to ensure its effective and ethical use. One of the foremost concerns is bias, as AI systems can inherit prejudices from skewed training data or flawed algorithms, potentially resulting in unjust treatment and the perpetuation of existing student inequalities (Zaman, 2023). Furthermore, the issue of privacy looms large, with AI's ability to collect and analyze vast amounts of student data raising legitimate concerns about the protection and appropriate use of sensitive information (Zaman, 2023, p.8).

With AI-related concepts in educational systems, administrators face a significant challenge in keeping their institutions up-to-date and relevant, given the rapid advancements in AI capabilities and their wide-ranging applications across various fields (Mohanty & Parida, 2022; Vinuesa et al., 2022). It has become increasingly essential for students to acquire knowledge and skills using AI tools and applications to compete in the job market. However, incorporating new AI themes into the existing curriculum structures poses two primary obstacles that education systems must overcome (Lockery & Gutteridge, 2022). First, there is the challenge of identifying the most impactful AI topics to include in the curriculum, and second, it can take time to determine which areas will have the most significant impact on future industries and job roles. Education administrators and industry leaders must carefully evaluate the potential long-term different AI themes and prioritize those most likely to shape the future landscape of work and society.

RETHINKING TEACHING AND LEARNING

AI helps teachers nurture the next generation of learners. The use of AI in the classroom has the potential to usher in a new era of student engagement and knowledge exchange through the development of dynamic, collaborative learning spaces. With the support of AI-driven tools, educators can cultivate more interactive and cooperative classrooms. Despite its many positive uses, how AI systems affect cultural norms, standards, and student-teacher interaction is still being determined. Student success is greatly affected by the learner-instructor relationship, defined by engagement, presence, support, and communication.

The rapid development of AI has brought about a sea change, challenging long-held beliefs in education and creating new opportunities for student success. Along with customization, AI gives teachers a cognitive augmentation tool that improves teaching skills. Teachers can maximize learning outcomes by adapting their teaching methods based on real-time insights provided by machine learning algorithms that examine large data sets for student knowledge trends (Nagar, 2024). In addition, AI shows great potential to revolutionize the appraisal process. Standardized testing and rote memorization are commonplace in traditional evaluation systems but do not capture the depth and breadth of students' knowledge and talents (Nagar, 2024, p.2).

AI is changing conventional teaching methods and influencing how the sector will use technology in the future. According to Mote (2024), AI applications have different educational benefits, such as personalized education, task automation, intelligent content creation, adaptable access, determining classroom vulnerabilities, closing skill gaps, customized data-based feedback, 24/7 assistance with conversational AI, and secure and decentralized learning systems (p. 108).

For example, focusing just on personalized education, AI has advantages over traditional education. The learner can choose their own pace, style, and content according to their strengths and interests. Immediate personalized feedback helps to improve performance. The most relevant content is provided to the individuals according to their strengths and needs to improve. Feedback is tailored to each student's mistakes or challenges, promoting targeted learning (Mote, 2024).

Integrating AI-powered educational technologies, such as intelligent tutoring systems and virtual simulations, has necessitated reevaluating traditional teaching methods in physical classrooms and online learning environments (Holmes et al., 2022). There is concern that if the role of human educators is not thoroughly reconsidered, AI technologies may inadvertently perpetuate passing learning dynamics (Jiang et al., 2021). According to constructivist learning theories, more than simply delivering content is required to foster meaningful skill development. Students also need opportunities for analytical discussions, critical assessment, creative expressions, and hands-on experiences (Wass & Golding, 2014).

THE PROS AND CONS

The digitization of society and education, a prominent trend supported by the transition to remote education in conjunction with the COVID-19 epidemic, drives the broad implementation of different formats for online learning worldwide (Almusaed et al., 2023). Moorhouse and Wong (2021) advocate for promoting new educational activities within the digital realm, facilitating innovative learning forms, and adapting to the evolving academic landscape shaped by technological advancement.

According to (Chetry, 2024; Jian, 2023; Y Feng et al., 2019) the pros of AI are:

1. *Personalized Learning*: AI algorithms analyze individual learning styles, preferences, and abilities to offer tailored learning experiences, enhancing student engagement and comprehension. AI-driven personalized learning experiences can transform andragogical strategies, incorporating innovations like e-learning modules and virtual tutors.
2. *Enhanced Efficiency*: AI-powered tools automate routine tasks such as grading, lesson planning, and administrative duties, allowing educators to focus more on personalized instruction and support.
3. *Accessibility*: AI technology, including speech-to-text transcription and language translation, improves access to educational content for students with disabilities or language barriers, fostering inclusivity in the learning environment. MOOCs, eLearning platforms, and cloud classrooms further facilitate the sharing of teaching resources.
4. *Data-driven Insights*: AI-driven analytics provide stakeholders valuable insights into learning trends and outcomes, enabling informed decision-making and targeted interventions to support student success.
5. *Adaptive Learning*: AI-powered adaptive learning platforms adjust instruction pace and content in real-time based on student progress, ensuring learning experiences are appropriately challenging and leading to improved outcomes.

According to (Chetry, 2024; Chaudhry & Kazim, 2021), the cons of AI are:

1. *Privacy Concerns*: AI systems' collection and analysis of large amounts of student data raise privacy concerns regarding personal information security and misuse, necessitating robust safeguards to protect student privacy rights. Addressing data privacy, algorithmic bias, and equitable access to AI-powered resources is essential for responsible and equitable AI implementation in education.
2. *Bias and Fairness*: AI algorithms may inadvertently perpetuate biases present in data, resulting in unfair treatment or discriminatory outcomes for specific student populations. Ensuring algorithmic fairness and mitigating bias are ongoing challenges in AI-driven education.
3. *Dependency on Technology*: Overreliance on AI technologies may lead to declining students' critical thinking, creativity, and interpersonal communication abilities, emphasizing the need to balance technology with teaching methods.
4. *Implementation Challenges*: Integrating AI into educational systems requires substantial investment in infrastructure, training, and ongoing support for educators, posing challenges for institutions with limited resources or technical expertise.
5. *Ethical Considerations*: The use of AI in education raises ethical questions related to transparency, accountability, and equity, necessitating careful consideration of ethical implications and responsible deployment of AI technologies in educational settings.

Pranav et al. (2024) identified the opportunities and challenges as:

Opportunities:

Reducing Instructors' Workload: AI significantly reduces educators' workloads by automating administrative tasks like proofreading and course material composition.

Personalized Learning: AI accommodates individual student needs that instructors might find challenging to address. This allows students to progress at their own pace.

Data-Drive Insights: AI-driven learning analytics empower teachers with comprehensive insights into student performance. By exposing and mitigating cognitive biases, AI contributes to a fairer educational environment regarding ethnicity and gender.

Improved Assessment Practices: AI enables a shift from periodic tests to continuous monitoring of student knowledge. This shift from standardized tests provides a more accurate representation of a student's understanding.

Integration with Digital Learning Applications: AI enhances existing digital learning resources by learning and adapting rules. AI optimizes learning outcomes with technologies like Virtual Reality (VR), Augmented Reality (AR), and serious games. However, caution is needed to ensure that knowledge gained in virtual environments aligns with real-world applicability and maintain the importance of less formalized knowledge acquired in traditional educational settings.

Challenges:

Impact on Educational Objectives: The overemphasis on technology in AI development risks educational objectives. When AI narrowly focuses on data and technology, there is a potential need for more alignment with academic goals. This could result in learning lacking essential elements like motivation or the entry of foreign actors into the education market, which may lead to a loss of control of educational processes.

Risk in Full Automation of Education: Full automation of education, particularly when students undergo the educational process without human intervention, raises concerns about the human nature of the learning experience. Excessive use of simulations for teaching adds another layer of risk, as knowledge and skills acquired in simulations may not be applicable in real-world scenarios.

Bias in AI from Human Data: Deploying AI introduces a significant risk related to biases in human data being incorporated into AI systems. Historical data may contain biases against ethnicity and gender, potentially leading to a feedback loop that systematically disadvantages certain minorities.

Impact on the Teacher Labor Market: Integrating AI could shift teachers' skills. Data-driven education is not currently part of teacher training, and if teachers cannot adapt, future educators may choose to become data scientists with a less robust educational background.

Dependency on Incomprehensive AI Systems: There is a risk of education becoming overly dependent on AI systems that need more transparency and understanding. Both teachers and AI systems need increased explainability and knowledge to navigate their challenges. Teachers cannot be held responsible for systems they find incomprehensible.

Implementing AI Without Prerequisites: Several prerequisites must be met before successful AI implementation in education, including a technical infrastructure and data availability. Raid implementation without meeting these conditions may lead to unmet expectations and potential aversion to AI in education.

Artificial Intelligence has emerged as a transformative technology in education. While the potential benefits of AI in education are numerous, it is essential to consider the associated challenges and risks to ensure that it is deployed ethically, equitably, and effectively for the benefit of students.

INFRASTRUCTURE AND RECOMMENDATIONS

There are infrastructure and policy frameworks, considerations, and strategies that educational institutions should consider when implementing AI in education. According to Zaman (2023, p.9), they are:

Scalability and Accessibility: To ensure that AI can benefit diverse learners, the needs of resource-rich and resource-constrained environments must be considered. Collaboration with technology providers and researchers can help tailor AI tools to different educational settings, making them more accessible to a broader audience. We must emphasize the importance of implementing AI in education from a technical perspective and establishing the proper governance.

Governance and Policy: Establishing comprehensive governance and policy frameworks to guide AI's ethical and practical use in education. This involves creating clear guidelines for collecting, storing, and sharing data. It also outlines procedures for handling data breaches and ensuring compliance with data protection regulations. These policies ensure that AI is used responsibly and within legal boundaries. Additionally, these policies address bias and fairness issues, setting standards for AI algorithms to minimize discrimination and promote fair learning opportunities.

Data Security and Privacy Protection: Sensitive student data is of the utmost importance when implementing AI. Institutions must implement security measures, encryption protocols, and access controls to safeguard against unauthorized access and data breaches. Using transparent communication with students about how their data is used and the privacy policies in place is essential for building and maintaining trust and ensuring compliance with privacy regulations.

Stakeholder Engagement: This involves all relevant stakeholders in the integration of AI. Their input can help shape AI-driven solutions that align with the specific needs and preferences of the educational community. Involving students in decision-making can enhance their sense of ownership and trust in AI-powered educational tools, making them more likely to embrace and benefit from these technologies.

GOVERNANCE AND POLICY

Policymakers must incorporate data science and machine learning into core frameworks. Self-paced learning platforms require new classroom dynamics. Assessments must prioritize higher-order thinking. An AI-driven education framework offers three crucial opportunities: broadening access, strengthening educators, and tailoring education (Huong, 2024).

Full integration of AI requires policies, institutional readiness, and public consciousness to be equally crucial in steering this transformation. Addressing issues through legislation can help set standards, provide solutions, and foster the growth of innovative ecosystems that can integrate AI into educational settings (Nagar, 2024). The foundations of policymaking need to be inclusion and fairness. Policymakers must incorporate data science and machine learning into core frameworks. Self-paced learning platforms require new classroom dynamics. Assessments must prioritize higher-order thinking. An AI-driven education framework offers three crucial opportunities: broadening access, strengthening educators, and tailoring education (Huong, 2024).

A collaborative ethos among educators, policymakers, AI developers, and other stakeholders ensures that AI integration aligns with the overarching educational goals and societal values. This collaborative framework should foster open discourse on ethical AI use, data governance, and potential impacts on educational equity and accessibility.

The integration of AI in education holds significant potential across various domains. The education sector welcomes, if not enthusiastically, the application of AI, particularly for automating administrative and specific educational tasks, such as test review and curriculum personalization. However, for AI to have a high impact, the role of instructors in AI implementation is a subject of ongoing discussion.

AlAli1 and Wardat (2024) offer recommendations to policymakers:

Invest in Comprehensive Training: Prioritize training programs for educators to enhance digital and data literacy and understand ethical considerations in AI integration. This will empower them to utilize AI tools and navigate challenges effectively.

Foster Collaboration: Encourage collaboration and transparency among stakeholders, including educators, technologists, and students, to ensure a holistic approach to AI integration. This collaboration can lead to better-informed decisions and strategies.

Develop Ethical Guidelines: Establish robust ethical guidelines for AI usage, emphasizing transparency, accountability, and fairness.

Enhance Data Privacy Measures: Implement stringent data privacy measures to safeguard sensitive student information. This includes compliance with data protection regulations and adopting robust security protocols to prevent unauthorized access.

Encourage Research and Evaluation: Promote research and evaluation efforts to continuously assess the impact of AI integration in education. This includes monitoring the effectiveness of AI tools, identifying areas for improvement, and ensuring alignment with andragogical goals and student needs.

Promote User Education: Provide educational resources for students to develop critical thinking skills and digital literacy when interacting with AI technologies. This will empower them to become responsible and informed users of AI-driven educational tools.

Ensure Equity and Accessibility: Prioritize equity and accessibility in AI integration efforts to ensure equitable access for all students. This includes addressing digital divides and providing support for marginalized or underserved communities.

Monitor and Adapt: Continuously monitor AI integration efforts and adapt strategies based on feedback and evolving needs. This iterative approach will help ensure that AI technologies effectively support teaching and learning goals while addressing emerging challenges and opportunities.

THE INTERSECTION OF AI AND EDUCATIONAL LEADERSHIP

The intersection of AI and educational leadership is an evolving trend with a broad perspective on enhancing different aspects of education. Educational management officials and staff members also use AI to reshape the future and gain the interest of the government, academia, and the public (Cox, 2021). The most crucial factor to be transformed is education leadership in the education system. The leadership role is perplexing and complicated (Mazurkiewicz & Fisher, 2021). Educational leadership improves practices and programs by applying effective methods. As AI has the potential to make the learning process more engaging and create a new form of interaction, leaders seek enhanced technology approaches for the development of their education institutes. According to Satya and Mohammed (2024), effective use of AI-based education systems enhances the value of educational leadership. The redefinition of school and education is necessary. The best way to do that is through educational leadership transformation. An original creative leadership is immediately required (Mazurkiewicz & Kolodziejcyk (2017). Leadership helps people in the growing stage fulfill their goals with satisfaction and respect for work and others. The world requires numerous efforts from education to create material and intellectual infrastructure.

AI is considered a powerful weapon for assisting original and creative paradigms for technological enhancement, instructional design, and education research, which cannot be improved with traditional education (Satya & Mohammed, 2024). AI increases the accuracy and efficiency of educational leaders. The most significant aspect of integrating AI in educational leadership is enhanced data-driven decision-making. AI is considered an approach for school leaders to finalize decisions related to the development of schools (Wang, 2021b). AI speeds up the potential to improve the data literacy of educational leaders

Additionally, AI modernizes administrative responsibilities. For example, AI systems automatically help with routine administrative processes, such as data management and scheduling. Since automation is implemented, leaders can concentrate more on instructional leadership, strategic preparation, and nurturing an optimistic learning atmosphere (Satya & Mohammed, 2024). Although AI usage requires careful planning, it is necessary in the age of technology to develop and improve the entire education environment.

AI COMPLEMENT AND COMPETENCY FOR TEACHERS

Continuous professional development should be prioritized to leverage AI effectively. This includes training educators in data literacy, AI concepts, and teaching methods that complement AI applications. By investing in the workforce's skills and knowledge, institutions can ensure that AI is a valuable tool to enhance teaching and learning rather than a substitute for human educators (Zaman, 2023).

AI enhances human teaching rather than substitutes for nuanced instructors, so teacher training programs must adapt to equip the next generation of educators with the necessary technical and socioemotional competencies to navigate the evolving educational landscape (Luckin et al., 2016). It is no longer sufficient for teachers to possess subject matter expertise solely; they must also be proficient in leveraging AI-enabled tools and understanding how to effectively integrate them into their teaching practices. The rise of AI-enabled educational technologies has revolutionized the field of teaching. By reimaging traditional teaching methods and equipping teachers with the necessary skills, we can create a harmonious blend of technology and human instruction that maximizes student learning outcomes (Huong, 2024).

Chetry (2024) posits that AI is a complement to teachers:

Human Connection: Teachers provide emotional support, encouragement, and mentorship to students, essential components of the learning process. AI may assist with certain aspects of instruction, but it cannot replicate the human connection and empathy that teachers offer.

Complex Interactions: Teaching involves dynamic interactions that require understanding, adaptation, and context awareness, which AI currently struggles to replicate. Teachers can assess students' needs, adjust instruction in real time, and provide personalized feedback considering individual differences and learning styles.

Critical Thinking and Creativity: Teaching goes beyond imparting knowledge; it involves fostering students' critical thinking skills, creativity, and problem-solving abilities. While AI can automate routine tasks and provide access to information, it lacks the capacity for independent thought and the ability to inspire and motivate students.

Ethical and Social Development: Teachers guide students' ethical and social development, teaching values, empathy, and responsible citizenship. These aspects of education require human judgment, moral reasoning, and social interaction, which AI cannot fully replace.

Adaptability and Flexibility: Education constantly evolves, and teachers must adapt to new andragogical approaches, technologies, and learning environments. While AI can support educators by providing data-driven insights and tools, human teachers possess the adaptability, flexibility, and creativity to meet the evolving needs of students and society.

Educators must be empowered to assess AI tools critically, interpret data, and mitigate biases to foster fair and inclusive learning environments (Mollman, 2022). Additionally, the successful integration of AI in education necessitates collaborative efforts among diverse stakeholders such as educators, policymakers, technologists, and students. The ethical, social, and pedagogical implications of AI adoption can be collectively addressed through interdisciplinary partnerships. Transparent communication, shared governance, and participatory design are crucial for promoting trust, accountability, and alignment with human-centric values.

CONCLUSION

Some individuals may question the use of AI in higher education for several reasons. One concern is the potential for AI to replace human educators, leading to job displacement and reduced personal interaction between students and teachers. Additionally, there are concerns about data privacy and security. AI systems may collect large amounts of sensitive information about students. Some critics argue that using AI could exacerbate educational inequalities by favoring students with access to the technology and resources needed to benefit from AI-based learning tools.

To the naysayers who are hesitant about integrating AI into higher education, it is essential to emphasize that AI can complement rather than replace human educators. By leveraging AI tools thoughtfully and ethically, universities can enhance personalized learning experiences, optimize administrative processes, and provide students with valuable skills for the future job market. Collaborative efforts between AI systems and human educators can lead to a more efficient, inclusive, and engaging learning environment that benefits all stakeholders in higher education.

As AI technology advances, we, as custodians of education and conduits of knowledge transfer, have the onus to navigate the turbulent waters of educational innovations proactively. These innovations could create more inclusive and effective learning environments that cater to students' diverse needs and abilities. By embracing AI responsibly, we can harness its full potential to revolutionize education and ultimately empower students to thrive in a rapidly changing world. Is not that the purpose of education?

REFERENCES

Akcayir, M., & Akcayir, G. (2017). Advantages and challenges associated with augmented reality for education: A systematic literature review. *Educational Research Review*, 20, 1–11. DOI: 10.1016/j.edurev.2016.11.002

AlAli, R., & Wardat, Y. (2024). Opportunities and challenges of integrating generative artificial intelligence in education. *International Journal of Religion*, 5(7), 784–793. DOI: 10.61707/8y29gv34

Almusaed, A., Almssad, A., Yitmen, I., & Homod, R. Z. (2023). Enhancing student engagement: Harnessing "AIED"'s power in hybrid education—A Review analysis. *Education Sciences*, 13(7), 632. DOI: 10.3390/educsci13070632

Baker, T., Smith, L., & Anissa, N. (2019). Educ-AI-tion rebooted? Exploring the future of artificial intelligence in schools and colleges. https://www.nesta.org. UK/report/education-rebooted/

Chen, L., Chen, P., & Lin, Z. (2020). Artificial intelligence in education: A review. *IEEE Access : Practical Innovations, Open Solutions*, 8, 75264–75278. DOI: 10.1109/ACCESS.2020.2988510

Chen, X., Xie, H., & Hwang, G. J. (2020). A multi-perspective study on artificial intelligence in education: Grants, conferences, journals, software tools, institutions, and researchers. *Computer & Education: Artificial Intelligence 1*.https://www.sciencedirect.com/science/article/pii/S2666920X20300059

Chetry, K. (2024). Transforming Education: How AI is Revolutionizing the Learning Experience. *International Journal of Research Publication and Reviews*, 5(5), 6352–6356. DOI: 10.55248/gengpi.5.0524.1277

Cope, B., Kalantzis, M., & Searsmith, D. (2021). Artificial intelligence for education: Knowledge and its assessment in AI-enabled learning ecologies. *Educational Philosophy and Theory*, 53(12), 1229–1245. DOI: 10.1080/00131857.2020.1728732

Cox, A. M. (2021). Exploring the impact of Artificial Intelligence and robots on higher education through literature-based design fiction. *International Journal of Educational Technology in Higher Education*, 18(1), 3. DOI: 10.1186/s41239-020-00237-8

Devedžić, V., Jovanović, J., Delić, V., Ševarac, Z., & Medenica, M. (2021). A framework for evaluating AIEd solutions' pedagogical, ethical, and privacy aspects. *Education Sciences*, 11(12), 840.

du Boulay, B. (2019). Can we learn from ITSs*? In International conference on intelligent tutoring systems,* 9-17. Springer.

Farrelly, T., & Baker, N. (2023). Generative Artificial Intelligence: Implications and Considerations for Higher Education Practice. *Education Sciences*, 13(11), 1109. https://www.mdpi.com/2227-7102/13/11/1109. DOI: 10.3390/educsci13111109

Feng, Y., Zhan, G., & Li, Z. (2019). Research on the co-construction of sharing of teaching resources under the "Internet Plus" environment. *10th International Conference on Information Technology in Medicine and Education,* Qingdao, China, pp. 498–502. DOI: 10.1109/ITME.2019.00117

Gasser, U., & Almeida, V. A. (2017). A layered model for AI governance. *IEEE Internet Computing*, 21(6), 58–62. DOI: 10.1109/MIC.2017.4180835

Halaweh, M. (2023). ChatGPT in education: Strategies for responsible implementation. *Contemporary Educational Technology*, 15(2), 15. DOI: 10.30935/cedtech/13036

Holmes, W., Anastopoulou, S., Schaumburg, H., & Mavrikis, M. (2018). *Technology-enhanced personalized learning: Untangling the evidence*. Rob Bosch Stiftung.

Holmes, W., Bialik, M., & Fadel, C. (2019). *Artificial intelligence in education: Promises and implications for teaching and learning*. Center for Curriculum Redesign.

Huang, J., & Chen, Z. (2016). The research and design of a web-based intelligent tutoring system. *International Journal of Multimedia and Ubiquitous Engineering*, 11(6), 337–348. DOI: 10.14257/ijmue.2016.11.6.30

Huong, X. V. (2024). The Implications of artificial intelligence for educational systems: Challenges, opportunities, and transformative potential. *The American Journal of Social Science and Education Innovations*, 6(03), 101–111. DOI: 10.37547/tajssei/Volume06Issue03-17

Hwang, G. J., Xie, H., Wah, B. W., & Gasevic, D. (2020). Vision, challenges, roles and research issues of artificial intelligence in education. *Computers & Education*, •••, 1.

Jerry, T., & Aaron, C. (2010). The impact of augmented reality software with inquiry-based learning on students' learning. *International Conference on Educational Technology and Computer, 2*(1). DOI: 10.1109/ICETC.2010.5529447

Kay, J. (2012). AI and education: Grand challenges. *IEEE Intelligent Systems*, 27(5), 66–69. DOI: 10.1109/MIS.2012.92

Liang, Zhang., Xiaomei, Zeng., & Ping, Lv. (2022). Higher Education-Oriented Recommendation Algorithm for Personalized Learning Resource. *International Journal of Emerging Technologies in Learning*.

Luckin, R., Holmes, W., Griffiths, M., & Forcier, L. B. (2016). *Intelligence Unleashed: An argument for AI in Education*. Pearson.

Ma, Y., & Siau, K. (2019). Intelligent tutoring systems and learning outcomes: A meta-analysis. *Journal of Educational Psychology*, 106(4), 901–918. DOI: 10.1037/a0037123

Mazurkiewicz, G., & Fischer, J. M. (2021). *The power of responsive educational leadership: Building schools for global challenges*. Routledge. DOI: 10.4324/9781003130277

Mazurkiewicz, G., & Kołodziejczyk, J. (2017). Management and education during the times of interregnum. ruj.uj.edu.pl, 149-158.

Mohanty, S., & Parida, A. K. (2022). Intelligent learning using artificial intelligence: Applications, challenges, and adaptation. *Education and Information Technologies*.

Moorhouse, B. J., & Wong, K. M. (2021). Blending asynchronous and synchronous digital technologies and instructional approaches to facilitate remote learning. *Journal of Computers in Education*, 9(1), 51–70. DOI: 10.1007/s40692-021-00195-8

Mote, A. P. (2024). Role of AI in personalized education. *International Journal of Advanced Research in Science. Tongxin Jishu*, 4(4). https://ijarsct.co.in/Paper15919.pdf

Nagar, N. (2024). Importance of artificial intelligence in education. *International Journal of Scientific Research in Engineering and Management*, 10(12), 387–392. https://www.ijres.org/papers/Volume-10/Issue-12/1012387392.pdf

Nandigam, D., Tavva, V., & Reddy, N. V. S. (2022). Applications of artificial intelligence in education for visually impaired people: A review. *Assistive Technology*, 1, 11.

Nurjanah, I. N. Salsabilla, A. Azzahra, Rahayu, R., & Marlina, N. (2024). Artificial intelligence (AI) usage in today's teaching and learning process. *Ridwan Institute*, 6.

Ouyang, F., & Jiao, P. (2021). Artificial intelligence in education: The three paradigms. *Computers & Education*, 2, •••. https://www.sciencedirect.com/science/article/pii/S2666920X2100014X

Perrigo, B. (2023). OpenAI Used Kenyan Workers on Less Than $2 Per Hour to Make ChatGPT Less Toxic. *Time*.

Pranav, S. S. Nausheen Noor Zaidi, & Rana, S. (2024). Application of AI in education: Dynamic course generation, International Journal for Research in Applied Science & Engineering Technology, 12(5). https://discovery.researcher.life/article/application-of-ai-in-the-field-of-education-dynamic-course-generation/26f15f04b11636a2b810554b7a617c7f

Rawan, G., Adnan, S., Abrar, M., & Al, S. (2022). Higher Education Transformation for Artificial Intelligence Revolution: Transformation Framework. *International Journal of Emerging Technologies in Learning*, 17(19). https://online-journals.org/index.php/i-jet/article/view/33309

Rojas-Contreras, M., & Ruiz-Bautista, L. E. (2020, December). Online laboratories are supported with virtual reality for higher education. In *Journal of Physics: Conference Series, 1708* (Vol. 1). IOP Publishing. DOI: 10.1088/1742-6596/1708/1/012036

Rose, C. P., McLaughlin, E. A., Liu, R., & Koedinger, K. R. (2019). Explanatory learner models: Why machine learning (alone) is not the answer. *British Journal of Educational Technology*, 50(6), 2943–2958. DOI: 10.1111/bjet.12858

Satya, R., & Mohammed, L. A. (2024). Interdisciplinary Insights: The Convergence of AI and Educational Leadership. *International Journal of Research and Innovation in Social Science*. https://rsisinternational.org/journals/ijriss/articles/interdisciplinary-insights-the-convergence-of-ai-and-educational-leadership/

Slimi, Z. (2023). The impact of artificial intelligence on higher education: An empirical study. Deusto University-Spain. *National University of Sciences and Technology*. https://files.eric.ed.gov/fulltext/EJ1384682.pdf

Starcic, A. I. (2019). Human learning and learning analytics in the age of artificial intelligence. *British Journal of Educational Technology*, 50(6), 2974–2976. DOI: 10.1111/bjet.12879

Steenbergen-Hu, S., & Cooper, H. (2014). A meta-analysis of the effectiveness of intelligent tutoring systems on college students' academic learning. *Journal of Educational Psychology*, 106(2), 331–347. DOI: 10.1037/a0034752

Tsai, Y. S., Poquet, O., Gasevic, D., Dawson, S., & Pardo, A. (2019). Complexity leadership in learning analytics: Drivers, challenges, and opportunities. *British Journal of Educational Technology*, 50(6), 2839–2854. DOI: 10.1111/bjet.12846

Vinuesa, R., Azizpour, H., Leite, I., Olsson, C., Boeva, V., Smith, D. M., Jamone, L., & Lourenco, A., Edsinger, & Brachmond, F. (2022). The role of artificial intelligence in achieving the Sustainable Development Goals. *Nature Communications*, 13(1), 1–13. PMID: 34983933 von Krogh, G., Roberson, Q., & Gruber, M. (2023). We recognize and utilize novel research opportunities with artificial intelligence. *Academy of Management Journal*, 66(2), 367–373. DOI: 10.5465/amj.2023.4002

Wang, T., Brady, D., Lund, D., Marengo, A., Pagano, A., Zoe, T., Pange, J., & Pange, W. (2023). Exploring the potential impact of artificial intelligence (AI) on international students in higher education: Generative AI, Chatbots, analytics, and international student success. Applied Sciences. https://www.mdpi.com/2076-3417/13/11/6716

Wass, R., & Golding, C. (2014). Sharpening a tool for teaching: The zone of proximal development. *Teaching in Higher Education*, 19(6), 671–684. DOI: 10.1080/13562517.2014.901958

Wolf, M. J., Miller, K. W., & Grodzinsky, F. S. (2017). Why we should have seen that coming: Comments on Microsoft's Tay experience and broader implications. *The ORBIT Journal*, 1(2), 1–12. DOI: 10.29297/orbit.v1i2.49

Zaman, B. (2023). Transforming education through AI, benefits, risks, and ethical considerations. *Education, Computer Science*. https://www.techrxiv.org/users/691638/articles/683292-transforming-education-through-ai-benefits-risks-and-ethical-considerations

Zawacki-Richter, O., Marin, V. I., Bond, M., & Gouverneur, F. (2019). Systematic review of research on artificial intelligence applications in higher education – where are the educators? *International Journal of Educational Technology in Higher Education*, 16(39), 39. https://educationaltechnologyjournal.springeropen.com/articles/10.1186/s41239-019-0171-0. DOI: 10.1186/s41239-019-0171-0

Chapter 4

Andragogy as a Theoretical Framework for AI Integration in Higher Education

Ashley L. Dockens
https://orcid.org/0000-0002-9707-975X
Lamar University, USA

Kaye Shelton
https://orcid.org/0000-0001-5024-5629
Lamar University, USA

ABSTRACT

This chapter examines the integration of artificial intelligence (AI) and andragogy in higher education, focusing on how adult learning principles can guide the ethical use of AI technologies. It provides an overview of andragogical principles, discusses AI's impact on adult learning, and presents strategies for aligning AI with andragogical approaches. Key areas include enhancing self-directed learning, supporting experiential and problem-centered learning, and fostering critical thinking with AI. The chapter explores practical implementation strategies, educator training, and ethical considerations such as data privacy and algorithmic bias. It also examines emerging AI technologies and their potential impact on andragogy, identifies areas for further research, and discusses preparing adult education for an AI-enhanced future. Throughout, the importance of balancing technological innovation with sound andragogical practices is emphasized, providing insights for educators, administrators, and policymakers in higher education.

DOI: 10.4018/979-8-3373-0502-8.ch004

INTRODUCTION

The landscape of higher education is undergoing profound change, driven by rapid technological advancements, changing societal needs, and evolving learner expectations. As we stand on the cusp of what some call the Fourth Industrial Revolution (Schwab, 2016), institutions of higher learning are grappling with the challenge of preparing students for a future characterized by uncertainty and constant change.

Recent research indicates a significant surge in AI-related publications in higher education, with a two to threefold increase in studies published in 2021 and 2022 compared to previous years (Crompton & Burke, 2023). This surge reflects the growing recognition of AI's transformative potential in academic settings. The integration of AI technologies, particularly the emergence of generative AI, such as large language models, is reshaping traditional approaches to teaching and learning (Zawacki-Richter et al., 2019). These advancements offer new possibilities for personalizing the university experience and providing tools for data-driven decision-making (Bond et al., 2024) while also raising important ethical considerations that demand careful examination (Crompton & Burke, 2023).

This chapter explores the intersection of artificial intelligence (AI) and andragogy in higher education, examining how adult learning principles can guide the effective and ethical integration of AI technologies in academic settings. By using AI to reveal objective skills indicators, institutions can better prepare students for evolving job markets and the uncertainties of the future workforce (Maslej et al., 2023). As education departments increasingly dominate AI-related research in higher education (Crompton & Burke, 2023), there is a growing emphasis on understanding these technologies' pedagogical and andragogical implications, ensuring that their implementation aligns with established principles of adult learning while embracing the innovative potential they offer.

BACKGROUND

Higher education in the 21st century faces numerous challenges and opportunities, shaped by globalization, demographic shifts, and economic pressures. These factors have led to increased competition among institutions and a growing emphasis on accountability and outcomes (Altbach & Peterson, 1999; Salmi, 2001). The impact of globalization on higher education is particularly significant, influencing the organization of higher education systems and necessitating fundamental changes to meet the demands of an increasingly interconnected world (Salmi, 2001).

Globalization has changed higher education into a more explicitly global enterprise, with institutions operating across sovereign borders (American Council on Education, 2011). This interconnectedness has created unprecedented opportunities for international collaboration, joint research projects, and exchange programs. Students can now access diverse learning experiences that transcend geographical boundaries and cultural barriers, fostering cross-cultural understanding and expanding intellectual horizons.

The changing structure of higher education is also characterized by the diversification of student populations, with a growing influx of non-traditional and adult learners. This shift has led to an increased demand for flexible, personalized learning experiences that can accommodate diverse learning styles and life circumstances. The rise of online education platforms and digital technologies has made educational resources more accessible, enabling students to enroll in courses offered by universities worldwide.

Furthermore, the nature of work is evolving rapidly, with many traditional jobs being automated or changed. This evolution has created a pressing need for lifelong learning and skill adaptability. Higher education institutions are now tasked with developing programs that promote the holistic development of students, incorporating educational technologies and innovative teaching methods to meet these new demands (Frontiers, 2023).

The current higher education ecosystem is also witnessing a growing emphasis on developing soft skills and higher-order thinking abilities alongside technical competencies. This shift reflects the evolving needs of the modern workforce and the importance of preparing students for the challenges of the 21st century.

Another significant trend is the move towards competency-based education and micro-credentialing to meet specific industry requirements more effectively. This approach allows for more targeted and efficient skill development, aligning education more closely with the needs of the job market.

The rising importance of digital literacy and technological fluency across all disciplines is reshaping curricula and teaching methodologies. Higher education institutions are increasingly embracing technology to enhance learning experiences and prepare students for an increasingly digital world (Frontiers, 2023).

However, these opportunities come with challenges. Globalization can exacerbate existing disparities in access to educational resources, potentially widening the gap between privileged and marginalized communities. Additionally, the pressure to publish in prestigious international journals and pursue research with commercial applications may incentivize researchers to prioritize quantity over quality, potentially undermining the integrity of academic scholarship.

In conclusion, the globalization of higher education presents both opportunities and challenges. While it offers unprecedented access to diverse learning experiences and fosters international collaboration, it also requires institutions to navigate complex issues of equity, quality, and cultural preservation. To thrive in this new landscape, higher education institutions must strike a balance between embracing global opportunities and addressing local needs, while continuously adapting to the rapidly changing demands of the 21st-century workforce and society.

The Rise of AI Technologies In Education

The rise of AI technologies in education has sparked significant changes and discussions about its impact on teaching, learning, and academic integrity. Artificial Intelligence has emerged as a tremendous force of change in various areas, and education is no exception. Integrating AI technologies into educational processes has opened new pathways for personalized learning, administrative efficiency, and data-driven decision-making.

Recent studies have begun to quantify the impact of generative AI on higher education. According to research by Yusuf et al. (2024), there is a high level of awareness and familiarity with generative AI tools among higher education stakeholders across 76 countries. This global study found that a significant portion of respondents had prior experience with these tools and expressed intention to continue using them, primarily for information retrieval and text paraphrasing.

Key developments in AI for education include but are not limited to:

- **Adaptive Learning Platforms**: These sophisticated systems utilize AI algorithms to tailor educational content and pacing to individual student needs.
- **Intelligent Tutoring Systems**: AI-powered tutoring systems provide personalized feedback and support to learners.
- **Automated Grading and Assessment Tools**: AI has revolutionized the assessment process by enabling the automated grading of both objective and subjective tasks.
- **Predictive Analytics for Student Success**: AI systems can predict student performance and identify those at risk of falling behind.
- **Natural Language Processing for Language Learning**: NLP technologies have significantly advanced language learning applications.
- **Virtual and Augmented Reality for Immersive Learning**: AI-enhanced virtual and augmented reality technologies create immersive learning experiences.

However, the integration of generative AI is not without challenges. A recent study by Garg (2024) explored the performance differences between AI-generated and human-generated content in higher education courses. The researcher found students achieved an average of 5.7% more points on quizzes after attending a purely human-generated and delivered course than a purely AI-generated and delivered course. Interestingly, a hybrid approach combining human-generated content with AI-delivered instruction resulted in students gaining an average of 4.3 additional points compared to a purely human approach.

The impact of generative AI extends beyond content creation and delivery. It has raised significant concerns about academic integrity and the need for new policies. The study by Yusuf et al. (2024) highlighted a strong correlation between cultural dimensions and respondents' views on the benefits and concerns related to generative AI, including its potential for academic dishonesty. Despite these challenges, many in the higher education community see potential benefits in the integration of generative AI. A recent EDUCAUSE QuickPoll survey revealed that 83% of respondents believe generative AI will profoundly change higher education in the next three to five years, with 65% seeing more benefits than drawbacks (McCormack, M., 2023).

Recent studies have predicted AI could automate up to 40% of current teaching tasks, potentially freeing up educators to focus on higher-value activities such as mentoring and complex problem-solving (McKinsey Global Institute, 2023). However, the integration of AI in education also raises important questions about the role of human educators, the fear of faculty replacement, the nature of learning, and the ethical implications of AI-driven decision-making in academic contexts.

As higher education institutions grapple with these changes, it is clear that the arrival of generative AI is not just a technological shift but a catalyst for reimagining teaching methodologies, assessment strategies, and the very nature of academic work. The challenge now lies in harnessing the potential of AI while preserving the core values of education and adapting to the evolving needs of students and society.

The Need for an Andragogical Perspective on AI Integration

The integration of AI in adult education should be guided by andragogical principles to ensure effective learning experiences. Knowles' theory of andragogy (Knowles, 1980) emphasizes self-directed learning, experiential learning, problem-centered approaches, intrinsic motivation, relevance, and recognition of diverse experiences (Milana et al., 2024). These principles provide a framework for evaluating and shaping AI integration in higher education.

Adopting an andragogical perspective on AI integration can help ensure that AI tools support learner autonomy, create personalized learning experiences, facilitate problem-based learning, and provide continuous assessment aligned with adult learning principles (Storey & Wagner, 2024). This approach can enhance the higher education experience for adult learners while addressing potential ethical concerns from a learner-centered standpoint.

AI technologies, such as adaptive learning systems, virtual reality, and chatbots, can be leveraged to support andragogical principles in adult education (Storey & Wagner, 2024). For example, AI-powered personalized learning paths can cater to diverse learning needs and styles, while virtual reality can provide immersive, experiential learning opportunities. By grounding AI integration in andragogical principles, higher education institutions can create learning environments that are both technologically advanced and attuned to the needs and motivations of adult learners in the 21st century (Milana et al., 2024; Story & Wagner., 2024).

ANDRAGOGY: PRINCIPLES AND APPLICATIONS IN HIGHER EDUCATION

Andragogy, the art and science of facilitating adult learning, serves as a cornerstone for understanding and enhancing educational experiences in higher education settings. Pioneered by Malcolm Knowles in the 1970s, this approach has evolved to become a fundamental framework in adult education theory and practice (Loeng, 2018). As we navigate the integration of AI technologies in adult learning contexts, it is imperative first to establish a robust foundation in andragogical principles and their applications. This understanding will not only inform our approach to AI implementation but also ensure that technological advancements align with and enhance the unique needs and motivations of adult learners. By examining the core tenets of andragogy and their practical implications, we can create a synergistic relationship between traditional adult learning theories and cutting-edge AI innovations, ultimately fostering more effective, engaging, and learner-centered educational environments in higher education (Pappas, 2014).

Overview of Andragogical Principles

Malcolm Knowles (1980), often called the "father of andragogy," initially proposed six core principles of adult learning. These principles have since been refined and expanded upon by subsequent researchers, but they continue to form the backbone of andragogical theory. The key principles include:

- **Self-concept**: Adults are self-directed learners who take responsibility for their own learning (Knowles et al., 2015).

- **Learner Experience:** Adults bring a wealth of life experiences to the learning process, which serve as both a resource and a potential barrier to new learning (Knowles et al., 2015).
- **Readiness to learn**: Adults are most motivated to learn when the content is immediately relevant to their personal or professional lives (Knowles et al., 2015).
- **Orientation to learning**: Adult learners prioritize practical problem-solving over content and abstract knowledge acquisition, emphasizing real-world applications of skills (Knowles et al., 2015).
- **Motivation to learn**: Internal factors such as self-esteem, quality of life, and job satisfaction are primary motivators for adult learners (Knowles et al., 2015).
- **Need to know**: Adults require a clear understanding of the purpose or relevance of new information before committing to learning (Knowles et al., 2015).

Recent research has expanded on these foundational principles. For example, Merriam and Bierema (2014) emphasized the importance of context in adult learning, highlighting how sociocultural factors influence the learning process. Additionally, transformative learning theory, as developed by Mezirow (1991) and others, has become an important aspect of andragogical thinking, focusing on how adults can experience fundamental shifts in perspective through critical reflection and dialogue.

Application of Andragogy in Higher Education Settings

Andragogical principles have significant implications for teaching and learning in higher education settings. Recent studies have demonstrated the effectiveness of andragogical approaches in higher education. For instance, a meta-analysis by Taylor and Hamdy (2013) found that andragogy-based instructional designs led to improved learning outcomes and higher student satisfaction in various disciplines. Similarly, Fornaciari and Dean (2014) reported that courses incorporating andragogical principles resulted in greater student engagement and deeper learning in management education.

Furthermore, Henschke (2011) conducted a comprehensive review of andragogy's impact on higher education, concluding that institutions adopting andragogical approaches improved student retention, academic performance, and overall satisfaction. These findings underscore the value of integrating andragogical principles into higher education practices to enhance the learning experience and outcomes for adult learners.

Key applications of andragogy include:

- **Learner-centered course design**: Structuring courses to allow for learner input, choice, and self-direction in terms of content, pace, and assessment methods (Knowles et al., 2015).
- **Experiential learning**: Incorporating real-world examples, case studies, and hands-on projects that allow learners to apply theoretical knowledge to practical situations (Kolb, 2014).
- **Problem-based learning**: Designing curricula around authentic, complex problems that require interdisciplinary thinking and collaborative problem-solving (Savery, 2006; Tawfik, 2015).
- **Reflective practice**: Encouraging critical reflection on learning experiences and their application to personal and professional contexts (Schön, 1992).
- **Flexible learning environments**: Offering multiple modes of instruction (e.g., face-to-face, online, hybrid) to accommodate diverse learner needs and preferences (Boettcher & Conrad, 2016).
- **Recognition of prior learning**: Developing mechanisms to assess and credit learners' existing knowledge and skills acquired through work and life experiences (Harris et al., 2014).
- **Collaborative learning**: Facilitating peer-to-peer learning and knowledge sharing through group projects, discussions, and peer assessments (Cross et al., 2014).

Challenges to Traditional Andragogical Approaches in the Digital Age

While andragogical principles remain relevant, the digital age presents new challenges and opportunities that necessitate re-examining how these principles are applied. Some key challenges include:

- **Digital literacy divide:** The varying levels of technological proficiency among adult learners can create disparities in their ability to engage with digital learning tools and environments (Zawacki-Richter et al., 2019).
- **Information overload:** The abundance of online information can overwhelm learners and make it difficult to discern credible sources from unreliable ones (Kidd & Keengwe, 2010).
- **Balancing flexibility and structure:** While digital technologies offer unprecedented flexibility in learning, some adult learners may struggle with the self-discipline required for successful online or blended learning (Bates, 2022).
- **Maintaining human connection:** The increased use of digital technologies in education can potentially reduce face-to-face interactions, challenging

the social aspects of learning emphasized in andragogical theory (Zawacki-Richter et al., 2019).

- **Adapting to rapid technological change:** The pace of technological advancement requires adult learners and educators to continually update their skills and knowledge, which can be challenging for some (Bates, 2022).
- **Ethical considerations:** The use of data-driven technologies in education raises questions about privacy, consent, and the potential for algorithmic bias in learning analytics and adaptive systems (Bates, 2022).
- **Redefining the role of the educator:** As AI and other technologies take on some traditional teaching tasks, educators must adapt to new roles as facilitators, mentors, and curators of learning experiences (Zawacki-Richter et al., 2019).

To address these challenges, researchers and practitioners are exploring new approaches that blend andragogical principles with digital age realities. For example, the concept of heutagogy, or self-determined learning, extends andragogical principles to emphasize learner agency in highly complex and networked learning environments (Hase & Kenyon, 2000). Similarly, connectivism offers a learning theory for the digital age that emphasizes the importance of networks and information flows in the learning process (Siemens, 2005).

As we explore the integration of AI in higher education, it is significant to consider how these evolving perspectives on adult learning can inform our approach. By grounding AI integration in sound andragogical principles while remaining open to new insights and adaptations, we can create learning environments that are both technologically advanced and deeply attuned to the needs of adult learners in the 21st century (Kidd & Keengwe, 2010).

THE IMPORTANCE OF AI IN HIGHER EDUCATION

As artificial intelligence (AI) continues to evolve and permeate various sectors, its impact on higher education is becoming increasingly significant. This section explores the current realm of AI applications in higher education, the potential benefits of AI integration, and the challenges and limitations that must be addressed.

Current Applications of AI in Higher Education

AI is already being utilized in numerous ways across higher education institutions, revolutionizing both administrative processes and teaching and learning experiences. The following are just a few of the many applications being successfully used in higher education.

Personalized Learning Systems

- Adaptive learning platforms use AI to tailor content, pacing, and assessments to individual student needs (Zawacki-Richter et al., 2019).
- Intelligent tutoring systems provide personalized guidance and feedback in specific subject areas (Holmes et al., 2019).
- Selected Examples:
    - **Knewton** (https://support.knewton.com/s/): Uses adaptive learning technology to provide personalized educational content based on student performance.
    - **Smart Sparrow** (https://www.smartsparrow.com/): Offers an adaptive learning platform that allows educators to create interactive and adaptive courseware.
    - **Realizeit** (https://www.realizeitlearning.com/): Provides personalized learning experiences by using artificial intelligence and data analytics to tailor content and pacing to individual student needs.
    - **ALEKS** (Assessment and Learning in Knowledge Spaces [https://www.aleks.com/]): Provides personalized learning and tutoring in mathematics and other subjects, adapting to individual student needs.
    - **Carnegie Learning's Cognitive Tutor** (https://www.carnegielearning.com/solutions/services-overview/instructional-services/): Uses cognitive science and AI to offer personalized math tutoring and feedback.
    - **Socratic** by Google (https://socratic.org/): An AI-powered tutoring app that provides personalized assistance and explanations for various subjects by using visual and text recognition.

Administrative Efficiency

- AI-powered chatbots assist with student inquiries and administrative tasks (Goel & Polepeddi, 2016).
- Predictive analytics tools help institutions identify at-risk students and implement early intervention strategies (Bates, 2024).
- Selected Examples:

- **Ivy.ai** (https://ivy.ai/): Ivy.ai provides AI-powered chatbots designed specifically for higher education institutions. Assists with student inquiries, provides information on admissions, financial aid, campus events, and more. Available 24/7 to respond to common questions and tasks.
- **Ada** (https://www.ada.cx/): Ada is an AI chatbot platform that automates interactions with students and prospective students. Provides instant responses to a wide range of inquiries, helps with administrative processes, and integrates with other systems for seamless support.
- **Druid** (https://www.druidai.com/): Druid is a chatbot platform designed to engage students, empower professors, and simplify operations. It uses natural language processing to provide timely, accurate responses.
- **Civitas Learning** (https://www.civitaslearning.com/): Civitas Learning offers predictive analytics tools to help higher education institutions improve student success. Identifies at-risk students, provides insights for early intervention, and tracks student progress. Uses data from various sources to generate actionable insights.
- **EAB Navigate360** (https://eab.com/solutions/navigate360/): EAB Navigate 360is a student success management system that uses predictive analytics to identify students who need support. Combines data from academic, engagement, and financial metrics to provide a holistic view of student risk. Offers tools for advising, intervention, and tracking student outcomes.
- **Starfish** (https://eab.com/solutions/starfish/): Starfish is a comprehensive student success platform that leverages predictive analytics to identify at-risk students. Provides early alerts, progress tracking, and communication tools to connect students with resources and support services.

Assessment and Feedback

- Automated essay scoring systems provide instant feedback on writing assignments (Zawacki-Richter et al., 2019).
- AI-enabled proctoring tools monitor online exams for academic integrity (Bates, 2024).
- Selected Examples:
  - **Grammarly** (https://www.grammarly.com/): An AI-powered writing assistant that provides instant feedback on grammar, punctuation, style, and plagiarism.
  - **Turnitin Revision Assistant** (https://www.turnitin.com/products/revision-assistant/): An AI-driven tool that offers instant formative feed-

back on student writing, focusing on aspects like content, structure, and style.

    - **ETS e-Rater** (https://www.ets.org/erater.html): Developed by Educational Testing Service (ETS), e-Rater is an automated essay scoring system used in various standardized tests.
    - **ProctorU** (https://www.proctoru.com/): An online proctoring service that uses AI to monitor and record exam sessions, ensuring academic integrity.
    - **ExamSoft** (https://examsoft.com/): A comprehensive exam management solution that includes AI-enabled proctoring tools to monitor test-takers and ensure the integrity of online exams.
    - Honorlock (https://honorlock.com/): An AI-driven proctoring service that monitors online exams using advanced algorithms to detect suspicious behavior.

Research and Discovery

- AI-powered literature review tools help researchers navigate vast amounts of academic literature (Kidd & Keengwe, 2010).
- Natural language processing algorithms assist in analyzing qualitative research data (Holmes et al., 2019).
- Selected Examples:
    - **ResearchRabbit** (https://www.researchrabbit.ai/): ResearchRabbit is an AI-powered tool for literature discovery and tracking. Provides AI-based recommendations for related research papers and tracks new publications in the user's area of interest.
    - **Zotero** (https://www.zotero.org/): Zotero is a free and open-source reference management software to manage bibliographic data and related research materials that uses AI features to discover, organize, and cite research literature.
    - **Rayyan** (https://www.rayyan.ai/): Rayyan is a free web application designed to help researchers working on systematic reviews and other knowledge synthesis projects. It uses machine learning to help researchers screen and select relevant studies efficiently.
    - **NVivo** (https://help-nv.qsrinternational.com/20/win/Content/welcome.htm): NVivo is a qualitative data analysis software that helps researchers organize, analyze, and find insights in unstructured or qualitative data. Utilizes NLP features such as text mining and machine learning techniques to analyze large volumes of text data.

- **ATLAS.ti** (https://atlasti.com/): ATLAS.ti is a qualitative data analysis software that provides tools for coding, analyzing, and visualizing qualitative data. Utilizes NLP features such as text analysis algorithms to facilitate the coding and analysis process.
- **MAXQDA** (https://www.maxqda.com/): MAXQDA is a software program for qualitative and mixed methods research, designed for analyzing qualitative data. Utilizes NLP features for text analysis, sentiment analysis, and thematic coding.

Accessibility and Inclusion

- AI-driven captioning and translation services improve accessibility for diverse learner populations (Bates, 2024).
- Text-to-speech and speech-to-text technologies enhance learning experiences for students with disabilities (Zawacki-Richter et al., 2019).
- Selected Examples:
    - **Otter.ai** (https://otter.ai/): An AI-powered transcription service that provides real-time captioning and transcription. It enhances accessibility for students by converting spoken content into text, supporting diverse learning needs.
    - **Rev** (https://www.rev.com/): Offers AI-driven captioning and translation services, providing accurate and timely captions for video content. It supports accessibility for learners who are deaf or hard of hearing and those who benefit from multilingual support.
    - **Google Live Transcribe** (https://www.google.com/intl/en_in/android/accessibility/live-transcribe/): A real-time transcription app that converts speech to text in real-time. It improves accessibility for students with hearing impairments by providing live captions during lectures and discussions.
    - **Kurzweil 3000** (https://www.kurzweiledu.com/kurzweil-3000.html): A comprehensive literacy support tool that provides text-to-speech and speech-to-text capabilities. It enhances learning experiences for students with dyslexia, visual impairments, and other learning disabilities.
    - **Read&Write** by Texthelp (https://www.texthelp.com/products/read-and-write/): An assistive technology software that offers text-to-speech, speech-to-text, and other literacy support tools. It supports students with reading and writing difficulties, helping them to engage more fully with their learning materials.
    - **Voice Dream Reader** (https://www.voicedream.com/reader/): A text-to-speech app that reads aloud text from various sources, including

PDFs, Word documents, and web pages. It helps students with visual impairments and reading difficulties to access written content more easily.

Career Services

- AI-powered platforms use machine learning to match students with relevant job opportunities (Kidd & Keengwe, 2010).
- Virtual career counselors provide personalized guidance on career planning and skill development (Holmes et al., 2019).
- Selected Examples:
  - **Handshake** (https://joinhandshake.com/): An AI-powered platform that uses machine learning to match students with relevant job opportunities. It connects students with employers and offers tools for job searching, event management, and networking.
  - **CareerExplorer** by Sokanu (https://www.careerexplorer.com/): An AI-driven platform that matches students with career paths based on their skills, interests, and personality. It provides personalized career recommendations and job opportunities.
  - **VMock** (https://www.vmock.com/): An AI-powered career preparation platform that offers instant feedback on resumes and LinkedIn profiles. It uses machine learning algorithms to enhance career documents and improve job matching.
  - **Parker Dewey** (https://www.parkerdewey.com/): An AI-enabled platform that connects students with micro-internships and project-based work opportunities. It helps students gain experience and skills relevant to their career goals.
  - **MyInterview** (https://myinterview.com/): An AI-driven video interview platform that helps students prepare for job interviews. It provides personalized feedback and matches students with job opportunities based on their interview performance.
  - **Career Coach** by Emsi (https://www.economicmodeling.com/career-coach/): An AI-powered virtual career counselor that provides personalized guidance on career planning and skill development. It offers tools for exploring career paths, identifying skills gaps, and finding relevant educational programs.

Potential Benefits of AI Integration

The potential of AI to transform higher education is significant, offering opportunities to enhance the quality, accessibility, and relevance of education in the 21st century. However, it is essential to approach AI integration thoughtfully, considering both its benefits and potential challenges.

The integration of AI in higher education offers numerous potential benefits:

- **Enhanced Personalization**: AI can provide tailored learning experiences that adapt to individual student needs, learning styles, and pace, potentially improving learning outcomes and student satisfaction (Holmes et al., 2019). This personalization can help address the diverse learning requirements of a heterogeneous student population.
- **Improved Efficiency:** Automation of routine tasks can free up educators' time for more high-value activities such as mentoring and complex problem-solving (Zawacki-Richter et al., 2019). This shift allows educators to focus on aspects of teaching that require human expertise and emotional intelligence.
- **Data-Driven Decision Making:** AI-powered analytics can provide insights into student performance, engagement, and institutional effectiveness, enabling more informed decision-making at all levels (Bates, 2024). These insights can help institutions optimize resource allocation and improve overall educational outcomes.
- **Expanded Access:** AI technologies can facilitate more flexible and accessible learning options, potentially broadening participation in higher education (Kidd & Keengwe, 2024). This expansion of access can help address educational inequalities and support diverse learner populations.
- **Innovative Pedagogies:** AI can enable new forms of immersive and interactive learning experiences, such as AI-powered simulations and virtual reality environments (Holmes et al., 2019). These innovative approaches can enhance student engagement and provide practical, hands-on learning opportunities.
- **Enhanced Research Capabilities:** AI tools can accelerate the research process, from literature reviews to data analysis, potentially leading to faster scientific discoveries (Zawacki-Richter et al., 2019). This acceleration can contribute to the advancement of knowledge across various disciplines.
- **Lifelong Learning Support:** AI can facilitate continuous learning and skill development beyond formal education, supporting the growing need for lifelong learning in a rapidly changing job market (Bates, 2024). This support is indispensable in an era where career paths are increasingly non-linear and require ongoing skill acquisition.

Challenges and Limitations of AI In Educational Contexts

Integrating AI in higher education presents significant challenges and limitations alongside its potential benefits. These challenges can be categorized into several key areas:

- **Ethical Concerns:** The use of AI in education raises vital ethical issues. Privacy and data security concerns emerge from the extensive collection and utilization of student data (Labadze et al., 2023). Algorithmic bias may perpetuate or exacerbate existing educational inequalities (Lim et al., 2023). Additionally, the use of AI-powered writing tools raises questions about authorship and academic integrity (Gökoğlu, 2024).
- **Digital Divide**: Unequal access to technology and varying levels of digital literacy among students can widen educational disparities (Luan et al., 2020). The cost of implementing and maintaining AI systems may be prohibitive for some institutions, further exacerbating this divide.
- **Quality of AI-Generated Content:** AI-generated content may lack the nuance, creativity, or critical thinking of human-generated content. Overreliance on AI tools could potentially hinder the development of essential skills in students (Kumar, 2023).
- **Human Interaction**: Excessive use of AI could reduce valuable face-to-face interactions between students and educators. The social and emotional aspects of learning may be challenging to replicate in AI-driven environments (Koumpouros, 2024).
- **Technological Limitations:** Current AI systems may struggle with complex, context-dependent tasks that are common in higher education. The rapid pace of AI development may make it difficult for institutions to keep up with the latest advancements (Leiker et al., 2023).
- **Workforce Implications:** The integration of AI may lead to job displacement or significant role changes for some higher education staff. Educators may need extensive training to effectively leverage AI tools in their teaching (Lim et al., 2023).
- **Regulatory and Accreditation Challenges:** The use of AI in education raises questions about quality assurance and accreditation standards. Legal and regulatory frameworks may need to evolve to address the unique challenges posed by AI in education (Kumar, 2023).

To address these challenges, higher education institutions must adopt a thoughtful and strategic approach to AI integration. This includes developing comprehensive AI governance frameworks, investing in digital literacy programs, and fostering collaboration between educators, technologists, and ethicists (Laupichler et al., 2022).

As we move forward, it is essential to view AI not as a replacement for human educators, but as a powerful tool that, when used judiciously, can enhance and change the educational experience. By aligning AI integration with sound andragogical principles and addressing the challenges head-on, higher education can harness the potential of AI to create more effective, inclusive, and innovative learning environments for adult learners (Knowles, 1980; Lim et al., 2023).

INTEGRATING ADULT LEARNING THEORY WITH AI

The successful integration of AI in higher education requires thoughtful alignment with established principles of adult learning. This section explores how AI capabilities can enhance andragogical approaches, focusing on self-directed learning, experiential and problem-centered learning, and the development of critical thinking and creativity (Knowles et al., 2015; Siemens, 2005).

Aligning AI Capabilities with Andragogical Principles

To effectively integrate AI with andragogical principles, we must consider how AI's capabilities can support and enhance each of the following core principle of adult learning (Pappas, 2014):

1. **Self-concept:** AI can provide personalized learning paths that respect learners' autonomy and self-direction. Adaptive systems can adjust to learners' preferences and pace, supporting their self-concept as independent learners (Ryan & Deci, 2000).
2. **Experience:** AI can help identify and leverage learners' prior experiences through sophisticated assessment tools. Recommender systems can suggest relevant content based on learners' backgrounds and experiences (Kolb, 2014).
3. **Readiness to learn:** AI-powered analytics can identify when learners are most receptive to new information. Just-in-time learning modules can be triggered based on learners' current needs and contexts (Merriam & Bierema, 2013).
4. **Orientation to learning**: AI simulations and virtual environments can provide problem-centered learning experiences. Intelligent tutoring systems can guide learners through real-world problem-solving scenarios (Zawacki-Richter et al., 2019).

5. **Motivation:** AI can help maintain learner motivation through personalized goal setting and progress tracking. Gamification elements powered by AI can enhance engagement and intrinsic motivation (Chen et al., 2020).
6. **Need to know:** AI can provide clear rationales for learning objectives, tailored to individual learner goals and career aspirations. Predictive analytics can demonstrate the future relevance of current learning topics (Luckin et al., 2016).

Enhancing Self-Directed Learning Through AI

AI offers numerous opportunities to support and enhance self-directed learning, a cornerstone of andragogy:

1. **Personalized Learning Paths:** AI algorithms can analyze learner data to create customized learning journeys that align with individual goals and preferences (Goel & Polepeddi, 2016).
2. **Intelligent Content Curation:** AI-powered recommendation systems can suggest relevant resources, articles, and learning materials based on learner interests and progress (Merchant et al., 2014).
3. **Adaptive Assessments:** AI can provide dynamic assessments that adjust in real-time based on learner responses, offering a more accurate measure of knowledge and skills (VanLehn, 2011).
4. **Progress Monitoring and Feedback:** AI systems can provide continuous feedback on learning progress, helping learners self-regulate their learning process (Baker & Inventado, 2014).
5. **Virtual Personal Assistants**: AI-powered chatbots can provide 24/7 support to learners, answering questions and offering guidance on self-directed learning strategies (Goel & Polepeddi, 2016).

Supporting Experiential and Problem-Centered Learning with AI

AI can significantly enhance experiential and problem-centered learning approaches, which are essential in andragogy:

1. **Immersive Simulations**: AI-powered virtual and augmented reality environments can provide realistic, hands-on learning experiences (Merchant et al., 2014).
2. **Intelligent Problem-Solving Assistants**: AI systems can guide learners through complex problem-solving processes, offering hints and feedback (VanLehn, 2011).

3. **Real-World Data Analysis**: AI tools can help learners analyze large datasets from real-world scenarios, bridging theory and practice (Baker & Inventado, 2014).
4. **Adaptive Case Studies:** AI can generate or modify case studies based on learners' backgrounds and learning objectives (Kolodner et al., 2005).
5. **Collaborative Problem-Solving:** AI can facilitate and enhance group problem-solving by matching learners with complementary skills and moderating discussions (Dillenbourg & Jermann, 2010).

Fostering Critical Thinking and Creativity in AI-Enhanced Environments

While there are concerns about AI potentially hindering critical thinking and creativity, when used thoughtfully, AI can actually enhance these important skills such as:

1. **Socratic Questioning**: AI chatbots can be programmed to engage learners in Socratic dialogues, encouraging deeper reflection and critical analysis (Graesser et al., 2001).
2. **Bias Detection and Analysis:** AI tools can help learners identify biases in information sources and their own thinking, promoting critical evaluation skills (Tsai et al., 2012).
3. **Idea Generation and Creativity Support:** AI-powered brainstorming tools can help generate novel ideas and connections, stimulating creative thinking (Lubart et al., 2013).
4. **Multimodal Learning and Expression:** AI can support the creation and analysis of diverse forms of content, encouraging creative expression and critical interpretation (Jewitt, 2013).
5. **Ethical Reasoning Scenarios:** AI simulations can present complex ethical dilemmas, encouraging critical thinking about the implications of AI in society (Borenstein & Howard, 2021).
6. **Metacognitive Support:** AI tools can prompt learners to reflect on their learning processes, fostering metacognitive skills crucial for critical thinking (Azevedo & Aleven, 2013).

By thoughtfully aligning AI capabilities with andragogical principles, we can create learning environments that not only leverage the power of technology but also respect and enhance the unique characteristics of adult learners. This integration has the potential to significantly improve the effectiveness and relevance of higher education in the digital age, preparing learners for the complexities of a rapidly evolving world.

PRACTICAL STRATEGIES FOR AI-ENHANCED ANDRAGOGICAL APPROACHES

As higher education institutions increasingly adopt AI technologies, it is imperative to implement these tools in ways that align with andragogical principles and enhance adult learning experiences. This section provides practical guidelines and best practices for educators and administrators seeking to integrate AI into their andragogical approaches.

Guidelines for Implementing AI While Adhering to Andragogical Principles

When integrating AI into educational settings for adult learners, institutions and educators must strike a balance between leveraging technological advancements and honoring these foundational andragogical principles. The following guidelines offer a framework for thoughtfully implementing AI in ways that enhance, rather than diminish, the unique characteristics of adult learning environments. By adhering to these guidelines, educators can harness the power of AI to create more personalized, engaging, and effective learning experiences that respect the autonomy and diverse needs of adult learners.

1. Learner-Centered Design:
   - Involve adult learners in the design and implementation of AI-enhanced learning experiences.
   - Ensure AI tools provide options for learner control and customization.
   - Example: Allow learners to set their own learning goals and pace within AI-powered adaptive learning platforms.
2. Transparency and Explainability:
   - Clearly communicate to learners how AI is being used in their educational experience.
   - Provide explanations for AI-generated recommendations or decisions.
   - Example: Offer a "Why am I seeing this?" feature in AI-powered content recommendation systems.
3. Experiential Integration:
   - Use AI to create opportunities for learners to apply knowledge to real-world scenarios.

   - Incorporate AI-enhanced simulations and problem-solving exercises that reflect workplace challenges.
   - Example: Implement AI-driven business simulations that adapt to learners' decisions and industry trends.
4. Continuous Feedback and Reflection:
   - Utilize AI to provide timely, constructive feedback that promotes self-reflection and metacognition.
   - Encourage learners to critically evaluate AI-generated feedback.
   - Example: Use natural language processing to provide detailed writing feedback, but prompt learners to reflect on and sometimes challenge the suggestions.
5. Collaborative Learning Support:
   - Leverage AI to facilitate meaningful peer-to-peer interactions and group work.
   - Use AI to form diverse learning groups based on complementary skills and experiences.
   - Example: Implement AI-powered discussion forums that suggest connections between learners based on shared interests or complementary expertise.
6. Ethical Considerations:
   - Develop clear ethical guidelines for AI use in educational settings.
   - Engage learners in discussions about the ethical implications of AI in their field of study.
   - Example: Incorporate modules on AI ethics into curriculum, using real-world case studies relevant to learners' professional contexts.
7. Accessibility and Inclusion:
   - Ensure AI-enhanced learning tools are accessible to learners with diverse needs and backgrounds.
   - Use AI to provide personalized accommodations and support.
   - Example: Implement AI-powered closed captioning and translation services for video content.

Best Practices for Educator Training and Development

Best practices for educator training and development in the realm of AI integration encompass several key areas. For example, comprehensive AI literacy programs are essential, offering ongoing training that covers both the technical aspects of AI and its pedagogical applications, including modules on AI ethics, data privacy, and potential biases. Providing hands-on experience with AI tools is also necessary, allowing educators to experiment with AI-enhanced teaching tools in low-stakes environments and encouraging peer-to-peer sharing of implementation experiences. Moreover, collaborative design workshops facilitate cooperation between educators, instructional designers, and AI specialists to integrate AI tools in ways that enhance rather than replace human instruction.

In addition, establishing ongoing support and a community of practice for educators implementing AI in their teaching is vital, providing continuous technical support and pedagogical guidance. Training should emphasize andragogical principles, ensuring all AI-related instruction is grounded in adult learning theory and encouraging critical evaluation of how AI tools align with these principles. Adaptive professional development, utilizing AI to personalize learning based on educators' needs and interests, can provide just-in-time resources for specific implementation challenges. Lastly, promoting research and reflection encourages action research on AI implementation in educators' own contexts and fosters reflective practice on the impact of AI on teaching and learning experiences. These best practices collectively aim to equip educators with the knowledge, skills, and support necessary to effectively integrate AI into their teaching practices.

By following these guidelines and implementing comprehensive educator training programs, higher education institutions can effectively integrate AI into their andragogical approaches. This thoughtful integration has the potential to significantly enhance the learning experience for adult students, preparing them for the complexities of a rapidly evolving professional arena while staying true to the core principles of adult learning theory.

ETHICAL CONSIDERATIONS AND CHALLENGES

The integration of AI in higher education, while offering numerous benefits, also presents significant ethical challenges that must be carefully addressed. This section explores key ethical considerations related to data privacy, algorithmic bias, inclusivity, and the balance between AI assistance and authentic learning.

Data Privacy and Security in AI-Enhanced Learning Environments

Data privacy and security in AI-enhanced learning environments require a comprehensive approach encompassing several key areas. Data collection and consent policies should be transparent, clearly communicating what data is collected and how it will be used. Obtaining informed consent from learners, with options to opt out of certain data collection practices, will become even more important. For instance, developing a comprehensive, easy-to-understand data policy that learners must review and accept before engaging with AI-enhanced learning tools can ensure transparency and informed participation.

Data protection and storage measures are equally important, involving the implementation of robust cybersecurity measures to protect learner data from breaches. Adherence to data protection regulations such as GDPR, FERPA, or relevant local laws is essential. This can be achieved through the utilization of encryption, secure cloud storage, and regular security audits to safeguard learner data.

Data minimization and retention practices should focus on collecting only necessary data and limiting retention periods. Providing learners with options to delete their data or request data portability empowers them to control their personal information. Implementing a data lifecycle management system that automatically deletes unnecessary data after a specified period can help maintain data minimization principles.

Careful vetting and monitoring of third-party AI providers' data handling practices is necessary, ensuring contractual agreements prioritize learner privacy and data security. Regular audits of third-party AI providers can help ensure compliance with institutional data privacy standards.

Lastly, transparency in AI decision-making is vital. Providing clear explanations of how AI systems use learner data to make decisions or recommendations and offering mechanisms for learners to challenge or seek clarification on AI-driven decisions, promotes trust and understanding. An "AI Transparency Dashboard" that shows learners what data is being used and how it influences their learning experience can be an effective tool for achieving this transparency.

Addressing Algorithmic Bias and Ensuring Inclusivity

Ensuring fairness and equity in AI-enhanced learning environments requires a multifaceted approach. First and foremost, it is essential to use diverse and representative training data for AI systems, ensuring they are trained on datasets that represent the full spectrum of learners. Regular audits of training data for potential biases are essential, and collaborating with diverse stakeholders to curate inclusive training datasets for AI learning systems can help achieve this goal.

Continuous bias monitoring is another essential aspect, involving the implementation of ongoing monitoring systems to detect and address potential biases in AI outputs. Regular equity audits of AI-enhanced learning experiences should be conducted, possibly through the development of an "Equity Impact Assessment" tool to evaluate the effects of AI systems on different learner demographics.

Adopting inclusive design principles in the development of AI-enhanced learning tools is also vital to ensure that AI systems can accommodate diverse learning needs and preferences. This could include implementing AI-powered accessibility features that automatically adapt content presentation based on individual learner needs.

Cultural sensitivity is equally important, requiring AI systems to be trained to recognize and respect cultural differences in learning styles and communication. Providing options for culturally relevant examples and contexts in AI-generated content, such as developing AI content generators that can adapt examples and case studies to reflect diverse cultural contexts, can enhance this aspect.

Lastly, transparent algorithmic decision-making is necessary, especially in high-stakes situations like admissions or assessment. Clear explanations of how AI algorithms make decisions should be provided, along with human oversight and appeal processes for significant AI-driven decisions. Implementing an "Algorithmic Fairness Statement" for each AI tool used in the institution, detailing how fairness is ensured and measured, can promote transparency and trust in the AI-enhanced learning environment.

Balancing AI Assistance with Authentic Learning and Assessment

Addressing ethical considerations and challenges in AI-enhanced learning environments requires a comprehensive approach that encompasses various aspects of the educational process. Defining appropriate AI use is an important first step, involving the development of clear guidelines on AI usage in learning and assessment contexts. Educating learners on the ethical use of AI tools and the importance of academic integrity is essential, potentially through the creation of an "AI Ethics in Learning" course that all students must complete before using AI-enhanced learning tools.

Authentic assessment design is another vital component, focusing on evaluating higher-order thinking skills and application of knowledge that are more challenging for AI to replicate. Incorporating real-world, context-specific tasks that require human creativity and analytical reasoning, such as project-based assessments, can help ensure the authenticity of student work.

Clearly differentiating between AI-assisted work and AI-generated work is also important, with policies developed on how AI-assisted work should be cited or acknowledged. Implementing a digital watermarking system that indicates which parts of a submission were created with AI assistance could provide transparency in this area.

Balancing personalization and standardization in AI-driven learning is central to ensure that adaptivity does not compromise the achievement of standardized learning outcomes. Developing AI systems that personalize the learning path while ensuring all learners achieve predefined competency benchmarks can help maintain this balance.

Human-AI collaboration in assessment processes is vital, using AI to support, not replace, human judgment. Implementing systems where AI provides initial assessment, which is then reviewed and finalized by human educators, can use the strengths of both AI and human expertise.

Promoting metacognitive skill development through AI can help learners understand their own learning processes and encourage critical evaluation of AI-generated suggestions or solutions. AI-powered learning journals that prompt learners to reflect on their learning strategies and decision-making processes could be an effective tool for this purpose.

Lastly, transparency in AI limitations is essential, clearly communicating the constraints of AI tools to learners and educators and encouraging a critical approach to AI-generated information or recommendations. Including "AI Limitation Disclaimers" alongside AI-generated content can remind users to evaluate the information critically.

Addressing these ethical considerations and challenges requires a multifaceted approach involving technology experts, educators, ethicists, and learners themselves. By proactively engaging with these issues, higher education institutions can harness the benefits of AI while upholding principles of privacy, fairness, and authentic learning, developing AI-enhanced learning environments that are not only effective but also ethical and inclusive.

FUTURE DIRECTIONS AND EMERGING TRENDS

As AI technologies continue to evolve at a rapid pace, their potential impact on andragogy and adult education is both exciting and challenging. This section explores emerging trends, identifies key areas for future research, and discusses strategies for preparing adult education for an AI-enhanced future.

Evolving AI Technologies and Their Potential Impact on Andragogy

The future of AI in adult education holds promising advancements across various technologies. Advanced Natural Language Processing (NLP) is expected to enable more sophisticated AI tutors and writing assistants capable of engaging in nuanced dialogue and providing contextual feedback. This enhancement could significantly support self-directed learning and offer personalized guidance aligned with adult learners' experiences and goals, such as AI tutors that can understand and respond to complex queries about theoretical concepts and their real-world applications.

Emotion AI and Affective Computing are poised to create more empathetic and responsive learning environments that address the holistic needs of adult learners. These systems could recognize and respond to learners' emotional states, adjusting content delivery and support accordingly. For instance, adaptive learning platforms might detect frustration or disengagement and offer timely interventions or motivational support.

The integration of Augmented and Virtual Reality (AR/VR) with AI promises immersive, AI-driven simulations that provide realistic, hands-on learning experiences. This technology could enhance experiential learning opportunities, bridging theory and practice in adult education. An example could be AI-powered VR simulations for medical students that adapt scenarios based on individual learning needs and performance.

Explainable AI (XAI) is set to increase transparency and trust in AI-enhanced learning by providing clear explanations for AI decisions and recommendations. This aligns with adult learners' need to understand the rationale behind learning activities. An AI-powered career guidance system that explains its recommendations based on labor market data and the learner's skills profile exemplifies this concept.

Quantum Computing in AI could dramatically increase processing power, enabling more complex AI models and real-time data analysis. This advancement could lead to highly sophisticated personalized learning experiences and predictive analytics in adult education, such as ultra-precise adaptive learning systems that can process vast amounts of data to create optimal learning paths in real-time.

Lastly, AI-Enhanced Brain-Computer Interfaces (BCIs) present new frontiers in cognitive support and personalized learning. These direct neural interfaces could potentially enhance cognitive processes or facilitate more intuitive human-AI interaction, raising profound questions about the nature of learning and knowledge acquisition. For example, BCI systems could help adult learners with cognitive disabilities more effectively engage with educational content.

These emerging technologies hold great potential for transforming adult education, offering more personalized, engaging, and effective learning experiences. However, their implementation will require careful consideration of ethical implications and pedagogical best practices to ensure they truly enhance the learning process for adult students.

Research Questions and Areas for Further Investigation

As the field of artificial intelligence continues to evolve and integrate with adult education, numerous questions and areas for further investigation emerge. This section addresses potential research questions and areas for further investigation in the intersection of andragogy and artificial intelligence. These inquiries aim to deepen our understanding of how AI can best serve adult learners, the potential impacts of AI-enhanced learning environments, and the challenges that need to be addressed to ensure equitable and effective implementation of AI in adult education.

The long-term impact of AI on adult learning outcomes is a vital area for investigation. Researchers need to explore how prolonged use of AI-enhanced learning tools affects adult learners' cognitive development, critical thinking skills, and knowledge retention. Additionally, studying the long-term career outcomes for adults who engage in AI-enhanced versus traditional learning environments could provide valuable insights into the effectiveness of these new technologies. The relationship between AI and metacognition in adult learners is another important area of study, focusing on how AI tools can be designed to enhance metacognitive skills and the connection between AI-assisted learning and the development of self-regulated learning skills in adults.

Cultural adaptivity of AI in global adult education presents another set of research questions. Investigating how AI systems can be designed to effectively adapt to diverse cultural contexts and the implications of AI-enhanced learning for cross-cultural competence development in adult learners is pivotal for ensuring inclusive and effective global education. The potential of AI in supporting non-traditional forms of adult learning, such as informal and non-formal learning experiences, and its role in recognizing and credentialing skills acquired through lifelong and life wide learning, also warrant further exploration.

Ethical considerations in AI decision-making within adult education contexts raise important questions about ensuring ethical practices in high-stakes educational situations while respecting adult learners' autonomy. Developing frameworks to guide the creation of AI systems that align with adult education ethics and values is a fundamental area for research. The alteration of adult educator roles in the face of AI integration is another key area of investigation, including the new skills and competencies that adult educators will need to effectively leverage AI in their practice.

Finally, accessibility and inclusivity of AI in adult education present crucial research questions. Investigating how AI-enhanced learning environments can be designed to be fully accessible and inclusive for adult learners with diverse needs and backgrounds is essential. Additionally, examining the potential risks of AI exacerbating existing educational inequalities in adult learning contexts is vital for ensuring that AI implementation in adult education promotes equity rather than widening gaps.

These research areas highlight the complex and multifaceted nature of integrating AI into adult education. By addressing these questions, researchers and practitioners can work towards developing AI-enhanced learning environments that are effective, ethical, and inclusive for adult learners.

Preparing for the Future of Ai in Adult Education

As artificial intelligence continues to advance and integrate into various aspects of education, it is necessary to prepare for its future impact on adult education. This section addresses thoughts and strategies for preparing for the future of AI in adult education, outlining key areas of focus and providing examples of potential initiatives. By proactively addressing these aspects, educational institutions and stakeholders can better position themselves to harness the benefits of AI while mitigating potential challenges.

Developing AI literacy programs is a fundamental step in preparing for the future of AI in adult education. Comprehensive AI literacy programs should be created for both educators and adult learners, focusing on understanding AI capabilities, limitations, and ethical implications. For instance, a modular "AI in Education" course could be developed and integrated into various adult education programs, ensuring a broad understanding of AI across different disciplines.

Tackling the intricate issues and potential benefits of AI in adult learning requires strong partnerships across different fields of expertise. Encouraging interdisciplinary collaboration between educators, AI specialists, ethicists, and policymakers can lead to more holistic and effective approaches. Establishing "AI in Adult Education" think tanks that bring together diverse experts to address emerging challenges and opportunities could be an effective way to facilitate this collaboration.

Developing adaptive policy frameworks is essential to keep pace with rapidly changing AI technologies. These frameworks should balance innovation with ethical considerations and learner protection. Implementing a regular "AI in Education Policy Review" process that involves stakeholders from various fields can help ensure policies remain relevant and effective.

Continuous professional development for educators is vital in preparing for the future of AI in adult education. Providing ongoing training on emerging AI technologies and their applications in adult education and encouraging educators to engage in action research on AI implementation in their contexts, can help keep the workforce up to date. Creating an "AI Innovation Fellowship" for educators to explore cutting-edge AI applications in adult learning could be an effective approach to fostering innovation and expertise.

Establishing ethical AI design principles specifically for adult education is crucial. These principles should be promoted and integrated into the development and implementation of AI educational tools. Collaborating with tech companies to create an "Ethical AI in Education" certification program could help ensure adherence to these principles across the industry.

Empowering learners and promoting agency in AI-enhanced environments is another important consideration. AI systems should be designed to empower adult learners to make informed choices about their learning experiences, providing transparency and control over AI-driven learning processes. Developing AI systems with customizable "learning agent" interfaces that allow learners to set preferences and goals could be an effective way to achieve this.

Finally, engaging in scenario planning and foresight activities can help prepare for various potential futures of AI in adult education. Regular scenario planning exercises and the use of foresight methodologies can help anticipate and prepare for multiple possible developments. Conducting annual "Future of AI in Adult Education" workshops that explore various scenarios and their implications could be a valuable tool for strategic planning.

By proactively addressing these areas, pursuing rigorous research, and preparing educational systems for change, we can harness the potential of AI to create more effective, accessible, and personalized learning experiences for adult learners. The key will be to remain grounded in andragogical principles while embracing the huge potential for change by AI technologies.

CONCLUSION

As we conclude this exploration of andragogy as a framework for AI integration in higher education, it is essential to synthesize the key insights, emphasize the essential balance between innovation and sound pedagogical practices, and provide a clear call to action for educators and institutions.

Key Takeaways from Each Section

The integration of AI in higher education represents not just a technological shift but a pedagogical revolution that must be grounded in adult learning principles. Andragogy provides a crucial framework for guiding the effective and ethical implementation of AI in adult learning contexts.

Andragogy: Principles and Applications in Higher Education

Core andragogical principles, including self-concept, experience, readiness to learn, orientation to learning, motivation, and need to know, remain relevant in the AI era. The digital age presents both challenges and opportunities for applying these andragogical principles in higher education settings.

The Importance of AI in Higher Education

AI offers significant potential benefits, including personalized learning, improved efficiency, and enhanced research capabilities. However, challenges such as ethical concerns, the digital divide, and the need to maintain human interaction must be carefully addressed.

Integrating Adult Learning Theory with AI

AI capabilities can be aligned with andragogical principles to enhance self-directed learning, support experiential and problem-centered learning, and foster analytical thinking and creativity. The integration of AI and andragogy has the potential to create more engaging, effective, and personalized learning experiences for adult learners.

Practical Strategies for AI-Enhanced Andragogical Approaches

Successful implementation requires clear guidelines, learning from best practices, and comprehensive educator training and development.

Ethical Considerations and Challenges

Data privacy, algorithmic bias, and maintaining authentic learning experiences are vital ethical considerations in AI integration. Addressing these challenges requires a multifaceted approach involving technology experts, educators, ethicists, and learners themselves.

Future Directions and Emerging Trends

Evolving AI technologies such as advanced NLP, emotion AI, and AI-enhanced AR/VR present new opportunities and challenges for adult education. Ongoing research and preparation are essential to harness the potential of AI while adhering to andragogical principles.

The Importance of Balancing Innovation with Sound Andragogical Practices

As we embrace the transformative potential of AI in higher education, it is necessary to maintain a balance between technological innovation and sound andragogical practices. This balance is essential for several reasons:

- **Preserving the human element**: While AI can enhance many aspects of education, the human connection and guidance that are central to effective adult learning must be preserved and augmented, not replaced.
- **Ensuring learner-centeredness**: Andragogical principles emphasize the importance of learner autonomy and experience. AI implementation must enhance, not diminish, the adult learner's role as an active participant in their educational journey.
- **Promoting critical thinking:** As AI systems become more sophisticated, it becomes increasingly important to develop learners' logical analysis skills to evaluate and contextualize AI-generated information and recommendations.
- **Addressing ethical concerns:** Andragogical practices, with their emphasis on respect for the learner and ethical conduct, provide a crucial framework for navigating the ethical challenges posed by AI in education.
- **Fostering adaptability:** By grounding AI integration in andragogical principles, we can create learning environments that not only utilize current technologies but are also adaptable to future developments and changing learner needs.

Call to Action for Educators and Institutions

As we stand at the intersection of AI and andragogy in higher education, there is a pressing need for proactive engagement from educators and institutions. Educators and institutions must shape the future of AI-enhanced adult learning. The following are recommended actions:

- Embracing continuous learning is essential; educators must commit to ongoing professional development to stay informed about AI advancements and their implications for adult education.
- Engaging in judicious implementation involves thoughtfully integrating AI tools in teaching practices, always evaluating their alignment with andragogical principles and their impact on learning outcomes.

- Participating in research is essential; educators should contribute to the growing body of knowledge by conducting action research on AI implementation in their specific contexts and sharing their findings.
- Advocating for ethical AI is paramount; educators must be vocal advocates for the ethical development and use of AI in education, ensuring that learner rights and well-being are always prioritized.
- Fostering digital literacy is key; developing and promoting comprehensive AI literacy programs for both educators and learners ensures informed and discerning engagement with AI technologies.
- Collaborating across disciplines is necessary to address the complex challenges of AI integration, bringing together expertise from education, technology, ethics, and policy.
- Empowering learners involves adult learners in decisions about AI integration, respecting their autonomy and employing their experiences and insights.
- Developing adaptive policies is key; working towards creating flexible institutional policies that can evolve with AI advancements while safeguarding educational quality and learner interests is essential.
- Prioritizing inclusivity ensures that AI implementation enhances rather than hinders accessibility and inclusivity in adult education.
- Envisioning the future through forward-thinking discussions and scenario planning is vital to anticipate and shape the future of AI in adult education.

By taking these actions, educators and institutions can play a pivotal role in shaping an AI-enhanced future for adult education that is effective, ethical, and deeply rooted in andragogical principles. The integration of AI in higher education presents an unprecedented opportunity to enhance adult learning experiences, but it is our responsibility to ensure that this integration serves the fundamental goals of education: empowering learners, fostering critical thinking, and preparing individuals for success in an ever-changing world.

As we move forward, let us embrace the potential of AI with enthusiasm, temper it with wisdom drawn from andragogical insights, and always keep the needs and aspirations of adult learners at the center of our educational innovations. The future of AI in adult education is not predetermined; it is ours to shape, guided by the timeless principles of effective adult learning and our commitment to educational excellence.

ACKNOWLEDGEMENT

This research received no specific grant from any funding agency in the public, commercial, or not-for-profit sectors.

REFERENCES

Altbach, P. G., & Peterson, P. M. (Eds.). (1999). *Higher education in the 21st Century: Global challenge and national response*. Institute of International Education.

American Council on Education. (2011). *Strength through global leadership and engagement: U.S. higher education in the 21st Century*. Report of the Blue Ribbon Panel on Global Engagement. Author. https://www.acenet.edu/Documents/2011-CIGE-BRPReport.pdf

Azevedo, R., & Aleven, V. (Eds.). (2013). *International handbook of metacognition and learning technologies*. Springer. DOI: 10.1007/978-1-4419-5546-3

Baker, R. S., & Inventado, P. S. (2014). Educational data mining and learning analytics. In J, Larusson, J., & B. White (Eds.,) *Learning analytics* (pp. 61-75). Springer. DOI: 10.1007/978-1-4614-3305-7_4

Bates, T. (2022). Teaching in a digital age (3rd ed.). BCcampus.

Boettcher, J. V., & Conrad, R. M. (2016). *The online teaching survival guide: Simple and practical pedagogical tips*. John Wiley & Sons.

Bond, M., Khosravi, H., De Laat, M., Bergdahl, N., Negrea, V., Oxley, E., Pham, P., Chong, S. W., & Siemen, G. (2024). A meta systematic review of artificial intelligence in higher education: A call for increased ethics, collaboration, and rigour. *International Journal of Educational Technology in Higher Education*, 21(4), 1–41. DOI: 10.1186/s41239-023-00436-z

Borenstein, J., & Howard, A. (2021). Emerging challenges in AI and the need for AI ethics education. *AI and Ethics*, 1(1), 61–65. DOI: 10.1007/s43681-020-00002-7 PMID: 38624388

Chen, L., Chen, P., & Lin, Z. (2020). Artificial intelligence in education: A review. *IEEE Access : Practical Innovations, Open Solutions*, 8, 75264–75278. DOI: 10.1109/ACCESS.2020.2988510

Crompton, H., & Burke, D. (2023). Artificial intelligence in higher education: The state of the field. *International Journal of Educational Technology in Higher Education*, 20(22), 1–22. DOI: 10.1186/s41239-023-00392-8

Cross, K. P., Major, C. H., & Barkley, E. F. (2014). *Collaborative learning techniques: A handbook for college faculty* (2nd ed.). John Wiley & Sons.

Dillenbourg, P., & Jermann, P. (2010). Technology for classroom orchestration. In Khine, M., & Saleh, I. (Eds.), *New Science of Learning* (pp. 525–552). Springer., DOI: 10.1007/978-1-4419-5716-0_26

Fornaciari, C. J., & Dean, K. L. (2014). The 21st-century syllabus: From pedagogy to andragogy. *Journal of Management Education*, 38(5), 701–723. DOI: 10.1177/1052562913504763

Frontiers. (2023). *Educational transformation: 21st Century skills and challenges for higher education*. Frontiers Research Topics.

Garg, R. (2024). The impact of generative artificial intelligence on higher education: Disruption or seamless integration? *Social Science Research Network*.https://ssrn.com/abstract=4762814

Goel, A. K., & Polepeddi, L. (2016). *Jill Watson: A virtual teaching assistant for online education*. Georgia Institute of Technology. http://hdl.handle.net/1853/59104

Gökoğlu, S. (2024). Challenges and limitations of Generative AI in education. In Sharma, R., & Bozkurt, A. (Eds.), *Transforming Education with Generative AI: Prompt Engineering and Synthetic Content Creation* (pp. 158–181). IGI Global., DOI: 10.4018/979-8-3693-1351-0.ch008

Graesser, A. C., VanLehn, K., Rosé, C. P., Jordan, P. W., & Harter, D. (2001). Intelligent tutoring systems with conversational dialogue. *AI Magazine*, 22(4), 39–39.

Harris, J., Wihak, C., & Van Kleef, J. (2014). *Handbook of the recognition of prior learning: Research into practice*. National Institute of Adult Continuing Education.

Hase, S., & Kenyon, C. (2000). From Andragogy to Heutagogy. *Ultibase Articles*, 5, 1–10.

Henschke, J. A. (2011). Considerations regarding the future of andragogy. *Adult Learning*, 22(1), 34–37. DOI: 10.1177/104515951102200109

Holmes, W., Bialik, M., & Fadel, C. (2019). *Artificial intelligence in education: Promises and implications for teaching and learning*. Center for Curriculum Redesign. https://curriculumredesign.org/our-work/artificial-intelligence-in-education/

Jewitt, C. (2013). Multimodal methods for researching digital technologies. In *The SAGE handbook of digital technology research* (pp. 250–265). SAGE Publications., DOI: 10.4135/9781446282229.n18

Kidd, T. T., & Keengwe, J. (Eds.). (2010). *Adult learning in the digital age: Perspectives on online technologies and outcomes*. IGI Global., DOI: 10.4018/978-1-60566-828-4

Knowles, M. (1980). *The modern practice of adult education: From andragogy to pedagogy*. Associated.

Knowles, M. S., Holton, E. F.III, & Swanson, R. A. (2015). *The adult learner: The definitive classic in adult education and human resource development* (8th ed.). Routledge.

Kolb, D. A. (2014). *Experiential learning: Experience as the source of learning and development*. FT press.

Kolodner, J. L., Cox, M. T., & González-Calero, P. A. (2005). Case-based reasoning-inspired approaches to education. *The Knowledge Engineering Review*, 20(3), 299–303. DOI: 10.1017/S0269888906000634

Koumpouros, Y. (2024). Revealing the true potential and prospects of augmented reality in education. *Smart Learning Environ*, 11(2), 2. DOI: 10.1186/s40561-023-00288-0

Kumar, D. (2023). How emerging technologies are transforming education and research: Trends, opportunities, and challenges. *Infinite Horizons: Exploring the Unknown*, 89-117.

Labadze, L., Grigolia, M., & Machaidze, L. (2023). Role of AI chatbots in education: Systematic literature review. *International Journal of Educational Technology in Higher Education*, 20(1), 56. DOI: 10.1186/s41239-023-00426-1

Laupichler, M. C., Aster, A., Schirch, J., & Raupach, T. (2022). Artificial intelligence literacy in higher and adult education: A scoping literature review. In *Computers and Education* (Vol. 3, p. 100101). Artificial Intelligence., DOI: 10.1016/j.caeai.2022.100101

Leiker, D., Finnigan, S., Gyllen, R., & Cukurova, M. (2023). Prototyping the use of Large Language Models (LLMs) for adult learning content creation at scale. CEUR Workshop proceedings. https://doi.org//arXiv.2306.01815DOI: 10.48550

Lim, W. M., Gunasekara, A., Pallant, J. L., Pallant, J. I., & Pechenkina, E. (2023). Generative AI and the future of education: Ragnarök or reformation? A paradoxical perspective from management educators. *International Journal of Management Education*, 21(2), 100790. DOI: 10.1016/j.ijme.2023.100790

Luan, L., Liang, J. C., Chai, C. S., Lin, T. B., & Dong, Y. (2020). Development of the new media literacy scale for EFL learners in China: A validation study. *Interactive Learning Environments*, 31(1), 244–257. DOI: 10.1080/10494820.2020.1774396

Lubart, T., Zenasni, F., & Barbot, B. (2013). Creative potential and its measurement. *International Journal for Talent Development and Creativity*, 1(2), 41–50.

Luckin, R., Holmes, W., Griffiths, M., & Forcier, L. B. (2016). *Intelligence unleashed. An argument for AI in education*. Pearson.

Masleg, N., Fattorini, L., Brynjolfsson, E., Etchemendy, J., Ligett, K., Lyons, T., Manyika, J., Ngo, H., Niebles, J. C., Parli, V., Shoham, Y., Wald, R., Clark, J., & Perrault, R. (2023). *The AI Index 2023 Annual Report*. AI Index Steering Committee, Stanford Institute for Human-Centered AI, Stanford University.

McCormack, M. (2023). EDUCAUSE QuickPoll results: Adopting and adapting to Generative AI in higher ed tech. *EDUCAUSE Review – EDUCAUSE Research Notes*. https://er.educause.edu/articles/2023/4/educause-quickpoll-results-adopting-and-adapting-to-generative-ai-in-higher-ed-tech

McKinsey Global Institute. (2023). *The economic potential of generative AI: The next productivity frontier*. McKinsey & Company. https://www.mckinsey.com/capabilities/mckinsey-digital/our-insights/the-economic-potential-of-generative-ai-the-next-productivity-frontier

Merchant, Z., Goetz, E. T., Cifuentes, L., Keeney-Kennicutt, W., & Davis, T. J. (2014). Effectiveness of virtual reality-based instruction on students' learning outcomes in K-12 and higher education: A meta-analysis. *Computers & Education*, 70, 29–40. DOI: 10.1016/j.compedu.2013.07.033

Merriam, S. B., & Baumgartner, L. M. (2020). *Learning in adulthood: A comprehensive guide* (4th ed.). Jossey-Bass.

Merriam, S. B., & Bierema, L. L. (2014). *Adult learning: Linking theory and practice*. Jossey-Bass.

Mezirow, J. (1991). *Transformative dimensions of adult learning*. Jossey-Bass.

Milana, M., Brandi, U., Hodge, S., & Hoggan-Kloubert, T. (2024). Artificial intelligence (AI), conversational agents, and generative AI: Implications for adult education practice and research. *International Journal of Lifelong Education*, 43(1), 1–7. DOI: 10.1080/02601370.2024.2310448

Pappas, C. (2014). *Nine tips to apply adult learning theory to eLearning*. eLearning Industry.

Ryan, R. M., & Deci, E. L. (2000). Self-determination theory and the facilitation of intrinsic motivation, social development, and well-being. *The American Psychologist*, 55(1), 68–78. DOI: 10.1037/0003-066X.55.1.68 PMID: 11392867

Salmi, J. (2001). Tertiary education in the Twenty-First Century: Challenges and opportunities. *Higher Education Management*, 3(2), 105–130.

Savery, J. R. (2006). Overview of problem-based learning: Definitions and distinctions. *The Interdisciplinary Journal of Problem-Based Learning*, 1(1). Advance online publication. DOI: 10.7771/1541-5015.1002

Schön, D. A. (1992). *The reflective practitioner: How professionals think in action*. Routledge Imprint of Taylor & Francis., DOI: 10.4324/9781315237473

Schwab, K. (2016). *The fourth industrial revolution*. World Economic Forum.

Siemens, G. (2005). Connectivism: A learning theory for the digital age. *International Journal of Instructional Technology and Distance Learning*, 2(1), 3–10.

Storey, V., & Wagner, A. (2024). Integrating artificial intelligence (AI) into adult education: Opportunities, challenges, and future directions. *International Journal of Adult Education and Technology*, 15(1), 1–15. DOI: 10.4018/IJAET.345921

Tawfik, A. A. (2015). Essential readings in problem-based learning: Exploring and extending the legacy of Howard S. Barrows. *The Interdisciplinary Journal of Problem-Based Learning*, 9(2). Advance online publication. DOI: 10.7771/1541-5015.1593

Taylor, D. C., & Hamdy, H. (2013). Adult learning theories: Implications for learning and teaching in medical education: AMEE Guide No. 83. *Medical Teacher*, 35(11), e1561–e1572. DOI: 10.3109/0142159X.2013.828153 PMID: 24004029

Taylor, E. W., & Cranton, P. (2012). *The handbook of transformative learning: Theory, research, and practice*. Jossey-Bass.

Tsai, M. J., Hsu, C. Y., & Tsai, C. C. (2012). Investigation of high school students' online science information searching performance: The role of implicit and explicit strategies. *Journal of Science Education and Technology*, 21(2), 246–254. DOI: 10.1007/s10956-011-9307-2

VanLehn, K. (2011). The relative effectiveness of human tutoring, intelligent tutoring systems, and other tutoring systems. *Educational Psychologist*, 46(4), 197–221. DOI: 10.1080/00461520.2011.611369

Yusuf, A., Pervin, N., & Román-González, M. (2024). Generative AI and the future of higher education: A threat to academic integrity or reformation? Evidence from multicultural perspectives. *International Journal of Educational Technology in Higher Education*, 21(1), 21. DOI: 10.1186/s41239-024-00453-6

Zawacki-Richter, O., Marín, V. I., Bond, M., & Gouverneur, F. (2019). Systematic review of research on artificial intelligence applications in higher education – Where are the educators? *International Journal of Educational Technology in Higher Education*, 16(39), 1–27. DOI: 10.1186/s41239-019-0171-0

Chapter 5
The AI Scholar: AI in Higher Education Research and Writing

Ashley L. Dockens
https://orcid.org/0000-0002-9707-975X
Lamar University, USA

Kaye Shelton
https://orcid.org/0000-0001-5024-5629
Lamar University, USA

ABSTRACT

This chapter focuses on the impact artificial intelligence is having on higher education, specifically in academic research and writing, and explores an array of AI tools tailored to enhance academic endeavors, providing insights into their significance, purpose, and impact within higher education settings. AI tools can greatly speed up the process for academic researchers in gathering, analyzing and presenting research data. In addition, the chapter reviews the use of AI tools for writing, editing, paraphrasing, and summarizing literature and recommends numerous tools for use. The potential organizational challenges are also addressed such as faculty resistance, the impact to technology support, and the ethics related to academic integrity associated with the use of artificial intelligence for both students and faculty. Recommendations for future research and a call to educators for next steps are included.

DOI: 10.4018/979-8-3373-0502-8.ch005

INTRODUCTION

Generative Artificial Intelligence (AI) has burst onto the higher education scene, revolutionizing academic research and writing while at the same time, sparking intense debate. Before 2022, AI's impact in academia was largely limited to predictive analytics for student performance, with higher education lagging behind other sectors in AI adoption (Bates et al., 2020). Interestingly, China, Turkey, and Spain led the charge in educational AI implementation (Zhang & Aslan, 2021). The landscape dramatically shifted in November 2022 with the launch of ChatGPT, a sophisticated large language model (LLM) developed by OpenAI. This AI powerhouse, capable of understanding and generating human-like text based on vast internet-sourced datasets, rapidly gained traction among college students (Silverman et al., 2023). Within a mere two months, ChatGPT's user base exploded to between 30 and 100 million, outpacing existing LLMs like Google's BARD (Roose, 2023; Silverman et al., 2024). By Spring 2023, educators were grappling with a new challenge: students submitting AI-generated work as their own (Cassidy, 2023), often without considering potential inaccuracies stemming from the AI's reliance on unverified online sources. This surge in AI usage has ignited a fierce debate about the future of academic integrity and the role of technology in education, for both faculty and students. Some institutions have responded by banning the usage of AI technology outright, while others are working to train faculty and help them integrate the tools responsibly into curricula.

As AI technology evolves, it is poised to revolutionize academia, offering innovative solutions to age-old challenges in research and writing. ChatGPT, for instance, is not just a writing tool; it's a multi-faceted assistant capable of idea generation, outlining, proofreading, and even providing feedback (Alshater, 2023; Atlas, 2023; Barrett & Pack, 2023). Its linguistic abilities allow for creating grammatically sound and fluent essays (Ljujić et al., 2023), potentially leveling the playing field for students struggling with language barriers. But AI's impact extends beyond writing assistance. These tools enhance the educational experience by fostering meaningful interactions, boosting student engagement, and tailoring assessments to individual needs (Zawacki-Richter et al., 2019; Zhang & Aslan, 2021). Perhaps what is most exciting is AI's potential to democratize education. When used responsibly, generative AI tools like ChatGPT can potentially break down barriers, empower learners, personalize education, and push faculty to embrace cutting-edge technologies (Yin, 2024; Ljujić et al., 2023). The possibilities for enhanced learning and scholarly output are tremendous. However, concerns about AI perpetuating biases and the need for digital literacy skills remain significant challenges we will need to address to prepare students for AI usage in their workplace.

From chatbots and expert systems to large language models and intelligent tutors, AI is reshaping the academic landscape (Zhang & Aslan, 2021). Khalifa and Albadaw (2024) assert artificial intelligence is a revolutionary tool for academic researchers. Their recent systematic review of 24 studies revealed six areas artificial intelligence can support academic writing: idea generation and research design; content and structuring; literature review and synthesis; data management and analysis; editing, review, and publishing; and assisting in communication, outreach, and ethical compliance, all a focus of this chapter.

This chapter illuminates how these tools can revolutionize research and writing in higher education, ushering in a new era of interactive learning, personalized education, and enhanced student support. AI's impact is far-reaching: boosting engagement, adapting to individual needs, enriching learning environments, and predicting student outcomes (Zawacki-Richter et al., 2019; Zhang & Aslan, 2021). As Walter (2024) aptly puts it, AI is not just another tech trend; it is fundamentally "reshaping the educational experiences at its core" (p. 1). The prescience of Bates et al. (2020) is striking - their prediction of an impending "tsunami" for educators made two years before the arrival of ChatGPT has indeed come to pass with the arrival of ChatGPT. Join us as we explore this AI wave sweeping through education and what it means for the future of learning as we review AI tools for research and writing. We'll also examine the ethical implications and necessary policy changes that higher education institutions must consider in this rapidly evolving landscape.

AI TOOLS FOR RESEARCH ASSISTANCE

The research landscape is transforming significantly as generative AI tools gain traction among scholars. Despite some journal editors' reservations, researchers are increasingly embracing AI for its remarkable efficiency and time-saving capabilities, potentially accelerating the publication process (Golan et al, 2023; Silverman et al., 2023). This shift is not limited to individual researchers; scholarly journals themselves are leveraging AI, with platforms like Research Exchange (ReX) streamlining the article submission process by automatically extracting relevant information from manuscripts (Hartel, 2022). However, the impact of AI in research extends far beyond submission assistance.

AI-driven tools streamline tasks and enhance research and writing outputs, enabling researchers to achieve higher levels of productivity (Silverman et al., 2023) without sacrificing quality, leading to greater scholarly impact. For example, large language models like ChatGPT have the potential to streamline research processes by summarizing articles, generating literature reviews, and assisting with data analysis (Atlas, 2023). According to Lixandru, (2024), "the synthesis capability of generative artificial intelligence becomes a cornerstone, providing researchers and analysts the ability to address complex texts with increased efficiency" (p. 66). In their recent article, Fabiano et al. (2024) provide a comprehensive and descriptive list of various AI tools that can assist with efficiency in the research process.

These sophisticated tools are revolutionizing information retrieval, helping with generating research ideas and questions, assisting with literature reviews, offering invaluable support in study design, enhancing data analysis efficiency, and even providing personalized recommendations to improve student learning experiences. In addition, AI tools can help with trends and large amounts of data analysis needed for grant funding, including providing in-depth information about the organization funding the grant. As AI continues to evolve, it promises to reshape the very foundations of academic research, offering unprecedented opportunities for innovation and discovery while simultaneously raising important questions about the future of scholarly work.

Enhanced Information Retrieval

AI-powered search engines and knowledge management systems serve as invaluable aids, guiding learners through vast amounts of information with precision and efficiency, thus augmenting the research process. These tools are designed to return more advanced search queries that retrieve more accurate results. Adelakun (2024) identified seven ways which AI has improved information retrieval compared to traditional keyword searches: Improved decision-making, enhanced relevance, efficient content organization, personalization, semantic understanding scalability and performance, and advanced search features such as voice searching and image recognition. AI-powered search engines can save considerable time in how quickly they can locate and quickly pinpointing seminal research papers and recognizing emerging trends in their field, potentially saving countless hours of manual searching and skimming. Recognizing the preferences of individuals, AI-based systems use algorithms to offer tailored guidance and facilitate personalized experiences for academic writers and researchers by recommending resources and suggestions specific to their search.

The following is a list of just a few of the many AI Search tools for academics and researchers:

- ChatGPT (https://openai.com/chatgpt/) is already, one of the most used AI tools with the ability to analyze large amounts of data, enhance writing, editing, and vocabulary, and quickly paraphrase, summarize, and synthesize text such as research study articles.

- Semantic Scholar (https://www.semanticscholar.org/) stands as one example at the forefront of this revolution. This AI-powered search engine harnesses the power of machine learning to deep dive into the content of scientific papers. Unlike traditional search engines that rely primarily on keyword matching, Semantic Scholar analyzes the context and relationships between concepts. This advanced approach yields more relevant search results and, crucially, identifies key insights that might otherwise be overlooked.
- Refseek (https://www.refseek.com/) developed for students and researchers, is an AI-powered web-based search engine that supports gathering academic research to make it more available and easier to access. According to their website, RefSeek has access to over five billion documents.
- BASE (https://www.base-search.net/) (Bielefeld Academic Search Engine) is an AI-powered web-based search engine with access to over 350 million resources. It was developed and operated by the Bielefeld University Library for searching academic resources and literature.
- CORE (https://core.ac.uk/) (COnnecting REpositories) provides a comprehensive database of open-access scholarly literature, collecting and indexing research from repositories and journals. They believe they offer the world's largest collection of full-text open-access research papers with a mission to index all research worldwide and deliver unrestricted access for all.
- Paper Digest (https://www.paperdigest.org) is an AI-powered platform using machine learning and natural language processing to search and provide information on current scientific research trends, provide literature reviews, and assist with editing and writing. This tool claims not to have AI hallucinations and provides citations for every sentence it creates.
- SCITE (https://scite/ai) is an AI-powered platform for finding and reviewing scientific articles via Smart Citations, which allow users to see how a publication has been cited by providing the context of the citation and a classification describing whether it provides supporting or contrasting evidence for the cited claim. Funded in part by the National Science Foundation and the National Institute on Drug Abuse of the National Institutes of Health, this powerful group of tools offers access to over 1.2 billion research citations, a reference checker, and customized dashboards.
- Consensus (https://consensus.app) is an academic AI-powered search engine using large language models and vector searching to find the most relevant research papers.
- Google Scholar (https://scholar.google.com/) is a web-based search engine using artificial intelligence and was developed by Google to specifically search scholarly literature and provides a link to both the information about the resource and the document itself if it is available in full text.

AI-Powered Literature Review Tools

One of the most time-consuming and critical aspects of academic research is conducting comprehensive literature reviews. This process, traditionally requiring weeks or even months of painstaking reading and analysis, is being revolutionized by AI tools. These sophisticated systems are transforming how researchers approach, synthesize, and utilize existing scholarship. While numerous AI-powered platforms are emerging in this space, we will explore a few notable examples to illustrate their potential.

Iris.ai (https://iris.ai) is an innovative tool whose platform leverages natural language processing to analyze research papers and generate visual maps of scientific concepts. The power of Iris.ai lies in its ability to uncover connections between different areas of research that might not be immediately apparent to human researchers. By visualizing these relationships, Iris.ai can spark new ideas, suggest novel research directions, and help researchers break out of siloed thinking within their disciplines.

Elsevier's Scival (https://www.elsevier.com/solutions/scival) takes a broader approach, using AI to analyze vast amounts of research data across institutions and disciplines. This platform is particularly valuable for institutions and researchers looking to position their research efforts strategically. By identifying research trends, potential collaborators, and funding opportunities, Scival helps researchers and institutions make data-driven decisions about where to focus their efforts and resources.

It is important to note that these tools are just a few examples in a rapidly growing field. Other platforms using AI technology like ResearchRabbit (https://www.researchrabbit.ai/), Scholarcy (https://www.scholarcy.com/), and Dimensions (https://www.dimensions.ai/) offer their own unique features and capabilities and range in pricing. As the field evolves, new tools are continually emerging, each with its own strengths and specializations.

These AI-powered literature review tools represent just the tip of the iceberg in AI-assisted research. As these technologies continue to evolve, they promise to not only speed up the research process but also to enhance the quality and depth of literature reviews. By helping researchers quickly grasp the state of knowledge in their field and identify gaps or contradictions in existing research (Khalifa & Albadawy, 2024), AI-powered literature review tools are poised to accelerate the pace of scientific discovery and publishing results.

However, while these tools offer powerful assistance, they do not replace the critical thinking and domain expertise of human researchers. Instead, they augment human capabilities, allowing researchers to spend less time on tedious searching and more time on analysis, synthesis, and original thinking. As these tools become more prevalent, developing skills in effectively leveraging AI for reviewing literature may become an essential part of research training in higher education. AI tools are truly revolutionizing this process.

Ai For Research Design, Data Collection and Analysis

AI tools are also transforming how researchers design research studies, improve research questions and method design, collect and analyze data, develop surveys, and code and analyze data. The following briefly highlights how AI can assist a researcher with increased efficiency and productivity:

- Automated Surveys: AI-powered chatbots can conduct surveys, adapting questions based on respondents' answers for more nuanced data collection.
- Natural Language Processing for Qualitative Data: Tools like NVivo, MAXQDA, RapidMiner, and ATLAS.ti incorporate AI to assist with coding and analyzing qualitative data from interviews and open-ended survey responses.
- Predictive Analytics: AI algorithms can identify patterns in large datasets that humans might miss, potentially leading to new hypotheses or research directions.

Extensive Large Language Models of AI such as ChatGPT and BARD can be used to assist researchers in developing research frameworks and analyzing data. For example, Elicit can assist with developing research questions. Research Rabbit App can recommend other articles based on the resources gathered in Zotero, an online reference manager. In addition, Graphmaker.AI can quickly create customized charts and graphs by simply uploading a data spreadsheet. In addition, AI tools can provide support for the administrative aspects of research:

- Trello with Butler: This project management tool incorporates AI to automate repetitive tasks, helping research teams stay organized.
- Asana's Workload feature: Uses AI to help distribute tasks among team members more efficiently, considering individual workloads and project deadlines.

Quantitative researchers can increase productivity by using AI tools to create data modeling and data analysis by using tools such as OpenAi's Advanced Data Analysis or Microsoft's Power BI. Qualitative researchers can effectively use AI tools (Lixandru, 2024) such as advanced transcription bots to transcribe interview data and tools such as Delve, Big Qual, or Remesh to sort through, code data, and develop themes, saving large amounts of time normally devoted to such tasks.

The modern world has an abundance of data, and AI algorithms offer invaluable assistance in unraveling complex datasets and extracting meaningful insights with ease. This powerful solution aids in the quality and depth of research. As higher education institutions become large data warehouses in the coming decades, educators and administrators will need to develop and outsource data-intensive technical capacities (Bates et al. 2020). AI data mining can use algorithms and decision trees to create learner profiles that can predict if a student is likely to drop a course (e.g. Dropout Detective) or even fail an assignment (Zawacki-Richter et al., 2019). In addition, it can predict at-risk students and identify gifted students in higher education settings, enabling educators to intervene appropriately and support student success (Zhang & Aslan, 2021).

However, it must be pointed out that some researchers resist sharing their data with AI for fear of data ownership and privacy concerns (Davison et al., 2024) and are concerned with existing biases with the AI tool possibly influencing the data analysis (Alshater, 2023). There are now recommendations that Institutional Review Boards (IRB) should need to consider AI in their approval process for participant protection (Davison et al., 2024; Ferretti et al., 2020; Friesen et al., 2021) and possible violation of the Belmont Report (Doerr & Meeder, 2022). While AI tools offer numerous benefits, researchers must consider potential ethical implications:

- Bias in AI algorithms: Researchers should be aware that AI tools may perpetuate existing biases in research literature or data sets.
- Over-reliance on AI: There's a risk of researchers becoming overly dependent on AI tools, potentially limiting creative thinking or novel approaches.
- Transparency: When using AI tools in research, users must be transparent about their use in publications and understand their limitations.

IMPROVING ACADEMIC WRITING AND EDITING WITH AI TOOLS

Academic writing is a formal style of structured writing used by students, educators, and researchers to present information, facts, arguments, reports, and results of research studies. For those originally trained to use unstructured writing, academic writing is a big paradigm shift, and have often struggled with mastering the style of concise reporting without opinion. Many students and academics have paid professional editors to help with editing and improving thesis papers and dissertations, with some academic programs and scholarly journals requiring the use of a professional editor. However, artificial intelligence can now provide that kind of support and many times, free of charge with today's powerful AI tools. For example, Microsoft Word now provides an AI-powered editing tool able to check for spelling, grammar, and even review for possible plagiarism.

Dirette (2024) suggested the following uses of AI for academic writing: "AI-assisted (editing, spell correction, word generation, and wordsmithing" and "AI-generated (brainstorming, outline development, summaries, writing examples, and tables and graphs" (p. 2). For example, Semantic Scholar's TLDR (Too Long Didn't Read) tool creates single-sentence summaries of scientific research articles, users to make quicker decisions on what articles to fully read.

In Table 1, Kassorla (2023) suggests new steps for students writing research papers with AI assistance. She also provides a great example of syllabus information and best practices to provide students in her article.

Table 1. Steps for students writing research papers with AI assistance

Writing Research before GAI	Writing Research after GAI
1. Identifying research interest 2. Identifying source material 3. Reading and writing research notes 4. Writing paper with documentation 5. Completing works cited or bibliography	1. Identifying research interest 2. Writing paper with GAI 3. Checking for hallucinations 4. Identifying academic knowledge 5. Identifying source material 6. Documenting sources 7. Completing works cited or bibliography

The following are additional examples of how AI tools can be used:
AI for Idea Generation and Outlining:

- Mind mapping tools with AI: Applications like MindMeister or Ayoa use AI to suggest related concepts and help researchers organize their thoughts.
- Outline generators: Tools like Writesonic, Article Forge, or ChatGPT can generate article outlines based on a topic or research question, providing a starting point for writers.

AI-Powered Plagiarism Detection:

- Turnitin's Originality Check: Uses AI to compare submitted work against a vast database of academic papers, websites, and other sources.
- iThenticate: Specifically designed for researchers and publishers to check for potential plagiarism in scholarly works before submission.

Automated Translation for International Collaboration:

- DeepL: Uses neural networks to provide more nuanced translations, particularly useful for academic writing.
- Papago: Developed by Naver, this tool is particularly effective for Asian languages, facilitating collaboration with researchers in these regions.

AI for Data Visualization:

- Tableau with Ask Data: Using natural language queries, this AI tool allows users to create visualizations making data presentation more accessible.
- Flourish: Offers AI-assisted chart recommendations based on the data input, helping researchers choose the most effective way to present their findings.

Tension does exist between students and instructors on just how much students can rely upon these tools to generate their classwork. Both students and instructors agree that the tools can be used for editing and brainstorming (Maphoto et al., 2024). However, there is less agreement when it comes to the tool generating the student's entire work and caution should be taken for students to not develop an overreliance as students need to develop their writing skills. Many have recommended instructors must provide clear guidelines on its use in coursework (Barrett & Pack, 2023; Ciampa et al., 2023; Jarrah et al., 2023; Maphoto et al., 2024; Sullivan et al., 2023). Nevertheless, the literature clearly shows the use of AI tools for academic writing is now widespread. Ciampa et al. (2023) remind us "It is possible to find a balance between utilizing AI technology and fostering students' abilities to think for themselves and develop their writing skills independently" (p. 192).

Grammar and Style Correction

AI-powered writing assistants provide real-time feedback on grammar and style, aiding scholars in refining academic writing and enhancing clarity, thereby improving the quality of scholarly publications. Tools like ChatGPT, Grammarly, PaperPal, Hyperwrite, Pigai, Wordtune, and Aithor can quickly help students with spelling, grammar, and concise writing. Recent research studies are showing students want to use AI in a variety of ways. For example, Picciano (2024) encouraged graduate students to use ChatGPT to write an essay and found that many of the students said the AI tool was good for generating ideas and providing an outline. Participants in a study by Niyozov et al. (2023) reported notable improvements in vocabulary acquisition, grammar comprehension, and overall language proficiency when utilizing ChatGPT for language learning.

However, students also highlighted a need for the university to teach them how to use various problem-solving methods, as AI tools are likely to become ubiquitous in their future workplaces (Smolansky et al., 2023). Bates et al. (2020) observed, "This reinforces the view that the role of the instructor or teacher needs to move away from content presentation, content management and testing of content comprehension – all of which can be done by computing – towards skills development" (p. 8).

Advanced Grammar and Style Correction:

- Context-aware corrections: Tools like ProWritingAid use AI to understand the context of writing, offering suggestions that go beyond basic grammar to improve clarity and style.
- Discipline-specific suggestions: Some AI writing assistants, like Trinka, are tailored for academic and technical writing, offering field-specific terminology and phrasing suggestions.

Automated Peer Review

AI-powered tools like those for computational peer review can enhance and facilitate various academic processes related to research and writing. AI platforms can facilitate collaborative peer review processes, offering constructive feedback and fostering scholarly discourse, thus enhancing the rigor and credibility of academic research (Tahiru, 2021). AI-powered tools can also offer personalized writing feedback to students, allowing for more targeted support and skill development (Atlas, 2023). For example, Banihashem et al. (2024) investigated the potential of ChatGPT, an AI-powered tool, to generate feedback on argumentative essays in higher education, comparing its performance to peer-generated feedback. Their study revealed significant differences like feedback provided by ChatGPT and peers, with the AI tool focusing more on descriptive elements while peers excelled at identifying problems within the essays. The findings suggest that ChatGPT and student-generated feedback could play complementary roles in the feedback process for essay writing tasks. They propose that the integration of ChatGPT as a feedback source could be particularly beneficial in higher education contexts, especially for courses with large enrollments and substantial essay-writing components.

Other researchers have found positive results with tutoring and feedback. For example, Wang et al. (2023) suggested the use of AI can improve learning for international students by using chatbots as personalized support. Escalante et al. (2023) found no significant difference in learning outcomes between English as New Language (ENL) students who received AI-generated feedback and those who received human tutor feedback over six weeks. They found that AI-generated feedback can likely be incorporated into ENL essay evaluation without affecting learning outcomes, although a blended approach utilizing the strengths of both forms of feedback is recommended (Escalante et al., 2023). Similarly, Tahiru's (2021) research on AI tutoring systems can match or outperform human tutors in certain educational tasks with free tools such as AI Tutor Pro, Atlas, TutorOcean, and Sizzle. However, more research is still needed regarding intelligent tutoring systems to fully convince faculty of the benefits which include promoting collaborative learning and increasing student motivation, and helping to scale very large courses such as MOOCs (Tahiru, 2021).

Reference Management

Conversational AIs and AI-specific programs can assist with citation formatting and reference management, ensuring adherence to academic standards and alleviating the burden of manual citation management. For example, Quillbot can generate an APA reference citation simply by uploading a PDF of the article; it can also provide a paraphrase, a summary, and check for plagiarism and includes a plug-in extension for the Google Chrome Internet browser. The citation generator part of this tool is free. Another example is Scite.Ai which is being used to evaluate scientific journal articles. Reference information can be exported from some journals in the Scite.Ai format. Additional AI Reference Manager applications quickly evolved such as Petal Reference Manager, Wisdom.AI, Trinka, Scholarcy, and Semantic Scholar, with some being free and some having an associated cost for whatever additional services it provides.

These new tools can manage the literature sources and at the same time, assist with finding new sources. Gone are the days of pouring over hundreds of journal articles to write a literature review if these tools' outputs are accurate! But as of now, there are still errors in the data output (incorrect citations, AI-created responses without fact) so scholars should always carefully examine the generated results. Students should be reminded to always check the results of the citations as there are errors or sometimes too much information is provided.

ADDRESSING ORGANIZATIONAL, ETHICAL, AND TECHNOLOGICAL CHALLENGES

Despite the promise of progress, organizational impact, ethical considerations, and technological challenges must be carefully traversed by educators to ensure responsible AI integration, safeguarding academic integrity, and promoting accessibility to AI-driven tools. The advancement of AI in education requires addressing critical issues such as ethics and usage, privacy concerns, and the need for interdisciplinary collaborations involving educators, researchers, and technology experts (Zhang & Aslan, 2021). There should also be additional awareness regarding user trust and acceptance and scalability and performance of the technologies (Adelakun, 2024).

Challenges also include a lack of clear guidelines for educators and limited AI expertise among educators. More interdisciplinary research with educational perspectives is needed (Zhang & Aslan, 2021) with Zawacki-Richter et al. (2019) noting educational researchers have been observing and critiquing from the sidelines without actively participating. To explore the potential improvements AI can bring to learning and pedagogy, educators must be willing to collaborate with computer scientists (Bates et al., 2020) and experiment with the possibilities.

Organizational Challenges

According to Bates et al. (2020), because things are changing so quickly, it will be crucial for higher institutions to be more agile and be able to quickly adopt new practices as artificial intelligence continues to develop and improve. Tarisayi (2024) suggests four key leadership strategies are needed for a successful implementation: articulation of a strategic vision, fostering an institutional culture, gathering and allocating resources, and seeking external partnerships. Tarisayi further notes a shared vision and effective communication can support campus buy-in but also surmises that "while AI holds transformative potential, realizing the full benefits requires strong governance, strategic investment, and a human-centric approach leveraging AI to augment human capabilities and educational excellence" (p. 11).

As many higher education faculty are slow to adopt new technologies, strategies are needed to overcome the resistance to the use of AI tools as faculty "can actively shape the conversation via creative experimentation and intervention in the evolution of writing genres through research and reflection on the processes and ethics of collaborating with AI to create new work" (Wise et al., 2024, p. 582). We suggest finding faculty champions that are successfully using artificial intelligence in teaching and writing and have them share their experience and provide demonstrations at perhaps, a faculty brown bag event or informational meeting. Pilot programs could be offered with faculty early adopters that have staff ready on the sidelines ready to support faculty and students to improve adoption.

To successfully roll out and support AI tools, a significant investment in training is necessary for both faculty and students. Ongoing training should be offered that demonstrates long-term support from the institution but also to improve faculty skills and confidence in the use of the tools. Discussions should include on potential limitations, possible AI biases (Jarrah et al., 2023), and institutional policy and guidelines. Faculty should be shown how to check for AI hallucinations The more faculty can see others successfully integrating the tools to reduce workload and engage students, the quicker the adoption rate will be.

However, when incorporating AI tools like ChatGPT into higher education, institutions must consider implications such as furthering bias and the potential impact on the workforce (Atlas, 2023) and understand there will be impacts to the institution regarding adoption, policy and continued training for the technologies that are evolving so quickly (Cotton et al., 2023). Higher education institutions need to develop data literacy and ethical frameworks to navigate the challenges and opportunities of AI and learning analytics (Bates et al., 2020). Brandon et al. (2023, para. 11) suggested the following questions be examined before developing an institutional AI policy (see their article for more in-depth recommendations for developing guidelines):

- Whom is the policy going to focus on? Students, faculty, staff, administration, third-party vendors, contractors, etc.?
- Can the same policy apply across the institution, or will different policies be needed for different parts of the organization?
- Will the policy stand on its own, or will there be room for adjustments (for example, will students encounter variations depending on whether instructors—under the notion of academic freedom—want to encourage or discourage certain uses of generative AI for the purposes of teaching)?
- What can or will be the implications of violating the policy?
- What methods of accountability with the policy can be created when it may be hard to actually detect generative AI text?
- Will there be differences between institutionally affiliated generative tools and those that are available to anyone?

The researchers further suggest an institutional AI policy framework should address the following areas: Policy Audience, Policy Timeline, Policy Tools, Academic Integrity Guidelines, Acceptable Use, Transparency, Security and Legal Considerations, Ethical Considerations, Institutional Resources, and Processes for Policy Violation.

Despite some faculty distrust in technology, artificial intelligence tools can assist by automating tasks like grading and record-keeping (Tahiru, 2021), providing quick and personalized feedback for students, and also helping students check their own classwork for needed improvements and increasing learning (Brown et al., 2023). Faculty challenges may exist for the institution as the literature identifies curriculum changes, training needs, and perception of AI replacing humans, (Tahiru, 2021) along with a lack of faculty adoption and overall understanding of the technology.

Walter (2024) surmised the initial and ongoing professional development is a barrier for educators in the use AI tools, AI literacy, and curriculum integration. Swindell et al. (2024) recommended faculty will need to be diligent in addressing how and when AI should be used by students. Bates et al. (2020) "AI supports teachers and instructors but does not replace them. Perhaps the less welcome news for some is that many teachers and instructors will need to change the way they teach, or they will become redundant" (para. 42).

Ethical Challenges

The literature identifies numerous ethical issues with the use of AI (Shaw et al., 2023; Zawacki-Richter et al., 2019; Zhang & Aslan, 2021) such as algorithmic bias, data security, responsible use (Webber & Zheng, 2024) along with accountability, job displacement, human rights and legitimacy (Tahiru, 2021). For example, bias may exist because many of the data sets AI uses in the large language model were created in the West (i.e., Australia, Western Europe, and North America). In higher education, faculty fear being replaced with an AI chatbot and therefore, push back on adoption. In addition, according to some researchers, the availability of ChatGPT to students has led to a substantial drop in the capacity of original assessment prompts to ensure academic integrity, according to both students and educators (Smolansky et al., 2023).

Students also expressed concerns about ethical issues, particularly plagiarism, in many studies as they found difficulty in determining the originality of work generated by AI tools (Chan & Hu, 2023; Farhi et al., 2023; Ghotbi et al., 2022; Han et al., 2023; McDonald & Pan, 2020). Dirette (2024) and Cotton et al. (2023) pointed to an increased risk of plagiarism since the AI tools like ChatGPT, gather the information from multiple sources sometimes with correct citations and quotations and other times, with no attribution at all. This can be confusing for both the student and the educator to determine if plagiarism exists, despite tools like Turnitin. In addition, Dirrette noted the recent lawsuits that have been filed regarding copyright and accuracy of information. Ciampa et al. (2023) asserted users should recognize risks associated with using AI such as repeating false information such as GAI hallucinations (if it cannot find information, it often makes it up) and of course, plagiarism.

Tiffin University encouraged and trained faculty to AI in their classes; at the same time, they developed a *Design Statement* that students are to include that addresses what process the student used to create the assignment (Tiffin University Online Resources, 2023). There are now tools available to check for AI-assisted writing such as GPTZero, Sappling, and Turnitin Tool; however, there are possible false positives in tracking so instructors should be careful with punitive decisions based on the results.

Educators should provide clear guidelines on the proper use of ChatGPT to avoid plagiarism and ensure academic integrity (Atlas, 2023; Bates, 2020; Cotton et al., 2023; Sedlbauer, 2024). Students should be informed of how they can ethically use an AI tool with their assignments and what is considered to be plagiarism and the guidelines for use should be discussed beforehand. When using AI technologies, students should ensure that their use aligns with ethical guidelines (Chan & Hu, 2023) provided by the institution.

The literature provides recommendations for ethical and use guidelines for AI. For example, Swindell et al. (2024) developed an ethical framework for student use of AI for both consumptive and humanizing action. Webber and Zheng (2024) recommend *Ethical Guidelines on the Use of Artificial Intelligence and Data in Teaching and Learning for Educators* by the European Commission (2022) as a guide for educators new to using AI. Ciampa et al. (2023) suggested having students sign a statement regarding whether they have or have not used AI to generate their work. Students and researchers must properly attribute the use of ChatGPT and other AI tools in their work to maintain transparency and credibility (Atlas, 2023; Webber & Zheng, 2024).

Technological Challenges

Technology challenges include data ownership, security, and trust in AI systems (Tahiru, 2021; Webber & Zheng, 2024). Among the key challenges discussed regarding AI adoption in education were concerns around data ownership, the specific technologies employed, system security, and establishing trust in the AI systems - these technological and trust factors were predominant across much of the literature examining challenges (Tahiru, 2021). For example, data privacy is a predominant concern in education as AI could obtain personal student information and inadvertently share it (Niyozov et al., 2023; Zawacki-Richter et al., 2019). In one study, students were concerned with the accuracy of the work generated by AI tools (Chan & Hu, 2023). Ljujić et al. (2023) discovered that ChatGPT was unable to incorporate texts into comprehensive theoretical frameworks, find meaningful relations with relevant scientific studies, and reflect on any kind of experience. They determined that ChatGPT-generated essays were predominantly descriptive and devoid of problematizing or polemicizing orientations, which were conspicuously present in students' assignments. They also noted that ChatGPT-generated essays merely contained existing insights and reproductions of online materials and therefore, they seemed unoriginal and lacked the distinctive creative elements observed in students' assignments. ChatGPT offered general statements and simple presentations of information lacking demonstration of contextual understanding of implied ideas, while students' assignments were thoughtful and comprehensively relational (Ljujić et al., 2023).

In addition to security challenges, institutions must provide the necessary infrastructure on which artificial intelligence tools can be used for both faculty and students (Almughairi & Bhaskar, 2024. AI tools need to work seamlessly with existing Learning Management Systems and other educational technologies along with expert staff to support the integration, which can be technically challenging and expensive. This is necessary though to be able to use predictive analytics on student success and create customized learning experiences for students. In addition, as institutions adopt multiple AI tools, ensuring these tools can work together effectively becomes crucial to overall success. Moreover, the field of AI is evolving rapidly. Institutions will need staff to keep up with these changes and ensure they use the most appropriate tools. Finally, AI tools are not infallible; human oversight and critical thinking will still be required to implement and use the AI tools seamlessly.

CONCLUSION

This chapter illustrates the wide range of AI-driven solutions ready to empower scholars and educators alike. The impact of AI tools in higher education is already and expected to be even more profound, offering increased productivity and enriched collaboration while presenting ethical and technological considerations that must be addressed to ensure responsible adoption and utilization. However, higher education institutions and classrooms generally lack preparedness for the emergence of generative AI technologies (Barrett & Pack, 2023). Institutions that block the use of AI tools could handicap their students who may be expected to be familiar with its use in the workplace (Yan et al., 2023). AI is expected to automate routine teaching tasks, but the role of human teachers will remain crucial in the future, with a focus on the emotional and social aspects of learning (Bates et al., 2020).

Key Takeaways from Each Section

This chapter discusses how artificial intelligence can revolutionize research and writing in higher education, creating a new era of interactive learning, and assisting students and faculty with personalized solutions and enhanced research support.

AI Tools for Research

AI-driven tools streamline tedious tasks and enhance research and writing outputs, enabling researchers to achieve higher levels of productivity. Tools such as highly productive search engines specific to research study articles, literature reviews, and data analysis can save time and help researchers be more efficient. These sophisticated tools are revolutionizing information retrieval, helping with generating research ideas and questions, offering support in study design, and further increasing data analysis accuracy.

Improving Academic Writing and Editing with AI Tools

AI tools can assist both students and faculty with academic writing by offering brainstorming, outlines, suggestions for grammar, editing, paraphrasing, article summary, and style formatting (APA). In addition, these tools can support peer review bibliographic organization, and reference management.

Addressing Organizational, Ethical, and Technological Challenges

During the adoption and implementation of artificial intelligence tools, institutions may be impacted by leadership challenges, faculty resistance, ethical concerns and legal compliance, and increased need for technology infrastructure and support.

Future Research Recommendations

Because the landscape is so quickly changing in the use of AI in higher education, we suggest the following topics for future research on how artificial intelligence impacts higher education:

- In a digital age with AI-assisted writing becoming only more prevalent, how do we maintain academic integrity?
- What constitutes original work when AI is involved in the writing process and who clearly owns the intellectual property?
- Should academic publishers offer researchers a way to opt out of having their research added to databases accessed by artificial intelligence?
- Despite the potential of AI tools for academic use, not all students or institutions will have equal access to the tools. How can we ensure that AI does not exacerbate existing inequalities in higher education and create a further digital divide?

- AI tools often require access to large amounts of student data to realize potential benefits such as predicting student success. How can institutions balance the benefits of AI with the need to protect student privacy?
- Faculty perceptions regarding the use of AI should be explored on an ongoing, long-term basis to gather best practices for use in the college classroom as well as better understand the fear faculty have of being replaced.
- As of now, there is a gap in the literature regarding student perceptions of the use of AI, and should be further explored on the benefits and their perspective on its use and plagiarism.
- The application of AI for developing research methodology for advanced studies should be further examined for sound practice and feasibility.
- Because academic integrity plays such an important role in a doctoral student's journey, how much are they utilizing AI for writing dissertations and is AI usage (if any) limited by universities?

Call to Action for Educators and Institutions

Crompton and Burke (2023) encourage all educators to better understand artificial intelligence technologies while others specifically urge institutions and researchers to include the use of artificial intelligence in research workflows but warn a balance of human insight and critical thinking is required (Golan et al., 2023; Jarrah et al., 2023; Khalifa & Albadawy, 2024; Maphoto et al., 2024). AI tools such as intelligent tutoring systems, personalized learning environments, and machine learning algorithms have the potential to provide adaptive learning materials, metacognitive support, and enriched educational experiences for students in higher education (Zawacki-Richter et al., 2019; Zhang & Aslan, 2021). However, in a recent survey by Tyton Partners, faculty are still significantly behind their students in the use of AI for education purposes (Shaw et al., 2023). Demonstrations, training, support, and encouragement for effective use will be needed for faculty to more readily adopt AI tools. Webber and Zheng (2024) asserted the use of AI tools could help us become better educators and elevate teaching and learning but for that to happen, we need to know its limits and potential.

As AI technology advances, educators and students should stay informed about new developments and best practices for using these tools effectively (Atlas, 2023). In addition, to fully realize the potential of AI tools in higher education research and writing, it is essential to develop explicit and practical guidelines for educators and foster their AI expertise through professional development opportunities for both existing and new AI applications (Barrett & Pack, 2023; Tahiru, 2021; Zhang & Aslan, 2021).

Artificial intelligence is and will continue to be a large disruptor for educators (Sullivan et al., 2023). We leave you with this profound observation from Bozhurt and Bae (2024), who remind us of our history with educational technology and how we seem to keep making the same mistakes, thinking the latest technology will increase student learning or it's going to make everything so much more engaging. The new wears off and the classroom stays the same. Will this be the same for artificial intelligence? We believe it will be different as AI technologies will continue to improve.

As we look to the future, AI's role in academic research and writing is likely to expand and evolve in several ways:

- Personalized Learning: AI could enable truly personalized learning experiences, adapting to each student's writing style and research interests.
- AI as a Collaborator: Future AI systems might act more as collaborators than tools, engaging in dialogue with researchers to refine ideas and methodologies.
- Ethical AI: As AI becomes more prevalent in academia, we may see the development of AI systems specifically designed to uphold academic integrity and ethical research practices.
- Interdisciplinary Research: AI could facilitate more interdisciplinary research by identifying unexpected connections between different fields of study.
- Global Collaboration: Advanced AI translation and collaboration tools could break down language barriers, leading to more global research partnerships.
- AI in Peer Review: The peer review process could be transformed by AI, potentially making it faster and more objective, while still maintaining human oversight.
- Lifelong Learning: As AI takes over more routine tasks, the emphasis in higher education may shift towards developing skills in critical thinking, creativity, and ethical decision-making - skills that complement rather than compete with AI.

We believe the use of artificial intelligence in higher education will continue to increase exponentially as the technology evolves and improves over time. Educators are encouraged to embrace AI tools responsibly, leveraging their potential to enhance student learning outcomes while remaining aware of potential pitfalls. At the same time, educators should encourage student use to be prepared for the workplace.

As we navigate this rapidly evolving landscape, it's clear that AI will play an increasingly important role in shaping the future of academic research and writing. By embracing these technologies thoughtfully and responsibly, we have the opportunity to enhance the quality, efficiency, and accessibility of higher education, preparing students for a future where human creativity and AI capabilities work in harmony.

Let us benefit from the power of AI to inspire and educate future generations, thereby shaping a more innovative and equitable academic landscape.

ACKNOWLEDGMENT

This research received no specific grant from any funding agency in the public, commercial, or not-for-profit sectors.

REFERENCES

Adelakun, N. O. (2024, May 14). Exploring the impact of artificial intelligence on information retrieval systems. *Information Matters, 4*(5). https://informationmatters.org/2024/05/exploring-the-impact-of-artificial-intelligence-on-information-retrieval-systems/

Al-Mughairi, H., & Bhaskar, P. (2024). Exploring the factors affecting the adoption AI techniques in higher education: Insights from teachers' perspectives on ChatGPT. *Journal of Research in Innovative Teaching & Learning*. DOI: 10.1108/JRIT-09-2023-0129

Alshater, M. (2023). Exploring the role of artificial intelligence in enhancing academic performance: a case study of ChatGPT. *SSRN*, (January 2023). DOI: 10.2139/ssrn.4312358

Atlas, S. (2023). *ChatGPT for higher education and professional development: A guide to conversational AI*. University of Rhode Island. https://digitalcommons.uri.edu/cba_facpubs/548

Banihashem, S. K., Taghizadeh Kerman, N., Noroozi, O., Moon, J., & Drachsler, H. (2024). Feedback sources in essay writing: Peer-generated or AI-generated feedback? *International Journal of Educational Technology in Higher Education*, 21(1), 23. DOI: 10.1186/s41239-024-00455-4

Barrett, A., & Pack, A. (2023). Not quite eye to A.I.: Student and teacher perspectives on the use of generative artificial intelligence in the writing process. *International Journal of Educational Technology in Higher Education*, 20(1), 59. DOI: 10.1186/s41239-023-00427-0

Bates, T., Cobo, C., Mariño, O., & Wheeler, S. (2020). Can artificial intelligence transform higher education? *International Journal of Educational Technology in Higher Education*, 17(42), 42. Advance online publication. DOI: 10.1186/s41239-020-00218-x

Bozhurt, A., & Bae, H. (2024). May the force be with you JedAI: Balancing the light and dark sides of Generative AI in the educational Landscape. *Online Learning : the Official Journal of the Online Learning Consortium*, 28(2), 1–6. https://www.doi.org/10.24059/olj.v28i2.4563

Brandon, E., Eaton, L., Gavin, D., & Papini, A. (2023), December 12). Cross-Campus approaches to building a Generative AI policy. *EDUCAUSE Review*. https://er.educause.edu/articles/2023/12/cross-campus-approaches-to-building-a-generative-ai-policy

Brown, H., Crawford, S., Miffitt, K., Mendolia-Moore, T., Nevins, D., & Weiss, J. (2023, December 6). 7 things you should know about Generative AI. *EDUCAUSE Review*.https://er.educause.edu/articles/2023/12/7-things-you-should-know-about-generative-ai

Cassidy, C. (2023, January 17). Lecturer detects bot-use in one fifth of assessments as concerns mount over AI in exams. *The Guardian*. https://www.theguardian.com/australianews/2023/jan/17/lecturer-detects-bot-use-in-one-fifth-of-assessments-as-concerns-mount-over-ai-in-exams

Chan, C. K. Y., & Hu, W. (2023). Students' voices on generative AI: Perceptions, benefits, and challenges in higher education. *International Journal of Educational Technology in Higher Education*, 20(1), 43. DOI: 10.1186/s41239-023-00411-8

Ciampa, K., Wolfe, Z. M., & Bronstein, B. (2023). ChatGPT in education. Transforming digital literacy practices. *Journal of Adolescent & Adult Literacy*, 67(3), 186–195. DOI: 10.1002/jaal.1310

Cotton, D. R. E., Cotton, P. A., & Shipway, J. R. (2023). Chatting and cheating: Ensuring academic integrity in the era of ChatGPT. *Innovations in Education and Teaching International*, 61(2), 228–239. DOI: 10.1080/14703297.2023.2190148

Crompton, H., & Burke, D. (2023). Artificial intelligence in higher education: The state of the field. *International Journal of Educational Technology in Higher Education, 20*(22). https://doi,org/DOI: 10.1186/s41239-023-00392-8

Davison, R. M., Chughtai, H., Nielsen, P., Marabelli, M., Iannacci, F., van Offenbeek, M., Tarafdar, M., Trenz, M., Techatassanasoontorn, A. A., Díaz Andrade, A., & Panteli, N. (2024, January). The ethics of using generative AI for qualitative data analysis. *Information Systems Journal*, 34(5), 1433–1439. Advance online publication. DOI: 10.1111/isj.12504

Dirette, D. P. (2024). Artificial intelligence: Analysis and guidelines for scholarly writing. *The Open Journal of Occupational Therapy*, 12(2), 1–5. DOI: 10.15453/2168-6408.2331

Doerr, M., & Meeder, S. (2022). Big health data research and group harm: The scope of IRB review. *Ethics & Human Research*, 44(4), 34–38. DOI: 10.1002/eahr.500130 PMID: 35802789

Escalante, J., Pack, A., & Barrett, A. (2023). AI-generated feedback on writing: Insights into efficacy and ENL student preference. *International Journal of Educational Technology in Higher Education*, 20(1), 57. DOI: 10.1186/s41239-023-00425-2

European Commission, Directorate-General for Education, Youth, Sport and Culture. (2022). *Ethical guidelines on the use of artificial intelligence (AI) and data in teaching and learning for educators*, Publications Office of the European Union. https://data.europa.eu/doi/10.2766/153756

Fabiano, N., Gupta, A., Bhambra, N., Luu, B., Wong, S., Maaz, M., Fiedorowicz, J. G., Smith, A. L., & Solmi, M. (2024). How to optimize the systematic review process using AI tools. *JCPP Advances*, 4(2), e12234. DOI: 10.1002/jcv2.12234 PMID: 38827982

Farhi, F., Jeljeli, R., Aburezeq, I., Dweikat, F. F., Al-Shami, S. A., & Slamene, R. (2023). Analyzing the students' views, concerns, and perceived ethics about chat GPT usage. *Computers and Education.Artificial Intelligence*, 5, 100180. DOI: 10.1016/j.caeai.2023.100180

Ferretti, A., Ienca, M., Hurst, S., & Vayena, E. (2020). Big data, biomedical research, and ethics review: New challenges for IRBs. *Ethics & Human Research*, 42(5), 17–28. DOI: 10.1002/eahr.500065 PMID: 32937036

Friesen, P., Douglas-Jones, R., Marks, M., Pierce, R., Fletcher, K., Mishra, A., Lorimer, J., Véliz, C., Hallowell, N., Graham, M., Chan, M. S., Davies, H., & Sallamuddin, T. (2021). Governing AI-Driven health research: Are IRBs up to the task? *Ethics & Human Research*, 43(2), 35–42. DOI: 10.1002/eahr.500085 PMID: 33683015

Ghotbi, N., Ho, M. T., & Mantello, P. (2022). Attitude of college students towards ethical issues of artificial intelligence in an international university in Japan. *AI & Society*, 37(1), 283–290. DOI: 10.1007/s00146-021-01168-2

Golan, R., Reddy, R., Muthigi, A., & Ramasamy, R. (2023). Artificial intelligence in academic writing: A paradigm-shifting technological advance. *Nature Reviews. Urology*, 20(6), 327–328. DOI: 10.1038/s41585-023-00746-x PMID: 36829078

Han, B., Nawaz, S., Buchanan, G., & McKay, D. (2023). Ethical and pedagogical impacts of AI in education. In N. Wang, N., G. Rebolledo-Mendez, N. Matsuda, O. C. Santos, & Dimitrova, V. (Eds.) *Artificial Intelligence in Education*. AIED 2023. *Lecture Notes in Computer Science, 13916*. Springer. DOI: 10.1007/978-3-031-36272-9_54

Hartel, R. (2022). ReX Submission Platform. *Journal of Food Science*, 87(8), 3333–3334. DOI: 10.1111/1750-3841.15279 PMID: 35962979

Jarrah, A. M., Wardat, Y., & Fidalgo, P. (2023). Using ChatGPT in academic writing is (not) a form of plagiarism: What does the literature say? *Online Journal of Communication and Media Technologies*, 13(4), e202346. DOI: 10.30935/ojcmt/13572

Kassorla, M. (2023, December 14). Teaching with GAI in mind. *EDUCAUSE Review*. https://er.educause.edu/articles/2023/12/teaching-with-gai-in-mind

Khalifa, M., & Albadawy, M. (2024). Using artificial intelligence in academic writing and research: An essential productivity tool. *Computer Methods and Programs in Biomedicine Update*, 5, 100145. Advance online publication. DOI: 10.1016/j.cmpbup.2024.100145

Lixandru, I. D. (2024). The use of artificial intelligence for qualitative data analysis: ChatGPT. *Informatică Economică, 28*(1/2024), 57–67. DOI: 10.24818/issn14531305/28.1.2024.05

Ljujić, B., Miljković, J., & Grozdić, V. (2023). ChatGPT and academic writing in higher education. In Radulović, M., & Trajković, M. (Eds.), *Towards a more equitable education: From research to change: Book of proceedings, 29th International Scientific Conference "Educational Research and School Practice"* (pp. 104–109). Institute for Educational Research., https://www.ipisr.org.rs/images/pdf/towards-a-more-equitable-education.pdf

Maphoto, K. B., Sevnarayan, K., Mohale, N. E., Suliman, Z., Ntsopi, T. J., & Mokoena, D. (2024). Advancing students' academic excellence in distance education: Exploring the potential of Generative AI integration to improve academic writing skills. *Open Praxis, 2–2*, 142–159. DOI: 10.55982/openpraxis.16.2.649

McDonald, N., & Pan, S. (2020). Intersectional AI: A study of how information science students think about ethics and their Impact. *PACM on Human-Computer Interaction, 4*, (Issue CSCW2). *Proceedings of the ACM on Human-Computer Interaction*, 147(CSCW2), 1–19. Advance online publication. DOI: 10.1145/3415218

Niyozov, N., Bijanov, A., Ganiyev, S., & Kurbonova, R. (2023). The pedagogical principles and effectiveness of utilizing ChatGPT for language learning. *E3S Web of Conferences, 461*, 01093. DOI: 10.1051/e3sconf/202346101093

Picciano, A. G. (2024). Graduate teacher education students use and evaluate ChatGPT as an essay-writing tool. *Online Learning : the Official Journal of the Online Learning Consortium*, 28(2). Advance online publication. DOI: 10.24059/olj.v28i2.4373

Roose, K. (2023, March 30). How should I use A.I. chatbots like ChatGPT? *The New York Times*.https://www.nytimes.com/2023/03/30/technology/ai-chatbot-chatgpt-uses-work-life.html

Sedlbauer, J., Cin, J., Slavík, M., Hartlová, A., & Sedlbauer, J. (2024). Students' reflections on their experience with ChatGPT. *Journal of Computer Assisted Learning*, 40(4), 1–9. DOI: 10.1111/jcal.12967

Shaw, C., Yuan, L., Brennan, D., Martin, S., Janson, N., Fox, K., & Bryant, G. (2023, October 23). Tyton Partners' *Generative AI in higher education: Fall update 2023.* https://www.tytonpartners.com/time-for-class-2023/GenAI-Update

Silverman, J. A., Ali, S. A., Rybak, A., van Goudoever, J. B., & Leleiko, N. S. (2023). Generative AI: Potential and pitfalls in academic publishing. *JPGN Reports*, 4(4), e387. DOI: 10.1097/PG9.0000000000000387 PMID: 38034432

Smolansky, A., Cram, A., Raduescu, C., Zeivots, S., Huber, E., & Kizilcec, R. F. (2023). Educator and student perspectives on the impact of Generative AI on assessments in higher education. *Proceedings of the Tenth ACM Conference on Learning @ Scale*, 378–382. DOI: 10.1145/3573051.3596191

Sullivan, M., Kelly, A., & McLaughlan, P. (2023). ChatGPT in higher education: Considerations for academic integrity and student learning. *Journal of Applied Learning and Teaching*, 6(1). Advance online publication. DOI: 10.37074/jalt.2023.6.1.17

Sutton, K. S., & DeSantis, J. (2017). Beyond change blindness: Embracing the technology revolution in higher education. *Innovations in Education and Teaching International*, 54(3), 223–228. DOI: 10.1080/14703297.2016.1174592

Swindell, A., Greeley, L., Farag, A., & Verdone, B. (2024). Against Artificial Education: Towards an ethical framework for Generative Artificial Intelligence (GAI) use in education. *Online Learning : the Official Journal of the Online Learning Consortium*, 28(2). Advance online publication. DOI: 10.24059/olj.v28i2.4438

Tahiru, F. (2021). AI in education: A systematic literature review. *Journal of Cases on Information Technology*, 23(1), 1–20. DOI: 10.4018/JCIT.2021010101

Tarisayi, K. S. (2024). Strategic leadership for responsible artificial intelligence adoption in higher education. *CTE Workshop Proceedings, 11*, 4-14. DOI: 10.55056/cte.616

Tiffin University Online Resources. (2023). *Design statements.* Tiffin University website. https://tuonlineresources.com/design-statement

Walter, Y. (2024). Embracing the future of artificial intelligence in the classroom: The relevance of AI literacy, prompt engineering, and critical thinking in modern education. *International Journal of Educational Technology in Higher Education*, 21(15), 15. Advance online publication. DOI: 10.1186/s41239-024-00448-3

Wang, T., Lund, B. D., Marengo, A., Pagano, A., Mannuru, N. R., Teel, Z. A., & Pange, J. (2023). Exploring the potential impact of artificial intelligence (AI) on international students in higher education: Generative AI, chatbots, analytics, and international student success. *Applied Sciences (Basel, Switzerland)*, 13(11), 6716. DOI: 10.3390/app13116716

Webber, K. L., & Zheng, H. Y. (2024). Artificial intelligence and advanced data analytics. Implications for higher education. *New Directions for Higher Education*, 2024(207), 1–9. DOI: 10.1002/he.20508

Wise, B., Emerson, L., Van Luyn, A., Dyson, B., Bjork, C., & Thomas, S. E. (2024). A scholarly dialogue: Writing scholarship, authorship, academic integrity and the challenges of AI. *Higher Education Research & Development*, 43(3), 578–590. DOI: 10.1080/07294360.2023.2280195

Yan, L., Sha, L., Zhao, L., Li, Y., Martinez-Maldonado, R., Chen, G., Li, X., Jin, Y., & Gašević, D. (2024). Practical and ethical challenges of large language models in education: A systematic scoping review. *British Journal of Educational Technology*, 55(1), 90–112. DOI: 10.1111/bjet.13370

Yin, W. J. (2024, January 24). Will our educational system keep pace with AI? A student's perspective on AI and learning. *EDUCAUSE Review*.https://er.educause.edu/articles/2024/1/will-our-educational-system-keep-pace-with-ai-a-students-perspective-on-ai-and-learning

Zawacki-Richter, O., Marín, V. I., Bond, M., & Gouverneur, F. (2019). Systematic review of research on artificial intelligence applications in higher education – where are the educators? *International Journal of Educational Technology in Higher Education*, 16(39), 39. Advance online publication. DOI: 10.1186/s41239-019-0171-0

Zhang, K., & Aslan, A. B. (2021). AI technologies for education: Recent research & future directions. *Computers and Education: Artificial Intelligence*, 2, 100025. DOI: 10.1016/j.caeai.2021.100025

Chapter 6
Are Critical Thinking and Problem-Solving Skills Enough to Help Prepare Students to Meet the Modern Workforce Demands With Artificial Intelligence?

James Andrew Martinez
https://orcid.org/0009-0000-5853-7300
Loma Linda University, USA

ABSTRACT

This chapter examines the transformative impact of Artificial Intelligence (AI) on education and workforce preparation. It delves into how AI technologies are redefining teaching methods, learning experiences, and the skillsets necessary in today's job market. The chapter explores AI's potential to personalize learning, boost student engagement, and develop critical thinking and problem-solving skills. It also addresses the challenges and opportunities of integrating AI into education, including the need for comprehensive educator training, AI literacy programs, and adaptive regulatory frameworks. Ethical considerations related to AI use in educational settings are discussed. Emphasizing the importance of balancing technological advancement with core educational values, the chapter advocates for approaches that nurture essential workforce skills while leveraging AI's capabilities. It concludes by underscoring the need for continued research and adaptation to ensure

DOI: 10.4018/979-8-3373-0502-8.ch006

that AI integration prepares students for an AI-driven future while preserving the fundamental objectives of education.

INTRODUCTION

Artificial Intelligence (AI) simulates human intelligence, encompassing problem-solving, learning, perception, understanding natural language, and decision-making (Russell & Norvig, 2010). In the realm of education, AI's potential to revolutionize teaching and learning methodologies has captured the imagination of educators, policymakers, and technologists alike. Recent advancements in AI and its evolving applications have expanded the potential to support Career and Technical Education (CTE) initiatives, industries, and modern workforce demands. This signifies a transformative moment in education, offering an opportunity to harness technology for teaching and learning (Jackson, 2024; Luckin et al., 2016; Russell & Norvig, 2010). As AI becomes more prevalent, it enhances students' abilities to gain foundational knowledge, practical applications, and innovative solutions to meet current job market needs (Lee & Kwon, 2024), including adapting to changes and improving traditional problem-solving methods (Darling-Hammond, Hyler, & Gardner, 2017). This chapter delves into the multifaceted impact of AI on education, exploring its potential to reshape learning experiences, enhance pedagogical approaches, and prepare students for an increasingly AI-driven workforce.

The integration of AI into educational systems signifies a pivotal shift, providing solutions to address diverse learner needs, enhance engagement, and develop the critical skills necessary for success in today's world. As Lee and Kwon (2024) argue, AI has the potential to not only facilitate the acquisition of foundational knowledge but also to encourage practical applications and drive innovative problem-solving approaches that meet current job market demands (Highland, 2023). This technological revolution in education arrives at a defining moment, as the global workforce undergoes rapid transformation, with automation and AI reshaping industries and job roles at an unprecedented pace (Filippucci et al., 2024; UNESCO, 2023). Consequently, the education sector faces the imperative to adapt and evolve, ensuring that students are equipped with the skills and knowledge required to thrive in this new landscape. The integration of AI across various subjects offers an opportunity to enrich academic instruction while fostering essential life skills such as critical thinking, adaptability, and self-directed learning (Highland, 2023; Kroeper, 2022).

However, the introduction of AI in education is not without its challenges. Concerns range from ethical considerations and data privacy issues to the potential exacerbation of existing educational inequalities. Moreover, the successful implementation of AI in educational settings requires a significant shift in pedagogical approaches, necessitating ongoing professional development for educators (Luckin, 2018; Luckin et al., 2022). By addressing modern workforce challenges, students must embrace innovation, a growth mindset, self-directed learning, and adaptability to rapidly changing industries (Kroeper, 2022; Highland, 2023). Technology benefits education and industry by enhancing efficiency, automating processes, and providing access to vast information (Filippucci, Gal, Jona-Lasinio, Leandro, & Nicoletti, 2024). Removing barriers to information and tools enhances students' creativity and problem-solving skills, empowering them to collaborate effectively and analyze, reason, and evaluate evidence comprehensively (Xu, Wang, & Wang, 2023).

This chapter aims to provide a comprehensive analysis of the role of AI in transforming educational landscapes and its implications for workforce development. We will explore key areas where AI is making significant inroads in education, including the personalization of learning experiences to address diverse learning styles and needs, the enhancement of student engagement through adaptive learning platforms and interactive technologies, the integration of AI across curricula to foster critical thinking, problem-solving, and adaptability, the challenges and opportunities presented by AI in distance learning and online education, and the necessity for ongoing professional development to enable educators to effectively leverage AI in their teaching practices. Furthermore, we will examine how these developments are reshaping the skills required for the modern workforce, considering the broader implications for educational policy, economic development, and social equity. We are at a pivotal moment in education with the rapid advancement of AI technologies. This shift has the potential to dramatically transform how we teach and learn; it is essential to critically examine both the potential benefits and the challenges necessary for its ethical and effective implementation. By doing so, we can harness the power of AI to create more effective, inclusive, and future-ready educational systems that prepare learners for success in an increasingly complex and technologically advanced world.

As we review literature and insights, it is important to recognize that integrating AI in education is not merely a technological upgrade but a fundamental reimagining of how we approach teaching and learning. The journey ahead is complex and multifaceted, requiring collaboration across disciplines and workforce sectors. However, with thoughtful implementation and continuous evaluation, AI has the potential to usher in a new era of educational excellence and workforce readiness, empowering learners to thrive in the dynamic landscape of the 21st century and beyond.

BACKGROUND ON ARTIFICIAL INTELLIGENCE IN EDUCATION

Artificial Intelligence (AI) has its roots in the mid-20th century, but its application in education has gained significant momentum in recent years (Table 1). The concept of using machines to enhance learning dates back to the 1920s when Sidney Pressey invented the first teaching machine (Benjamin, 1988). However, it wasn't until the 1950s and 1960s that the term "Artificial Intelligence" was coined, and the field began to take shape. Early AI applications in education were primarily focused on computer-aided instruction (CAI) and intelligent tutoring systems (ITS) (Woolf, 2010). The 1980s and 1990s saw the development of more sophisticated ITS, capable of modeling student knowledge and providing personalized instruction. However, these systems were limited by the computational power and data availability of the time (VanLehn, 2011). The 21st century brought about a renaissance in AI, driven by advancements in machine learning, increased computational power, and the availability of big data. This new wave of AI technologies has dramatically expanded the possibilities for AI in education, leading to the current landscape of adaptive learning platforms, personalized recommendation systems, and AI-powered educational tools (Holmes et al., 2019).

Table 1. Milestones in the evolution of AI in education

Year	*Milestone*
1920s	• Sidney Pressey invents the first teaching machine
1950s	• The term "Artificial Intelligence" is coined
1960s	• Early development of Computer-Aided Instruction (CAI) begins
1980s-1990s	• More sophisticated Intelligent Tutoring Systems (ITS) are developed
	• These systems can model student knowledge and provide personalized instruction
	• Limited by computational power and data availability of the time
2000s-2010s	• AI renaissance in education begins
	• Advancements in machine learning
	• Increased computational power
	• Availability of big data
2010	• Publication of Woolf's book on building intelligent interactive tutors
2011	• VanLehn's study on the effectiveness of different tutoring systems is published
2017	• Introduction of the Transformer architecture by Google researchers,
	• laying the groundwork for GPT models

continued on following page

Table 1. Continued

Year	Milestone
2018	• OpenAI releases GPT-1, the first in the series of GPT models
2019	• Holmes et al. publish work on AI promises and implications for teaching and learning
	• OpenAI releases GPT-2, showing significant improvements in language generation
2020	• OpenAI releases GPT-3, marking a major leap in generative AI capabilities
	• Increased interest in using generative AI for educational purposes
2022	• Release of ChatGPT, based on GPT-3.5,
	• sparking widespread public interest and discussions about AI in education
2023-Present	• Rapid adoption and integration of generative AI tools in educational settings
	• Development of adaptive learning platforms incorporating generative AI
	• Creation of personalized recommendation systems powered by advanced language models
	• Emergence of various AI-powered educational tools leveraging generative capabilities

Several AI technologies are particularly relevant to the field of education. Machine learning (ML) stands at the forefront of this revolution, empowering educators with data-driven insights. By analyzing vast datasets, ML algorithms can create personalized learning paths, predict student performance, and identify at-risk students early. AI-driven platforms such as DreamBox and Khan Academy use machine learning algorithms to adapt content and difficulty levels based on individual student performance. This personalized approach helps address each student's unique learning pace and needs, making education more effective (Al-khresheh, 2024).

Natural Language Processing (NLP) enables computers to understand, interpret, and generate human language. In education, NLP enhances student engagement and assessment through a variety of applications. Tools like Grammarly and Turnitin employ natural language processing to provide real-time writing assistance and plagiarism detection. Additionally, AI-powered chatbots, such as those used by Carnegie Mellon University, offer students immediate support for academic queries and administrative help, improving accessibility and engagement. Chatbots provide instant assistance, automated essay grading systems offer rapid feedback, and sophisticated language learning tools adapt to individual needs. These NLP-powered tools create a more interactive and responsive learning environment, supporting students around the clock and freeing educators to focus on higher-order teaching tasks (Celik et al., 2022).

Computer Vision allows computers to interpret and understand visual information from the world. In education, it enables secure online proctoring through facial recognition and creates immersive learning experiences through augmented reality

(AR) and virtual reality (VR). Platforms like ClassVR and Google Expeditions use computer vision and augmented reality (AR) to create immersive learning experiences. For example, ClassVR's AR capabilities allow students to explore historical sites or complex scientific concepts in 3D, while Google Expeditions offers virtual field trips to locations around the world, enhancing experiential learning. These technologies not only enhance the integrity of online assessments but also provide dynamic, interactive learning environments that can simulate complex real-world scenarios, bridging the gap between theory and practice (Ng et al., 2023).

Deep Learning, a subset of machine learning, uses neural networks with many layers to analyze complex patterns. Deep Learning can process and interpret complex data such as images and audio. It enables the creation of sophisticated adaptive learning systems that can understand and respond to nuanced student inputs. AI applications like Google's AutoML and IBM Watson use deep learning to analyze and generate educational content. For instance, AutoML can help create customized quizzes and learning materials, while IBM Watson's Speech to Text and Text to Speech technologies facilitate language learning by converting spoken language into text and vice versa. This technology is paving the way for more personalized and effective learning experiences, capable of adjusting in real time to a student's progress and learning style (Wang et al., 2023).

Expert systems, designed to simulate human expertise, are bringing specialized knowledge directly to students through intelligent tutoring systems. Intelligent tutoring systems such as Pearson's MyLab and Carnegie Learning's MATHia use expert systems to offer personalized tutoring and support. These systems simulate human expertise to provide tailored feedback and guidance, helping students master complex subjects through adaptive learning technologies. These AI-powered tutors offer on-demand access to expert-level guidance, complementing traditional teaching methods and enabling more flexible, self-paced learning. They can provide detailed explanations, answer questions, and offer practice exercises tailored to each student's level of understanding (Luckin et al., 2022).

Large Language Models (LLMs), a subset of AI, have significantly advanced Natural Language Processing (NLP) and become more accessible. OpenAI's ChatGPT, for example, is a Machine Learning model designed to understand and analyze natural language data (OpenAI, n.d.). LLMs represent a major NLP breakthrough with the potential to transform industries by generating human-like text and engaging in conversational interactions (Heaven, 2020). In education, AI-powered NLP shows promise in developing adaptive learning platforms, real-time feedback mechanisms, active engagement strategies, and personalized learning experiences (Hwang, Sung, Chang & Huang, 2020; Gupta, 2023). These innovations address diverse learning styles and modalities, ensuring a rich and inclusive educational approach (Dumont & Ready, 2023). By leveraging AI for personalized learning, educators can tailor instruction to individual needs, promoting equity and accessibility and empowering all students to thrive (McNulty, 2024).

Integrating AI into pedagogical approaches and curricula enhances student-centered and inquiry-based learning (Tuomi, 2018). AI tools enable educators to create personalized learning experiences that connect theoretical concepts with real-world applications (Shemshack, 2020; Yue, Jong, & Ng, 2024). This approach supports CTE initiatives and encourages student engagement and practical exploration of topics, preparing them for future careers (Gupta, 2023; Meyer et al., 2024). A dynamic learning environment empowers students to take active, self-directed roles in their academic and professional journeys, developing the skills, confidence, and motivation to pursue their goals (Lee & Kwon, 2024; Meyer et al., 2024). The shift toward AI and student-centered learning supports critical thinking, problem-solving, and lifelong learning, preparing students for diverse academic and professional contexts (Lee & Kwon, 2024).

Educators are at the forefront of innovation, leveraging AI and emerging technologies to enhance teaching and student engagement. Ongoing support and collaboration with stakeholders and experts are essential when integrating new technologies like AI into classrooms (Kim, 2023). Working together, educators, administrators, developers, and specialists can ensure AI technologies' relevance and alignment with educational standards and learning objectives (Celik, Dindar, Muukkonen, & Jarvela, 2022). By utilizing AI in distance learning platforms, educators can create dynamic, interactive, and effective learning environments catering to diverse student needs (Dimitriadou & Lantis, 2023). Integrating new technologies into existing curricula can be costly and challenging due to the lack of ready-made resources and instructional materials aligned with standards and objectives. Teachers and administrators may also lack the infrastructure, knowledge, and skills to integrate AI effectively (Ng et al., 2023; Yue, Jong, & Ng, 2024). Continuous learning and support are vital to help educators adapt to the evolving educational landscape and align their teaching strategies (Luckin, 2018; Luckin, Cukutoca, Kent, & Boulay, 2022).

THE ROLE OF TEACHER EDUCATION PROGRAMS

As the educational landscape increasingly incorporates AI technologies, teacher education programs must evolve to prepare future educators for this new reality. These programs should prioritize integrating AI literacy as a fundamental component, ensuring that aspiring teachers understand the capabilities, limitations, and potential applications of AI in education (UNESCO, 2023). Simultaneously, there needs to be a strong emphasis on developing adaptable educators who can navigate and embrace ongoing technological changes, fostering a mindset of continuous learning and innovation (Otto et al., 2023). Ethical considerations surrounding AI in education are paramount, and teacher preparation programs must equip future educators with the knowledge and skills to address these challenges responsibly. This includes understanding issues such as data privacy, algorithmic bias, and the appropriate balance between AI and human instruction (Haleem et al., 2022). Furthermore, practical experience with AI educational tools should be a core part of teacher training, allowing future educators to gain hands-on familiarity with these technologies and develop strategies for their effective integration in the classroom (Nguyen, 2021).

Professional development for educators in the AI era is crucial for the successful integration of AI technologies in education. By focusing on these areas, teacher education programs can produce educators who are not only technologically literate but also adaptable, ethically conscious, and practically skilled in leveraging AI to enhance learning outcomes (Levy, 2020). This requires a multifaceted approach that goes beyond mere technical training to include pedagogical strategies, ethical considerations, and critical evaluation skills. By investing in comprehensive and ongoing professional development, we can empower educators to harness the potential of AI to enhance teaching and learning while navigating the challenges it presents. As AI continues to evolve, so too must our approaches to educator professional development, ensuring that teachers remain at the forefront of educational innovation (Dimitriadou & Lantis, 2023).

The adoption of AI in education has been accelerated by several factors, including the increasing digitization of education, the need for personalized learning experiences, and the demand for skills relevant to an AI-driven economy (Bhutoria, 2022). Distance learning platforms, powered by AI and advanced technologies, offer transformative opportunities in education. During the COVID-19 pandemic, distance learning accelerated the adoption of digital technologies (UNESCO, 2023). This period led to significant shifts in educational practices, including the widespread adoption of online learning platforms and digital tools for remote instruction (Otto et al., 2023; Haleem et al., 2022). Educators enhanced their skills in online teaching, instructional design, technology integration, and student engagement. AI-powered tools and innovative teaching solutions like gamification, simulations, virtual reality (VR), and augmented reality (AR) can significantly enhance student engagement and understanding of complex concepts (ACTE, 2022; Bhutoria, 2022). During the pandemic, many children used platforms like Minecraft and Roblox for self-directed learning and entertainment (Levy, 2020). These platforms, which incorporate AI technologies, effectively engage students in active learning experiences, promoting collaboration, problem-solving skills, and deeper understanding across subjects (Nguyen, 2021). By integrating similar technologies into teaching practices, educators can empower students to develop analytical, creative, and resilient mindsets for success in a continuously evolving era (Nguyen, 2021).

However, the integration of AI in education raises important questions and challenges. These include concerns about data privacy and security (Grosso et al., 2024), the potential for bias in AI systems (Dumont & Ready, 2023), the digital divide and issues of equity in access to AI-enhanced education (Tuomi, 2018), and the need for AI literacy among educators and students (Lee & Kwon, 2024). As we move forward, it's crucial to approach the implementation of AI in education with a critical and ethical mindset, ensuring that these powerful technologies are used to enhance and support human learning and teaching, rather than replace them. The following sections will delve deeper into specific applications of AI in education and their implications for learners, educators, and the broader society.

AI TECHNOLOGIES TRANSFORMING EDUCATIONAL LANDSCAPES

The integration of Artificial Intelligence (AI) is revolutionizing both education and the modern workforce in significant ways. AI supports social learning and self-efficacy within social cognitive theory by creating virtual peer models, offering personalized feedback, providing safe environments for social skills training, and assisting in goal setting. These tools help students observe successful behaviors, track their progress, and build confidence. In constructivist learning, AI contributes by creating interactive environments through adaptive virtual worlds, intelligent simulations, dynamic storytelling, and personalized learning paths. These features support students in actively constructing knowledge through experimentation, decision-making, and reflection, aligning with constructivist principles. Additionally, AI enhances collaborative learning by forming optimal groups, supporting real-time collaboration, analyzing individual contributions, enabling cross-cultural interactions, managing virtual spaces, and enhancing peer feedback. These applications enrich social cognitive and constructivist approaches, complementing traditional teaching methods with unique opportunities for observation, interaction, and collaborative knowledge construction.

Educators can leverage AI tools to design engaging instruction, develop practical skills, and bridge the gap between classroom learning and real-world experiences (Jackson, 2024). However, integrating AI into education also requires careful consideration of ethical issues. Educators must address concerns related to academic plagiarism, privacy violations, and compliance with regulations such as FERPA, COPPA, and HIPAA (Grosso et al., 2024). When incorporating AI and career and technical education (CTE) initiatives, it is vital to ensure that AI tools are suitable, aligned with academic standards, culturally relevant, accessible, engaging, and instructional effective, thus empowering all students to succeed.

The integration of AI in education has profound implications for teaching, learning, and workforce preparation. AI technologies are transforming industries and job markets, necessitating educational evolution to prepare students for this new reality (Filippucci et al., 2024; UNESCO, 2023). Routine tasks are increasingly automated, elevating the value of jobs requiring complex problem-solving, creativity, and emotional intelligence (Holmes et al., 2019; Russell & Norvig, 2021). To thrive in an AI-driven workforce, education must emphasize skills that complement AI technologies, such as adaptability, lifelong learning, critical thinking, creativity, digital and AI literacy, emotional intelligence, interdisciplinary thinking, and ethical reasoning (Jackson, 2024; Meyer et al., 2024). These skills will enable students to collaborate effectively with AI systems and navigate the complexities of an AI-enhanced workplace (Wang et al., 2023; Ng et al., 2023).

Educators must adapt to the evolving demands of the modern workforce to effectively prepare students for success in an AI-driven and technology-focused job market. With the rise of remote and hybrid work models, new skills and mindsets are required. Educators should integrate training on digital communication, virtual collaboration tools, and self-management skills to prepare students for these work environments (Haleem et al., 2022). Additionally, digital literacy and a foundational understanding of AI are crucial for equipping students to work effectively with AI tools and systems, thereby enhancing their job market relevance (Filippucci et al., 2024). As the workforce becomes more globalized, developing global and cross-cultural competence is also essential. Educators should incorporate global perspectives and cross-cultural skills into their curricula to prepare students for international and multicultural work settings (Dumont & Ready, 2023).

Strategies for aligning education with workforce needs include integrating AI across curricula (Touretzky et al., 2019), emphasizing project-based learning (Nguyen, 2021), implementing personalized learning paths (Hwang et al., 2020; Shemshack & Spector, 2020), fostering industry partnerships (ACTE, 2022), focusing on soft skills development (Kroeper, 2022), encouraging an entrepreneurial mindset, and establishing continuous assessment and skill credentialing systems. These approaches ensure students acquire the diverse skill set required for success in an AI-driven economy (Al-khresheh, 2024; Pawar, 2023). Another key concern is the emphasis on adaptability and the commitment to lifelong learning. As technology evolves rapidly, career paths are becoming less linear and more dynamic. Educators must foster adaptability and encourage a commitment to continuous learning, helping students update their skills and knowledge regularly (Lee & Kwon, 2024; Meyer et al., 2024).

However, challenges such as keeping pace with rapid technological changes (Holmes et al., 2019), ensuring educational equity (Dumont & Ready, 2023; McNulty, 2024), balancing specialization with versatility (Highland, 2023), preparing teachers for new educational landscapes (Luckin et al., 2022; Kim, 2023), and addressing ethical implications (ISTE, 2024; Grosso et al., 2024) must be addressed. By tackling these challenges and implementing innovative strategies, education systems can effectively prepare students for the evolving demands of an AI-enhanced workforce, cultivating adaptable, skilled, and ethically conscious professionals ready for the complexities of the future job market (Yue et al., 2024; Celik et al., 2022).

AI's potential to personalize learning experiences revolutionizes education by enabling tailored learning paths based on students' strengths, weaknesses, and preferences (Lee & Kwon, 2024). AI enhances student engagement through adaptive learning platforms that adjust content difficulty and style according to performance, providing real-time feedback, and supporting 24/7 assistance via AI-driven chatbots (Dimitriadou & Lantis, 2023). Integrating AI across curricula fosters critical thinking, problem-solving, and adaptability skills that are crucial for the modern workforce (Highland, 2023). AI also presents challenges in distance learning, such as ensuring equitable access and maintaining motivation, but offers opportunities through virtual tutors and adaptive materials (UNESCO, 2023; Otto et al., 2023).

Professional development for educators is crucial as AI continues to reshape education. Teachers need to master the integration of AI tools into their teaching practices, accurately interpret AI-generated data, and effectively combine AI with traditional instructional methods. Additionally, educators must focus on helping students develop skills that complement AI advancements, including adaptability, digital literacy, critical thinking, creativity, emotional intelligence, and the ability to navigate ongoing technological changes (Jackson, 2024; Meyer et al., 2024).

The transformative impact of AI extends beyond education, profoundly affecting industries such as marketing, legal services, and healthcare. For instance, AI-driven technologies like DALL-E, an image generation tool, and advanced data analytics platforms are revolutionizing content creation and customer engagement. DALL-E can generate highly creative and customized visuals based on textual descriptions, streamlining the design process and enabling marketers to produce unique content rapidly. Similarly, AI-driven analytics tools help marketers understand consumer behavior through data insights, allowing for more targeted and effective advertising strategies. This shift has transformed traditional marketing roles, requiring professionals to develop skills in AI tool management, data analysis, and digital strategy (Haleem et al., 2022).

In the legal industry, AI is automating tasks such as document review and legal research. Tools like ROSS Intelligence and LegalZoom leverage natural language processing to assist with case law research and legal document preparation, significantly reducing the time and effort required for these tasks. These advancements are changing the nature of legal work, necessitating that legal professionals acquire new skills in managing and interpreting AI outputs, as well as integrating AI tools into their practice (Filippucci et al., 2024).

The healthcare sector is another example, experiencing profound changes due to AI. Technologies such as IBM Watson Health and AI-powered diagnostic tools are enhancing patient care through more accurate diagnostics and personalized treatment plans. AI algorithms can analyze medical imaging to detect conditions like cancer at earlier stages, while predictive analytics can help manage patient care more effectively. Healthcare professionals now need to be adept at using these advanced tools and interpreting their results, as well as staying current with ongoing technological advancements (Ng et al., 2023).

These industry shifts highlight the critical need for students to develop adaptability and technological proficiency to meet the changing demands of the modern workforce. Emphasizing skills in technology adaptation and continuous learning is crucial. As AI continues to advance, both educators and professionals must cultivate a blend of technical proficiency, critical thinking, and adaptability to thrive in an environment increasingly shaped by AI innovations.

The integration of AI necessitates a reimagining of pedagogical approaches, focusing on skills that complement AI technologies and addressing educational inequalities. AI has the potential to democratize access to quality learning, but this must be balanced with policies ensuring equitable access. Lifelong learning and adaptability are essential, supported by AI's ability to facilitate micro-learning and personalized career development (Gupta, 2023; Hwang et al., 2020).

Ongoing collaboration among educators, industry leaders, and policymakers is essential to harness AI's potential while mitigating risks. This ensures that education systems prepare students effectively for the future workforce (Association for Career and Technical Education, 2022; Celik et al., 2022). As AI continues to advance, the need for a well-rounded skill set, combining technical proficiency with critical thinking and adaptability, will only grow, underscoring the importance of these educational transformations.

CONCLUSION

The integration of Artificial Intelligence (AI) into education and workforce development marks a transformative shift with significant implications. AI, while a powerful tool, should be seen as an enhancement rather than a replacement for human teaching and learning. The evolving role of AI is reshaping educational foundations, fostering creativity, and advancing problem-solving skills (Xu et al.,

2023). This evolution emphasizes the necessity to leverage AI to empower educators, engage students, and prepare learners for a future where human skills and AI capabilities complement each other.

This chapter has delved into how AI technologies are transforming educational landscapes and influencing the skills needed for the modern workforce. The rapid changes in the job market underscore the importance of continuous skill development and adaptability. Educational institutions face a dual responsibility: nurturing adaptability and instilling a passion for lifelong learning (Lee & Kwon, 2024; Meyer et al., 2024). This focus is critical for equipping students with resilience in an environment of constant change and uncertainty.

The development of adaptive AI frameworks is vital in today's educational context (Lee & Kwon, 2024). Both educators and students need to be adept at navigating AI's capabilities, limitations, and ethical considerations. These frameworks must be flexible to accommodate technological advancements while upholding educational integrity and ethical standards. For educators, AI literacy involves not only using AI tools effectively but also critically evaluating AI resources and guiding students in their use. For students, AI literacy means understanding AI's societal role, interacting with AI systems, and developing critical thinking skills to assess AI-generated information.

The integration of AI supports the development of critical thinking and problem-solving skills by personalizing learning experiences to address diverse learning styles and enhancing student engagement through adaptive platforms, real-time feedback, and interactive technologies. AI's role in fostering these skills aligns with preparing students for the modern workforce (Dumont & Ready, 2023; Huang, Sung, Chang, & Huang, 2020). By integrating AI across curricula, educators can promote critical thinking, problem-solving, and adaptability, crucial for success in an AI-driven economy (Filippucci et al., 2024).

However, critical thinking and problem-solving alone may not be sufficient. The modern workforce requires a broader set of skills, including adaptability, digital literacy, creativity, and emotional intelligence (Holmes et al., 2019; Jackson, 2024). As the global workforce becomes increasingly prominent, students must develop global and cross-cultural competence. To achieve this, educators should weave global perspectives and cross-cultural skills into their curricula, ensuring students are well-prepared for international and multicultural work environments (Dumont & Ready, 2023). AI-enhanced education must go beyond merely fostering these skills and address ethical considerations, such as data privacy, algorithmic bias, and the balance between AI and human instruction (ISTE, 2024; Grosso et al., 2024). This comprehensive approach ensures that students are well-prepared for a future where AI is an integral part of the job market.

The rapid pace of technological advancement underscores the need for lifelong learning. Education systems must evolve to support continuous skill development throughout an individual's career, shifting from traditional models to frameworks that emphasize ongoing learning (Lee & Kwon, 2024; Meyer et al., 2024). AI plays a crucial role in facilitating this transition by enabling micro-learning and on-demand skill acquisition, aligning education with the dynamic demands of the workforce (Gupta, 2023). While critical thinking and problem-solving skills are essential, they must be integrated into a broader educational strategy that also fosters adaptability, digital literacy, creativity, and ethical understanding. The incorporation of AI into education supports these objectives by enhancing learning experiences and preparing students for the complexities of an AI-driven job market. This comprehensive approach ensures that students are well-equipped to thrive in a future where AI is increasingly prevalent, making meaningful contributions to an evolving world.

REFERENCES

Al-khresheh, M. H. (2024). Bridging technology and pedagogy from a global lens: Teachers' perspectives on integrating ChatGPT in English language teaching. Computers & Education. *Artificial Intelligence*, 100218, 100218. Advance online publication. DOI: 10.1016/j.caeai.2024.100218

Association for Career and Technical Education. (2022, January 10). Leveraging VR, AR & AI for CTE student success. https://www.acteonline.org/tech-changes-how-we-learn/

Benjamin, L. T. (1988). A history of teaching machines. *The American Psychologist*, 43(9), 703–712. DOI: 10.1037/0003-066X.43.9.703

Bhutoria, A. (2022). Personalized education and artificial intelligence in United States, China, and India: A systematic Review using a Human-In-The-Loop model. *Computers and Education: Artificial Intelligence*, 3, 100068. DOI: 10.1016/j.caeai.2022.100068

Celik, I., Dindar, M., Muukkonen, H., & Järvelä, S. (2022). The promises and challenges of artificial intelligence for teachers: A systematic review of research. *TechTrends*, 66(4), 616–630. Advance online publication. DOI: 10.1007/s11528-022-00715-y

Darling-Hammond, L., Hyler, M. E., & Gardner, M. (2017). *Effective teacher professional development*. Learning Policy Institute., DOI: 10.54300/122.311

Dimitriadou, E., & Lanitis, A. (2023). A critical evaluation, challenges, and future perspectives of using artificial intelligence and emerging technologies in smart classrooms. *Smart Learning Environments*, 10(1), 12. Advance online publication. DOI: 10.1186/s40561-023-00231-3

Dumont, H., & Ready, D. D. (2023). On the promise of personalized learning for educational equity. *NPJ Science of Learning*, 8(1), 26. Advance online publication. DOI: 10.1038/s41539-023-00174-x PMID: 37542046

Filippucci, F., Gal, P., Jona-Lasinio, C., Leandro, A., & Nicoletti, G. (2024, April 16). The impact of Artificial Intelligence on productivity, distribution and growth: Key mechanisms, initial evidence and policy challenges. OECD iLibrary. https://www.oecd-ilibrary.org/docserver/8d900037-en.pdf

Grosso, D., Bowling, M., Chun, S., & Delaney, B. (2024). Protecting student data privacy in light of artificial intelligence. *National Law Review*. https://www.natlawreview.com/article/development-ai-and-protecting-student-data-privacy

Gupta, G. (2023, September 18). The AI advantage: Boosting student engagement in self-paced learning through AI. Faculty Focus. https://www.facultyfocus.com/articles/teaching-with-technology-articles/the-ai-advantage-boosting-student-engagement-in-self-paced-learning-through-ai/

Haleem, A., Javaid, M., Qadri, M. A., & Suman, R. (2022). Understanding the role of digital technologies in education: A review. *Sustainable Operations and Computers, 3*(3), 275–285. https://www.sciencedirect.com/science/article/pii/S2666412722000137

Heaven, W. (2020, July 20). OpenAI's new language generator GPT-3 is shockingly good—and completely mindless. *MIT Technology Review*. https://www.technologyreview.com/2020/07/20/1005454/openai-machine-learning-language-generator-gpt-3-nlp/

Highland, S. (2023, January 17). Designing modern CTE classrooms: Four keys to success. *Essentials Magazine*. https://essentials.edmarket.org/2023/01/designing-modern-cte-classrooms-four-keys-to-success/

Holmes, W., Bialik, M., & Fadel, C. (2019). *Artificial intelligence in education: Promises and implications for teaching and learning*. Center for Curriculum Redesign.

Hwang, G. J., Sung, H. Y., Chang, S. C., & Huang, X. C. (2020). A fuzzy expert system-based adaptive learning approach to improving students' learning performances by considering affective and cognitive factors. *Computers and Education: Artificial Intelligence*, 1, 100003. DOI: 10.1016/j.caeai.2020.100003

ISTE. (2024). A guide on ethics and AI for the classroom hands-on. https://iste.org/ai

Jackson, E. A. (2024). The evolution of artificial intelligence: A theoretical review of its impact on teaching and learning in the digital age. EconStor *Preprints*. https://ideas.repec.org/p/zbw/esprep/280893.html

Kim, J. H. (2023). Leading teachers' perspective on teacher-AI collaboration in education. *Education and Information Technologies*. Advance online publication. DOI: 10.1007/s10639-023-12109-5

Kroeper, K. (2022). Identifying teaching behaviors that foster growth mindset classroom cultures. *American Psychological Association*. https://www.apa.org/ed/precollege/psychology-teacher-network/introductory-psychology/growth-mindset-classroom-cultures

Lee, S. J., & Kwon, K. (2024). A systematic review of AI education in K-12 classrooms from 2018 to 2023: Topics, strategies, and learning outcomes. *Computers and Education: Artificial Intelligence*, 6, 100211. DOI: 10.1016/j.caeai.2024.100211

Levy, A. (2020, April 8). While parents Zoom, their kids are flocking to an app called Roblox to hang out and play 3D games. CNBC. https://www.cnbc.com/2020/04/08/roblox-is-seeing-a-surge-during-coronavirus-shelter-in-place.html

Luckin, R. (2018). *Machine learning and human intelligence: The future of education for the 21st century*. UCL IOE Press.

Luckin, R., Cukurova, M., Kent, C., & Du Boulay, B. (2022). Empowering educators to be AI-ready. *Computers and Education: Artificial Intelligence*, 3, 100076. DOI: 10.1016/j.caeai.2022.100076

McNulty, N. (2024, January 24). AI for inclusive education: Enhancing learning opportunities for all. https://www.niallmcnulty.com/2024/01/ai-for-inclusive-education/

Meyer, J., Jansen, T., Schiller, R., Liebenow, L., Steinbach, M., Horbach, A., & Fleckenstein, J. (2024). Using LLMs to bring evidence-based feedback into the classroom: AI-generated feedback increases secondary students' text revision, motivation, and positive emotions. *Computers & Education: Artificial Intelligence*, 6, 100199. DOI: 10.1016/j.caeai.2023.100199

Ng, D. T. K., Leung, J. K. L., Su, J., Ng, R. C. W., & Chu, S. K. W. (2023). Teachers' AI digital competencies and twenty-first century skills in the post-pandemic world. *Educational Technology Research and Development*, 71(1), 137–161. Advance online publication. DOI: 10.1007/s11423-023-10203-6 PMID: 36844361

Nguyen, H. (2021, March 26). How to use gameplay to enhance classroom learning. Edutopia. https://www.edutopia.org/article/how-use-gameplay-enhance-classroom-learning

Open, A. I. (n.d.). GPT-3 powers the next generation of apps. https://openai.com/blog/gpt-3-apps?ref=digitvibe

Otto, S., Bertel, L. B., Ruan, E., Markman, A. O., Andersen, T. F., & Ryberg, T. (2023). Emerging digital practices supporting student-centered learning environments in higher education: A review of literature and lessons learned from the Covid-19 Pandemic. *Education and Information Technologies*. Advance online publication. DOI: 10.1007/s10639-023-11789-3 PMID: 37361841

Pawar, P. (2023). AI-enhanced education: Personalized learning and educational technology. https://doi.org/DOI: 10.25215/9358791152.01

Russell, S., & Norvig, P. (2021). *Artificial intelligence: A modern approach* (4th ed.). Pearson.

Shemshack, A., & Spector, J. M. (2020). A systematic literature review of personalized learning terms. *Smart Learning Environments*, 7(1), 33. Advance online publication. DOI: 10.1186/s40561-020-00140-9

Tuomi, I. (2018). *The impact of artificial intelligence on learning, teaching, and education policies for the future*. JRC Science for Policy Report., DOI: 10.2760/12297

UNESCO. (2023). Global education monitoring report, 2023: technology in education: A tool on whose terms? https://unesdoc.unesco.org/ark:/48223/pf0000385723

VanLehn, K. (2011). The relative effectiveness of human tutoring, intelligent tutoring systems, and other tutoring systems. *Educational Psychologist*, 46(4), 197–221. DOI: 10.1080/00461520.2011.611369

Wang, X., Li, L., Tan, S. C., Yang, L., & Lei, J. (2023). Preparing for AI-enhanced education: Conceptualizing and empirically examining teachers' AI readiness. *Computers in Human Behavior*, 146, 107798. DOI: 10.1016/j.chb.2023.107798

Woolf, B. P. (2010). *Building intelligent interactive tutors: Student-centered strategies for revolutionizing e-learning*. Morgan Kaufmann.

Xu, E., Wang, W., & Wang, Q. (2023). The effectiveness of collaborative problem solving in promoting students' critical thinking: A meta-analysis based on empirical literature. *Humanities & Social Sciences Communications*, 10(1), 1–11. DOI: 10.1057/s41599-023-01508-1 PMID: 37192950

Yue, M., Jong, M. S.-Y., & Ng, K. (2024). Understanding K–12 teachers' technological pedagogical content knowledge readiness and attitudes toward artificial intelligence education. *Education and Information Technologies*, 29(15), 19505–19536. Advance online publication. DOI: 10.1007/s10639-024-12621-2

Chapter 7
Co-creating Intercultural Scenes With Gen AI Using a Case Study Framework

Patricia Goodman Hayward
https://orcid.org/0000-0002-8616-6102
Northeastern University, USA

Lucy Bunning
Northeastern University, USA

Wallace Lages
https://orcid.org/0000-0003-2942-5793
Northeastern University, USA

ABSTRACT

Higher education and workplaces have expressed an increased need and priority for intercultural training to facilitate collaboration in a global workforce (World Economic Forum, 2023). This chapter proposes an andragogical approach to intercultural exploration using large language models (LLMs), specifically a generative AI (Gen AI) tool. This approach takes advantage of the inherent bias in these models to create customized case studies which are relatable for rich learner discussions. Researchers will discuss the supporting theory and provide examples on how educators can best use LLMs to support inclusive learning environments. The Researchers offer both a tested Gen AI case study template for learning activities and a LEAP (Launch, Experiment, Assess, and Ponder) workshop format available for execution.

DOI: 10.4018/979-8-3373-0502-8.ch007

CO-CREATING INTERCULTURAL SCENES WITH GEN AI USING A CASE STUDY FRAMEWORK

Based on the Future of Jobs Report 2023, institutions and workplaces are becoming increasingly diverse with a significant need for people to work effectively across cultural differences (World Economic Forum, 2023). However, diversity training rarely delivers positive results, partially because they are disconnected from one's actual experience and sense of agency (Dobbin & Kalev, 2018). Could a learner become aware of intercultural cues through the creation and analysis of a personalized case study? This chapter offers practical tools and insights for educators and adult learners on how to employ Gen AI to co-create a customizable case study for critical reflection. The framework incorporates case studies for relevance to learners' present and future education, along with proposing use in professional settings.

TAKING AN ANDRAGOGICAL APPROACH TO PROMOTE INTERCULTURAL EXPLORATION

When taking an andragogical approach to education, and case development, learners make decisions about what is important and relevant to their own lives. Andragogy supports the diversity of adult learners both their backgrounds and experiences because of the focus on practical applications, such as experiential learning (Knowles et al., 2020). Based on recent research, one effective and engaging form of experiential learning is using a case study, especially a relatable case study (Neubert et al., 2020). Hence, this chapter proposes an andragogical approach to intercultural exploration using customizable case studies. We will further discuss supporting theory and provide examples of how instructors can best apply case study analysis to support diversity in a learning environment.

Case study analysis offers learners opportunities for real-life scenarios to apply knowledge and enhance learner engagement. At a foundational level, case studies promote analytical skills, critical thinking, strategic decision-making, and solution generation (Chern & Cheeb, 2022; Nohria, 2021). Will positive outcomes be associated with any case? Research has confirmed that relatable cases and stories strengthen constructive meaning for learners (Hoffer, 2020). Adult learners, in particular, may be more engaged in a context that is known to them, described as perspective meanings (Mezirow, 1991), cognitive scripts formed from direct or indirect experiences.

Case studies are valuable to the development of intercultural competence because they provide a dilemma embedded within a defined sociocultural context. Han's (2022) Integrative Model of Intercultural Effectiveness provides a pathway to outcomes that begin with intercultural situations, the foundation necessary for intercultural development. Deliberate attention to the intercultural aspects of a situation addresses Hofstede's (1994) argument that one must acknowledge cultural differences before learning can occur. The dilemmas in case studies and subsequent analysis hold potential for sparking a *disorienting dilemma*, a key component for transformative learning (Mezirow, 1991).

Engaging with case studies with a group promotes dialogue that mobilizes participants' knowledge, attitudes, skills, and values which inform decision-making and action in real-world situations (Sales et al., 2023). When taking an andragogical approach to education - and specifically case study development - learners make decisions about what is important and relevant to their own lives. Additionally, when learners create their own scenes, there is a shift from common pitfalls of diversity training- shame about holding implicit biases and fear of legal action (Banaji & Dobbin, 2023) to agency in creating inclusive environments.

DRAWING ON LARGE LANGUAGE MODELS TO CREATE PERSONALIZED CASE STUDIES

One challenge for using personalized intercultural case studies is that educators have limited time and resources to generate customized cases that enhance the learning experience and connection. Educators often rely on published cases because they are more efficient than writing one's own cases for their specific subject area and group of learners. When educators create their own case studies, they are limited by their own education and experiences. Thus, it is practically unfeasible for educators to gather or create individual cases that are relatable for each student.

Large language models (LLMs) support various professional fields in analyzing, creating, and summarizing data (Forbes Expert Panel, 2024). Because of its generative capabilities, the researchers hypothesize that an LLM would be a perfect tool for educators attempting to generate relevant case studies. LLMs, thus, seem to be a well-tailored tool to support an andragogical approach in developing customized intercultural case studies. The use of LLMs can address the time-consuming nature of writing and open the possibility for individual cases for instruction.

Unfortunately, creating a prompt for an LLMs that leads to a desired outcome is nuanced and can involve a frustrating learning curve. This can prevent beginners from taking advantage of generative AI tools. As a solution, we propose a customizable case study prompt template that would allow instructors to more easily use generative artificial intelligence tools. This template would enable educators to create specialized cases while being replicable and scalable. More specifically, this approach would allow learners to generate intercultural scenes relevant to their cultural backgrounds, future education, and professional prospects.

When using LLMs to create intercultural case studies, it is important to acknowledge, respond to, and ideally leverage their potential limitations. LLMs are trained on human-authored data and therefore produce text with cultural bias (Cao et al., 2023; Shwartz, 2024). For example, Naous et al. (2024) examined culture-related biases in LLMs in languages other than English. They found that even LLMs using Arabic produced text with pro-Western bias. Additionally, an in-depth computation survey was completed confirming that LLMs can create, perpetuate, and amplify social media biases (Gallegos, Rossi, Barrow, Tanjim, Kim, Dernoncourt, Yu, Zhang, & Ahmed, 2024).

Considering these findings, we sought to develop a case study prompt with an LLM. However, we recognized that this could create a problematically biased or stereotypical scenario. With such a buzz around the use of *Gen AI* in education, a potential guiding principle for early adopters and skeptics is "educational purpose". In other words, how can the use of LLM, Gen AI, enhance or facilitate learning objectives (Kostka, & Toncelli, 2023)? As suggested through Gallegos, et al. (2024), this "human in the loop" practice is recommended when using LLMs. It would then be the learners' role to critically analyze the output before applying it. We synthesized the following five areas to examine as we tested the process:

1. Recognize the missing case/scenario cultural cues
2. Question the nuances of different perspectives
3. Draw on critical thinking and curiosity to generate a robust case/scenario and conclusions
4. Check for "machine" characteristics and inconsistencies in the case/scenario
5. Identify cultural stereotypes in the case/scenario

Based on our experience, we have identified the above five points that are particularly important to examine when seeking to focus on intercultural effectiveness in a learning environment.

In the following sections, we describe and analyze the development of a case study prompt, along with an intercultural case development workshop. A resulting revised prompt and workshop framework is offered for readers to leverage LLMs with an andragogical approach to engage learners in intercultural communication scenarios relevant to their own lives.

EXPLORATION INTO THE IMPLEMENTATION OF AN LLM TOOL FOR LEARNING

Case Study Prompt Development

First, we created a customizable prompt template for learners to use with LLMs to generate rich learning opportunities through mini-cases or scenarios. To ensure the output of coherent cases, the researchers designed a prompt template based on a traditional storytelling arc including information to establish the context, develop the characters then move into a rising action and climax. The downward side of the arc is the character's resolution and conclusion.

We initially played with a few prompts across multiple Gen AI tools to gain an understanding of how many details were necessary to produce an output that could be unique. This process is referred to as prompt engineering. Prompt engineering is a technical concept for the effective development of a prompt within Gen AI, which often requires the developer to know the output sought being crafted (Korzynski, Mazurek, Krzypkowska, & Kurasinski, 2023). We invested time into multiple trials, rewriting the prompt until the desired output was generated. The challenge was the output needed to have enough similarity to promote peer discussion in an intercultural communications workshop. We found a balance of key case study terms drawing on a storytelling model to be effective across three different Gen AI tools: Microsoft Copilot, Google Gemini, and Chat GPT-4. The final prompt tested in all three Gen AI tools was the following:

Create a case with the following key elements: an international organization with headquarters in Brazil focused on promoting online marketing with international influencers. The case should have a communication's director, marketing director, and information technology director, along with 5 international influencers. The case will discuss collaboration to most effectively promote the influencers to market various international corporations. The conflict relates to an error in a social media post about one of the influencers. The resolution will support conflict management processes. The conclusion will be a reflective learning question about the case.

The responses created by that prompt provided some common formats that could be easily shared with peers and some biases as anticipated. The table below shows the exact responses from the same prompt across the Gen AI tools as a comparison of a couple of interesting outcomes (See Table 1). We determined that the prompt provided enough details for the generated cases to offer rich data to be analyzed. For example, even though the prompt did not identify the five international influencers, there was diversity among the groups of five influencers. Some of the generated names are names of real people from those locations, but the descriptions are not accurate for real people with the generated names. When reviewing the generated case study conflicts, each provided a scenario supporting the prompt and relevant to the field. The context articulated in the prompt supported enough complexity for the case study to provoke a peer discussion.

Table 1. Initial Case Study Content Comparisons from Gen AI Outputs

Gen AI Tool, Case Study Title	5 International Influencers	Case Study Conflicts
Microsoft Copilot, *Navigating Influencer Marketing Challenges: A Global Organization's Dilemma*	Sophia: A lifestyle vlogger from Italy. Raj: A tech-savvy YouTuber from India. Léa: A fashion influencer from France. Diego: A fitness guru from Argentina. Yuki: A beauty blogger from Japan.	Scenario: During a high-profile campaign, an error occurs in a social media post featuring Sophia. Her sponsored content mistakenly promotes a competitor's product instead of the intended brand. Impact: The organization faces backlash from followers, and Sophia's credibility is at stake. Conflict: Maria (Communications Director) blames Carlos (Marketing Director) for inadequate oversight, while Ana (IT Director) investigates the technical glitch.
Google Gemini, *Case: The Influencer Mishap*	Anika Khan (India) - Beauty & Fashion (20M followers) Liam Jones (UK) - Travel & Adventure (15M followers) Keisha Davis (USA) - Food & Lifestyle (12M followers) Hiro Tanaka (Japan) - Gaming (8M followers) Mamadou Diallo (Senegal) - Education (5M followers)	As part of the campaign, a social media post showcased Anika Khan with a caption highlighting her expertise in "South Asian Beauty." Unfortunately, Gabriela, overwhelmed with system updates, accidentally published the post with the caption reading "Southeast Asian Beauty." A crisis meeting ensued. Sofia (Communication Director) stressed the importance of immediate damage control. Miguel, (Marketing Director) worried about Anika's reputation, advocated for a personal apology from Conectar. Gabriela, (Information Technology Director) feeling responsible, apologized profusely but remained concerned about the potential legal ramifications of the error.

continued on following page

Table 1. Continued

Gen AI Tool, Case Study Title	5 International Influencers	Case Study Conflicts
Chat GPT – 4, *Case Study: Harmonizing Global Influence – A Strategic Approach to International Influencer Marketing*	Emily Carter (USA) - A fashion icon with a significant following on Instagram and YouTube. - Akira Kobayashi (Japan) - A travel vlogger with a strong presence on YouTube and TikTok. - Sophie Dubois (France) - A culinary expert with a popular blog and Instagram account. - Arjun Singh (India) - A tech guru with a large following on Twitter and a tech review channel on YouTube. - Pedro Alvarez (Mexico) - A fitness coach with an engaging Instagram profile and a motivational podcast.	An error occurred when an intern, managing the social media calendar, inadvertently published a post on IOMA's official Twitter account. The post contained an outdated promotional image for Emily Carter, which included a logo of a brand she no longer endorses. This mistake created a conflict with Emily's current contractual obligations and sparked a negative reaction from her fan base and the brand involved.

Moreover, the case studies generated articulated resolutions that supported the conflict management process as directed. Across the three Gen AI platforms, there were different formats for documenting the suggestions, but all emphasized the need for coordination and direct communication. However, there is no discussion emphasizing the perspectives from the different roles or impact on cross-cultural communication needs (See Table 2).

Table 2. Initial Case Study Resolution from Gen AI Outputs

Gen AI Tool, Case Study Title	Resolution
Microsoft Copilot, *Navigating Influencer Marketing Challenges: A Global Organization's Dilemma*	Collaboration: The three directors convene to address the issue: Maria (Communications Director) emphasizes transparent communication with Sophia's followers. Carlos (Marketing Director) proposes a public apology and a corrected post. Ana (Information Technology Director) ensures IT systems are audited to prevent future errors.
Google Gemini, *Case: The Influencer Mishap*	Following established conflict management protocols, Sofia (Communication Director) facilitated a calm discussion. They decided on a multi-pronged approach: Transparency and Apology: Conectar issued a public apology acknowledging the error and highlighting Anika's South Asian heritage. Direct Communication: Sofia personally reached out to Anika, expressing sincere regret and offering a platform for her to address the situation directly with her fans. Internal Review: Gabriela (Information Technology Director), with Miguel's input (Marketing Director), implemented stricter review processes for future social media content.
Chat GPT – 4, *Case Study: Harmonizing Global Influence – A Strategic Approach to International Influencer Marketing*	Upon discovery of the error, the Communications Director, João Silva, immediately implemented the following conflict management processes: 1. Quick Response: The post was promptly deleted, and an official statement was issued across all platforms, acknowledging the mistake and clarifying the situation. 2. Internal Review: An emergency meeting was called with the marketing and IT directors to assess the situation and prevent future occurrences. 3. Stakeholder Communication: Personalized apologies were extended to Emily Carter and the affected brand, along with a corrective action plan. 4. Training and Procedures: Carlos Rocha, the IT Director, introduced advanced content management software with approval workflows to prevent unauthorized posts. Additionally, all staff, including interns, received training on the new system and protocols. 5. Monitoring and Feedback: Maria Fernandes, the Marketing Director, established a real-time monitoring system to track the sentiments of the audience and the response to the corrective actions taken.

We were impressed that the closing, as directed in the prompt, the Gen AI promoted reflective learning. The questions appeared to be relevant and insightful for the participant to discuss with a peer (See Table 3). Hence, engineering the prompt with a reflective inquiry appeared to be a valuable element in the development.

Table 3. Initial Case Study Conclusion from Gen AI Outputs

Gen AI Tool, Case Study Title	Prompted Reflective Learning Questions
Microsoft Copilot, *Navigating Influencer Marketing Challenges: A Global Organization's Dilemma*	How can organizations strike a balance between influencer creativity and brand consistency? Purpose: Encourages critical thinking about influencer marketing challenges.
Google Gemini, *Case: The Influencer Mishap*	How important is a clear communication strategy for mitigating social media crises? Considering the case, discuss the role of transparency and ownership in maintaining brand reputation.
Chat GPT – 4, *Case Study: Harmonizing Global Influence – A Strategic Approach to International Influencer Marketing*	How could the implementation of a robust digital content management system and effective training protocols prevent future conflicts in social media marketing, and what other proactive measures could organizations take to mitigate risks when collaborating with influencers?

After a couple of trials of prompt engineering, there was a consistent output from all the LLMs based on our final structured prompt. From this trial, the researchers identified key elements to include in a prompt that learners can use to develop cases with intercultural interactions that encourage specificity and critical thinking. We dissected the final prompt into six key elements, which then needed to be formatted for others to easily recreate the prompt while adding their own context. As previous research supported, andragogy promotes the individual construction of knowledge from experiences. We felt a storytelling model was a general and familiar framework to build the template for the prompt. Based on the comprehensive prompt engineering exercise, the template below articulates six elements that are mapped nicely to a storytelling framework.

The case study prompt template includes storytelling descriptions for the learners to build upon from their own experiences:

A. Context - state the environment and/or location to set the scene.
B. Character development - identify the type of roles that will interact in the case.
C. Rising action - provide a situation that leads to a climax.
D. Climax - describe a potential critical incident, communication conflict, challenge, or tragedy.
E. Character resolution - offer a possible concept or process that is employed, such as conflict management.
F. Conclusion - propose a solution is generated or a reflective question is developed for the closure.

By employing patience in the prompt engineering process, we were able to address the challenge of initially being too general, while avoiding a tendency of becoming overly specific in the prompt instructions. With this storytelling template, our expected outcome was visualized. Case studies generated by the participants could easily be compared, discussed, and analyzed while allowing for some variation in their contents.

Initial Workshop Framework

To perform an initial evaluation of the case study template prompt, we created a workshop focusing on intercultural exploration and leading participants in creating a personalized intercultural case study. We promoted the workshop to explore Gen AI with intercultural team effectiveness through case study analysis. The workshop was divided into four sections: introduction, ice breaking, case study development with Gen AI, analysis of Gen AI-created cases, and feedback on workshop activities. It is important to recognize our initial workshop framework here to experience the transition based on the workshop feedback and reflection. The Gen AI tools and case study prompt are tools embedded in a larger learning experience rather than being a stand-alone lesson. See the table below for the first basic workshop structure (Table 4).

Table 4. Initial Workshop Agenda and Objectives

Agenda Item	Objective
Introduction to the workshop and facilitators	Establish a shared understanding of the workshop agenda and objectives.
Ice breaking	Orient students start thinking about cultures broadly and cultures with which they identify. Initiate conversations among participants to start building rapport and noticing similarities and differences.
Case study development	Develop intercultural case studies using a prompt template and information relevant to participants' professional or academic experience.
Analysis of Gen AI-created cases	Analyze cases to raise awareness of potential bias and cultural cues.
Debrief on workshop activities	Reflect on the experience of creating and analyzing cases to inform future work with Gen AI tools and case study development.

As educators, we often develop learning environments anticipating specific outcomes. However, a workshop integrating a Gen AI activity opens the learning experience to unknowns. Hence, we will step through a more detailed account of the workshop activities, outcomes and observations, and resulting revisions in the following sections.

Pilot Workshop and Interesting Participant Insights

To implement and evaluate the case study framework and prompt template, we offered, conducted, and analyzed an intercultural team workshop. The workshop was promoted as an intercultural case study exploration of Gen AI and advertised along with various events held by an international department at a large research university. Participation had no impact on attendees' coursework, grades, or professional standing.

Two of the three researchers were participant observers during the workshop. One researcher facilitated the case study activity, debriefed, and conversed with a participant about their case when their partner left early. One researcher facilitated the icebreaker and partnered with a participant for the case study activity. One researcher was primarily taking notes but offered technical guidance. After the workshop, we met to compare notes and identify findings to inform revision of the workshop framework and prompt template.

Seven adult learners showed up for this pilot workshop and consented to observational data being collected during the workshop. Five of the participants completed written tasks and consented to the data being collected for research. The workshop participants who completed the written tasks reported being from China, Iran, Taiwan, and the United States. Of the seven workshop participants, only two self-reported using generative AI tools before. When asked about how they felt about AI tools, one participant expressed concerns about the correctness or accuracy of the tools. Anecdotally, none of the participants voiced excitement about using Gen AI or having confidence in LLMs.

Stepping Through the Pilot Workshop

To begin, we introduced ourselves, the agenda, and the goals. After the introductions, a warm-up activity primed participants to start thinking about intercultural issues. Students wrote one-word descriptions of communities and cultures they identify with (e.g., academic, professional, national, interests, etc.) on post-it notes. They then arranged the post-its on the wall in categories and discussed commonalities and differences. Following this activity, students moved into pairs to start generating ideas that could potentially be developed into a story or case study using the guiding question: "What are two intercultural communication interactions you have experienced that were positive or challenging?" The participants showed an understanding of intercultural interactions, and sharing experiences associated with different ethnicities. There was a brief discussion about how professional roles can have unique values and be viewed as a culture, i.e. accountants as compared to artists.

After the warm-up, the researchers introduced participants to the prompt template for creating case studies with Gen AI by talking through a sample. Before they got started, participants selected the tool they would use (researchers confirmed all given options were selected): Microsoft Co-pilot, OpenAI Chat GPT, or Google Gemini. We encouraged participants to work with an LLM that they might be less familiar with to increase their exploration of "play" in this process. Instructions on how to access the various tools were provided. To generate their case studies, participants used the template below and replaced the items in brackets with what they wanted for their case.

Write a case study with the following elements:

Context- [state the type of environment and/or location to set the scene]

Character development- [identify the type of roles who will interact in the case]

Rising action- [provide a situation that leads to a climax]

Climax- [describe a potential critical incident, communication conflict, challenge, or tragedy]

Character resolution- [offer a possible concept or process that is employed, such as conflict management]

Conclusion- The conclusion will be a reflective or critical thinking question about the case.

After creating the case studies, the participants filled out a questionnaire that guided them through a reflection on the process. The questionnaire asked students to evaluate their overall satisfaction with their case study and the six storytelling elements from the prompt they wrote. The questionnaire also encouraged the case study developer to reflect on their own case study based on the key elements in their customized prompt. A matrix with the case study template key elements directed critical thinking as related to expectations (See Image 1). In the survey itself, the matrix appeared twice for both the individual reflection and to gain a peer's perspective. The purpose of this matrix completed at both levels was to promote intercultural interactions by offering a framework to interview the peer about their unique case study generated. This data gathered provided helpful insights into the case study template usability. When the template was not accurately applied, the participant was dissatisfied with their case study output. After being redirected to apply the case study template as provided, the output was easier to compare with their peer.

Figure 1. Workshop Reflection Questionnaire

	Strongly disagree	Somewhat disagree	Neither agree nor disagree	Somewhat agree	Strongly agree
The context was clear and believable.	○	○	○	○	○
The character development was on target.	○	○	○	○	○
The rising action was sufficiently explained.	○	○	○	○	○
The climax had a probable situation.	○	○	○	○	○
The resolution included a realistic process.	○	○	○	○	○
The conclusion was insightful.	○	○	○	○	○

The questionnaire also elicited additional open-ended comments to gather individual reflections. This was an opportunity for the participants to consider concepts that might not have been apparent in their case study and reflect further between expectations and the actual output. Below are a couple of the related open-text questions from the survey to elicit this data.

- "Please provide more description related to your responses above. Were there cultural biases discovered? Was there missing content or problematic statements in the case study Gen AI generated?"
- "What do you think would make the case study more accurate?"
- "What is an insight gained through this discussion about your Gen AI case study?"

While the matrix focuses more on the form of the case study. These questions directed participants to think more about the disciplinary focus, i.e. intercultural interactions, of the workshop. A critical analysis component in the debrief was for the participants to share notable aspects of their experience with the case study activity with the group.

Pilot Workshop Observations and Questionnaire Results

Overall, the workshop was a positive experience for the participants. It supported participants in reevaluating their expectations about what the LLM tools can do. What didn't work as anticipated? There was also some confusion about how to add the prompt template and their own information into the prompt box in the LLMs. Before the case generation, we were surprised about the participants' uncertainty about what a case study was and how it related to storytelling. During the case study generation, some participants needed support on how to incorporate their experiences into the template. We needed to specify that storytelling is not always real. The participants wanted to create something interesting, but not necessarily realistic.

What old-school basic best practice teaching technique shined in the workshop? We shared our final version of the storytelling prompt due to our prompt engineering. By providing our example prompt and generated case study, participants gained insights on multiple levels. It offered a visual on how to incorporate their experiences into the prompt template, along with ideas on what type of experience to draw from in their professional lives. Initially, the participants started with broad statements and played, rather than following the template. For example, one participant mentioned that he did not want to limit the tool to enable it to make a very creative story. However, he was unsatisfied with that story and ended up using the provided case study template. Interestingly, the participants tested a couple of versions of the prompt template to build in cultural dimensions and deeper descriptors. Another participant wanted to quickly switch the background of her original story to a Chinese cultural background, and it translated the story into Mandarin language. When asked again, the tool refused to do so (Gemini). One participant asked for the case context to include a sensitive topic, suicide, but the output did not contain any reference to that prompt context (Copilot). In general, the participants found by using the structure of the prompt template, they were able to have a discussion opening the conversation for easy comparisons and differences.

How could we confirm the participants were engaged in the learning process and not just going through the motions? We gathered key data points from the observation of participants using the questionnaire to interview their peers and from the data submitted in the questionnaire. There were interesting comments from the participants related to the character development and arch of the case study generated. Some participants felt the characters were too archetypical and that the story (i.e. case study) was not very creative. For example, in the questionnaire, one participant noted, "The Chinese culture sounds very conservative." However, participants pointed out that they could easily provide additional instructions to fine-tune the outcome (e.g., create a negative resolution). One participant mentioned that by changing the context of the case study from a hypothetical to reflect a known organization, it was considered much better since it was "very relatable". Another participant was impressed when one of the characters had the same age and last name (the character development description was to create a Chinese name - using Copilot). However, this literal connection generated discomfort and a negative emotion in the case study. There was some thought that the participant signed into the tool, and was aware of their credentials when generating the case study (This feature has not been validated as part of the Gen AI tool functionality). One participant who created a case study about a group discussing music identified generalizations and stereotyping of musical genres based on the ethnicities of the characters. The participant shared, "It made everyone too easy, too polite." It was intriguing how the output was overly simplified, lacking depth in the diversity of musical options.

Could this workshop be replicated? In the following sections, we will share specific tools to promote future implementation. A couple of simple tips include opening the workshop with clear definitions for all main terms: culture, case study, and generative AI tools. Additionally, the facilitators should test out the storytelling prompt template themselves to secure their comfort with the process. Another thought is to provide detailed instructions to support participants in a smoother transition from reviewing the example to creating their own case study. If funding or technical skills are available, consider creating a chatbot to navigate the participant's actions through each step in the process.

TOOLS FOR EDUCATORS

What are the major takeaways for Educators? First, this type of case study development workshop sets up learners to have a common skeleton of a prompt to support future discussion and applications. Second, we found it helpful to identify key concepts in a specific structure of the case study template to promote peer discussion. Ultimately, we recognized the value of incorporating an andragogical approach to promote individual descriptions into the key concepts of the case study framework. Next, this exercise opened the door to observe how Gen AI produces generalities associated with characters, roles, intercultural interactions, and stereotypes in various LLMs' outputs. We demonstrated the value in navigating through the process to observe the pitfalls and avoid acceptance of generic scenes. Hence, this workshop activity promotes a learning environment to deepen both critical thinking and reflection, along with creativity in generating a meaningful case study.

Throughout this chapter, several elements have been discussed about the strengths and challenges of the workshop design. Is there an easy way to ensure key elements are replicated for future workshops? As we reflected on these key takeaways, we realized the workshop could have a plan to build on the additional scaffolding and support the rich peer discussion in being replicated. How can the workshop intentionally involve intercultural cues and conflicts? Know the audience for the workshop. In general, it would be beneficial to incorporate activities and definitions associated with culture, intercultural communications, and cross-cultural conflicts. Additionally, don't assume the participants understand the similarities and differences between a case study and a storytelling framework. Given societies varied levels of experience using LLMs, it would also be helpful to add in an activity for participants to experiment with different Gen AIs. Moreover, prompt engineering is a competency all on its own. However, there could be a benefit in encouraging the participants to play with creating a prompt before using the storytelling prompt template to create their own case study. These major findings lead us to construct a strategy to promote the flow of the workshop (See Image 2). By using the acronym LEAP, Launch, Experiment, Assess, and Ponder as the workshop framework, the activities can be strategically organized.

LEAP can be further described with the following concepts:

- **L**aunch (Introduce, define, describe)
- **E**xperiment (Play, try, create)
- **A**ssess (Evaluate, analyze)
- **P**onder (Reflect, debrief)

As a point of interest, this acronym was developed by employing the assistance of Copilot to produce four to five-letter words that started with a letter using the descriptions above.

Figure 2. LEAP: Developing a Custom Gen AI Case Study Exploring Cultural Cues

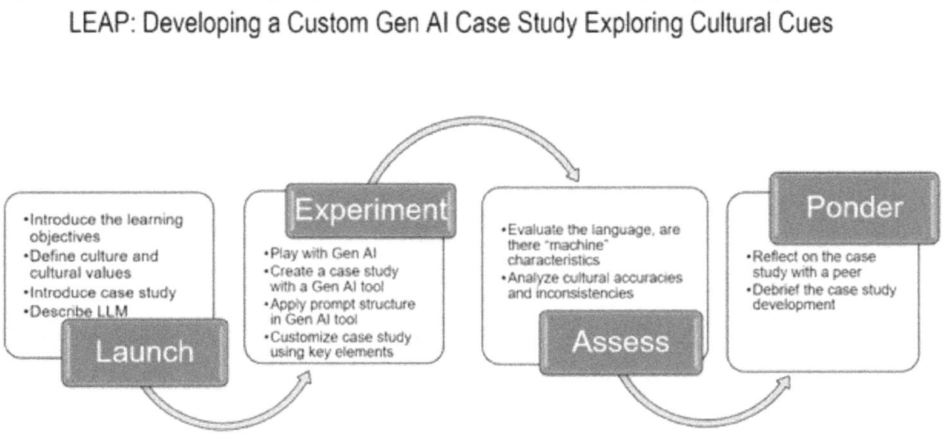

As confirmation, this LEAP framework is a result of our experiences in running the workshop with the Gen AI case studies. To further support educators, a detailed workshop agenda below articulates key learning elements throughout the workshop (See Table 5). It is intended to facilitate other educators' use of Gen AI to guide learners in an andragogical approach to unique case study development. Elaboration and customization on this agenda are enthusiastically encouraged.

Table 5. Revised Workshop Agenda and Activities Employing the LEAP Strategy

Agenda Item	Objective	Activities
Launch		
Introduction to the workshop and facilitators	Establish a shared understanding of the workshop agenda and objectives.	Facilitators ● introduce themselves and the workshop agenda and objectives
Ice breaking	Orient students to think about cultures broadly and cultures with which they identify. Initiate conversations among participants to start building rapport and noticing similarities and differences.	Facilitators ● define culture ● ask participants to use post-it-notes write cultures they identify with (one culture per note) Participants ● arrange notes on the wall into agreed-upon categories Facilitators ● pose a discussion question based on the categories and notes: "What are some of the commonalities and differences across the categories?" ● pose discussion questions to start thinking about case study topics: "What are two intercultural communication interactions (in a professional, academic, or social setting) you have experienced positive/ challenging?"
Experiment		
Warm-up with LLM	Play with the LLM	Facilitators ● introduce a list of Gen AI tools to experiment with and directions to access them ● ask participants to work with a partner and use different LLM, enter prompts "What is the difference between a story and a case study?" and/or "How can a case study be used as a learning tool?" Participants ● share notable results of their explorations with the group

continued on following page

Table 5. Continued

Agenda Item	Objective	Activities
Case study development	Develop intercultural case studies using a prompt template and information relevant to participants' professional or academic experience.	Facilitator ● show an example of a completed prompt template, explaining each element, and the case generated from the prompt ● instruct participants to create their own cases using the prompt template Participants ● use their preferred Gen AI tool and the template to create a case study about an intercultural situation they have experienced
Assess		
Analysis of Gen AI-created cases	Analyze cases to raise awareness of potential bias and cultural cues.	Facilitator: ● provide questions to guide the analysis of the case studies Participants ● use the questions in analyzing their own case ● ask someone else to read their case and interview the reader about their impressions
Ponder		
Debrief on workshop activities	Reflect on the experience of creating and analyzing cases to inform future work with Gen AI tools and case study development.	Facilitator: ● prompts reflective questions of what new insights were gained through this activity Participants ● Consider recalling the introduction of concepts ● Share unexpected findings and outcomes from the activities and discussion

For future use of this LEAP workshop, we observed that by applying the storytelling template we did generate more consistent and complete outcomes. It was important to be direct with the participants that they needed to copy the entire template within the quote and replace the items in brackets with what they wanted for their case. The one slight adjustment in one of the key elements was changing *Character resolution* to simply *Resolution* to decrease confusion over multiple characters requiring a recommendation. The following is the revised storytelling prompt template to be applied:

Write a case study with the following elements:
Context- [state the type of environment and/or location to set the scene]
Character development- [identify the type of roles who will interact in the case]
Rising action- [provide a situation that leads to a climax]
Climax- [describe a potential critical incident, communication conflict, challenge, or tragedy]

Resolution- [offer a possible concept or process that is employed, such as conflict management]

Conclusion- The conclusion will be a reflective or critical thinking question about the case. "

What can educators expect if they try LEAP? Educators can expect that this specific storytelling prompt template will support the participants in generating unique case studies, which will also promote a similar structure to promote discussions between the participants. The participants will be engaged in the workshop activity because of the andragogical approach to constructing their own situations or ideas. By adopting the questionnaire matrix, crosstalk will describe why they chose their context, characters, and climax. Based on the comfort of the learning environment, this framework can lead to open discussions about preferences and perspectives.

One contradictory point is there was an advantage in being flexible with participants to play with the process. Through that *freedom of play*, the participants questioned some of their grounded assumptions and explored intercultural concepts as addressed previously in the examples. What is the risk? Too much time to play can create a loss of momentum in the learning objectives for the workshop. Moreover, too many distractions can lead to sidebar conversations and discourse, which might not have time available for resolutions. In one situation, we decided to enact the "let's place that idea in a parking lot" technique often employed in team meetings. Ultimately, our trials and revisions allowed us to create a learning experience for participants to employ Gen AI tools. They drew upon critical thinking constructed their case study and reflected upon biases in Gen AI output. Most significantly, the case studies became the catalyst for participants to discuss approaches for successful intercultural interactions in academic and work settings.

CONCLUSION

In this chapter, research was conducted to explore an alternative way for educators to support learners in co-creating a case study with an LLM. By employing a consistent storytelling template as a Gen AI prompt, participants can create a customized case study that is relevant to their personal or professional lives. This has the potential for transformative learning while saving time and resources for the educator. Using the terminology of Mezirow's (1991) transformative learning could be a bold claim, yet as described through the workshop observations and findings, participants shared how their perspectives shifted as new information was gained and tried. We cannot guarantee that all learners engaged in this LEAP workshop will have a changed behavior. Nevertheless, we can antidotally share we observed a shift in how the participants initially spoke with negative expressions about their perceptions of Gen AI tools to more of an open intrigue. The realization of how the process of constructing a personalized case study with a Gen AI tool opened opportunities for deeper discussions as compared to everyone speaking about the same case study in general terms.

By implementing the LEAP framework in developing the workshop, educators who might have limited experience with LLM tools can apply an andragogical approach while guiding learners in the basic use of LLM tools. Moreover, we detailed the process we went through to validate our comprehensive efforts in developing helpful resources. Our strategy of being transparent about the decisions we make, ideally will save others time in not repeating our missteps. Plus, we highlight the need for experimentation and iteration when working with LLM tools. To continue our exploration of using LLMs to create intercultural case studies, we have identified several areas for future development.

FURTHER RESEARCH

The LEAP workshop with the case study prompt template provides a scaffolded learning experience. The participants in our pilot had a range of previous experiences with LLMs. Given the rapid development and spread of Gen AI technology, it is reasonable to assume that when these tools are used in educational settings, learners will approach them with different levels of understanding or experience. As we experienced, learners using the tools for the first time experienced a heavy cognitive load, meaning they needed to make connections between the prompt, their experience, using the LLM, and interactions with other workshop participants. This may require a significant amount of cognitive energy and openness to inquiry or draw upon working memory resources. As a result, there is value in examining the impact of time management on the workshop. What amount of time should be identified to support participants needing extra space to orient themselves to the task and practice? This is consistent with research on cognitive load in collaborative learning (Kirschner et al., 2018) and multimedia learning environments (Noetel et al., 2022). One way to consider reducing the cognitive load is to develop a blueprint to lead users through the information they need to include in the prompt engineering process. This would help to explain why the steps are part of the process and what can be expected. Additionally, this support can reduce the anxiety that some might have in working with technology, unknown tools, or ambiguity in outcomes. One current resource addressing this is Mollick and Mollick (2024), which provides an accessible guide with examples of how to provide a blueprint.

In our case, we could test how an in-depth analysis of elements of the case study template impacts the participant's experience. Plus, there could be an expansion of or develop an additional element in the case study template structure. Another alternative could be altering the prompt to develop scripts for role plays or promoting discourse among the participants with further inquiry being created in the case study.

Another research exploration is associated with cultural biases that are inherent in LLMs, which present challenges and opportunities for developing intercultural skills. The LEAP workshop was designed for participants to critique the case studies they created and engage in peer discussion to benefit from other participants' perspectives. Participants' initial wariness of the Gen AI content encouraged their critical reading of the case studies. As LLMs continue to be refined with users' feedback altering and improving machine learning, it will be interesting to note how this influences the outputs. Users can produce LLM agents to have deeper knowledge and generate fewer errors (Schwartz, Yaeli, & Shlomov, 2023). These agents could alter the way users trust and evaluate the LLM output. Hence, further research is necessary to support educators who might not have technical backgrounds on how they can gain skills to design a topic-focused LLM agent. Specifically, a future direction would go to pursue how to develop LLM agents trained in intercultural and cross-cultural areas of study.

At this stage of using LLMs in education, the opportunities seem limitless. For example, this work could be extended into activities examining intercultural interactions through virtual reality. For any of the paths being pursued, we recommend two guiding principles. First, with the incredible potential of LLMs, we believe the focus should be on a learner's experience to meet a specific andragogical goal. Next, we suggest simplifying the learners' interaction with the LLMs in a way that allows them to integrate personal experiences while critiquing for biases. In closing, further exploration and research will benefit learners, educators, and LLM tool development.

REFERENCES

Banaji, M., & Dobbin, F. (2023, September 18). Why DEI Training Doesn't Work -- And How to Fix It -- WSJ. *Dow Jones Institutional News*https://link.ezproxy.neu.edu/login?url=https://www.proquest.com/wire-feeds/why-dei-training-doesnt-work-how-fix-wsj/docview/2865953838/se-2

Cao, Y., Zhou, L., Lee, S., Cabello, L., Chen, M., & Hershcovich, D. (2023). Assessing cross-cultural alignment between ChatGPT and human societies: An empirical study. Proceedings of the First Workshop on Cross-Cultural Considerations in NLP. https://aclanthology.org/2023.c3nlp-1.7.pdf

Chern, O. S., & Cheeb, L. C. (2022). Examining the Use of Scaffolding Approach in Teaching Case Study: An Approach Towards Enhancing Students' Critical Thinking and Problem-Solving Skills. In *Proceeding of the 7th Inspirational Scholar Symposium* (pp. 180-192).

Dobbin, F., & Kalev, A. (2018). Why doesn't diversity training work?: The challenge for industry and academia. *Anthropology Now*, 10(2), 48–55. DOI: 10.1080/19428200.2018.1493182

Gallegos, I. O., Rossi, R. A., Barrow, J., Tanjim, M. M., Kim, S., Dernoncourt, F., Yu, T., Zhang, R., & Ahmed, N. K. (2024). Bias and fairness in large language models: A survey. *Computational Linguistics*, 50(3), 1–79. DOI: 10.1162/coli_a_00524

Han, P.-C. (2022). Creating a developmental pathway for developing intercultural effectiveness competencies. *International Forum of Teaching and Studies, 18*(1), 27-60).

Hoffer, E. R. (2020). Case-based teaching: Using stories for engagement and inclusion. *International Journal on Social and Education Sciences*, 2(2), 75–80.

Kirschner, P. A., Sweller, J., Kirschner, F., & Zambrano, R. J. (2018). From cognitive load theory to collaborative cognitive load theory. *International Journal of Computer-Supported Collaborative Learning*, 13(2), 213–233. DOI: 10.1007/s11412-018-9277-y PMID: 30996713

Knowles, M. S., Holton, E. F., III, Swanson, R. A., & Robinson, P. A. (2020). *The adult learner: The definitive classic in adult education and human resource development* (9th ed.). Routledge/Taylor & Francis Group. DOI: 10.4324/9780429299612

Korzynski, P., Mazurek, G., Krzypkowska, P., & Kurasinski, A. (2023). Artificial intelligence prompt engineering as a new digital competence: Analysis of generative AI technologies such as ChatGPT. *Entrepreneurial Business and Economics Review*, 11(3), 25–37. DOI: 10.15678/EBER.2023.110302

Kostka, I., & Toncelli, R. (2023). Exploring applications of ChatGPT to English language teaching: Opportunities, challenges, and recommendations. *TESL-EJ*, 27(3), n3. DOI: 10.55593/ej.27107int

Mezirow, J. (1991). *Transformative dimensions of adult learning*. Jossey-Bass.

Mollick, E., & Mollick, L. (2024). Instructors as innovators: A future-focused approach to new AI learning opportunities, with prompts. *arXiv.Org*. https://doi.org//arxiv.2407.05181DOI: 10.48550

Naous, T., Ryan, M. J., Ritter, A., & Xu, W. (2024). Having Beer after Prayer? Measuring Cultural Bias in Large Language Models. *arXiv.Org*. https://doi.org//arxiv.2305.14456DOI: 10.18653/v1/2024.acl-long.862

Neubert, M., Rams, W., & Utikal, H. (2020). Experiential learning with live case studies. *International Journal of Teaching and Case Studies*, 11(2), 173–190. DOI: 10.1504/IJTCS.2020.109726

Noetel, M., Griffith, S., Delaney, O., Harris, N. R., Sanders, T., Parker, P., del Pozo Cruz, B., & Lonsdale, C. (2022). Multimedia design for learning: An overview of reviews with meta-meta-analysis. *Review of Educational Research*, 92(3), 413–454. https://doi-org.ezproxy.neu.edu/10.3102/00346543211052329. DOI: 10.3102/00346543211052329

Nohria, N. (2021). What the case study method really teaches. *Harvard Business Review*, •••, 21.

Sales, A., Portera, A., & Milani, M. (2023). Developing intercultural competences through participatory strategies: A multiple case study. *Intercultural Education*, 34(4), 426–445. https://doi-org.ezproxy.neu.edu/10.1080/14675986.2023.2211854. DOI: 10.1080/14675986.2023.2211854

Schwartz, S., Yaeli, A., & Shlomov, S. (2023). Enhancing trust in LLM-based AI automation agents: New considerations and future challenges. *arXiv.Org*. https://doi.org//arxiv.2308.05391DOI: 10.48550

Shwartz, V. (2024, Feb 13). Artificial intelligence needs to be trained on culturally diverse datasets to avoid bias. *The Conversation*.https://theconversation.com/artificial-intelligence-needs-to-be-trained-on-culturally-diverse-datasets-to-avoid-bias-222811

Successful Real-World Use Cases for LLMs and Lessons They Teach. (Mar 8, 2024). Forbes Tech Council. https://www.forbes.com/sites/forbestechcouncil/2024/03/07/successful-real-world-use-cases-for-llms-and-lessons-they-teach/

The Future of Jobs Report. (2023). World Economic Forum https://www.weforum.org/reports/future-of-jobs-report-2023

Chapter 8 Integrating Artificial Intelligence in Higher Education: Enhancing Pedagogy, Instruction, and Administration

Praveen Kumar Dubey
https://orcid.org/0000-0003-1060-2278
Montana State University Northern, USA

Angela R. Crevar
https://orcid.org/0000-0002-0596-9174
Mercer University, USA

ABSTRACT

This chapter explores the integration of Artificial Intelligence (AI) in higher education with an emphasis on pedagogy, instruction, and administration for student learning and achievement. The paradigm shift moved the focus from teacher-centered to learner-centered systems involving AI-powered tools for personalized learning systems such as intelligent tutoring, adaptive learning systems, natural language processing (NLP), machine learning (ML), robotics, automated grading, and feedback to offer enhanced learning opportunities for teaching and learning. However, the AI technological transformation presented challenges in the form of ethical considerations, algorithm biases, curriculum development, lack of infrastructure, and accessibility issues. The chapter discusses the history and evolution of AI, AI technologies in higher education, enhancing pedagogy with AI in higher education, faculty support, and administrative efficiency. Additionally, it addresses the ethical considerations and future trends for AI adoption in higher education.

DOI: 10.4018/979-8-3373-0502-8.ch008

OVERVIEW OF AI IN HIGHER EDUCATION

Education is going through digital transformation and has started using artificial intelligence (AI) to derive and explore new educational opportunities for teaching and learning (Bozkurt, 2021). In recent years, the trend in education has moved from teacher-centered to learner-centered education. This trend has opened new doors for AI-powered teaching and learning processes. It has initiated an approach to consider AI embedded tools for pedagogical advantage to a broader scale and to understand how AI impacts teaching and learning at higher education. The emergence of new technologies such as intelligent tutoring, adaptive learning, robotics, and human-computer interaction has created a paradigm shift for student learning in an overall education landscape (Li et al., 2021). As the traditional roles of educators are changing, it is imperative to enhance teaching-learning with AI enhanced tools. However, the adoption of AI in higher education introduces different challenges such as lack of ethical consideration in AI applications, issues of curriculum development, and proper infrastructure (Bond et al., 2024).

The advanced tools of AI bring exciting opportunities to education and provide a wide range of technologies, features and functions to improve educational outcomes (Zhang & Aslan, 2021). While developing adaptive learning systems, it is important to consider the cognitive and affective factors for better student learning achievement (Hwang et al., 2020). Even though AI technologies use human generated data, it lacks regulation on how to use these data amid missing applications of AI ethics (Dogan et al., 2023). Zhang and Aslan (2021) highlighted that to utilize the full potential of AI in education "it is critical to bridge the gaps between AI technological innovations and its educational applications" (p. 6). Thus, considering the collaboration among different stakeholders, it is essential in creating AI-powered classroom instructions. According to Zhang and Aslan (2021), the most important initiative to advance AI technologies in education is to invite educators and educational researchers to participate in the process of technological innovation. Additionally, including feedback from educational communities, integrating features of theoretical, conceptual, practical and empirical support from educational literature, and aligning current research are part of successful adoption of AI in higher education.

In a meta-analysis, the researchers found that in online distance learning programs, the most often used artificial intelligence applications, are for purely technical studies which ignored the issues of pedagogy, curriculum, and instructional/learning design (Dogan et al., 2023). The key considerations of promoting AI in education include costs, scalability, ethics, and privacy (Baker et al., 2019; Zhang & Aslan, 2021). Additional challenges are the lack of actionable guidelines for implementation and AI expertise among educators (Zhang & Aslan, 2021). Furthermore, AI supported technologies are mediating and demonstrating support for pedagogical design and the role it plays in personalized teaching and learning in effective language acquisition (Yang & Kyun, 2022). Thus, intersecting teacher intervention and configuration for AI-supported services contains a myriad of options for AI enabled classrooms.

For the purpose of this chapter, a broad scope of the development of AI in higher education is considered. Specifically, the history of AI in higher education, use of different technologies such as machine learning, natural language processing, and robotics are explored. Learner centric pedagogy with AI such as Personalized Learning, Blended Learning, Adaptive Learning Systems, and Intelligent Tutoring Systems (ITS) are addressed considering their value for student learning outcomes. The topics of Automated Assessment and Feedback are discussed along with Professional Development demands for AI. Further, the advances in Administrative Efficiency for higher education institutions along with advances in Library Services and Facilities Management are discussed. Finally, the chapter concludes with Ethical Considerations and Future Trends of AI in higher education institutions.

History and Evolution of AI in Higher Education

The term Artificial Intelligence (AI) was first introduced by John McCarthy in 1956. AI has capabilities to perform different human cognitive tasks of problem solving, learning, and communication, etc. (Nilsson, 1998). Later, MIT professor Joseph Weizenbaum built a natural language processing (NLP) programme ELIZA which was used to establish a communication interface between machine and human beings (Weizenbaum, 1966). Throughout the next few decades several researchers furthered the field using different features such as adaptive learning tools, virtual reality, national language procession (NLP) programs, robotics, etc. as useful tools to improve student learning experiences through AI. In the last decade, several educational technology (Ed Tech) companies have developed Adaptive Learning Systems (ALS) which promote personalized learning and enhanced student learning experiences. Innovation added several other AI learning tools in higher education such as Aided Teaching System (ATS), grading, evaluation, robotics, second-language learning tool, Intelligent Tutoring Systems (ITS), and Institute Administration System (IAS) to help with student teaching and learning processes (Guan et al., 2020).

The definitions of AI had varied among the researchers, educators, and policymakers. In their report, Baker et al (2019) defined AI as "Computers which perform cognitive tasks, usually associated with human minds, particularly learning and problem-solving" (p. 10). With such extensive definition, AI is considered as a combination of tools which not only provides the new learning systems for education; instead, it adds sophisticated layers of learning processes with enhanced learning opportunities. AI in education has a wide range of tools for higher education which are grouped in three categories: learner-facing, teacher-facing and system-facing (Baker et al., 2019).

Baker et al. (2019) describe learner-facing AI in Education as 'intelligent tutoring systems', or 'adaptive', 'personalized' or 'differentiated' learning platforms; Teacher-facing AI tools help reduce teachers' workload, inject innovation in classrooms, and gain insights about student learning. System-facing AI tools provide help to administrators to make program decisions for the system as a whole (Baker et al., 2019). These AI tools have shown a positive impact on student learning, teacher performance, and program management. In fact, a meta-analysis suggests that the use of AI in online higher education has shown positive effects on high quality learning, improved academic performances, and online engagement with participation (Ouyang et al., 2022).

AI Technologies in Higher Education

The future of higher education is linked to the development and deployment of newer technologies and its capacity to transform the learning needs of students (Popenici & Kerr, 2017). In recent years, AI played an important role in opening the doors with new possibilities for teaching and learning in higher education. Considering the potential to fundamentally change the internal structure of higher education, it is essential to adopt the advancements of AI technologies such as machine learning, natural language processing, and robotics. In this section we are discussing the scope of machine learning, natural language processing, and robotics as they have the potential to change the realm of teaching and learning at higher education.

Types of AI Technologies

Machine learning, natural language processing, and robotics have shown increased instructional outcomes in higher education (Zawacki-Richter, 2019). This section discusses their scope and significance in higher education while imposing relevance of their importance in student learning, assessment, data management, and language processing systems.

Machine learning, natural language processing and robotics are subsets of AI that enable programs to learn from data and improve performance over time without the need of programming (Zawacki-Richter, 2019; Baker et al., 2019).

Machine Learning (ML). Popenici & Kerr (2017) define machine learning "as a subfield of artificial intelligence that includes software able to recognize patterns, make predictions, and apply newly discovered patterns to situations that were not included or covered by their initial design" (p. 2). Moreover, AI is used as a broad term to describe different technologies such as machine learning, natural language processing, data mining, neural networks, and/or an algorithm (Baker et al., 2019). In general, all these technologies play a foundational role in the development of AI enabled learning tools in higher education. Machine learning in higher education not only improves the teaching and learning processes, but also opens doors of opportunities for innovation (Popenici & Kerr, 2017). In their systemic review, Zawacki-Richter et al (2019) found that researchers have been using machine learning algorithms to evaluate and assess student academic performance, their academic integrity, need for interventions, and adaptive learning systems for machine-human learning interfaces. These results have proved that machine learning is a promising field of artificial intelligence which needs proper attention from educators, administrators, and policymakers.

Online higher education values learner-centered learning. Human intelligence and machine learning can facilitate the transformation of traditional education to learner-centered learning (Ouyang & Jiao, 2021). Looking at these promises and widespread usage, it is significant to note that "machine learning and artificial intelligence open new possibilities and challenges for higher education, it is important to observe that education is eminently a human-centric endeavor, not a technology centric solution" (Popenici & Kerr, 2017, p. 3). Ultimately, how human-machine interaction takes place, who plays what role, and how information is extracted depends on the user. In the end, considering these sophisticated tools and their abilities, new opportunities are presented as a potential avenue for the way new information is acquired, created, and used for learning.

Natural Language Processing (NLP). Natural language processing is a field which studies how AI technology provides computers with an ability to interpret, comprehend, and manipulate human languages. AI technologies teach computers to understand, comprehend, and characterize many facets of language such as semantics, syntax, pragmatics, and phonology (Duong, 2017). The models of NLP had been explored for the last several decades but gained momentum in recent years with the development of deep learning techniques (Kang et al., 2020). In fact, the introduction of Open AI tools created a set of new resources and educational opportunities for higher education. The relevance of NLP tasks is so eminent in higher education that the adoption of open sources such as HuggingFace and OpenAI solutions are very economical and achieve comparable accuracy regarding student performance predictions with reduced cost for institutions (Lin et al., 2024).

In higher education, NLP has significance in analyzing large amounts of text such as academic papers, study materials, and textbooks which provides students an opportunity for personalized learning based on their learning preferences and needs (Fuchs, 2023). Additionally, it is an effective approach to predict the students' learning outcomes and interpret behaviors (Lin et al., 2024). Thus, the use of NLP in higher education creates an opportunity as well as challenges in cultivating a flexible and adaptive learning environment (Alqahtani et al., 2023).

As the landscape of higher education evolves, adopting AI technologies such as NLP will help educators improve student learning experiences.

Robotics. Robotics is a technology used to develop robots in different fields such as education, military, medicine, etc. to replicate human actions (Wang & Siau, 2019). Robotics has been used as an educational tool in higher education to improve the teaching of mathematics, physics, and development of research work (Sánchez et al., 2019). In addition to teaching, robotics should be used as the continuation of education and retraining with proper attention to creativity, social and human skills (Wang & Siau, 2019). In other words, robotics is standing out as an educational tool to improve teaching and learning outcomes in higher education. Research suggests that when grounded in learning theory, robotics has potential to support learning in higher education and interdisciplinary teaching (Spolaôr & Benitti, 2017). Increased student motivation (Gabriele et al., 2017) and improved problem-solving using project-based learning has been shown to improve learning outcomes (Bada et al., 2013). Interestingly, these findings have not been without challenges in higher education contexts. Gerecke and Wagner (2007) suggest that to effectively use robots in higher education, there are challenges that need to be met. First, appropriate software and hardware must be acquired. Next, strategies on how to integrate teachable concepts need to be solidified. Finally, interdisciplinary sharing must occur. With proper planning, collaboration, and assessment of program needs, higher education institutes can achieve the goals of integrating robotics within their programs.

Enhancing Pedagogy with AI in Higher Education

AI enhances pedagogy in higher education by providing adaptive instructional design through both learner centric and instructor centric focused AI applications (Zhang & Aslan, 2021). Learner centric applications are those applications which focus on improving the learning processes for students (Shoaib et al., 2024). Instructor centric applications are those which focus on streamlining student and course management through attendance, grading, and planning efforts (Popencini & Kerr, 2017). Both of these foci rely on data analysis and predictive algorithms to inform pedagogical decisions and improve course design (Ouyang & Jiao, 2021).

Instructional Design and AI

Generative AI is poised to transform instructional design in higher education (Baïdoo-Anu & Owusu Ansah, 2023; Kurtz et al., 2024). Just as breakthroughs in large language models disrupt business and industry to transform individual access to information, the same is occurring in higher education (Arogundade, 2023). Institutions have unprecedented access to real-time data and analysis (Selwyn, 2022). With this access, institutions of higher education have the opportunity to reevaluate their approach to these technologies and data analysis to harness the benefits to enhance the relevance and sustainability of higher education systems, especially in instructional design (Crawford et al., 2023). Generative AI offers educator support, interactivity, personalization, and scalability of education offerings to improve and streamline instructional processes (Crompton & Song, 2021). The apprehension around generative AI exists, but the use of AI for instruction in higher education has increased over the last several years (Crompton & Burke, 2023; Selwyn, 2022). Large language models combined with generative AI are enhancing course development through improved accessibility, and blended learning opportunities that are prescriptive for each student. As new technologies emerge, it is essential for higher education educators to understand how AI can both improve instructional design and introduce new challenges.

Enhanced Course Development

The convergence of AI and educational technologies streamlines course development while enhancing interactivity between the student and platforms (CIPD, 2024). The creation of courses that are rigorous, engaging, and aligned with learning objectives has traditionally been a labor-intensive process that requires instructor expertise in the content area (Shoaib et al., 2024). Then academic oversight is required to ensure consistency across multiple disciplines. The automated analyses provided by AI reduces both the staffing needs and time constraints in course development and oversight (Shoaib et al., 2024). For example, AI offers tools which support content creation, curricular design, and the generation of assessments instantaneously. Generative AI aims to automate such educational tasks to increase the time available to the instructor for higher order critical thinking tasks such as personalized interactions with students (CIPD,2024). This reduces the time needed to plan or source course content, freeing professors to focus on more critical components of course design to better enhance instruction (Arogundade, 2023).

AI powered platforms generate pedagogically sound content such as quizzes, study guides, case scenarios, creation of sample datasets, and interactive modules which are aligned to designated learning objectives (Baykasoğlu et al., 2018). Recent advances enable AI to synthesize instructional concepts from other sources to create instructional resources such as a teaching slide deck to complement that resource, generation of a notetaking guide for the lecture, and creation of assignments to evaluate learning along those prescribed objectives instantaneously (Verdú et al., 2017). Additionally, AI harbors the ability to analyze large scale datasets of student formative and summative data to determine content area weaknesses and disparities in course outcomes (Ismail et al., 2023). Thus, the efficacy of instructional methods and the usage of digital materials can be analyzed to evaluate course performance and future efforts in instructional design (Roski et al., 2024). Additionally, these insights reveal nuances that lead to targeted revision of courses and curricula vastly reducing the necessary human capital to complete such analyses (Shoaib et al., 2024).

Enhanced Accessibility

The needs of vulnerable, historically marginalized, English language learners, and economically disadvantaged students are unique (Han et al, 2022). AI serves as a powerful weapon to remove barriers for a wide range of needs to enhance instructional design (Goldman et al., 2024). For example, speech recognition software can transcribe lectures in real time, making them accessible to students with hearing impairments. Similarly, large language models offer on-demand translation of text offering English language learners immediate access to translated information. Text can be reworded for different levels of readability and enhanced for accessibility improving efforts toward Universal Design for Learning (UDL) (Roski et al., 2024). Rather than investing in additional resources to meet these needs, AI can adjust the same text on-demand (Goldman et al., 2024). For students who begin without the necessary prior knowledge, instructors use AI to bridge learner readiness with higher rigor content, as AI produces scaffolded instruction. These advances offer tremendous benefit; however, there is trepidation in regard to privacy, bias, and accountability (Prinsloo et al., 2024). For example, Algorithmic decision-making processes do not consider the emotional needs of a vulnerable learner (Perez Vallejos, 2021). Centric norms govern these processes and may not reflect appropriate norms for historically marginalized learners. Differing combinations of demographic backgrounds such as race, gender, ethnicity, ability, and age are not easily disentangled and may remain unobserved in the algorithms (Kurtz et al., 2024).

AI lacks quality control measures to ensure the accuracy sourcing of content that is produced. Content may include material that is hallucinated, inaccurate, or contains overt biases (Niewint-Gori, 2023; Prinsloo et al., 2024). This is a significant concern regarding integrity and scholarly accuracy of content (Roski et al., 2024). The nuanced understandings needed for deep critical thinking may be missing with AI generated content. In the goal to differentiate, AI may oversimplify a concept and offer a shallow understanding of the content that lacks the depth and rigor required for higher education (Perez Vallejos et al., 2021).

Personalized Learning

The role of AI in higher education is significant in providing quality education, practical teaching-learning, and opportunities for better careers. Such goals of excellence can be achieved through use of AI tools: Personalized Learning (PL). Research suggests that the implementation of personalized learning (PL) improves students' learning outcomes and increases their satisfaction, motivation, and engagement (Fariani et al., 2022). It creates a learning environment which optimizes for the learners' needs and provides an adaptation for a student-centered learning environment. In higher education, PL has potential to switch the focus from teacher-centered to learner-centered environments (Alamri et al., 2020). To transform higher education with AI, institutions need to be more relevant to teaching and learning with proper use of AI tools such as personalized and adaptive learning systems, innovative approach, and awareness with reality. The goals of better higher education can be achieved through planning, development and implementation of digital skills to train professionals, and deployment of technological tools such as PL based on learners' needs. Bates et al (2020) recommend that institutions of higher education need to produce multidisciplinary research, involving educators in planning, streamlining between AI applications and educational theories, and recognize threats created to teachers and instructors.

Blended and Personalized Learning

The emergence and accessibility of AI has dramatically increased the feasibility of blended and personalized learning without the excessive costs of increased faculty planning. Blended learning combines the traditional methods of classroom instruction with online personalized learning (NEA, 2021). Personalized learning with AI harnesses learning analytics to optimize the online learning environment (Shoaib et al., 2024). Learning analytics uses data mining, data analysis, and algorithms to monitor student learning, identify knowledge gaps, and adapt instructional content to meet the unique needs of learners (Shu & Ye, 2023). Personalized learning evaluates learning styles, bridges learning gaps, and identifies preferences of the individual student (Kew & Tasir, 2022). These analyses then form the instructional core of online learning in blended learning. Virtual tutors and virtual course assistants increase the breadth of coursework while reducing demands on the instructor. Even standardized college entrance tests such as the SAT have become personalized (College Board, 2024). These exams adjust in real-time for individual students based on ongoing analytics as students complete the exam offering a streamline experience with reduced time to results.

While AI is poised to improve personalized learning, there are concerns that AI could diminish the human interaction between professors and students, especially in larger courses (Perez Vallejos, 2021). AI may miss the subtleties of student emotions, motivations, and individual barriers that human interaction reveals. Professors and instructors bring a dynamic element to a course that motivates and inspires students. The algorithms of AI lack the personal connection that can drive student engagement and perseverance, especially in difficult coursework or content areas (Shoaib et al., 2023).

Adaptive Learning Systems

The purpose of AI in education is to provide personalized learning to students based on their learning preferences, status, or personal characteristics (Hwang et al., 2020). Higher education institutes have used multiple AI algorithms to facilitate students' academic recommendations, academic predictions, or student performance assessments (Ouyang et al., 2022). The findings suggest that the adaptive learning system with the affective and cognitive performance analysis mechanism could reduce students' mathematical anxiety compared to the conventional learning system with no adaptive mechanism (Hwang et al., 2020). The research suggests that the main applications of AI in higher education are students' performance prediction, resource recommendation, automatic assessment, and improvement of learning experiences and higher education institutions have been using AI algorithms to facilitate these purposes (Ouyang et al., 2022). Thus, while developing learning with AI embedded tools, considering these components would help achieve the goals of higher student learning.

The research suggests that AI learning tools such as adaptive learning systems with affective and cognitive performance analysis mechanisms are advantageous to facilitating students' learning achievement (Hwang et al., 2020). The systematic research review suggests "the importance of data collection and analysis of learning process data in addition to summative data in order to achieve a high quality of AI-enabled prediction or recommendation" (Ouyang et al., 2022, p. 7909). Furthermore, collecting real-time data will achieve the desired goals of student learning as it provides current data for adaptive learning systems to make adjustments.

Intelligent Tutoring Systems

Intelligent tutoring systems (ITS) is a computer-led learning that provides students' immediate and tailored instruction or feedback with no intervention from a human instructor (Steenbergen-Hu & Cooper, 2014). ITS is a stimulated one-to-one personal tutoring based on algorithms and neural networks (Bond et al., 2024; Zawacki-Richter et al., 2019). This technology makes decisions on individual student learning paths and selection of content to provide appropriate cognitive scaffolding and to engage the student in dialogue about the content (Zawacki-Richter et al., 2019). The SCHOLAR system was the first ITS launched in 1970 to exchange the questions between teacher and student regarding South American geography and provided instant feedback in natural language about the response quality of a learner's responses (Carbonell, 1970; Welham, 2008). Guan et al. (2020) suggests that research on ITS should focus on pedagogical issues to provide better one-on-one instructional guidance and advanced systems as these models are associated with improved teaching and learning processes. Thus, the importance lies in adopting an ITS that not only provides one-on-one learning but improved learning experiences for students' learning needs. In a study, researchers found that the use of ITS improved the learners' skills on language learning and reduced anxiety levels for learning languages (Yang & Kyun, 2022).

When evaluating the usage of technology, ample consideration must be given to the topics of pedagogical, cultural, social, economic, ethical and psychological aspects of education (Guan et al., 2020). In other words, as an educator, we should consider learners' culture, pedagogical knowledge, social standing, economics, ethics, and psychology when designing the learning. In online higher education, Ouyang et al. (2022) recommend theoretical, technological, and practical implications for applications of AI to strengthen interactions between students, educators, and AI. Intelligent tutoring systems are implemented based on the cognitive capabilities of used AI techniques, and these techniques are deployed based on interacting components such as the knowledge base, the student model, the pedagogical module, and the user interface (Sedlmeier, 2001). Guan et al (2020) described that while developing ITS, special attention was given to functionality assessment of these components such as granularity, generality, interoperability, and reliability. Thus, to provide students with versatility of learning opportunities, ITS should focus on learners' learning needs while considering the flexibility of learning environments. Research suggests that the ITS enhances the learners' personalized learning experiences by providing tailored learning based on their knowledge and preferences (Yang & Kyun, 2022).

Faculty Support with AI

AI augments teacher capabilities by automating routine tasks. Enhanced efficiency of AI reduces the time spent on grading, taking attendance, creating content, and lesson delivery (Zawacki-Richter, 2019). An AI augmented LMS provides real time feedback and develops personalized plans for each student based on individual knowledge and readiness (Dever et al., 2020). Learning Management Systems (LMS) create customized learning paths to differentiate based on specific student learning needs, reducing the time instructors spend analyzing data on student performance and creating individual plans (Kurtz et al, 2024). Instructors can instantaneously refine instructional plans based on immediately available data (Bahadir, 2016). Data driven dynamic content creation provides diversity in instructional delivery with the added advantage of automatic curricular updates (Alamri et al., 2020). While not always perfect, large language models are able to use algorithms to evaluate written work for grammar, adherence to directions, coherence, and provide specific feedback to improve writing which vastly reduces the instructor grading load (Baker et al., 2019).

Automated Assessment and Feedback

Automated Assessment Tools (AAT) are AI enabled grading systems used in teaching and learning environments which automate student evaluation in the program, and such tools are used in computer classes to provide feedback to students and highlight their areas of improvement (Cipriano & Fachada, 2022). In other words, AAT is an assessment tool to provide automated evaluation of student work and provide immediate feedback for learning improvements. The meta-analysis suggests that the AI assessment tools can perform assessment and evaluation with high efficiency and accuracy; however, due to calibration and supervised machine learning requirements, they are applicable to high enrolled classes (Zawacki-Richter, 2019). In other words, AI assessment tools such as ML can perform assessment and evaluation seamlessly with high efficiency and accuracy but need more resource allocation due to calibration and supervised requirements.

Teacher feedback is crucial for student learning; however, providing students immediate one-to-one feedback in real-time is not achievable on a regular basis as teachers have limited time and resources during instruction (Demszky et al., 2024; Deeva et al., 2021; Osakwe et al., 2022). The efficacy of feedback depends on four levels such as feedback about the self, task, process, or self-regulation (Osakwe et al., 2022). Fortunately, such goals are achievable through the proper use of technology such as Automated Feedback Tools (AFT). During the learning process, the AFT can provide the necessary feedback in education to improve students' learning which involves the use of natural language processes (Osakwe et al., 2022). The AFT's allows feedback processing with speed, precision, and scale which exceeds human capabilities and effectively exercises teacher feedback competently (Buckingham Shum et al., 2023).

Professional Development

Business and industries use AI to facilitate employee on the job training with the same features that engage students instructionally (George & Wooden, 2023). Capitalizing on methods found in business, higher education leaders have the option to provide professional development that is delivered through an AI platform (Maio & Yao, 2021). Such professional development programs use student achievement data, observations, and instructor responses to training to build customized plans to improve pedagogy (Baker et al., 2019). Such training provides professional development experiences that are designed to move instructors through the material while closing knowledge gaps and providing learning scenarios that are specific to the course objectives (Lu et. al., 2024). AI collaboration tools encourage peer to peer conversations and build the online community (al-Zyoud, 2020). More advanced options may analyze individual learning styles and build prescriptive training modules around those needs on demand (George & Wooden, 2023). Continual data tracking provides the avenue for coordinated learning with multiple pathways to ensure instructors are equipped with current theory and practice with greatly reduced need for direct input from administrative faculty (Miao & Yao, 2021).

AI for Administrative Efficiency

AI is poised to lower university costs through improved administrative efficiency (Chen & Do, 2014). Generative AI offers the ability to automate and streamline admissions, enrollment, and scheduling processes autonomously (Schiff, 2022). Through access to rapid data analytics accessed in student information systems (SIS), AI models are able to predict student success at particular institutions with up to 97% accuracy and have been doing so for over a decade (Acikkar & Akay, 2009). Predictors of at-risk students through data in the admissions process can equip higher education institutions to provide the resources needed by incoming students. These same data analysis processes are able to analyze admission patterns, identify trends, and identify possible biases and geographic patterns in admission decisions (Andris et al., 2012; Çağataylı & Çelebi, 2022). Models using artificial neural networks in China identified geographic patterns to higher education enrollment decisions that had gone unobserved previously (Feng et al., 2011). Having access to this type of analysis during the admission season affords universities the opportunity to identify observed and unobserved admission patterns that marginalize students in time to avert such outcomes, as well as building optimal systems to support learners (Çağataylı & Çelebi, 2022).

AI neural networks provide valuable institutional insight for institutional planning and educational services (Chen & Do, 2014). Large scale data analysis using SIS course plans, student transcripts, prior course taking behavior, and available faculty provide high level analysis for planning course offerings, educational supports, and faculty lines within programs (Kardan et al., 2013). Higher education institutions are able to identify trends in course taking (Bahadir, 2016) and determine alignment with current marketplace demands (Zawacki-Richter, 2019). Higher education institutions are also able to use data analysis to predict high demand fields and to allocate capital for maximum benefit of investment (George & Wooden, 2023).

Facilities Management

Integration of AI into facilities management in higher education offers key advancements in the efficiency, sustainability, and overall management of campus operations (Lavy, 2008). Higher education campuses consist of multiple buildings with differing purposes as compared to other sectors (Amaratunga & Baldry, 2000). AI driven systems have the capacity to monitor and analyze data from multiple buildings and multiple control systems such as HVAC, lighting, and security. The integration of AI technologies allows for consistent monitoring of those different building systems, enabling real-time adjustments that optimize energy usage, reduce operational costs and enhance the comfort of campus in an area of oversight which is historically short staff and budget constrained (Wright & Wilton, 2012). AI autonomously tracks trends in work orders and identifies when significant maintenance or replacement is optimal (Pampana et al., 2022). In regard to energy management, AI optimizes climate control and building systems in real time thereby reducing energy consumption costs (George & Wooden,2023). Further analytics can include sustainability initiatives to align with the institution's environmental goals.

Proactive management of schedules, space planning, and maintenance operations allows institutions to optimize allocations of resources (Pampana et al., 2022). Similarly to the way AI functions with student SIS data, facilities using AI gather data from multiple campus operations to offer predictive maintenance schedules (Lavy, 2008). Optimally scheduled maintenance is strategically coordinated during low usage times or with minimal equipment downtime (Amaratunga & Baldry, 2000). Additionally, space usage analytics allow higher education institutions to optimize the allocation of resources, ensuring that facilities are used efficiently and evolve with the needs of students and faculty (Yoon et al., 2021). While the adoption of AI analysis in facilities management offers multiple cost savings, these measures also require consideration of data privacy and cybersecurity given the sensitive nature of the information involved (Pampana et al., 2022).

Library Services

Instruction and reference librarians with information technology expertise are ideally situated to collaboratively build policies between the institution, faculty, and staff for ethical adoption of AI technologies (Federer, 2018). Educators and administrators acknowledge the importance of AI literacy and education for entry into the workforce, and librarians are information specialists (Cox, 2022). A librarians' expertise in data management has shifted from data storage to data services, by which librarians provide access to a combined networked data system (Koltay, 2019). Librarians are poised to instruct students and faculty in higher education to create effective prompts for ethical AI use (Martin & Armstrong, 2024). Critical thought instruction on prompt writing can be implemented through authentic research during interactions with the librarian (Cox, 2022).

Future Trends and Innovations

The integration of AI into academic institutions is rapidly reshaping the landscape of higher education (Zawacki-Richter, 2019). As AI increasingly permeates postsecondary systems, it offers both transformative potential as well as possible pitfalls. The complexities of these resources place additional demands on educators even though processes are streamlined. Institutions will need advances in infrastructure development and increased digital literacy by those using the technologies (George & Wooten, 2023). In higher education, the nature of work is expected to change with the implementation of AI technologies. Implementation of such tools requires thoughtful planning for adequate human oversight and management of AI tools. Educating faculty to participate in the ethical and effective usage of AI will require increased professional development to address the needs in digital literacy and AI usage (Miao &Ya0, 2021). The shift in instruction should allow more room for human-centric teaching, augmenting rather than replacing the instructor's role. Reskilling the current institution faculty and staff members must include professional development on AI technology usage.

AI technologies are merging and overlapping which creates more powerful applications. Neural networks, large language models, and deep learning technologies are melding into ever more powerful applications in rapid cycles (Taylor, 2020). Different types of AI working together offer interdisciplinary applications for both the academic and administrative benefit of universities and students (Niewint-Gori, 2023). Improved integration of systems is predicted to envelop students from multiple perspectives. Ongoing data analytics will improve to provide more accurate recommendations and prescriptive instruction for course design, intelligent tutoring, and personalized learning to increase the automation and responsiveness of instruction (George & Wooden, 2023). AI systems have enormous potential to support students, faculty, administrators, and facility managers throughout the higher education system (Zawacki-Rickter, 2019). Integrated learning experiences with AI technologies will work together between the students, instructors, and administrators with instantaneous data flow and analytics. The discourse in AI technologies underscores the necessity of leveraging AI to support instruction and administration but to also ethically examine the implications of AI decisions (Schiff, 2022). Instructors will need to adapt their pedagogy to the complexities of AI technologies as institutional policies lag behind the rapid pace of evolving AI technologies and integrations (Niewint-Gori, 2023). These technologies will require design collaboration to ensure equity in implementation and access across the institution (Selwyn, 2022).

Ethical Considerations and Challenges

AI in education is believed to have significant potential to facilitate personalized learning for students and raises ethical concerns and biases in educational communities. The uncertainty of which AI algorithms are commonly used and how they influence online higher education raises concern (Ouyang et al., 2022). To reduce the biases or ethical considerations, technological perspectives are expected to consider the potential of integrating students' learning processes with interactions between AI, educators, and students to address the issues of biases and the non-transparency of why and how of AI algorithms decisions (Hwang et al., 2020). To reduce the biases or ethical considerations, technological perspectives are expected to consider potentials of integrating students' learning processes which strengthens interactions among AI developers, educators, and students (Hwang et al., 2020). In other words, to address the issues of biases and non-transparency of why and how AI algorithms decisions are made, the process should consider collaboration among students, teachers, and AI algorithms writers. While designing AI in education courses, awareness that AI technologies are the part of larger educational systems with several components such as learners, instructors, information and resources, etc. is extremely important (Riedl, 2019). Additionally, to improve the opportunities for students' learning outcomes, the adopted advanced AI technologies should collect and analyze real-time data processing.

In higher education, to achieve high quality predictions, assessments or recommendations, AI-enabled systems should consider student diversity for both learning and overall performance, and it is recommended to use advanced AI algorithms to improve student learning motivation, engagement and performance (Ouyang et al.,

2022). Dogan et al., (2023) emphasized the importance of ethical consideration of AI in higher education with the following statement, "developing policies and strategies is a high priority for educational institutions to better benefit from artificial intelligence technologies and design human-centered online learning processes" (p. 10). The research suggests that while using the AI-supported language learning tools, learners still prefer working with their peers collaboratively (Yang & Kyun, 2022). This indicates that AI course designers should include components of student collaboration in designing AI tools (Yang & Kyun, 2022). Thus, the recommendations of course designers is to consider these characteristics to improve student-centered personalized learning with proper considerations for learning preferences, ethics, fairness, and biases (Hwang et al., 2020).

CONCLUSION

AI in higher education has existed as an instructional tool for the last few decades. Adoption of AI in higher education, particularly the personalized learning system, has triggered a debate in the educational community about its potential, usefulness, and impact. Additionally, despite the growing use, higher educational institutions are still trying to find the balance to fully use its potential of AI for student learning outcomes. Given the current understanding of AI in higher education, several tools have made their ways to produce and provide improved student learning experiences. Learning systems such as intelligent tutoring, NLP, robotics, etc. have become a part of teaching and learning processes. These learning systems have stimulated one-to-one personalized learning based on student learning needs, classroom environment, and content area requirements while providing cognitive scaffolding, engaged student dialogue, and higher content retainment.

Integrating AI into higher education represents a transformative shift in how higher education institutions enhance pedagogy, instruction, and administration. As AI technologies have evolved over the years, their impact on higher education has grown significantly, providing multiple tools and systems that enhance the learning experience and streamline administrative processes. The broad applications of AI in higher education have grown from simple automation tools to sophisticated systems that fundamentally reshape how instruction is delivered and managed. From the development of rule-based systems that performed specific tasks such as grading multiple choice exams, AI has morphed into increasingly complex competencies. NLP, machine learning algorithms, and intelligent tutoring systems are capable of responding to human behavior and inputs through data analysis in nuanced ways to improve learning.

AI's application has expanded from enhancing course development and improving accessibility to personalizing learning experiences. For example, NLP enables chatbots and personal assistants to interact with students and address learning needs in real time, providing instantaneous support and feedback. Adaptive learning systems analyze student performance and adjust instructional content to meet individual learning needs, offering personalized learning experiences that accommodate different learning styles and needs. These technologies can provide tailored educational experiences to increase engagement and ensure adequate support for success in content mastery.

Enhanced instructional design includes not only these types of individually tailored educational experiences but also offers the ability to analyze vast amounts of educational data to identify patterns and trends, providing insights into which instructional methods are most effective for different types of learners. These insights inform the development of instructional materials tailored to student needs to create more relevant and impactful instructional experiences. Instructional design is enhanced when accessibility increases. Speech recognition software, AI translation tools, and formatting makes instruction accessible to students with special education needs. To further personalize learning, AI technologies continuously analyze student performance data and adapt instructional content accordingly. Additionally, AI technologies enhance the educational experience in blended learning by facilitating the integration of online and offline learning environments, providing individualized online experiences to scaffold students to success in face-to-face environments. Educators receive comprehensive views of student performance and recommended pacing and pathways for students to achieve instructional goals.

AI's role in higher education is not limited to enhancing instructional design and pedagogy; it also streamlines administrative tasks, supports faculty through automated assessments, and promotes professional development. AI powered systems can improve library services, ensuring that resources are available to meet research and learning needs. Librarians hold the key to efficient access to information services. For example, librarians can provide training and collaboration in how to effectively use AI systems to obtain the most effective search outcomes. By automating routine tasks, AI allows educators to focus more time on teaching and mentoring students. AI platforms recommend professional development courses based on individual educator needs and content. By supporting faculty development, AI technologies strengthen and hone the skills of instructors. Facilities management efficiency is increased with AI systems monitoring. Environmental controls such as air conditioning and heating automatically adjust with building usage to reduce energy consumption and costs. Streamlining administrative tasks in coursework, library science, and facility maintenance increases the resources to support instruction in higher education.

With the increased use of AI tools in higher education, morality has been questioned. The concerns of AI use in higher education have been raised due to algorithmic biases, lack of awareness of AI technologies, issues of automation, and matters surrounding academic integrity. The need is to understand how notions of Fairness, Accountability, Transparency, and Ethics are defined and how challenges are related to creating the capacity to make ethical changes or integrations in a timely manner (Memarian & Doleck, 2023). To achieve the goals of unbiased AI tools usage, anti-biased frameworks should be adopted. In the end, such processes can be analyzed with "everyday decision-making against best practices and get to label processes that are fair vs. need further improvement" (Memarian & Doleck, 2023, p. 10). As AI technologies use human-generated data, a lack of regulation on how to use that data exists; therefore, appropriate AI policies on ethics must be put into place (Dogan et al., 2023).

REFERENCES

Acikkar, M., & Akay, M. F. (2009). Support vector machines for predicting the admission decision of a candidate to the School of Physical Education and Sports at Cukurova University. *Expert Systems with Applications*, 36(3), 7228–7233. DOI: 10.1016/j.eswa.2008.09.007

al-Zyoud, H. M. M. (2020). The role of artificial intelligence in teacher professional development. *Universal Journal of Educational Research*, 8(11B), 6263–6272. DOI: 10.13189/ujer.2020.082265

Alamri, H. A., Watson, S., & Watson, W. (2020). Learning technology models that support personalization within blended learning environments in higher education. *TechTrends*, 65(1), 62–78. DOI: 10.1007/s11528-020-00530-3

Alqahtani, T., Badreldin, H. A., Alrashed, M., Alshaya, A. I., Alghamdi, S. S., Bin Saleh, K., Alowais, S. A., Alshaya, O. A., Rahman, I., Al Yami, M. S., & Albekairy, A. M. (2023). The emergent role of artificial intelligence, natural learning processing, and large language models in higher education and research. *Research in Social & Administrative Pharmacy*, 19(8), 1236–1242. DOI: 10.1016/j.sapharm.2023.05.016 PMID: 37321925

Amaratunga, D., & Baldry, D. (2000). Assessment of facilities management performance in higher education properties. *Facilities*, 18(7/8), 293–301. DOI: 10.1108/02632770010340681

Andris, C., Cowen, D., & Wittenbach, J. (2013). Support vector machine for spatial variation. *Transactions in GIS*, 17(1), 41–61. DOI: 10.1111/j.1467-9671.2012.01354.x

Arogundade, O. (2023). Structuring Knowledge Bases with AI and Machine Learning. *Information and Knowledge Management*, 13(1), 27–35. DOI: 10.7176/IKM/13-1-03

Bada, J. K., Laamanen, M., & Miiro, E. (2013). A project-based learning approach for teaching robotics to undergraduates. *Makerere Journal of Higher Education*, 5(1), 35–47. DOI: 10.4314/majohe.v5i1.3

Bahadır, E. (2016). Using Neural Network and Logistic Regression Analysis to Predict Prospective Mathematics Teachers' Academic Success upon Entering Graduate Education. *Educational Sciences: Theory & Practice*. Advance online publication. DOI: 10.12738/estp.2016.3.0214

Baídoo-Anu, D., & Owusu Ansah, L. (2023). Education in the era of generative artificial intelligence (AI): Understanding the potential benefits of chatgpt in promoting teaching and learning. *Journal of AI*, 7(1), 52–62. DOI: 10.61969/jai.1337500

Baker, T., Smith, L., & Anissa, N. (2019). Educ-AI-tion rebooted? Exploring the future of artificial intelligence in schools and colleges. https://media.nesta.org.uk/documents/Future_of_AI_and_education_v5_WEB.pdf

Bates, T., Cobo, C., Mariño, O., & Wheeler, S. (2020). Can artificial intelligence transform higher education? *International Journal of Educational Technology in Higher Education*, 17(1), 42. Advance online publication. DOI: 10.1186/s41239-020-00218-x

Baykasoğlu, A., Özbel, B. K., Dudaklı, N., Subulan, K., & Şenol, M. E. (2018). Process mining based approach to performance evaluation in computer-aided examinations. *Computer Applications in Engineering Education*, 26(5), 1841–1861. DOI: 10.1002/cae.21971

Bond, M., Khosravi, H., De Laat, M., Bergdahl, N., Negrea, V., Oxley, E., & Siemens, G. (2024). A meta systematic review of artificial intelligence in higher education: A call for increased ethics, collaboration, and rigour. *International Journal of Educational Technology in Higher Education*, 21(1), 4.

Bozkurt, A., Karadeniz, A., Baneres, D., Guerrero-Roldán, A. E., & Rodríguez, M. E. (2021). Artificial intelligence and reflections from educational landscape: A review of AI studies in half a century. *Sustainability (Basel)*, 13(2), 800. DOI: 10.3390/su13020800

Buckingham Shum, S., Lim, L., Boud, D., Bearman, M., & Dawson, P. (2023). A comparative analysis of the skilled use of automated feedback tools through the lens of teacher feedback literacy. *International Journal of Educational Technology in Higher Education*, 20(1), 40. Advance online publication. DOI: 10.1186/s41239-023-00410-9

Çağataylı, M., & Çelebi, E. (2022). Estimating academic success in higher education using big five personality traits, a machine learning approach. *Arabian Journal for Science and Engineering*, 47(2), 1289–1298. DOI: 10.1007/s13369-021-05873-4

Carbonell, J. (1970). AI in CAI: an artificial intelligence approach to computer aided instruction. *Science, 167*, 190e202.

Chen, J.-F., & Do, Q. H. (2014). Training neural networks to predict student academic performance: A comparison of cuckoo search and gravitational search algorithms. *International Journal of Computational Intelligence and Applications*, 13(01), 1450005. DOI: 10.1142/S1469026814500059

CIPD. (2024). *AI generated content: Considerations for course design*. Center for Integrated Professional Development, Illinois State. https://prodev.illinoisstate.edu/pedagogy/ai/

Cipriano, B. P., Fachada, N., & Alves, P. (2022). Drop project: An automatic assessment tool for programming assignments. *SoftwareX*, 18, 101079. DOI: 10.1016/j.softx.2022.101079

College Board. (2024, March 12). *Digital SAT launches across the country, completing the transition to digital and providing a simpler testing experience for students and educators*. College Board. https://newsroom.collegeboard.org/digital-sat-launches-across-country-completing-transition-digital-and-providing-simpler-testing

Cox, A. (2023). How artificial intelligence might change academic library work: Applying the competencies literature and the theory of the professions. *Journal of the Association for Information Science and Technology*, 74(3), 367–380. DOI: 10.1002/asi.24635

Crawford, J., Cowling, M., & Allen, K.-A. (2023). Leadership is needed for ethical ChatGPT: Character, assessment, and learning using artificial intelligence (AI). *Journal of University Teaching & Learning Practice*, 20(3). Advance online publication. DOI: 10.53761/1.20.3.02

Crompton, H., & Burke, D. (2023). Artificial intelligence in higher education: The state of the field. *International Journal of Educational Technology in Higher Education*, 20(1), 22. DOI: 10.1186/s41239-023-00392-8

Crompton, H., & Song, D. (2021). The potential of artificial intelligence in higher education. *Revista Virtual Universidad Católica del Norte*, 62(62), 1–4. DOI: 10.35575/rvucn.n62a1

Deeva, G., Bogdanova, D., Serral, E., Snoeck, M., & De Weerdt, J. (2021). A review of automated feedback systems for learners: Classification framework, challenges and opportunities. *Computers & Education*, 162, 104094. DOI: 10.1016/j.compedu.2020.104094

Demszky, D., Liu, J., Hill, H. C., Jurafsky, D., & Piech, C. (2024). Can Automated Feedback Improve Teachers' Uptake of Student Ideas? Evidence From a Randomized Controlled Trial in a Large-Scale Online Course. *Educational Evaluation and Policy Analysis*, 46(3), 483–505. DOI: 10.3102/01623737231169270

Dever, D. A., Azevedo, R., Cloude, E. B., & Wiedbusch, M. (2020). The impact of autonomy and types of informational text presentations in game-based environments on learning: Converging multi-channel processes data and learning outcomes. *International Journal of Artificial Intelligence in Education*, 30(4), 581–615. DOI: 10.1007/s40593-020-00215-1

Dogan, M. E., Goru Dogan, T., & Bozkurt, A. (2023). The use of artificial intelligence (AI) in online learning and distance education processes: A systematic review of empirical studies. *Applied Sciences (Basel, Switzerland)*, 13(5), 3056. DOI: 10.3390/app13053056

Duong, L. (2017). *Natural language processing for resource-poor languages*. University of Melbourne.

Fariani, R. I., Junus, K., & Santoso, H. B. (2022). A systematic literature review on personalised learning in the higher education context. *Technology. Knowledge and Learning*, 28(2), 449–476. DOI: 10.1007/s10758-022-09628-4

Federer, L. (2018). Defining data librarianship: A survey of competencies, skills, and training. *Journal of the Medical Library Association: JMLA*, 106(3). Advance online publication. DOI: 10.5195/jmla.2018.306 PMID: 29962907

Feng, S., Zhou, S., & Liu, Y. (2011). Research on data mining in university admissions decision-making. *International Journal of Advancements in Computing Technology*, 3(6), 176–186. DOI: 10.4156/ijact.vol3.issue6.21

Fuchs, K. (2023). Exploring the opportunities and challenges of NLP models in higher education: Is chat GPT a blessing or a curse? *Frontiers in Education*, 8, 1166682. Advance online publication. DOI: 10.3389/feduc.2023.1166682

Gabriele, L., Marocco, D., Bertacchini, F., Pantano, P., & Bilotta, E. (2017). An educational robotics lab to investigate cognitive strategies and to foster learning in an arts and humanities course degree. *International Journal of Online Engineering*, 13(4), 7–19. DOI: 10.3991/ijoe.v13i04.6962

George, B., & Wooden, O. (2023). Managing the strategic transformation of higher education through artificial intelligence. *Administrative Sciences*, 13(9), 196. DOI: 10.3390/admsci13090196

Gerecke, U., & Wagner, B. (2007). The Challenges and Benefits of Using Robots in Higher Education. *Intelligent Automation & Soft Computing*, 13(1), 29–43. DOI: 10.1080/10798587.2007.10642948

Goldman, S. R., Taylor, J., Carreon, A., & Smith, S. J. (2024). Using ai to support special education teacher workload. *Journal of Special Education Technology*, 39(3), 434–447. DOI: 10.1177/01626434241257240

Guan, C., Mou, J., & Jiang, Z. (2020). Artificial intelligence innovation in education: A twenty-year data-driven historical analysis. *International Journal of Innovation Studies*, 4(4), 134–147. DOI: 10.1016/j.ijis.2020.09.001

Han, K. (2021). Fostering students' autonomy and engagement in efl classroom through proximal classroom factors: Autonomy-supportive behaviors and student-teacher relationships. *Frontiers in Psychology*, 12, 767079. DOI: 10.3389/fpsyg.2021.767079 PMID: 34744946

Hwang, G., Sung, H., Chang, S., & Huang, X. (2020). A fuzzy expert system-based adaptive learning approach to improving students' learning performances by considering affective and cognitive factors. *Computers and Education: Artificial Intelligence*, 1, 100003. DOI: 10.1016/j.caeai.2020.100003

Hwang, G. J., Xie, H., Wah, B. W., & Gašević, D. (2020). Vision, challenges, roles and research issues of artificial intelligence in education. *Computers and Education: Artificial Intelligence*, 1, 100001. DOI: 10.1016/j.caeai.2020.100001

Ismail, H., Hussein, N., Harous, S., & Khalil, A. (2023). Survey of personalized learning software systems: A taxonomy of environments, learning content, and user models. *Education Sciences*, 13(7), 741. DOI: 10.3390/educsci13070741

Kang, Y., Cai, Z., Tan, C. W., Huang, Q., & Liu, H. (2020). Natural language processing (NLP) in management research: A literature review. J. Manag. *Analyt.*, 7(2), 139–172. DOI: 10.1080/23270012.2020.1756939

Kardan, A. A., Sadeghi, H., Ghidary, S. S., & Sani, M. R. F. (2013). Prediction of student course selection in online higher education institutes using neural network. *Computers & Education*, 65, 1–11. DOI: 10.1016/j.compedu.2013.01.015

Kay, R. H., & Lauricella, S. (2011). Exploring the benefits and challenges of using laptop computers in higher education classrooms: A formative analysis. *Canadian Journal of Learning and Technology / La revue canadienne de l'apprentissage et de la technologie, 37*(1). DOI: 10.21432/T2S598

Kew, S. N., & Tasir, Z. (2022). Learning analytics in online learning environment: A systematic review on the focuses and the types of student-related analytics data. *Technology. Knowledge and Learning*, 27(2), 405–427. DOI: 10.1007/s10758-021-09541-2

Koltay, T. (2019). Accepted and emerging roles of academic libraries in supporting research 2.0. *Journal of Academic Librarianship*, 45(2), 75–80. DOI: 10.1016/j.acalib.2019.01.001

Kurtz, G., Amzalag, M., Shaked, N., Zaguri, Y., Kohen-Vacs, D., Gal, E., Zailer, G., & Barak-Medina, E. (2024). Strategies for integrating generative AI into higher education: Navigating challenges and leveraging opportunities. *Education Sciences*, 14(5), 503. DOI: 10.3390/educsci14050503

Lavy, S. (2008). Facility management practices in higher education buildings: A case study. *Journal of Facilities Management*, 6(4), 303–315. DOI: 10.1108/14725960810908163

Li, F., He, Y., & Xue, Q. (2021). Progress, Challenges and Countermeasures of Adaptive Learning: A Systematic Review. *Educational Technology and Society, 24*(3), 238–255. https:// eric. ed. gov/? id= EJ130 5781

Lin, C., Cheng, E. S., Huang, A. Y., & Yang, S. J. (2024). DNA of learning behaviors: A novel approach of learning performance prediction by NLP. *Computers and Education: Artificial Intelligence*, 6, 100227. DOI: 10.1016/j.caeai.2024.100227

Lu, J., Zheng, R., Gong, Z., & Xu, H. (2024). Supporting teachers' professional development with generative AI: The effects on higher order thinking and self-efficacy. *IEEE Transactions on Learning Technologies*, 17, 1279–1289. DOI: 10.1109/TLT.2024.3369690

Martin, J., & Armstrong, M. (2024, April 12). *Tips and trends: AI developments and resources for academic librarians*. Association of College & Research Libraries https://acrl.ala.org/IS/tips-and-trends-ai-developments-and-resources-for-academic-librarians/

Memarian, B., & Doleck, T. (2023). Fairness, accountability, transparency, and ethics (FATE) in artificial intelligence (AI) and higher education: A systematic review. *Computers and Education: Artificial Intelligence*, 5, 100152. DOI: 10.1016/j.caeai.2023.100152

Miao, Y., & Yao, Y. (2021). Professional development of college teachers in the era of artificial intelligence: Role rebuilding and development path. In Sugumaran, V., Xu, Z., & Zhou, H. (Eds.), *Application of intelligent systems in multi-modal information analytics* (Vol. 1233, pp. 618–626). Springer International Publishing., DOI: 10.1007/978-3-030-51431-0_89

NEA. (2021, March 25). *Rethinking the classroom for blended learning.* National Education Association. https://www.nea.org/professional-excellence/student-engagement/tools-tips/rethinking-classroom-blended-learning

Niewint-Gori, J. (2023). *A snapshot of the evolving landscape of artificial intelligence in education.* Ital-IA. https://www.semanticscholar.org/paper/A-snapshot-of-the-evolving landscape-of-artificial-Niewint-Gori/cc5410f5cd3dc0fd230e31182d-cff204468b6dbf

Nilsson, N. J. (1998). *Artificial intelligence: A new synthesis.* Morgan Kaufmann Publishers, Inc.

Osakwe, I., Chen, G., Whitelock-Wainwright, A., Gašević, D., Pinheiro Cavalcanti, A., & Ferreira Mello, R. (2022). Towards automated content analysis of educational feedback: A multi-language study. *Computers and Education: Artificial Intelligence*, 3, 100059. DOI: 10.1016/j.caeai.2022.100059

Ouyang, F., & Jiao, P. (2021). Artificial intelligence in education: The three paradigms. *Computers & Education: Artificial Intelligence*, 100020, 100020. Advance online publication. DOI: 10.1016/j.caeai.2021.100020

Ouyang, F., Zheng, L., & Jiao, P. (2022). Artificial intelligence in online higher education: A systematic review of empirical research from 2011 to 2020. *Education and Information Technologies*, 27(6), 7893–7925. DOI: 10.1007/s10639-022-10925-9

Pampana, A. K., Jeon, J., Yoon, S., Weidner, T. J., & Hastak, M. (2022). Data-driven analysis for facility management in higher education institution. *Buildings (Basel, Switzerland)*, 12(12), 2094. DOI: 10.3390/buildings12122094

Perez Vallejos, E., Dowthwaite, L., Creswich, H., Portillo, V., Koene, A., Jirotka, M., McCarthy, A., & McAuley, D. (2021). The impact of algorithmic decision-making processes on young people's well-being. *Health Informatics Journal*, 27(1), 146045822097275. DOI: 10.1177/1460458220972750 PMID: 33446031

Popenici, S., & Kerr, S. (2017). Exploring the impact of artificial intelligence on teaching and learning in higher education. *Research and Practice in Technology Enhanced Learning*, 12(1), 22. Advance online publication. DOI: 10.1186/s41039-017-0062-8 PMID: 30595727

Prinsloo, P., Khalil, M., & Slade, S. (2024). Vulnerable student digital well-being in AI-powered educational decision support systems in higher education. *British Journal of Educational Technology*, 55(5), 2075–2092. DOI: 10.1111/bjet.13508

Riedl, M. O. (2019). Human-centered artificial intelligence and machine learning. *Human Behavior and Emerging Technologies*, 1(1), 33–36. DOI: 10.1002/hbe2.117

Roski, M., Sebastian, R., Ewerth, R., Hoppe, A., & Nehring, A. (2024). Learning analytics and the Universal Design for Learning (UDL): A clustering approach. *Computers & Education*, 214, 105028. DOI: 10.1016/j.compedu.2024.105028

Sánchez, H., Martínez, L. S., & González, J. D. (2019). Educational robotics as a teaching tool in higher education institutions: A bibliographical analysis. *Journal of Physics: Conference Series*, 1391(1), 012128. DOI: 10.1088/1742-6596/1391/1/012128

Schiff, D. (2022). Education for AI, not AI for education: The role of education and ethics in national AI policy strategies. *International Journal of Artificial Intelligence in Education*, 32(3), 527–563. DOI: 10.1007/s40593-021-00270-2

Sedlmeier, P. (2001). Intelligent tutoring systems. In Neil. J. Smelser, & Paul. B. Baltes (Eds.), International Encyclopedia of the Social & Behavioral Sciences (pp. 7674e7678). Pergamon. https://doi.org/DOI: 10.1016/B0-08-043076-7/01618-1

Selwyn, N. (2022). The future of AI and education: Some cautionary notes. *European Journal of Education*, 57(4), 620–631. DOI: 10.1111/ejed.12532

Shoaib, M., Sayed, N., Singh, J., Shafi, J., Khan, S., & Ali, F. (2024). AI student success predictor: Enhancing personalized learning in campus management systems. *Computers in Human Behavior*, 158, 108301. DOI: 10.1016/j.chb.2024.108301

Shu, X., & Ye, Y. (2023). Knowledge discovery: Methods from data mining and machine learning. *Social Science Research*, 110, 102817. DOI: 10.1016/j.ssresearch.2022.102817 PMID: 36796993

Spolaôr, N., & Benitti, F. B. V. (2017). Robotics applications grounded in learning theories on tertiary education: A systematic review. *Computers & Education*, 112, 97–107. DOI: 10.1016/j.compedu.2017.05.001

Steenbergen-Hu, S., & Cooper, H. (2014). A meta-analysis of the effectiveness of intelligent tutoring systems on college students' academic learning. *J. Educ.Psychol., 106*(2), 331e347. https://psycnet.apa.org/doi/10.1037/a0034752

Taylor, R. D. (2020). Quantum artificial intelligence: A "precautionary" U.S. approach? *Telecommunications Policy*, 44(6), 101909. DOI: 10.1016/j.telpol.2020.101909

Verdú, E., Regueras, L. M., Gal, E., De Castro, J. P., Verdú, M. J., & Kohen-Vacs, D. (2017). Integration of an intelligent tutoring system in a course of computer network design. *Educational Technology Research and Development*, 65(3), 653–677. DOI: 10.1007/s11423-016-9503-0

Wang, W., & Siau, K. (2019). Artificial intelligence, machine learning, automation, robotics, future of work and future of humanity. *Journal of Database Management*, 30(1), 61–79. DOI: 10.4018/JDM.2019010104

Weizenbaum, J. (1966). ELIZA d a computer program for the study of natural language communication between man and machine. *Commun. ACM, 26*(1), 23e28. https://doi.org/. January 1983.DOI: 10.1145/357980.357991

Welham, D. (2008). AI in training (1980–2000): Foundation for the future or misplaced optimism? *British Journal of Educational Technology*, 39(2), 287–303. DOI: 10.1111/j.1467-8535.2008.00818.x

Wright, T. S. A., & Wilton, H. (2012). Facilities management directors' conceptualizations of sustainability in higher education. *Journal of Cleaner Production*, 31, 118–125. DOI: 10.1016/j.jclepro.2012.02.030

Yang, H., & Kyun, S. (2022). The current research trend of artificial intelligence in language learning: A systematic empirical literature review from an activity theory perspective. *Australasian Journal of Educational Technology*, •••, 180–210. DOI: 10.14742/ajet.7492

Yoon, S., Weidner, T., & Hastak, M. (2021). Total-package-prioritization mitigation strategy for deferred maintenance of a campus-sized institution. *Journal of Construction Engineering and Management*, 147(3), 04020185. DOI: 10.1061/(ASCE) CO.1943-7862.0001956

Zawacki-Richter, O., Marín, V. I., Bond, M., & Gouverneur, F. (2019). Systematic review of research on artificial intelligence applications in higher education – where are the educators? *International Journal of Educational Technology in Higher Education*, 16(1), 39. Advance online publication. DOI: 10.1186/s41239-019-0171-0

Zhang, K., & Aslan, A. B. (2021). AI technologies for education: Recent research & future directions. *Computers and Education: Artificial Intelligence*, 2, 100025. DOI: 10.1016/j.caeai.2021.100025

Chapter 9
AI and the Humans in Higher Education

Geraldine Torrisi-Steele
https://orcid.org/0000-0002-6045-4114
Griffith University, Australia

ABSTRACT

This chapter, AI and the Humans in Higher Education delves into the evolving role of Artificial Intelligence (AI) in higher education, emphasizing the need for a human-centered approach to its integration. As AI technologies continue to advance, they bring both opportunities and challenges for educators and students alike. While AI has the potential to transform educational practices, there is a growing concern that techno-centric perspectives might overshadow the essential human elements of teaching and learning. This chapter argues for the importance of keeping human needs, experiences, and ethical considerations at the forefront of AI adoption in education. By advocating for a balanced approach, the chapter encourages educators to view AI as a tool that should be thoughtfully integrated into pedagogical strategies, always aiming to enhance students' educational experience.

INTRODUCTION

Artificial Intelligence (AI) is at the center stage of higher education discourse about learning and teaching. Undeniably, the sophistication and capabilities of AI technologies bring excitement, uncertainty, and even apprehension, to all the stakeholders in education contexts. The great challenge is how can (more precisely, *how should)* AI be used for the mutual benefit of educators and students? Due to the inevitable complexity of human behavior and learning and the incessant evolution

DOI: 10.4018/979-8-3373-0502-8.ch009

of technologies, the challenge and the accompanying exploratory process of integrating AI in education remains ongoing.

Although AI in education is a nascent field, the vast volumes of literature on AI and education are a testament to the scale of exploration and adoption already taking place. Literature is already rife with claims that AI is transforming higher education (Breines & Gallagher, 2020). Reflecting on the history of technology in education, it is evident that techno-centric perspectives tend to dominate. This is one reason why now is the opportune time to ensure that humans rather than technology are at the center of AI in education discourse. Another reason for ensuring that humans remain at the center of discussions is the anthropomorphic language that is commonly used in the field of AI. The term AI itself ascribes the human quality of intelligence to the technology. Applications of AI such as chatbots easily bring human qualities to technological systems. The danger of anthropomorphism in AI is that the attribution of human qualities tends to "exaggerate AI capabilities and performance" and muddies the ethical aspects such as responsibility and trust (Placani, 2024, p. 1). Amid this, it is imperative to not lose sight of the real human who is experiencing the technology. Placani (2024, p. 3) summarizes well the issue with anthropomorphic language in AI: anthropomorphic language is problematic because "it asserts an out-o-place human-centric perspective that conceals the reality of how [AI systems] work as well as their limitations". Consequently, the risk of losing sight of the human at the center is conceivably greater for AI technologies than for other existing technologies. Adopting a human-centered perspective of AI in learning and teaching in higher education is imperative.

The core intent of the present chapter is adding emphasis to the necessity human centered discussion of AI in higher education. It is hoped that the chapter evokes reflection, fuels human-centered discussion of AI in education, and helps to inform best practices. The author encourages the view of AI as part of the technological toolkit which human educators, which based on the needs of their human students and demands of discipline, decide to integrate into their learning strategies.

The concept of human-centered AI is not peculiar to the context of higher education. Human-centered AI is an emerging philosophy in the broader field of AI. AI technologies develop further and permeate more deeply human existence, the human-centered AI 'movement' is (thankfully) gaining momentum. Subsequently, before embarking on a discussion of AI in education, and human-centered AI in education it is instructive to first understand the principle of human-centered AI in the broader context.

HUMAN-CENTERED AI

With all the attention AI is receiving it may seem that AI is a very recent development. AI has been present and been used in varied contexts for several decades. The birth of AI (often referred to as the "Spring" of AI) can be considered to occur in 1950. In 1950 Alan Turing published the seminal article "Computing Machinery and Intelligence" in which he discussed machine intelligence and developed the 'Turing Test' – a machine intelligence test still used today. The article was a product of Turing's reflection on his development of a code-breaking machine (The Bombe) for the British government to break the German Enigma code used in World War II (Haenlein & Kaplan, 2019). Given that the machine he had developed broke code that was beyond human capability to do so, Turing became fascinated with the apparent intelligence of such machines. Turing himself didn't use the term artificial intelligence, the term 'artificial intelligence' was 'officially' coined six years later when Marvin Minskey and John McCarthy hosted an eight-week Dartmouth Summer Research Project on Artificial Intelligence.

Historically, AI has emerged from a techno-centric perspective, from a focus on the potential capabilities of machines and how machines might be able to do tasks that humans cannot. This techno-centric perspective persists. Techno-centric perspectives dominate the design and development of AI right across many application contexts, education included. The dominance of techno-centric perspectives in AI is increasingly problematic. To push ahead with the development of AI in a way that positions machines as superior to humans, that are autonomous with little or no regard to human agency, is detrimental to the ethical and responsible development and use of AI. Challenging the techno-centric perspectives in AI is a growing group of scientists and researchers espousing Human-centered AI. Human-centered AI is an emergent philosophy to guide the design, development, and implementation of AI technologies. Advocates of human-centered AI maintain that the design and development of AI is driven by the desire to advance technology with little regard to the effect of AI "on the human condition" (Ozmen Gariby, et al., 2023). Worryingly, the effect of AI on humans is poorly understood leaving AI open to unintended negative consequences (Ozmen Gariby, et al., 2023). None articulate the situation better than Shneiderman, a computer scientist and leading advocate of human-centeredness in AI:

"In early 1997, before Alexa and Siri were conceived, I engaged in several public debates with MIT Media Lab professor Pattie Maes about the future of computing and artificial intelligence. The starting place for our disagreement was the question of control. Maes was advancing a vision of machine autonomy, of the "proactive "software agent" that " can take initiative because it knows what your interests are". I offered a different vision: software designs that give

users high levels of understanding and control over their AI-enabled devices to preserve human agency.

Although both views of AI design have their value, I believe that pursuing a vision of AI and technology design that starts with machine autonomy is dangerous for the future of human beings, our societies, and our environment...Autonomy first-first elevates the dangers of hidden biases in algorithms for making decisions... As AI-enabled devices proliferate in the economy and our daily lives we are at a decisive moment. What will it take to put humanity on a path where humans steer AI to advance their own values and aspirations...? [Human centered AI] is a vision of how machines might augment humans, and even encourage our best impulses towards each other, rather than how they might replace humans with something supposedly better...[the goal of Human centered AI] is to amplify rather than erode human agency" (Shneiderman, 2021, p. 56).

While Shneiderman's conceptualization of human-centered AI provides a useful basis for understanding the human-centered AI philosophy, a pivotal question remains open for exploration: How can the goal of human-centered AI as amplifying rather than eroding human agency be achieved? Fulfilling the goal is complicated because AI is applied across diverse contexts. Also, the technologies are constantly and quickly evolving. Human-centered AI likely looks or even means different things in different contexts. Furthermore, as AI technologies continue to evolve the philosophies of human-centered will also need to evolve. Already researchers such as Schmager, Pappas, and Vassilakopoulou (2023) are noticing that across literature, there is some differentiation in the points of emphasis in the various definitions of human-centered AI being used by researchers (and in some cases, there is a complete absence of definition). In agreement with Schmager, Pappas, and Vassilakopoulou (2023), defining human-centered AI is non-trivial because definitions and in particular, shared definitions are important for unambiguous communication, discussion, and the formulation of strategies and action.

The Human-centered AI community is growing as evidenced by the growing volumes of literature on the topic. Human-centered AI mustn't be considered the domain of any single discipline but rather that all who are involved with AI, in whatever context or capacity, adopt the human-centered AI "ways of thinking" (Schmager, Pappas, & Vassilakopoulou, 2023, p. 4) and, importantly, continue to explore their understandings and goals to enable an AI future that is humanistic and positively influences the human condition. Refocusing on the context of education means that educators need to meld their knowledge of learning and teaching with human-centered AI thinking. Educators will need to explore what human-centered AI means and looks like as they seek to integrate AI into their strategies and classrooms.

A BRIEF HISTORY OF AI AND EDUCATION

Briefly examining the history of AI in education is important to moving forward with the implementation of AI in education in a human-centered way since our worldviews are inevitably influenced by the past.

The release of ChatGPT in November 2022 'took the world' and especially higher education by storm. Since then, AI, particularly generative AI, has dominated discussions around teaching and learning in higher education. With all the fuss it may seem that AI is a new phenomenon in higher education. However, although nascent, the use of AI in educational settings is not exactly new. AI has a long history in education. Its beginnings can be traced to EILIZA – a natural language processing program developed in the 1960s by Josepah Weizenbaum (1966). ELIZA is the predecessor for the natural language models such as ChatGPT being used today.

Soon after ELIZA Jaime R. Carbonell, set out to "show that a new and more powerful type of computer-assisted instruction CAI, based on extensive application of artificial intelligence techniques, is feasible" (Carbonell, 1970, p. 190). Carbonell wrote a set of computer programs called SCHOLAR which enabled interaction of students with the system. SCHOLAR could generate text as well as questions and answers, and impressively, could answer questions that the students posed (Carbonell, 1970). Interestingly, Carbonell observed that the system could replace most of the drill and practice systems, but they do not advocate eliminating the drill and practice system because "it will have its role for some time to come" (1970, p. 201). SCHOLAR formed the basis of what would later be referred to as an Intelligent Tutoring System. These systems could engage in dialogue with students, answer questions, and importantly provide some tailoring of educational content to help 'individualize' instruction. Throughout the 70's and 80's there were significant advancements in AI, both in theory and in the application in education. Expert systems were soon developed. These systems mimic the decision-making abilities of the human expert.

Intelligent tutoring systems and later adaptive learning systems for personalized learning became the backbone of the evolution of AI in higher education and firmly established AI in education as a field of academic study.

Realizing the promise of AI is always constrained by the technical limitations of the time. In the late 1980's through to the 1990's is what's often referred to as the "AI winter". During this time the high expectations surrounding AI were tempered by the technical limitations of the era. Many early AI projects failed to deliver on their promises resulting in reduced funding and interest. In higher education, this period was marked by a slowing in AI research and development. Despite the slowdown, the foundational work done in earlier decades helped AI remain a topic of interest, albeit with more cautious expectations. The slowdown does have a positive side. With the failure of projects to meet expectations, researchers were prompted to rethink their approaches. Thus, the AI winter served as a critical learning period which helped to lay groundwork for more robust AI systems in the future.

The late 1980s - early 90's was the second AI winter, the first being in the 1960's. The term AI winter refers to the event of slowdown that comes after each cycle of hype because reality does not match the high hopes held for the technology. Some maintain that we will soon experience another AI winter given the recent AI hype (Karim, 2024).

In the late 1990's through to the early 2000's the advent of the internet and associated world wide web and various communication technologies gave cause for a renewed interest in AI in higher education. The growing accessibility and ubiquity of personal computers, digital technologies, and connectivity prompted educators to reflect on teaching approaches and to consider how these new technologies might be used to enhance learning and teaching in higher education. At about the same time, there were greatly increased economic and competitive pressures on higher education institutions to attract and retain students. The need to support and attract students together with the increased competitive pressures on higher education institutions and the increased availabilities of new digital technologies resulted in an increased focus on student-centered learning and constructivist approaches to learning and teaching (Guan, Mou, & Jiang, 2020). Interest in AI resurged, fueled by the promise of AI to offer individualized learning, student-centered approaches along efficiencies for educators. The release of CHAT GPT, which put AI firmly in public hands, catalyzed the explosion of interest in AI in higher education.

THE ROLE OF AI IN ENHANCING LEARNING EXPERIENCES

The role and perceptions of AI in education are well captured by the definitions of AI in education over time. In the definitions of AI in education collated by Guan, Mou, and Jiang (2020) it is clear that the main contribution of AI in higher education is intelligent tutoring which, through human-like interactions and processes, can be adaptive and offer individualized interaction to remediate or guide progression based on learner activity or learner profile.

Reviews of literature on AI in higher education such as those conducted by Crompton and Burke (2023), Moroianu, Iacob and Constantin (2023), Zhai et. al. (2021), and, Zhang and Aslan (2021) provide a comprehensive summary of the key roles played by AI in higher education Key roles of AI in higher education include: AI-enabled learning environments (especially learning management systems), chatbots (for stimulating conversations, thinking and increasing learning interest and engagement), expert systems (assisting with pedagogical planning and leveraging learning management systems), intelligent tutors or agents (providing customized and timely feedback along with customizing the learning experience based on needs, preferences, and prior knowledge), machine learning (for analyzing student data at scale and creating predictive models to assist with preventative and adaptive intervention), personalized learning systems/environments (to facilitate e-learning and providing custom learning materials and tailored resources for learning), visualizations and virtual learning environments (to support collaborative learning, engagement and visual feedback as well as the visualization of information and creating immersive learning environments) (Zhang & Aslan, 2021).

From a learning perspective, the emphasis remains on the potential of AI to provide individualized or personalized learning. One developing area is AI in the domain of learning management systems (LMS) such as Moodle, Canvas, BlackBoard, and Web CT among others (Kabudi, Pappas, & Olsen, 2021). In higher education, the use of LMSs is almost ubiquitous as a way of delivering learning materials to students in flexible and efficient ways. LMSs usually offer mechanisms for facilitating collaboration, availability of course materials 24/7, multimodal methods of presenting content, and the capability for interactions such as quizzes and other interactive multimedia learning materials. However, technical aspects dominate these learning platforms and they are traditionally not perceived as adaptive to their needs (Kabudi, Pappas, & Olsen, 2021). Advances in data analytics and AI techniques have now enabled the development of AI-enabled learning systems. AI-enabled learning systems are much more adaptive and responsive and are key in providing more personalized learning in educational settings (Kabudi, Pappas, & Olsen, 2021). Contemporary AI learning systems are extending personalization capabilities by being adaptable not just to the performance of students as they work through materials but also can create student profiles and have knowledge of student backgrounds.

One example of an AI-enabled learning system is Brightspace LeaP™ (Learning and Performance Training Machine) (https://community.d2l.com/brightspace/kb/articles/4554-about-leap) is a cutting-edge AI-driven platform designed to enhance learning and performance in educational and professional settings. Developed as a response to the growing need for personalized and adaptive learning environments, Brightspace LeaP™ integrates machine learning algorithms, data analytics, and cognitive science principles to provide tailored training and educational experiences.

At its core, Brightspace LeaP™ operates by continuously analyzing user interactions, performance data, and learning patterns. This analysis enables the system to adapt content delivery in real time, ensuring that each user receives information in a manner that best suits their learning style and pace. For instance, if a learner struggles with a particular concept, Brightspace LeaP™ can offer additional resources, alternative explanations, or practice exercises to reinforce understanding.

Conversely, if a learner excels in a specific area, the system can accelerate content delivery, presenting more advanced material to maintain engagement and challenge.

One of the standout features of Brightspace LeaP™ is its ability to provide detailed feedback and performance metrics. The system tracks progress across various dimensions, such as knowledge retention, skill acquisition, and problem-solving abilities. This data is then used to generate comprehensive reports that can guide instructors or trainers in making informed decisions about curriculum adjustments, intervention strategies, or personalized coaching.

Brightspace LeaP™ is particularly valuable in environments where continuous learning and skill development are critical, such as corporate training programs, higher education, and specialized technical fields. Its adaptability, coupled with its data-driven approach, ensures that learners are not only acquiring knowledge but also applying it effectively in real-world scenarios. As AI and machine learning continue to evolve, systems like Brightspace LeaP™ are poised to play an increasingly significant role in shaping the future of education and professional development. Shelle et. al (2018) pilot-tested Birghtspace Leap and reported positive outcomes from the trial but also emphasized the necessity of the educators following appropriate principles of learning and teaching to ensure the effectiveness of the system.

Data analytics are increasingly appearing hand in hand with AI tools in higher education. With the advent and ubiquity of online learning in higher education the vast volumes of data generated are being harnessed for several purposes including to support student learning in personalized and adaptive learning systems and to provide feedback to educators and institutions about students' university experiences (Crompton & Burke, 2023). At a time when attracting and retaining students is a priority for higher education institutions big data and AI analysis of it has become indispensable for administrative and strategic directions of universities (Crompton & Burke, 2023). Literature reviews such as that by Crompton & Burke (2023) show that the focus of AI tools remains on students as intended users (72%) with a strong but lesser focus on instructors and managers as the intended users.

AI tools are also cast in the role of an AI assistant. Often referred to in the literature by a variety of names such as virtual assistant, virtual agent, intelligent tutor, etc, these systems, which include chatbots, are designed to help learners by answering questions and providing other forms of outreach and guidance to students (Crompton & Burke, 2023). An example of such an assistant is Alex who supported mathematics students by asking diagnostic questions and offering differential support depending on student needs (Kim & Bennekin, 2016 cited in Crompton & Burke 2023). Chatbots are growing a strong presence in higher education as educators seek to provide more personalized learning experiences to students while at the same time seeking efficiencies especially when working with very large student cohorts.

With the economic pressures bearing down on universities, alongside pressures for improving the student experience, seeking efficiencies in learning and teaching is becoming increasingly important. It is not surprising then that one of the most common roles of AI in higher education is in the automation assessment and feedback (Crompton & Burke, 2023). Efficiencies aside the use of AI in assessment delivery and feedback is being shown to have the potential to improve the student experience by catering to a variety of students with diverse needs and from diverse cultural backgrounds (Crompton & Burke, 2023).

It is in the domain of assessment/evaluation and feedback that the presence of AI in higher education is being felt most strongly. There are two main reasons for this. Firstly, assessment and feedback practices are consistently in the limelight since it is well-established that assessment and feedback is a critical element of student learning as well as the determinant of student performance. Secondly, given the criticality of assessment for the evaluation of student learning, the issue of academic integrity is a long-standing concern and with the evolution of digital technologies is becoming increasingly complicated. It is unsurprising then that of all aspects of teaching and learning in higher education, the impact of AI is being felt most about assessment. The entrance of generative AI (the type of AI to which Chat GPT belongs) catalyzed calls for reform to assessment and education throughout the education sector. Such reform is seen as imperative to quality assurance in higher education. For example, in Australia, the Tertiary Education Quality and Standards Agency (TESQA) calls for universities to attend to how they are dealing with AI with their assessment practices, and this is becoming a requirement of the quality assurance processes. TESQA's stance on AI in assessment, though intended for quality assurance in Australian universities distills well the key perspectives on AI in higher education:

> *The emergence of generative artificial intelligence (AI), while creating new possibilities for learning and teaching, has exacerbated existing assessment challenges within higher education. However, there is considerable expertise, based on evidence, theory and practice, about how to design assessment for a digital world, which includes artificial intelligence. AI is not new, after all, even if the current iterations of generative AI are. This document, constructed through expert collaboration, draws on this body of knowledge and outlines directions for the future of assessment. It seeks to provide guidance for the sector on ways assessment practices can take advantage of the opportunities, and manage the risks, of AI, specifically generative AI... The most immediate concern is that students may use generative AI in assessment tasks, calling into question their personal learning attainment... Moreover, we adhere to core principles underpinning an inclusive higher education system...These foundational principles include fairness, accessibility, transparency, equity, a right to privacy, and respecting students as individuals among diverse student cohorts, in alignment*

with the school sector (as per National Artificial Intelligence Taskforce, 2023). The right of students to be partners in their learning underpins all representations in this document. Given this position, we highlight the importance of ensuring learners are not disadvantaged by the inclusion of AI in assessment (Australian Government - Tertiary Education quality and Standards Agency, 2023, pp. 1-2).

TESQA (2023) goes on to provide guiding principles and propositions for the use of AI in higher education:

Principle 1 Assessment and learning experiences equip students to participate ethically and actively in a society where AI is ubiquitous (p. 2)

Principle 2 "Forming trustworthy judgments about student learning in a time of AI requires multiple, inclusive, and contextualized approaches to assessment) (p. 3)

The propositions under these guiding principles are that assessment should emphasize appropriate, authentic engagement with AI, a systemic approach to program assessment aligned with discipline; lines/qualifications, give evidence of the learning process over time and in context, and opportunities for students to work with each other and with AI, and finally, there must be security at meaningful points across a program to inform decisions about progression and completion" (pp 4-6).

With the acknowledgment of the expanding integration of AI in education, it is also been seen that AI in education has a potential role in not only providing customized learning but also in addressing issues of inclusiveness in education. In 2024, the Center for Innovation, Design, and Digital Learning (housed at the University of Kansas) published a report entitled "Inclusive Intelligence, the Impact of AI on Education for All Learners making the key points that:

AI has the potential to revolutionize teaching and learning through personalization efficiency and innovation in a way that can benefit special education programs but achieving this "requires collaboration, planning and open dialogue among all stakeholders and ensuring that decisions on the use of AI are "student-centered and focused on privacy and fairness. It is only through such careful management and collaboration with the community and parents that the significant advantages of AI for students with disabilities can be realized. Ethical considerations are paramount to the endeavor (Centre for Innovation, Design and Digital Learning, 2024, p. 7).

PUTTING THE HUMAN IN HUMAN-CENTERED AI IN EDUCATION

"The greater the impact that AI has on humans, the greater the need is for us to understand it" (Yang, Ogata, Matsui, & Chen, 2021, p. 4).

It seems that AI has much potential in education and can play an important role in student learning, institutional efficiency, and teaching practices. The discourse around AI in education is dense with terms like "individualized learning", "personalized learning" "inclusive education" and so on. These are crucial elements of the discussion around AI in education. It is good to see that the learning and the learner are occupying a lot of space in the discussion of AI in education. Emphasis on the learner and their needs rather than purely the technology is a move in the right direction. However, for most stakeholders in education, how AI works is not well understood. This is highly problematic. With other digital technologies such as online tools, understanding how the technology worked was of secondary importance (or even irrelevant) to knowing what the technology could do. Knowing the affordances of the technology enables the educator to exploit those affordances to the benefit of student learning. Knowing the affordances of AI is important too but ensuring a human-centered effective use of AI also requires understanding how the technology works, at the very least at a conceptual level. That's not to say that educators need to become AI technical experts but they need to understand how AI works to be able to strip away the apparent 'beyond human' powers of AI. The anthropomorphic language found in the field of AI taken together with the seeming neutrality of technology imbues excessive power to AI and gives it a seemingly autonomous nature. Lack of a high level of understanding of how AI technologies work masks the humans behind the AI and consistently reduces or even eliminates awareness of the human biases inherent in AI technologies.

Hence, achieving a human-centered mindset of AI among educators, students, administrators, policy makers, and all education stakeholders requires an understanding of what AI is and how it is made. The human-centered AI mindset extends beyond student-centeredness, beyond concern for learning and learning outcomes to a more contextual view that reflects the realities and complexities of the real world. To explain further and reinforce this view, it is instructive to consider Shneiderman's (2021) views on the difference between AI and human-centered AI:

Shneiderman (2021, p 57) maintains that "the difference between artificial intelligence and Human-centered AI reflects a historical and philosophical clash between two approaches to gaining knowledge about the world – Aristotle's rationalism and Leonardo da Vinci's empiricism" Rationalists, Shneiderman (2021) explains "believe in logical thinking…they believe in the perfectibility of the rules, the strength of formal methods and the constancy between different categories of things [but]…as useful as strong rules and categories are for allowing clarity of thought, they limit seeing other options and the middle ground" leading to a more mechanistic view of things. In contrast, empricists understand that "beliefs have to be continuously refined to respond to the changing realities and new concepts…

Empiricism, pursued through the empathic observation of people is the basis for much of the HCAI community [human centered AI community]".

Against the background of Shneiderman's (2021) perspectives, decisions about how AI is integrated in the instructional methods of student-centered learning and teaching must be surrounded and permeated by a more empiricist, human mindset. (On the "other side of the coin", a human mindset is also required by those developing AI and those designing and making AI systems). Following Shneiderman (2021) decision-making about how AI is used in higher education is necessarily driven by engagement with human users and stakeholders along with "naturalistic observations and a strong empathy" for the humans who are experiencing rather than simply 'using' the technology. Educators and other decision-makers involved in AI in education need to do as Shneiderman advocates, "push forward with humility about the limits of machines and people" (p. 58) and most importantly recognize the complexities, capabilities, and nuances of AI as coming from its human designers. Furthermore, adopting this mindset means that the use of AI in education is not geared toward replacing humans but to empowering humans to harness technology for positive impact.

With a human-centered mindset, when educators are decision-making about how they will use AI in their classrooms, it is not just about how their students will learn best. With the lens of human-centered AI, educators are "not blinded by the technology" and realize that while personalized learning is a great idea and that personalized learning is facilitated by profiling learners, the AI tools that do this are anything but neutral. For example in machine learning applications, data is curated and fed into the system to facilitate the training of the system. Acknowledging the complexity of context and the human element, educators should question whether data are being fed into the system. Who determined what data sets are used? What are their biases and world views? Where has the data been generated from? and are there neglected populations (e.g. economically poor who may not have the technology to engage with technology and are therefore excluded from the data sets by lack of access). A human approach demands that educators dig deep into what they are doing, and what they are using in their classroom, and remain alert to inherent human biases including their own. This critical thinking approach gives educators and all stakeholders greater control over how AI is used and the impact it will have on the humans involved in its use.

A significant element of individualized/personalized learning with AI is learning analytics. The use of learning analytics in higher education is widespread and is used across contexts from the level of the classroom to the strategic level of decision-making in institutions and at the level of policymakers in the sector. Although learning analytics have clear potential for augmenting decision-making (we often talk about evidence-based learning and data-driven decision-making), the inherent biases, lack of transparency, "lack of accountability, and threat to human autonomy and agency mitigate their benefits" (Alfredo et al., 2024). Because learning analytics is so widely used in higher education decision-making at all levels, the impact of learning analytics behind AI systems is doubtlessly significant. The impact can be positive or negative, depending on the extent to which the core principles of human-centered AI (safety, reliability, trustworthiness, and human control) are taken into consideration in both the design of the system and in how the decision-makers work with the analytics. Unfortunately, but unsurprisingly given the nascent state of AI in education, there is only minimal consideration and understanding of "human control, safety, reliability, and trustworthiness in the design and implementation of these systems". An overall and deep understanding of these crucial elements of learning analytics systems remains lacking (Alfredo, et al., 2024). What is the impact of this lack of understanding? How many educators and policymakers are making decisions based predominantly on the face value of the analytics they have access to?

It is apparent that there is limited end-user involvement right throughout the design process and a potential lack of understanding of AI and analytics at the implementation phase of the systems (Alfredo, et al., 2024). Recommendations for moving towards human-centered learning analytics and AI in education include:

1) Carefully balancing stakeholders's involvement in designing and deploying… systems throughout all design phases. 2) actively involving target end-users especially students, to delineate the balance between human control and automation, and 3) exploring safety, reliability, and trustworthiness as principles in future human-centered systems (Alfredo, et al., 2024, p. 1).

Learning analytics warrant some special but not exclusive attention in the discussion of human-centered AI in education because of their growing usage and impact on decision-making at all levels of the educational systems. However, the whole business of education, by its very nature, impacts greatly on individuals and society. If we accept that education is about preparing millions of individuals for productive, satisfying work and function in ways that benefit (rather than erode) the human condition in all societies, then human-centered AI is not just a priority but an imperative in education.

"Education aims to nurture individuals and prepare them for a society that values human-centered centered approaches. It's essential to ponder whether AI can support educational goals without compromising its fundamental values. Human-centered AI (HCAI) in education emerges as an acrucial element in this context" (Gattupalli & Maloy, 2024).

The philosophy of human-centered AI is clear although the principles and its implementation in different contexts still require a lot of work. Thoughts and 'theories' are emerging but a translation to practice is still quite a distance away. Furthermore, the landscape is ever-changing and what might be sensible or works for now will undoubtedly require revision in times to come. Delivering human-centered AI in education is a formidable challenge. A good starting point for working on human-centered AI in education is to bring to the fore the grand challenges of AI for humanity more broadly. Ozemen et. al. (2023, p. 3) articulate six human-centered AI grand challenges which are not unlike those challenges identified for AI in the broader context:

Developing AI that

(1) is human well-being oriented
(2) is responsible
(3) respects privacy,
(4) incorporates human-centered design and evaluation frameworks, and
(5) is governance and oversight enabled
(6) respects human cognitive processes at the human-AI interaction frontier – represents the ultimate product of HCAI, the vision of future human-AI interaction.

Human well-being can be impacted by AI technology in multiple ways, for good or harm. Highly automated AI can relieve humans of mundane tasks but the lack of human input can also result in a lack of control that may be needed in some situations. Because the AI lacks human common sense, values, or ethics, it may cause harm that is not anticipated in certain circumstances. The algorithms that are trained on certain data sets may have implicit biases or may not have a wide enough data set to cater to the complex contexts that occur in reality, again causing negative consequences. What is or is not included in the machine learning models underlying AI systems is not apparent or transparent to human users, removing the ability of humans to make informed decisions or judgments (Ozmen Gariby, et al., 2023).

Conversely, some aspects of AI can support well-being, since AI systems can have predictive value and can help people with health systems such as stress management and independent living (Ozmen Gariby, et al., 2023).

The nature of AI and the level of interaction humans may have with it means that there is a need to reconsider what we mean and include it in the traditional ideas of usability and also an urgent need to develop methods that can evaluate and remediate potential risks to humans in AI systems (Ozmen Gariby, et al., 2023). The impact of AI systems on humans is poorly understood. Alongside technical developments, there must be concerted efforts in research to understand people's experiences and the impact of AI systems on people.

The responsible design of AI includes the development of initiatives and standards to regulate AI and guide AI design and development. There is much work to be done on attributing accountability and liability, moral and legal in AI systems (Ozmen Gariby, et al., 2023). And of course, there is much work to be done by ethicists in coming to a good understanding of where responsibilities and liabilities may lay (Ozmen Gariby, et al., 2023). This also ties in with the obvious issues around data privacy and collection and even the right of individuals to control their data or how personal data might/could be controlled by others. Developing effective governance frameworks for AI systems and data as well as the impacts of these systems is critical to the future of AI (Ozmen Gariby, et al., 2023).

Like all other technologies, it is the design of the technology itself that ultimately impacts on the human users. The need for user-centered approaches, or more accurately participatory approaches to the design and development of AI is central to supporting a human-centered approach. When computers first emerged and then permeated society, the discipline of Human-Computer Interaction (HCI) came into being out of necessity to support non-expert users to use computers in ways that were effective and efficient. Since the development of HCI the design of technology and digital media has been (at least somewhat) informed by the theory and principles related to usability, user experience, interface design, and so on. The roots of HCI are in computer systems and most of what is known is for systems that involve screens and other interactive elements, predominantly on computers but also in other artifacts and objects that humans interact with daily.

AI is a different technology than other online and digital technologies that we are accustomed to. Although AI is developing technically there is a dearth of knowledge about the user experience and what constitutes human-centered interactions with it. Thus it is necessary to revisit conventional HCI wisdom and this requires renewal in user research, evaluation, and the whole of the design and development process (Ozmen Gariby, et al., 2023). There are many outstanding questions related to the design process of AI systems, including "What are the specific design principles and standards to support HCI in AI"? Do the principles we already have still hold? Are new ones required? "How do we effectively measure and test the evolving performance of AI systems?" What metrics and measures can we use? What new methods or approaches are needed to put humans at the center? "What new methods or frameworks do we need, along with what metrics, research methods, and design principles are necessary to "increase benevolence and decrease maleficence in AI research and development"? (Ozmen Gariby, et al., 2023, p. 35).

WHERE TO FROM HERE?

High-level thinking and directions about human-centered AI in education are emerging. The emerging principles resonate with the broader perspectives on human-centered AI across contexts. Implementing effective human-centered AI practices in education requires extrapolating from broad perspectives to a more pragmatic level.

There is a desperate need to bring actionable principles to the proverbial table of AI in higher education. Various policymakers and influential groups in education are making headway into developing actionable items to move forward with AI in education. In May 2023, the US Department of Education, Office of Educational Technology published the report on Artificial Intelligence and the Future of Teaching and Learning: Insights and Recommendations. The report is representative of the state of play among policymakers regarding AI in education.

In the report, three reasons are given as to why it is crucial to address AI in education now. The reasons include: (1) AI helping to achieve educational priorities in better ways, at scale and with lower costs. AI could help teachers to extend their support to students and the students may have better adaptive learning resources. The time and effort investment in the customisation of curricular resources can be reduced and finally using assistive AI can enhance educational services (Office of Educational Technology, 2023, p. 2).

(2) Urgency to address and raise awareness of system-level risks and anxiety about future potential risks including the need to increase transparency and thus trust. It is of the "highest importance" to ensure that there is efficacy in the ability to discern authentic information from that which though it appears authentic is inaccurate or lacks basis of reality or is subject to algorithmic biases leading to unfairness in learning opportunities (Office of Educational Technology, 2023, p. 3)

(3) With at-scale automation and implementation of AI the risk of unintended or unexpected consequences is monumental (Office of Educational Technology, 2023)

Seven recommendations are made in the report designed to align AI to policy objectives and to call education leaders to action.

The recommendations are:

> Recommendation #1: Emphasize Humans in the Loop (the author advocates this should be center humans in the loop)
> Recommendation #2: Align AI models to a Shared Vision for Education
> Recommendation # 3: Design using Modern learning principles
> Recommendation # 4 Prioritize strengthening trust
> Recommendation # 5 Inform and involve educators
> Recommendation #6 Focus R&D on addressing context and enhancing trust and safety
> Recommendation #7 Develop Education education-specific guidelines and Gaurdrails

(Office of Educational Technology, 2023)

At this juncture, a view of the state of AI and in particular human-centered AI becomes evident. The deep proliferation of AI in education is relatively recent. Awareness and urgency about the need to formulate principles and pragmatic guidelines is growing. There is a large gap between the emerging theory and the largely experimental practices in place. The necessity of human-centered AI in education and the broader AI context is rising to the surface but there is also much to be done to properly understand what human-centered AI entails or should entail both in theory and practice of education. Human-centered AI is a noble guiding philosophy for the future development and implementation of AI in education but moving forward also requires critical thinking and empathic approaches to innovation for educators, policymakers, students, communities, and the designers and developers of AI technologies.

CONCLUSION

AI is dominating the discourse in higher education. Amid the considerable excitement and some trepidation about the possibilities of AI technologies in education and broader society, it is easy to be swept away by this anthropomorphic technology, beguiled or perhaps frightened by its apparent magical qualities and its ability to perhaps be somehow more than or better than humans. Much of the discussion around AI in higher education is characteristically about the technology although there is now emerging some solid discourse that brings attention to the humans who are actually at the very center of the technology. With this in mind, the author has sought to add a voice to the growing community of proponents of human-centered AI particularly in the context of education. The author couldn't agree more with the view expressed by Shneiderman (2021) and the larger human-centered AI community that "AI should empower not replace humans".

It is hoped that from the preceding discussion in the chapter, it is abundantly clear that the integration of AI in education will, like all educational endeavors should, play a role in imparting knowledge and, most importantly, in shaping the values, beliefs, and norms of a future society. From this standpoint, it is clear that we cannot afford to focus purely on technology or consider it a replacement for humans in any way. More so, we cannot afford to blindly use AI technologies, merely considering what it can do in the absence of some understanding of what AI is and how humans make it. Biases and assumptions are a part of what it means to be human and everything that humans design or embodies those biases and assumptions. Without understanding what AI is and how it works leaves us open to the risk of accepting its products and information as true to reality and being more authoritative than the humans using it. Although there is work being done in the technical domain on developing transparent, explainable AI, AI is a persistently magical artefact for the time being at least, thus the author urges educators to question and seek knowledge about how AI works as part of the decision making in their adoption. The author also encourages educators to augment their knowledge of the theory and practice of student-centered with their understanding of not only what AI can do, but how it does what it does.

Responsibly using AI in education means taking the responsibility to adopt a critical, questioning mindset, bringing to the surface and making explicit the assumptions and values that reside in us and those that reside within the systems we use. This can only happen when we don't just acknowledge the presence of humans in AI systems but recognize the humans (i.e.student, teachers, policymakers, technology designers, and developers) involved as being at the center of AI, in education and elsewhere.

"The time of reckoning for Artificial Intelligence is now" if we are not to be faced with an "uncertain and potentially unpredictable socio-technological future [but instead] lead humanity to a future of prosperity, fairness, and well-being" (Ozmen Gariby et al., 2023, p. 38).

Given the power of education to shape the future of society, our use of AI in education needs careful consideration.

REFERENCES

Alfredo, V., Echeverria, V., Jin, Y., Yan, L., Swiecki, A., Gasevic, D., & Martinez-Maldonado, R. (2024). Human-centred learning analytics and AI in education: A systematic literature review. *Computers and education. Artificial Intelligence*, 6, 1–23.

Australian Government - Tertiary Education quality and Standards Agency. (2023). *Assessment reform for the age of artificial intelligence.* Retrieved from TESQA: https://www.teqsa.gov.au/sites/default/files/2023-09/assessment-reform-age-artificial-intelligence-discussion-paper.pdf

Breines, M., & Gallagher, M. (2020). A return to Teacherbot: Rethinking the development of educational technology at the University of Edinburgh. *Teaching in Higher Education*, 28(3), 517–531. DOI: 10.1080/13562517.2020.1825373

Carbonell, J. R. (1970). AI in CAI: An artifical-intelligence approach to computer-assisted instruction. *IEEE transactions on Man-Mahine Systems, MMS-11*(4), 190-202.

Centre for Innovation. Design and Digital Learning. (2024). *CIDDL.* The Impact of AI on Education: https://ciddl.org/wp-content/uploads/2024/04/InclusiveIntelligence_a11y_navadded.pdf

Crompton, H., & Burke, D. (2023). Artificial intelligence in higher education: State of the field. *International Journal of Educational Technology in Higher Education*, 20(22), 1–22. DOI: 10.1186/s41239-023-00392-8

Gattupalli, S., & Maloy, R. (2024, August 10). *On human centered AI in education.* https://scholarworks.umass.edu/items/5cdf7696-2916-444c-bb4c-e237755ec6b6

Guan, C., Mou, J., & Jiang, Z. (2020). Artificial intelligence innovation in education: A twenty-year data-driven historical analysis. *International Journal of Innovation Studies*, 4(4), 134–147. DOI: 10.1016/j.ijis.2020.09.001

Haenlein, M., & Kaplan, A. (2019). A Brief History of Artificial Intelligence: On the Past, Present, and Future of Artificial Intelligence. *California Management Review*, 61(4), 1–10. DOI: 10.1177/0008125619864925

Kabudi, T., Pappas, I., & Olsen, D. (2021). AI-enabled adaptive learning systems: A systematic mapping of the literature. *Computers and Education: Artificial Intelligence*, 2, 1–12. DOI: 10.1016/j.caeai.2021.100017

Karim, R. (2024, June 25). *Is an AI winter coming?: Navigating the cycles of AI hype and just regulation.* https://lens.monash.edu/@business-economy/2024/06/25/1386756/is-an-ai-winter-coming-navigating-the-cycles-of-ai-hype-and-just-regulation

Moronianu, N., Iacob, S., & Constantin, A. (2023). Artificial intelligence in education: a systematic review. *Proceedings of the 6th International Conference on Economics and Social Sciences*, (pp. 906-921). Romania.

Office of Educational Technology. (2023). *Artificial intelligence and the future of teaching and learning: insights and recommendations*. U.S. Department of Education.

Ozmen Gariby, O., Winslow, B., Andolina, S., Antona, M., Bodenschatz, A., & Coursaris, C.. (2023). Six Human centered Artificial Intelligence Grand Challenges. *International Journal of Human-Computer Interaction*, 39(3), 391–347. DOI: 10.1080/10447318.2022.2153320

Placani, A. (2024). Anthropomorphism in AI: Hype and fallacy. *AI and Ethics*, 4(3), 1–6. DOI: 10.1007/s43681-024-00419-4

Schmager, S., Pappas, I., & Vassilakopoulou, P. (2023). Defining human centered AI: A comprehensive review of HCAI literature. *The 15th Mediterranean Conference on Information Systems (MCIS) and the 6th Middle East & North Africa Conference on Digital Information Systems (MENACIS), Madrid 2023*, (pp. 1-12). Retrieved from Easycha.

Shelle, G., Earnesty, D., Pilkenton, A., & Powell, E. (2018). Adaptive Learning: An Innovative Method for Online Teaching and Learning. *Journal of Extension*, 56(5). Advance online publication. DOI: 10.34068/joe.56.05.17

Shneiderman, B. (2021). Human centered AI. *Issues in Science and Technology*, (Winter), 56–61.

Weizenbaum, J. (1966). ELIZA - a computer program for the study of natural language communication between man and machine. *Communications of the ACM*, 25(1), 23–28. DOI: 10.1145/357980.357991

Yang, S., Ogata, H., Matsui, T., & Chen, N. (2021). Human centered artificial intelligence in education: Seeing the invisible through the visible. *Computers and Education: Artificial Intelligence*, 2, 1–5. DOI: 10.1016/j.caeai.2021.100008

Zhai, X., Chu, X., Chai, C., Jong, M., Istenic, A., Spector, M., & Li, Y. (2021). A review of artificial intelligence (AI) in education from 2010 to 2020. *Complexity*, 2021(1), 1–18. DOI: 10.1155/2021/8812542

Zhang, K., & Aslan, A. (2021). AI technologies for education: Recent research & future directions. *Computers and Education: Artificial Intelligence*, 2(2), 1–11. DOI: 10.1016/j.caeai.2021.100025

Chapter 10
Ethics and Equity in AI-Driven Education

Viktor Wang
https://orcid.org/0000-0001-9557-0054
California State University, San Bernardino, USA

ABSTRACT

Ethics and Equity in AI-Driven Education, explores the critical ethical considerations and challenges that arise as artificial intelligence becomes increasingly integrated into educational systems. This chapter examines issues such as data privacy, bias in AI algorithms, and the transparency of AI decision-making processes, emphasizing the need for ethical frameworks to guide the use of AI in education. It also addresses the importance of ensuring equity in access to AI tools and resources, particularly for underserved and marginalized student populations. By highlighting the ethical implications of AI in education, this chapter underscores the responsibility of educators, developers, and policymakers to ensure that AI technologies are used in ways that promote fairness, inclusivity, and student well-being.

INTRODUCTION

As artificial intelligence (AI) continues to reshape various sectors, its impact on education is profound and far-reaching. AI offers the potential to transform the educational landscape in ways that were previously unimaginable. From personalized learning experiences (Association of College and University Educators, 2024) to predictive analytics that can improve student outcomes, AI promises to revolutionize how students learn, how educators teach, and how institutions operate. AI-powered tools and platforms, such as intelligent tutoring systems, adaptive learning technologies, and data-driven administrative systems, are already enhancing classroom instruction,

DOI: 10.4018/979-8-3373-0502-8.ch010

enabling educators to cater to the individual needs of their students, while reducing administrative burdens. These advancements could make education more accessible, efficient, and tailored to the needs of each learner, particularly for those who have historically been underserved or left behind by traditional educational methods.

Despite the immense promise that AI holds, the integration of AI into education is not without its challenges. These challenges primarily stem from ethical concerns about the way AI is used, the potential for unintended negative consequences, and the need for responsible, equitable implementation. As AI continues to gain traction in educational settings, questions of fairness, transparency, and bias are at the forefront. AI algorithms are designed to process and analyze vast amounts of data, but if the data that these systems use is biased or unrepresentative, AI tools may reinforce existing inequalities in education. For instance, an AI-powered grading system that is trained on historical data might unintentionally disadvantage students from certain backgrounds or fail to recognize the value of non-traditional learning approaches (Luan & Tsai, 2021). This type of bias can perpetuate systemic issues in education and deepen existing disparities, which raises significant concerns for educators, policymakers, and communities alike.

One of the most pressing ethical concerns related to AI in education is data privacy. The vast amount of data collected by AI systems—ranging from academic performance to behavioral patterns and even social-emotional data—raises serious questions about the protection of student privacy. AI platforms that track and analyze student data could inadvertently expose students to breaches of privacy or misuse of sensitive information. Furthermore, the storage and sharing of this data must adhere to stringent data protection laws and ethical guidelines to safeguard students' rights. As educational institutions increasingly rely on AI to guide decisions, from academic interventions to admissions and beyond, the issue of data security becomes even more critical. Ensuring that students' personal information remains confidential and is used only for its intended purposes is a fundamental responsibility of educators and institutions.

Another critical aspect of AI in education is ensuring equitable access to these technologies. While AI has the potential to revolutionize education, not all students and schools have equal access to the tools and resources needed to benefit from it. Schools in underserved or rural areas, for instance, may struggle to afford the technology infrastructure or to provide the necessary training for educators to effectively use AI-driven tools. This digital divide can exacerbate existing inequalities, leaving some students without the opportunities (Alasadi & Baiz, 2023) that AI-powered learning offers. Ensuring that all students, regardless of their socioeconomic status or geographical location, have access to the benefits of AI is essential for achieving educational equity (Ainscow, 2020). In this context, it is crucial that policymakers and educators prioritize efforts to bridge the digital divide and ensure that AI is accessible to all learners, especially those from marginalized groups.

To navigate these challenges, it is essential to establish ethical guidelines and frameworks for the development, implementation, and use of AI in education. Transparency is key to ensuring that AI systems are used responsibly and that their decision-making processes are understandable and accountable. Educators, students, and parents must be able to trust the AI systems that are shaping the educational experience. To achieve this, AI systems must be designed with transparency in mind, providing clear explanations of how decisions are made and what data is being used. This would help prevent the potential for misuse and allow stakeholders to hold AI systems accountable for their actions.

In addition to transparency, fairness is another cornerstone of ethical AI use in education. AI systems must be designed and implemented in a way that prevents discrimination and ensures that all students have an equal opportunity to succeed. This includes addressing biases in the data that AI systems rely on, as well as ensuring that algorithms are tested and refined to be as inclusive as possible. Developers and educators must work together to identify potential sources of bias and take steps to mitigate them, ensuring that AI tools are used to promote equity rather than exacerbate existing inequalities.

This chapter aims to explore the ethical considerations surrounding AI in education, focusing on key issues such as fairness, transparency, and data privacy. It will also examine strategies for promoting equity in AI implementation, ensuring that all students, regardless of background or circumstance, can benefit from AI-driven innovations. By addressing these ethical concerns, we can better understand how to integrate AI into education in a way that maximizes its potential while minimizing its risks. Ultimately, the goal is to ensure that AI becomes a tool for advancing educational equity and success, rather than a force that perpetuates disparities.

As AI becomes more deeply embedded in educational systems, the need for ethical guidelines and robust oversight will continue to grow. The potential for AI to enhance learning and improve educational outcomes is undeniable, but its implementation must be approached with caution and consideration for the broader societal impacts. Educators, policymakers, and AI developers must work collaboratively to ensure that AI is used in ways that align with the core values of education: equity, inclusivity, and respect for students' rights (Berendt, ittlejohn, & Blakemore, 2020) and dignity. By doing so, we can help shape a future where AI contributes to a more just and effective educational system, one that meets the needs of all learners and helps them thrive in an increasingly digital world.

In conclusion, while AI offers tremendous potential to improve education, it also raises complex ethical questions that must be carefully considered and addressed. Issues of data privacy, bias, and equitable access are central to the responsible use of AI in education, and it is imperative that stakeholders work together to ensure that AI is used in ways that are fair, transparent, and inclusive. As we move forward, it is crucial to develop policies and practices that protect students, promote equity, and ensure that AI technologies enhance, rather than hinder, the learning experience. Only then can we unlock the full potential of AI to transform education for the better.

THE PROMISE AND PERILS OF AI IN EDUCATION

Artificial intelligence (AI) holds the promise to revolutionize the educational landscape, offering immense opportunities to create personalized learning experiences, enhance teaching practices, and streamline administrative processes. By harnessing the power of AI, educators can tailor instruction to the unique needs and abilities of each student, thereby improving engagement and learning outcomes. AI systems can analyze vast amounts of data, identifying patterns in student performance, behavior, and engagement that human educators might miss. This capability allows for the creation of adaptive learning environments that can adjust in real-time, ensuring students are appropriately challenged while receiving the support they need to succeed. Additionally, AI tools can reduce the administrative burden on teachers by automating tasks such as grading, scheduling, and resource allocation, enabling educators to focus more on student interaction and pedagogy (Holmes & Preston, 2020). However, despite these promising benefits, the rapid adoption of AI in education raises significant ethical concerns that must be carefully addressed to ensure that these technologies are deployed in a manner that is both responsible and equitable.

The first major ethical issue surrounding AI in education is bias and discrimination. AI systems are only as good as the data on which they are trained. If the data used to develop these systems is biased or unrepresentative, the AI models can perpetuate and even amplify existing inequalities in education. For example, if an AI system is trained on historical data that reflects systemic biases, such as lower test scores among certain racial or socioeconomic groups, the AI could unfairly predict that these students are less likely to succeed, thereby reinforcing the very disparities the system was designed to overcome. In educational contexts, this could lead to biased decision-making in areas like student admissions, academic support, and even the allocation of resources. Furthermore, biased algorithms can disproportionately affect marginalized or vulnerable groups, such as students of color, students with disabilities, or students from low-income families, making it even more crucial to ensure that AI systems are designed and tested with fairness in mind. Addressing this issue requires a concerted effort to ensure that the data used to train AI models is diverse, inclusive, and representative of all student populations.

Privacy and data protection are another critical ethical concern in AI-driven education. AI tools collect vast amounts of data on students, including sensitive information such as academic performance, attendance records, behavioral data, and even social-emotional learning indicators. This data, if mishandled or improperly secured, could expose students to significant privacy risks, including identity theft, unauthorized access to personal information, or surveillance. As AI systems become more pervasive in educational settings, it is essential to establish robust data protection policies that safeguard students' privacy rights and ensure that their data is used only for its intended purpose. Additionally, educational institutions must comply with data protection regulations such as the Family Educational Rights and Privacy Act (FERPA) in the United States, the General Data Protection Regulation (GDPR) in the European Union, or similar privacy laws in other jurisdictions. These regulations are designed to protect the privacy of students and ensure that their personal information is handled with care. Ensuring transparency in how student data is collected, used, and shared is crucial to maintaining trust between educational institutions, students, and their families.

Equitable access to AI technologies is another significant ethical issue. While AI has the potential to level the playing field by providing personalized learning experiences, it also risks exacerbating the digital divide between students who have access to advanced technologies and those who do not. Students in underserved or rural areas may have limited access to the necessary devices, high-speed internet, or technical support to fully benefit from AI-driven educational tools. Moreover, students from low-income families may not have the financial resources to afford the technology (Nazaretsky et al., 2022) required to participate in AI-enhanced learning environments. This digital divide could create a situation where only students in wealthier or more well-resourced schools are able to benefit from AI advancements, leaving disadvantaged students further behind. To ensure that AI fulfills its potential as an equalizer in education, it is essential to focus on policies and initiatives that promote equitable access to AI technologies for all students. This includes providing the necessary infrastructure, support, and training to schools and communities that are struggling to keep up with technological advancements. Governments, educational institutions, and technology developers must work together to bridge this divide and ensure that AI tools are accessible to all learners, regardless of their socio-economic background.

Accountability and transparency are essential in addressing the ethical challenges (Akgun & Greenhow, 2022) posed by AI in education. As AI systems are increasingly relied upon to make important decisions—such as predicting student success, recommending interventions, or evaluating teacher effectiveness—it is vital that these systems be transparent and accountable. Educators, students, and parents must have a clear understanding of how AI models make decisions, what data is being used, and how those decisions impact students. Without transparency, there is a risk that AI systems will be seen as "black boxes" whose decisions cannot be questioned or understood, eroding trust in the technology and undermining its effectiveness. To address this issue, AI developers must prioritize creating systems that are explainable and understandable to all stakeholders. This includes providing clear, accessible information about how the AI works, how decisions are made, and the steps taken to ensure fairness and accuracy. Furthermore, there must be mechanisms in place to hold AI systems accountable for their outcomes. For example, if an AI system makes an error or causes harm, there should be a clear process for identifying the source of the problem, correcting the error, and compensating affected students or stakeholders.

In conclusion, while AI holds enormous promise for transforming education, it also raises important ethical issues that must be carefully considered. Bias and discrimination, privacy and data protection, equitable access, and accountability and transparency are central concerns that require thoughtful, responsible approaches (Mollick & Mollick, 2023) to address. To ensure that AI is used ethically in education, stakeholders—including educators, policymakers, technology developers, and students—must work together to create systems that are fair, transparent, and accessible to all. By addressing these ethical challenges (Fuchs, 2023) head-on, we can help ensure that AI fulfills its potential to enhance learning outcomes and create a more inclusive, equitable educational environment for all students. As AI continues to play an increasingly prominent role in education, ongoing dialogue, research, and collaboration will be essential to creating a future where AI supports, rather than undermines, the principles of fairness and equity in education.

BIAS AND DISCRIMINATION: ENSURING FAIRNESS IN AI SYSTEMS

Artificial intelligence (AI) has emerged as a transformative tool in education, offering the potential to personalize learning experiences, optimize teaching strategies, and improve overall educational outcomes. However, as with any powerful technology, AI also brings with it a host of ethical concerns, chief among them being the potential for bias. AI systems are only as unbiased as the data they are trained on, and when those datasets reflect historical inequalities and societal prejudices, AI can perpetuate and even amplify these biases. This can result in discriminatory outcomes that disproportionately affect marginalized groups, further entrenching the inequalities that AI was designed to help address. In the context of education, biased AI systems pose a particular risk because they can influence critical decisions such as admissions, resource allocation, and student support in ways that disadvantage certain groups.

Types of Bias in AI Education Systems

There are several different types of bias that can manifest in AI systems used in education. Understanding these various forms of bias is essential to addressing the ethical concerns associated with AI in the classroom.

Data Bias: One of the most common sources of bias in AI systems is the data used to train these systems. AI algorithms learn patterns from historical data, and if that data is inherently biased—reflecting societal inequalities such as racial, gender, or socioeconomic disparities—the AI will inevitably learn and reproduce those biases. For example, if an AI system is trained on historical data that shows a disproportionate number of male students excelling in STEM (Science, Technology, Engineering, and Mathematics) fields, the AI may assume that male students are better suited for STEM-related courses and may recommend these courses to them more frequently than to female students. This reinforcement of gender stereotypes can contribute to the underrepresentation of women in STEM fields. Similarly, data bias can lead to the underrepresentation of students from marginalized racial or socioeconomic backgrounds in advanced academic tracks, perpetuating existing educational inequities.

Algorithmic Bias: Another form of bias arises from the design of the AI algorithms themselves. Even if the data used to train an AI system is diverse and representative, the way in which an algorithm processes that data can introduce bias. Algorithmic bias often results from the underlying assumptions made during the development of the model. For instance, an AI system used for grading may place undue emphasis on certain types of assessment or preferred learning styles, which could unintentionally favor students from particular backgrounds, such as those who have access to better educational resources. In predictive systems, such as those designed to assess student performance or predict college readiness, algorithms may favor students who are already academically privileged, overlooking students who may have potential but lack access to necessary resources or support.

Cultural Bias: AI systems are often developed within specific cultural and geographical contexts, and as a result, they may not always be appropriate for diverse or international student populations. A system trained on data from one country or region may not fully understand or accurately interpret the needs and experiences of students from different cultural backgrounds. For example, an AI system trained primarily on data from Western educational contexts may struggle to understand the challenges (Kasneci et al., 2023) faced by students from other parts of the world, particularly those in countries with different languages, teaching methods, or societal structures. This can lead to mismatches between the recommendations provided by the AI system and the actual needs of students from diverse backgrounds, exacerbating the digital divide and leaving certain groups at a disadvantage.

Addressing Bias in AI

To ensure that AI in education serves all students equitably and ethically, it is essential to address bias at every stage of the AI development and implementation process. Below are several key strategies for mitigating bias in AI-driven education systems.

Diverse and Representative Data: The first step in minimizing bias is to ensure that the data used to train AI systems is as diverse and representative as possible. AI systems should be trained on datasets that reflect a broad range of student experiences across various demographic groups, including different racial, ethnic, socioeconomic, and gender backgrounds. This requires collecting data that accounts for the experiences of marginalized and underrepresented groups, such as students with disabilities, students from low-income households, and students who identify as LGBTQ+. Without diverse data, AI systems risk reinforcing existing biases and failing to account for the complexities and nuances of student experiences across different contexts. Moreover, this data must not only be diverse but also accurate, ensuring that it is free from historical inaccuracies or discriminatory practices that may have influenced the data collection process in the past.

Bias Detection and Mitigation: Developers of AI systems must implement ongoing checks for bias throughout the lifecycle of the AI tool. This includes continuously monitoring and auditing AI-driven tools for discriminatory outcomes, identifying any patterns of bias, and adjusting the algorithms to correct those biases. Bias detection is not a one-time task; it is an ongoing process that requires regular testing and recalibration of AI models. For example, when using AI to predict student performance, educators and administrators should routinely check whether the system disproportionately predicts lower success rates for certain groups of students and work to refine the model if such biases are detected. Mitigation strategies might involve adjusting the weight of certain factors in the AI algorithm or incorporating corrective mechanisms that ensure fairer outcomes. Developers must also be transparent about the methods and metrics used to detect and address bias, allowing for public scrutiny and accountability.

Transparency in Algorithm Design: One of the most important steps toward ensuring fairness in AI systems is to increase transparency in the design (Bhimdiwala, Neri, & Gomez, 2022) of the algorithms themselves. Educators, administrators, students, and parents must be able to understand how AI systems make decisions, what data is being used, and how those decisions impact students. Without transparency,

AI systems can appear as "black boxes," where decisions are made without clear rationale, making it difficult for stakeholders to understand why certain outcomes occur or to challenge unfair decisions. Transparent AI systems should provide clear explanations of how they process data and make recommendations, as well as detailed documentation of the data sources and assumptions that underpin the algorithms. Additionally, educators and administrators should be trained to interpret and understand the outputs of AI systems, ensuring that they can make informed decisions based on the insights provided. This transparency can help build trust in AI systems and ensure that they are used in ways that are both effective and ethical.

Inclusive Development and Testing: To further address bias, AI systems should be developed and tested with input from diverse stakeholders, including educators, students, parents, and experts in equity and social justice. Inclusive development ensures that AI systems are designed with a broader understanding of the challenges (Luan et al., 2020) faced by different student populations. This can involve collaboration with sociologists, psychologists, and other experts to ensure that AI systems are developed with a comprehensive understanding of the various factors that influence student success. Additionally, AI systems should undergo rigorous testing in real-world educational environments to ensure that they perform equitably across diverse student populations. These tests should specifically assess whether the system treats all demographic groups fairly and whether any unintentional biases are present. By incorporating diverse perspectives (Kaplan-Rakowski et al., 2023) in both development and testing, AI systems can be more effective at meeting the needs of all students.

Policy and Regulation: Finally, addressing bias in AI requires a strong regulatory framework that establishes standards for fairness and accountability. Governments, educational institutions, and industry leaders must collaborate to create policies that regulate the use of AI in education. These policies should require regular audits of AI systems for bias, mandate transparency in algorithmic decision-making, and ensure that AI tools comply with privacy and data protection laws. Moreover, policymakers should prioritize creating standards for ethical AI that are aligned with broader goals of educational equity and social justice. This can help prevent the widespread use of AI systems that disproportionately harm vulnerable or marginalized students. By establishing clear ethical guidelines and accountability measures, policymakers can ensure that AI in education serves to benefit all students, rather than exacerbating existing inequalities.

AI has the potential to significantly enhance education by providing personalized learning experiences, optimizing teaching practices, and improving overall efficiency. However, as AI systems become more integrated into the educational landscape, it is crucial to address the ethical concerns related to bias. Data bias, algorithmic bias, and cultural bias can all lead to discriminatory outcomes that disproportionately affect marginalized students, undermining the potential benefits of AI. To mitigate these risks, AI systems must be developed using diverse and representative datasets, undergo continuous bias detection and mitigation, and be designed with transparency and fairness in mind. By ensuring that AI is used ethically and equitably, we can help ensure that all students have the opportunity to benefit from the transformative potential of AI in education.

PRIVACY AND DATA PROTECTION: SAFEGUARDING STUDENT INFORMATION

The widespread integration of artificial intelligence (AI) in education brings immense potential to transform teaching and learning, offering personalized learning experiences, predictive insights, and data-driven decision-making. However, this also requires the collection and analysis of large amounts of student data, which includes personal information, academic records, engagement patterns, and even social-emotional data. As AI systems become more central to the educational process, it is critical to prioritize privacy and ensure robust data protection measures to safeguard sensitive student information.

Data Privacy Challenges

With the growing reliance on AI to drive educational tools, platforms, and strategies, various privacy challenges have emerged, which need to be addressed to avoid harm to students and preserve their rights.

Sensitive Information: AI systems often collect a wide range of sensitive data about students. This includes academic performance, grades, learning preferences, behavioral data, and increasingly, emotional and mental health data. For example, AI systems that track student engagement may collect data on how often a student interacts with specific course materials or their emotional responses to particular topics. While these insights can be valuable for personalizing learning, this sensitive information also carries significant risks if not handled properly. Data breaches, unauthorized access, or malicious use of this data could lead to identity theft, cyberbullying, or even psychological harm to students. If student data is not adequately protected, it could be misused in ways that negatively affect their future educational or professional opportunities.

Surveillance and Tracking: Another concern associated with AI in education is the potential for over-surveillance. AI-powered tools can monitor various aspects of student behavior, such as tracking academic progress, engagement levels, and even social interactions in online learning environments. While these systems can provide valuable feedback (Messer et al., 2024) for educators and administrators, there is a risk of infringing on students' right to privacy, particularly if students are unaware of the full extent of data being collected. Over-surveillance can create a sense of constant monitoring, leading to stress, anxiety, or even behavioral changes that may not accurately reflect students' true capabilities. Additionally, if students are not fully informed about how their data is being used or if they have no say in what is collected, they may feel disempowered, leading to a loss of trust in the education system and in AI tools more broadly.

Consent and Control: A major issue with data privacy in AI education systems is the lack of clarity and control over how data is collected and used. In many cases, students and parents may not fully understand the implications of AI data collection or the ways in which their data will be used. Educational institutions must ensure that students and their families are properly informed and given the opportunity to provide informed consent for data collection. This includes providing clear explanations about the types of data being collected, the specific purposes for which it will be used, and who will have access to it. Furthermore, it is essential that students and parents have control over how their data is used, with the option to opt out of certain types of data collection or sharing. The lack of transparency and control over data usage can lead to discomfort or reluctance among students and parents to fully embrace AI-driven educational tools.

Ensuring Data Protection

Given the privacy challenges associated with AI, it is imperative that educational institutions take proactive steps to ensure data protection. A robust framework for handling student data is necessary to mitigate risks, foster trust, and comply with regulatory standards.

Compliance with Regulations: Educational institutions must adhere to national and international data privacy regulations to ensure that student data is handled properly. In the United States, the Family Educational Rights and Privacy Act (FERPA) governs how student information can be shared and protects students' privacy rights. FERPA gives students and parents control over their educational records, including the right to access, review, and request amendments to their records. Institutions must comply with these provisions, especially when using AI systems to collect or process student data. Similarly, the European Union's General Data Protection Regulation (GDPR) sets a high standard for data protection, requiring that data collection be transparent, lawful, and based on explicit consent. The GDPR also mandates that organizations implement strict measures to protect personal data, including the right for individuals to request access to, correction of, or deletion of their data. AI systems used in educational settings must comply with these regulations, ensuring that data collection, storage, and sharing practices are in line with legal requirements. Educational institutions should regularly review their policies and practices to ensure they remain compliant with the latest data protection laws.

Data Anonymization: To further protect privacy, AI systems should employ data anonymization or pseudonymization techniques whenever possible. Anonymization involves removing or obfuscating personally identifiable information so that it cannot be traced back to an individual student. This is particularly important when AI systems aggregate large datasets for analysis or use for predictive modeling. If student data is anonymized, even in the event of a data breach or unauthorized access, it would be difficult to link the data to specific individuals. Pseudonymization is another approach where personal identifiers are replaced with pseudonyms, ensuring that the data remains useful for analysis while still offering a level of protection. These measures help minimize the risks associated with data breaches and provide an added layer of security for students. Anonymization and pseudonymization can also promote the use of educational data for research purposes, allowing for the improvement of AI systems and educational practices without compromising individual privacy.

Transparency and Informed Consent: For AI systems to be used ethically in education, transparency is key. Students and their parents must be fully informed about the types of data being collected, the specific purpose for which it will be used, and how it will be shared. Clear and accessible consent forms should be provided to ensure that individuals understand what they are agreeing to. This consent process should not be buried in dense legal language but should be presented in a simple, straightforward manner that is easy for non-experts to comprehend. Additionally, students and parents should have the ability to opt in or opt out of certain data collection practices. For example, they should be able to choose whether they want their social-emotional data to be collected or whether they are comfortable with AI tools tracking their behavioral patterns. This level of control is vital for building trust and ensuring that students feel empowered in the data collection process. Furthermore, institutions must periodically review consent forms and update them to reflect any changes in data collection practices, ensuring that students and parents have up-to-date information.

Data Minimization: Another best practice for protecting student privacy is the principle of data minimization, which involves collecting only the data that is necessary for the specific purpose at hand. AI systems should be designed to gather minimal information, focusing only on the data that directly supports the learning process or educational goals. By minimizing the amount of data collected, institutions can reduce the risk of exposing sensitive information and limit the potential for misuse. Data minimization also involves ensuring that data is retained only for as long as necessary, with proper protocols in place for securely deleting data once it is no longer needed.

Secure Data Storage and Access: It is also crucial to ensure that student data is stored securely and that access is tightly controlled. This requires implementing robust cybersecurity measures, such as encryption, to protect data from unauthorized access. Data should be stored in secure, compliant environments, with regular security audits to identify and address vulnerabilities. Additionally, only authorized personnel should have access to student data, and institutions must establish clear protocols for handling and sharing sensitive information. Restricting access and ensuring that all data transactions are properly logged and monitored will help reduce the risk of breaches or misuse.

As AI continues to shape the future of education, it is essential to prioritize student privacy and data protection. While AI offers the potential to enhance learning and improve educational outcomes, it also brings significant privacy challenges that must be addressed. Educational institutions must ensure compliance with data protection regulations, such as FERPA and GDPR, and implement robust data protection measures, including anonymization, transparency, and informed consent. By taking these steps, institutions can protect student privacy, build trust, and create a safe environment for students to benefit from the opportunities AI offers. Ultimately, data privacy and security should be at the forefront of the conversation surrounding AI in education, ensuring that students' rights are safeguarded while AI is used to enhance the educational experience.

EQUITABLE ACCESS TO AI TECHNOLOGIES: BRIDGING THE DIGITAL DIVIDE

As artificial intelligence (AI) technology continues to permeate educational environments, its integration has the potential to revolutionize teaching and learning. AI tools, from personalized learning platforms to predictive analytics, promise to enhance educational experiences by tailoring content to individual students' needs and helping educators provide more effective support. However, as these tools become more widespread, it is critical to ensure that all students, regardless of background, have equitable access to these advancements. The digital divide—the gap between those with access to advanced technologies and those without—remains a significant challenge that could further deepen educational inequities. This divide is not only evident across socioeconomic, geographic, racial, and disability-related lines, but it also has the potential to shape the future of educational opportunities for generations to come.

Barriers to Access

Several barriers contribute to the digital divide, limiting equitable access to AI-powered educational tools for various student groups. These challenges are multifaceted and require a comprehensive approach to address them.

Socioeconomic Inequities: One of the primary barriers (Renz & Hilbig, 2020) to access is socioeconomic status. Students from low-income families often lack the financial resources to purchase the necessary technology, such as computers, tablets, or smartphones, required to engage with AI-driven learning platforms. Additionally, these students may not have access to high-speed internet, which is essential for seamless interaction with cloud-based educational tools. For many students, this means that even if AI technologies are available at their schools, they are unable to access them at home or outside of school hours. This creates a disparity where wealthier students with access to personal devices and reliable internet connections can engage with AI-enhanced learning opportunities, while their peers in low-income households are left behind, unable to benefit from these advancements. This inequity in access further exacerbates the achievement gap, as students without access to these tools miss out on opportunities to improve their academic performance and gain skills that are increasingly valuable in the modern workforce.

Geographic Inequities: Geographic location is another major factor contributing to the digital divide. Students living in rural or remote areas face unique challenges in accessing the infrastructure needed to take full advantage of AI-powered learning. In many rural areas, broadband internet access is limited or non-existent, making it difficult for students to use online learning platforms, participate in virtual classrooms, or access resources like digital textbooks. Without access to reliable internet, students in these areas are effectively excluded from the full benefits of AI-enhanced education. Additionally, schools in rural areas may not have the budget to invest in modern technology or provide students with the latest devices, leading to further disparities in the quality of education offered. Similarly, in developing countries where infrastructure is often lacking, AI-based educational solutions are not always a viable option. Students in these regions may not have access to the necessary technological devices or may struggle with inconsistent power supply, further widening the gap between affluent and underserved populations.

Disability Access: Another critical issue in ensuring equitable access to AI in education is the inclusion of students with disabilities. Many AI-powered tools are designed for the general population without consideration for the diverse needs of students with disabilities. For students with visual impairments, for example, AI interfaces may not be compatible with screen readers, making it difficult or impossible for them to navigate learning platforms. Similarly, students with hearing impairments may face challenges with voice-based AI tools that do not provide alternative text-based options. Motor impairments may prevent students from interacting with devices that rely on physical input methods, such as touchscreens or keyboards. If AI tools are not designed with these accessibility needs in mind, they can inadvertently exclude students with disabilities, further perpetuating educational inequities and limiting opportunities for these students to succeed. Ensuring that AI tools are inclusive and accessible is crucial to ensuring that all students can benefit from the educational potential of these technologies.

Promoting Equitable Access

To address the challenges posed by the digital divide, stakeholders in the education sector—policymakers, educators, and technology providers—must work together to promote equitable access to AI-powered educational tools. Several key strategies can help bridge this gap and ensure that all students have the opportunity to engage with these technologies.

Affordability and Infrastructure: One of the most effective ways to promote equitable access to AI in education is by improving the affordability and infrastructure required to use these tools. Policymakers and educational institutions must prioritize investments in technology and internet access, particularly for underserved communities. This could involve subsidizing technology for low-income students, ensuring that devices such as laptops and tablets are available to those who cannot afford them. Additionally, providing access to high-speed internet is essential to ensuring that students can fully engage with AI-powered learning platforms. In rural and underserved areas, governments and private companies could collaborate to expand broadband access, helping to address the geographic inequities that limit students' ability to participate in digital learning. Schools could also explore solutions like providing students with devices on loan, allowing them to take home the technology they need to continue learning outside of the classroom. By addressing affordability and infrastructure, we can begin to level the playing field and give all students the tools they need to succeed in an AI-powered education system.

Inclusive Design: Another essential strategy for promoting equitable access is ensuring that AI tools are designed with accessibility in mind. Inclusive design involves creating products and systems that can be used by a wide range of people, including those with disabilities. AI tools should be developed with features that support students with visual, auditory, motor, and cognitive impairments. For example, AI systems could integrate voice recognition and text-to-speech features, allowing students with visual impairments to navigate digital platforms with ease. Similarly, interfaces should be designed to work with screen readers and other assistive technologies to accommodate students with disabilities. Providing customizable settings that allow students to adjust the interface to meet their specific needs can also improve accessibility. By prioritizing inclusive (Xia et al., 2022) design, developers can ensure that AI tools are accessible to all students, regardless of their abilities, and that students with disabilities are not excluded from the educational opportunities AI provides.

Global Collaboration: The digital divide is not limited to specific countries or regions but is a global issue that requires international cooperation to address. Governments, international organizations, and educational institutions must collaborate to reduce the global digital divide and ensure that all students, regardless of their location, can access AI-powered educational tools. This collaboration could involve sharing resources, knowledge, and expertise to help low-income countries or regions with limited infrastructure implement AI-based learning solutions. Furthermore, educational technology providers can help bridge the gap by developing low-cost or open-source AI tools that are accessible to underserved communities. By creating affordable, adaptable solutions and making them available to the global community, we can help ensure that the benefits of AI-powered education reach students in even the most remote or resource-poor areas. International collaboration also involves advocating for policy changes that prioritize equitable access to technology and internet infrastructure, ensuring that all students can benefit from AI-driven learning.

As AI technology continues to reshape the landscape of education, it is essential that we prioritize equitable access to these tools for all students. The digital divide, driven by socioeconomic, geographic, and disability-related barriers, poses significant challenges to ensuring that every student has the opportunity to benefit from AI-powered education. By addressing these barriers through policies that improve affordability and infrastructure, designing AI tools with accessibility in mind, and fostering global collaboration to reduce the digital divide, we can create a more inclusive and equitable educational system. Ultimately, ensuring equitable access to AI in education will help empower all students to succeed and thrive in an increasingly technology-driven world.

ACCOUNTABILITY AND TRANSPARENCY: WHO IS RESPONSIBLE?

As artificial intelligence (AI) becomes more integrated into educational systems, it is critical to address questions of accountability. AI systems are increasingly involved in making decisions that directly impact students' learning experiences—ranging from assessing performance and recommending resources to predicting academic success or failure. With such significant implications, the issue of who is ultimately responsible for these decisions must be addressed to ensure that the use of AI in education remains ethical, transparent, and fair. Understanding accountability in the context of AI decision-making is crucial to maintaining trust in these systems and ensuring that they align with the broader goals of education.

Accountability in AI Decision-Making

AI System Developers: The role of AI developers is fundamental when it comes to ensuring ethical decision-making. Developers of AI tools bear significant responsibility for creating systems that are both effective and fair. This responsibility begins at the design stage, where developers must ensure that their algorithms are free from bias and discrimination. Since AI systems learn from data, it is essential that the data used to train these models is representative and does not reflect existing societal biases. For example, an AI system used for grading or academic performance prediction must not be influenced by factors such as race, gender, or socioeconomic status, as this could lead to unfair outcomes. Ensuring that AI tools are designed to be free of bias requires rigorous testing, monitoring, and validation throughout the development process. Developers must also ensure that their AI systems are transparent—providing clear explanations of how decisions are made, so that both students and educators can understand the reasoning behind the outcomes produced by the system. Transparency is a critical element of accountability, as it helps build trust in AI systems and allows for greater scrutiny. Moreover, developers must align their AI tools with educational goals, ensuring that they serve the interests of students and support teachers in delivering high-quality education.

AI developers must also be proactive in addressing potential risks associated with AI systems. For example, AI-based decision-making processes should not lead to "automated" judgments that ignore the complexities of individual students' learning experiences. Instead, developers should design systems that offer flexible, contextualized support for educators, allowing them to override or adjust recommendations when needed. In this way, developers can help mitigate the potential harms that could arise from over-reliance on AI in educational settings.

Educators and Administrators: While AI can support decision-making in the classroom, the ultimate responsibility for educational outcomes rests with educators and administrators. AI systems are tools that provide insights, recommendations, and predictions based on data, but these tools should not replace the professional judgment of teachers and school leaders. Educators and administrators must remain informed and involved in the decision-making process. They must understand how AI tools work and be capable of interpreting the data these systems produce.

For example, AI systems may offer recommendations on which resources or interventions may be beneficial for a student based on performance data. While this may be valuable information, it is crucial for educators to evaluate these recommendations in the context of the student's individual learning needs. Teachers should use

AI suggestions as one piece of the puzzle, not as a definitive answer. Furthermore, educators should have the ability to intervene if AI-generated recommendations or assessments appear to be inappropriate or harmful. This could include challenging AI-generated grades, revising content recommendations, or even disregarding AI predictions when they conflict with their own professional judgment.

Administrators also have a role (Harry, 2023) in ensuring that AI systems are used ethically and that students' privacy and rights are protected. They must work with educators to establish clear guidelines for the responsible use of AI in the classroom, ensuring that AI tools are being used to enhance—not replace—the educational experience. Furthermore, administrators must advocate for transparency, ensuring that AI systems are implemented in ways that are accessible to all stakeholders, including students, parents, and teachers.

AI Governance: To further support accountability, educational institutions should establish governance structures for the use of AI tools. Governance refers to the processes, policies, and practices that guide the implementation and use of AI systems in educational settings. By setting up clear oversight mechanisms, educational institutions can ensure that AI systems align with the institution's values and ethical standards. Governance structures help create accountability by establishing who is responsible for monitoring the use of AI, ensuring compliance with ethical guidelines, and addressing any issues that arise.

A key component of AI governance is the formation of committees or working groups that are tasked with overseeing the use of AI tools in education. These committees can include a diverse range of stakeholders, including educators, administrators, data scientists, ethicists, and legal experts. By involving people with different areas of expertise, institutions can ensure that AI systems are being used responsibly and in ways that benefit students. These groups can be tasked with regularly reviewing the AI tools in use, evaluating their impact on student outcomes, and providing recommendations for improvement. They can also serve as a forum for discussing ethical concerns, such as the potential for bias or misuse of student data.

Regular reviews (Zhai et al., 2021) of AI tools are necessary to ensure that they continue to meet ethical standards and align with educational goals. As AI technology evolves, it is essential for educational institutions to stay informed about new developments and assess the potential risks and benefits associated with emerging AI applications. Additionally, these governance bodies should be responsible for setting up transparent policies regarding data privacy (Yang & Beil, 2024) and student consent. This includes ensuring that AI systems comply with data protection regulations and that students and parents are fully informed about how their data is being used.

One key aspect of AI governance is developing accountability frameworks that include clear channels for addressing concerns or grievances related to AI decision-making. For example, if a student believes that an AI system has unfairly assessed their performance, there should be a process for appealing the decision and rectifying any mistakes. This ensures that students are not unfairly penalized or overlooked due to AI errors or biases.

Moreover, institutions should ensure that AI tools do not disproportionately affect vulnerable or marginalized student groups. For instance, there should be checks in place to prevent AI systems from reinforcing existing inequalities in education. Bias in AI tools, whether due to skewed data sets or flawed algorithms, can exacerbate disparities in educational outcomes. Through strong governance, educational institutions can mitigate such risks and ensure that AI systems are used in ways that promote fairness and inclusivity.

As AI systems play an increasingly central role in educational decision-making, it is essential to establish clear accountability structures that involve AI developers, educators, administrators, and educational institutions as a whole. Developers must ensure that AI tools are ethically designed, free from bias, and transparent in their decision-making processes. Educators and administrators must remain responsible for the educational outcomes of their students, using AI tools as aids rather than replacements for their professional judgment. Additionally, robust governance structures should be established within educational institutions to oversee the ethical use of AI, promote transparency, and safeguard against bias or misuse. Only by addressing these questions of accountability can AI truly fulfill its potential as a tool for enhancing education while ensuring fairness, transparency, and equity for all students.

CONCLUSION

Ethics (Schiff, 2022) and equity are paramount when integrating AI-driven systems into education, as these technologies have the potential to reshape how students learn, engage, and succeed. However, without careful attention to ethical principles, AI systems could unintentionally exacerbate existing disparities or create new forms of discrimination. One of the most pressing ethical concerns is bias in AI algorithms. AI systems are often trained on historical data, and if that data reflects societal biases, the algorithms can perpetuate and even amplify those biases. For instance, AI systems used for grading or predicting academic success may be influenced by factors such as race, gender, or socioeconomic status, leading to unequal treatment of students. It is essential that developers address these biases during the design and training phases, ensuring that AI tools are fair, impartial, and built on diverse, representative data sets.

Privacy concerns are also central to the ethical use of AI in education. AI systems often rely on large volumes of student data, including sensitive personal information, academic performance, and even social-emotional indicators. Without proper safeguards, there is a risk that this data could be misused, exposed, or accessed by unauthorized third parties. Protecting student privacy means adhering to strict data protection regulations such as FERPA in the U.S. or GDPR in the EU, as well as ensuring transparency in how data is collected, stored, and used. Educational institutions must be proactive in obtaining informed consent from students and parents and offering clear explanations of how their data will be used. By prioritizing data security and privacy, schools can foster trust among students and parents while protecting individual rights.

Equitable access is another critical consideration in the ethical deployment of AI in education. The digital divide—the gap between students who have access to advanced technologies and those who do not—remains a significant barrier to ensuring that all students benefit from AI-driven educational tools. Students from low-income backgrounds, rural areas, or developing countries often face challenges in accessing the necessary devices, internet connectivity, or infrastructure to fully engage with AI-powered platforms. Additionally, students with disabilities may encounter accessibility barriers if AI tools are not designed with inclusive features. To address these inequities, it is crucial that policymakers, educational institutions, and tech developers work together to ensure that all students, regardless of their background or abilities, have the resources and opportunities they need to succeed. This can involve expanding access to technology, offering financial assistance, and ensuring that AI tools are designed with accessibility in mind.

Finally, establishing clear accountability frameworks (Bravo et al., 2021) is essential to the ethical use of AI in education. AI systems are powerful tools, but they cannot replace human judgment and responsibility. Educators, administrators, and AI developers must work collaboratively to ensure that AI systems are used to support—not replace—human decision-making. Educators must be equipped to understand how AI tools work, interpret the data they provide, and intervene when AI-generated recommendations may not align with the needs of students. Moreover, educational institutions should have robust governance structures in place to monitor the use of AI tools, review their impact on student outcomes, and address any ethical concerns that arise. By ensuring that AI is developed and used responsibly, we can create educational environments where fairness, transparency, and inclusivity are at the forefront, empowering all students to reach their full potential.

REFERENCES

Ainscow, M. (2020). Inclusion and equity in education: Making sense of global challenges. *Prospects*, 49(3), 123–134. DOI: 10.1007/s11125-020-09506-w

Akgun, S., & Greenhow, C. (2022). Artificial intelligence in education: Addressing ethical challenges in K-12 settings. *AI and Ethics*, 2(3), 431–440. DOI: 10.1007/s43681-021-00096-7 PMID: 34790956

Alasadi, E. A., & Baiz, C. R. (2023). Generative AI in education and research: Opportunities, concerns, and solutions. *Journal of Chemical Education*, 100(8), 2965–2971. DOI: 10.1021/acs.jchemed.3c00323

Association of College and University Educators. (2024). *Teaching with AI: Inclusive and AI-resistant learning experiences.* Association of College and University Educators.

Berendt, B., Littlejohn, A., & Blakemore, M. (2020). AI in education: Learner choice and fundamental rights. *Learning, Media and Technology*, 45(3), 312–324. DOI: 10.1080/17439884.2020.1786399

Bhimdiwala, A., Neri, R. C., & Gomez, L. M. (2022). Advancing the design and implementation of artificial intelligence in education through continuous improvement. *International Journal of Artificial Intelligence in Education*, 32(3), 1–27. DOI: 10.1007/s40593-021-00278-8

Bravo, M. C. M., Chalezquer, C. S., & Serrano-Puche, J. (2021). Meta-framework of digital literacy: A comparative analysis of 21st-century skills frameworks. *Revista Latina de Comunicacion Social*, (79), 76–109.

Fuchs, K. (2023, May). Exploring the opportunities and challenges of NLP models in higher education: Is Chat GPT a blessing or a curse? []. Frontiers Media SA.]. *Frontiers in Education*, 8, 1166682. DOI: 10.3389/feduc.2023.1166682

Harry, A. (2023). Role of AI in Education. [INJURITY]. *Interdiciplinary Journal and Hummanity*, 2(3), 260–268.

Holmes, K., & Preston, G. (2020). Concept of pedagogy and andragogy education. *Community Medicine and Education Journal*, 1(1), 12–18. DOI: 10.37275/cmej.v1i1.166

Kaplan-Rakowski, R., Grotewold, K., Hartwick, P., & Papin, K. (2023). Generative AI and teachers' perspectives on its implementation in education. *Journal of Interactive Learning Research*, 34(2), 313–338.

Kasneci, E., Seßler, K., Küchemann, S., Bannert, M., Dementieva, D., Fischer, F., Gasser, U., Groh, G., Günnemann, S., Hüllermeier, E., Krusche, S., Kutyniok, G., Michaeli, T., Nerdel, C., Pfeffer, J., Poquet, O., Sailer, M., Schmidt, A., Seidel, T., & Kasneci, G. (2023). ChatGPT for good? On opportunities and challenges of large language models for education. *Learning and Individual Differences*, 103, 102274. DOI: 10.1016/j.lindif.2023.102274

Luan, H., Geczy, P., Lai, H., Gobert, J., Yang, S. J., Ogata, H., Baltes, J., Guerra, R., Li, P., & Tsai, C. C. (2020). Challenges and future directions of big data and artificial intelligence in education. *Frontiers in Psychology*, 11, 580820. DOI: 10.3389/fpsyg.2020.580820 PMID: 33192896

Luan, H., & Tsai, C. C. (2021). A review of using machine learning approaches for precision education. *Journal of Educational Technology & Society*, 24(1), 250–266.

Messer, M., Brown, N. C., Kölling, M., & Shi, M. (2024). Automated grading and feedback tools for programming education: A systematic review. *ACM Transactions on Computing Education*, 24(1), 1–43. DOI: 10.1145/3636515

Mollick, E. R., & Mollick, L. (2023). Assigning AI: Seven Approaches for Students, with Prompts. *SSRN*. DOI: 10.2139/ssrn.4475995

Nazaretsky, T., Ariely, M., Cukurova, M., & Alexandron, G. (2022). Teachers' trust in AI-powered educational technology and a professional development program to improve it. *British Journal of Educational Technology*, 53(4), 914–931. DOI: 10.1111/bjet.13232

Renz, A., & Hilbig, R. (2020). Prerequisites for artificial intelligence in further education: Identification of drivers, barriers, and business models of educational technology companies. *International Journal of Educational Technology in Higher Education*, 17(1), 14. DOI: 10.1186/s41239-020-00193-3

Schiff, D. (2022). Education for AI, not AI for education: The role of education and ethics in national AI policy strategies. *International Journal of Artificial Intelligence in Education*, 32(3), 527–563. DOI: 10.1007/s40593-021-00270-2

Xia, Q., Chiu, T., Lee, M., Temitayo Sanusi, I., Dai, Y., & Sing Chai, C. (2022). A self-determination theory (SDT) design approach for inclusive and diverse artificial intelligence (AI) education. *Computers & Education*, 189, 189. DOI: 10.1016/j.compedu.2022.104582

Yang, E., & Beil, C. (2024). Ensuring data privacy in AI/ML implementation. *New Directions for Higher Education*, 2024(207), 63–78. DOI: 10.1002/he.20509

Zhai, X., Chu, X., Chai, C. S., Jong, M. S. Y., Istenic, A., Spector, M., Liu, J., & Li, Y. (2021). A Review of Artificial Intelligence (AI) in Education from 2010 to 2020. *Complexity*, 2021(1), 8812542. DOI: 10.1155/2021/8812542

Chapter 11
Revolutionizing CTE: AI-Driven Andragogical Practices for Social Justice in Urban Education

Sailesh Maharjan
California State University, San Bernardino, USA

Marvin Espinoza
https://orcid.org/0009-0009-5662-8239
California State University, San Bernardino, USA

Thomas Robles
https://orcid.org/0009-0006-7946-8635
California State University, San Bernardino, USA

Leon P. Strayer
https://orcid.org/0009-0002-7789-8712
California State University, San Bernardino, USA

ABSTRACT

The level of student engagement is a critical factor in determining a student's continuation at a university. Adult learners, one of the fastest-growing student demographics in higher education, often bring unique life experiences that interconnect with their online classes, family responsibilities, work, and other commitments. Artificial Intelligence (AI) chatbots in online learning environments have proven effective in revolutionizing student engagement through intentional communication and providing timely academic assistance. This four-part chapter explores how AI-driven practices can transform Career and Technical Education (CTE) by addressing systemic inequities and advancing social justice in urban education. The chapter

DOI: 10.4018/979-8-3373-0502-8.ch011

emphasizes the importance of ensuring that the benefits of AI are distributed equitably, particularly in the context of lifelong learning and community empowerment. Furthermore, AI can enhance andragogical practices in urban settings by improving strategic planning, resource allocation, and personalized learning experiences.

Urban education is a multifaceted domain that extends far beyond its traditional association with large city schools and districts. Defined through critical dimensions such as population, enrollment, demographic composition, resource availability, disparities, educational inequalities, and socioeconomic context (Welsh & Swain, 2020), urban education presents challenges and opportunities. Integrating Artificial Intelligence (AI) into this landscape offers a promising avenue to address these challenges by enhancing learning, strategic planning, and family engagement within diverse educational environments. This chapter delves into AI's transformative potential in urban education, examining its capacity to empower school district trustee boards, optimize resource allocation, personalize learning experiences, support strategic decision-making, and strengthen family engagement. As urban schools navigate complex challenges, the thoughtful implementation of AI can redefine success and equity in education, particularly by addressing systemic inequities and empowering marginalized communities.

The rapid integration of AI into educational systems raises significant questions about its impact on adult learning, or andragogy, a domain that has gained importance in our continuously evolving world. AI technologies promise to revolutionize education by offering personalized learning experiences, automating administrative tasks, and providing innovative tools for educators and learners. However, these technologies also carry risks, mainly when implemented without considering the diverse needs of all learners, especially those from marginalized communities. The potential for AI to perpetuate existing inequalities is a pressing concern, as these technologies often reflect the biases and assumptions of the societies in which they are developed.

The authors critically examine the intersection of AI and social justice within andragogical education, highlighting the implications for addressing disparities and enhancing community engagement. AI's role in education transcends merely improving efficiency or enhancing learning outcomes; it is also about ensuring that these advancements are accessible to all, regardless of their background. In this context, Ayeni (2024) defines AI as a branch of computer science dedicated to creating intelligent machines capable of learning and problem-solving, thus establishing a unique and essential role in the educational landscape. The chapter will further explore the exponential growth of AI technology, tracing its origins and evolution, its rapid expansion in educational settings, and its impact on the cognitive, behavioral, and emotional aspects of adult learning. Additionally, it will analyze the ethical considerations of AI integration in education, particularly in urban environments, and explore the potential future role of AI in shaping andragogy.

In higher education, particularly in the context of online learning, AI's influence is increasingly evident. The COVID-19 pandemic accelerated the shift from in-person instruction to online modalities, bringing to the forefront the need to understand online pedagogy's implications on student transition and engagement (Brown et al., 2022). Students' experiences within sophisticated learning management systems (LMS) vary, and these platforms have proven effective at collecting data about learner behaviors and providing feedback to improve teaching, learning, and decision-making. The meaning of engagement is nuanced, and in the context of online learning, engagement involves behaviors where students are continuously interacting with the resources and activities that promote learning within the online environment (Brown et al., 2022).

Learning Analytics (LA), a tool often leveraged within these systems, monitors online and learner engagement, providing valuable insights into student activity, contact frequency with course content, and overall performance (Brown et al., 2022). This data-driven approach allows educational institutions to make informed decisions about early interventions and the support needed to promote student engagement and confidence, particularly for low/non-engaged students. As AI expands across higher education, its role in andragogy, particularly in urban settings, is expected to grow. This chapter seeks to critically analyze these developments, offering insights into how AI can be harnessed to support adult learners in navigating the complexities of urban education, ultimately contributing to a more equitable and just educational landscape.

SECTION ONE: AI IN URBAN EDUCATION: ENHANCING LEARNING, STRATEGIC PLANNING, AND FAMILY ENGAGEMENT

Urban education, a term often associated with large city schools and districts, encompasses much more than just geographical location. Welsh and Swain (2020) define urban education through six key dimensions, i.e., population, enrollment, demographic composition, resource availability, disparities and educational inequalities, and the socioeconomic context. Despite the challenges often highlighted in urban education, integrating Artificial Intelligence (AI) presents promising opportunities to enhance learning, strategic planning, and family engagement within these diverse educational environments. This chapter explores the transformative potential of AI in urban education, addressing how AI can empower school district trustee boards, optimize resource allocation, personalize learning experiences, support strategic decision-making, and strengthen family engagement. As urban schools navigate complex challenges, the thoughtful implementation of AI could redefine success and equity in education.

1.1 AI Support for District Trustee Boards

1.1a Empowering District Trustee Boards with AI Support

Integrating AI within school district trustee boards is increasingly recognized as a critical component in enhancing the efficacy of decision-making processes and the overall educational outcomes within districts. Torre et al. (2019) present compelling evidence supporting this assertion, demonstrating how AI's ability to analyze vast and complex datasets can uncover critical trends and patterns that might go unnoticed. This capability is crucial in enabling trustees to make more informed, objective, and data-driven policy decisions, which are essential for effectively addressing the diverse needs of students and communities. By harnessing the power of AI, school boards are equipped to allocate resources more efficiently, ensuring that funds, personnel, and other resources are directed where they are most needed. Additionally, AI supports personalized learning experiences for students by tailoring educational approaches to individual needs and learning styles, thus fostering better academic performance and engagement. This empowerment through AI instills confidence and capability in school district trustee boards.

Torre et al. (2019) highlighted AI's role in identifying at-risk students through predictive analytics, enabling early interventions that positively alter academic trajectories. This proactive use of AI is essential for improving educational outcomes. Automating administrative tasks allows trustees to focus on strategic initiatives like long-term planning and policy development, leading to more efficient governance. However, Torre et al. also discussed challenges in AI implementation, emphasizing the need for careful consideration of data privacy and adequate training for board members to use AI tools effectively and ethically. Moreover, Torre et al. (2019) advocated for a thoughtful and measured approach to AI integration, recognizing its benefits while acknowledging risks like potential biases in AI algorithms and the need for transparency in AI-driven decision-making. They argue that AI is beneficial and necessary for school district trustee boards to navigate modern education's complex, data-driven landscape. Effectively harnessing AI can determine a school board's ability to achieve its goals and fulfill its mission of providing high-quality education for all students.

1.1b Relieving the Burden of Resource Allocation with AI

AI plays a crucial role in relieving the burden of resource allocation, particularly in the context of cloud-native applications, by automating and optimizing the management of infrastructure resources. Tatineni and Chakilam (2024) discuss that integrating AI with DevOps practices allows for a more intelligent and dynamic approach to resource allocation, which is traditionally a complex and labor-intensive process. AI systems continuously analyze real-time data, predict future resource demands, and adjust resource distribution automatically, ensuring that resources are over-provisioned and underutilized. This dynamic adaptability not only improves resource utilization efficiency but also minimizes the risks associated with manual resource management, such as human error and delayed response to changes in demand. The predictive capabilities of AI enable proactive management of resources, where potential bottlenecks or resource shortages are identified and mitigated before they impact system performance. Tatineni and Chakilam (2024) emphasize that AI-driven resource allocation optimizes performance and cost-efficiency and frees up valuable time for IT professionals, allowing them to focus on more strategic tasks rather than routine monitoring and adjustments. This shift towards AI-managed infrastructure represents a significant advancement in intelligent infrastructure management, highlighting the transformative impact of AI on reducing the operational burdens associated with resource allocation in modern cloud environments. This emphasis on AI's role in relieving the burden of resource allocation can make the audience feel relieved and less stressed about this aspect of their work.

1.2 Enhancing Learning Experiences with AI

Onesi-Ozigagun et al. (2024) provide robust evidence that AI can significantly enhance learning experiences by revolutionizing how educational content is personalized and delivered. The authors underscore the capability of AI-driven tools to individualize education by adapting instructional materials to the unique needs of each student. Through sophisticated algorithms, AI can analyze individual learning patterns, strengths, and areas of difficulty, creating customized learning paths that cater to learners' specific pace and preferences. As detailed in the article, this personalized approach addresses the limitations of traditional educational models that often employ a uniform teaching method, thereby improving learning outcomes and fostering a deeper understanding of the material. This potential of AI to enhance learning experiences can make the audience feel excited and optimistic about the future of education.

Onesi-Ozigagun et al. (2024) also highlight the potential of AI to enhance student engagement. The article discusses how AI technologies, such as virtual tutors and intelligent learning platforms, create dynamic educational experiences involving students in their learning process. These AI-powered systems are designed to provide immediate feedback, employ gamification strategies, and present adaptive challenges that maintain student interest and motivation. As the authors argue, the integration of AI makes learning more interactive and enjoyable. It extends the learning process beyond the confines of the traditional classroom, facilitating continuous and self-directed learning. This comprehensive review demonstrates how AI can potentially transform educational practices and significantly enhance the learning experience (Onesi-Ozigagun et al., 2024).

1.3 Strategic Planning

Biloslavo et al. (2024) present compelling evidence that AI significantly enhances strategic planning in volatile, uncertain, complex, and ambiguous (VUCA) environments by processing vast data quickly and accurately, generating predictive analytics crucial for navigating these complexities. Integrating AI into strategic planning equips leaders with tools to anticipate trends, identify emerging opportunities and threats, and adjust strategies in real time, ensuring organizational agility and resilience. In educational leadership, AI's capacity to analyze complex datasets, including student performance and resource management, provides actionable insights that enhance strategic foresight and foster more informed, data-driven decisions. Moreover, AI-driven insights can inspire innovation in curriculum development, teaching methodologies, and resource allocation, driving continuous improvement and transformative educational changes. This comprehensive AI integration is poised to significantly impact the future of education in a rapidly evolving world (Biloslavo et al., 2024).

Chklovski et al. (2021) provide compelling evidence that AI can significantly support families in solving real-world problems by enhancing communication, fostering collaborative decision-making, and improving overall quality of life. Their two-year study highlights AI's adaptability across various familial contexts and its transformative impact on addressing complex, everyday challenges. Additionally, the study emphasizes AI's role in democratizing access to problem-solving resources, making advanced tools more accessible to diverse family structures. AI's ability to personalize and adapt to individual family needs fosters a more inclusive and supportive environment, empowering families to navigate modern life and become more resilient and self-sufficient. Furthermore, the authors underscore AI's potential in promoting long-term behavioral changes within families, as AI systems, through consistent interaction and feedback, help develop healthier habits and stronger communication patterns. This contributes to improved well-being and sustainable changes in family dynamics, showcasing AI's capacity as both an immediate problem-solving tool and a catalyst for lasting positive change in family life (Chklovski et al., 2021).

1.4 Addressing Ethical and Practical Concerns

Integrating AI in healthcare presents profound ethical implications (Li et al., 2022). One primary concern is the potential for AI systems to exacerbate existing biases in healthcare delivery. The authors underscore that AI algorithms, often trained on historical data, can inadvertently perpetuate systemic inequities, particularly in diagnosing and treating marginalized populations. This concern is further complicated by the opacity of AI decision-making processes, which can obscure the reasons behind specific clinical recommendations, potentially leading to distrust among patients and healthcare providers alike (Li et al., 2022).

Another significant ethical challenge discussed in the article is the issue of data privacy and consent. Li et al. (2022) argue that the widespread deployment of AI in healthcare necessitates collecting and analyzing vast amounts of personal health data. While this data is invaluable for improving AI accuracy, it raises concerns about the potential for misuse or unauthorized access, especially in the absence of robust regulatory frameworks. The authors highlight the need for clear guidelines and strategies to ensure that patient data is handled with the utmost care, balancing the benefits of AI advancements with the protection of individual privacy (Li et al., 2022). They emphasize the importance of accountability and transparency in AI systems to address ethical concerns. They further suggested that for AI to be ethically integrated into healthcare, there must be mechanisms to hold developers and healthcare providers accountable for the outcomes of AI-driven decisions. The lack of clear accountability can lead to a diffusion of responsibility, where no single entity is held responsible for errors or adverse consequences. Therefore, the authors advocate for developing ethical guidelines and governance structures that promote transparency in AI systems, ensuring that they are designed and implemented to align with the principles of fairness, justice, and respect for human dignity (Li et al., 2022).

AI's potential to support urban education extends beyond the classroom. It can play a significant role in strategic planning and decision-making at the district level, particularly in resource allocation and addressing disparities. By analyzing large datasets, AI can help urban school districts identify trends and gaps in resource distribution, ensuring that resources are allocated where they are most needed. This data-driven approach can help address the longstanding inequities that often characterize urban education environments. Additionally, AI can enhance family engagement by providing platforms that facilitate better communication between schools and families, ensuring that parents are informed and involved in their children's education. As AI continues to develop, its role in supporting and transforming urban education will likely expand, offering new tools to educators and administrators working to create more equitable and effective educational environments.

SECTION TWO: AI, SOCIAL JUSTICE, AND ANDRAGOGICAL EDUCATION

2.1 Transformative Impact of Technologies

This section critically examines the intersection of AI and social justice within andragogical education. It aims to elucidate how AI, as a transformative technology, influences educational practices and its implications for addressing systemic inequities and empowering marginalized communities (Knox, 2020; Selwyn, 2019). The rapid integration of AI into education raises significant questions about how these technologies might reshape educational landscapes, especially in adult learning, which is increasingly important in a world that demands continuous skill development and lifelong learning (Williamson, 2018).

AI technologies promise to revolutionize education by providing personalized learning experiences, automating administrative tasks, and offering new tools for both teachers and students (West et al., 2019). However, these technologies also pose risks, mainly when implemented without considering the diverse needs of all learners, especially those from marginalized communities (Eubanks, 2018). The potential for AI to perpetuate existing inequalities is significant, as these technologies often reflect the biases and assumptions of the societies in which they are developed (O'Neil, 2016).

Bucella (2024) discusses the socio-political implications that arise when AI is considered through the lens of social justice or the Capability Approach, highlighting the transformative effects of technology on society. The Capability Approach, developed by economist Amartya Sen and furthered by philosopher Martha Nussbaum, emphasizes enabling individuals to achieve capabilities they have reason to value. When applied to AI and education, this approach challenges educators and policymakers to consider the efficiency of AI tools and their ability to support the development of learners' full potential.

This exploration sets the stage for understanding the different types of transformative technologies outlined by Gruetzemacher and Whittlestone (2022), which include General-purpose Technologies (GPTs). These technologies, such as telephones and electricity, have become widespread and multipurpose, deeply integrated into everyday life. In the context of AI, GPTs represent tools and systems that are not just specialized for one task but can be adapted across various domains, including education, healthcare, and public services. AI's transformative potential as a GPT lies in its ability to create new opportunities for learning and growth, particularly for those who have been historically marginalized.

2.2 Quick and Dramatic Impact Technologies:

These technologies significantly influence specific aspects of life, like nuclear energy's impact on warfare and international relations. AI, when deployed in educational settings, can have similarly dramatic impacts. For instance, AI-driven platforms can rapidly scale personalized education to millions of learners, offering tailored content that adapts to the learner's progress in real time. This capability can transform traditional education systems, which often need help to meet students' diverse needs. However, the rapid adoption of such technologies also raises concerns about the readiness of educational institutions to integrate these tools effectively, the potential loss of human elements in teaching, and the ethical implications of data-driven learning.

2.3 Fundamental and Unprecedented Societal Change Technologies:

These technologies bring about gradual and profound societal changes, such as during the industrial and agricultural revolutions. AI has the potential to be such a technology within the educational sphere. Over time, AI could fundamentally change how education is perceived, delivered, and valued. For example, the traditional model of education, centered around physical classrooms, scheduled classes, and standardized curricula, could be replaced by more flexible, on-demand learning experiences customized to each learner's needs. This shift could democratize access to education, making high-quality learning opportunities available to people regardless of their location, economic status, or prior educational background. However, these changes also raise important questions about the future role of teachers, the potential for increased surveillance and control in educational environments, and the need to ensure that AI-driven education systems are designed to promote equity and inclusion.

Bucella (2022) argues that AI, as a profoundly transformative technology, has introduced new possibilities and raised standards of well-being in society, making it crucial for all individuals to access it. The challenge, however, lies in ensuring that access to AI-driven educational tools is equitable and inclusive. For example, while AI can provide personalized learning experiences that cater to individual needs, there is a risk that these tools may only be accessible to those with the resources and infrastructure to support them. This could exacerbate existing inequalities rather than reduce them. Considering these possibilities, Ayeni et al. (2024) emphasize that integrating AI into educational technologies reshapes the learning infrastructure and redefines pedagogical paradigms, mainly through personalized education. Personalized education allows for a more tailored approach to learning, where students can progress at their own pace, focus on areas where they need more support, and receive immediate feedback on their performance. This approach contrasts with traditional education models, where all students are expected to learn the same material at the same pace, regardless of their needs or abilities. However, this shift necessitates critically examining how such technologies can perpetuate or mitigate educational disparities. For instance, if AI systems are designed with inherent biases or rely on data that reflects existing societal inequalities, they may inadvertently reinforce those inequalities.

2.4 Andragogical Education

Andragogy, often defined as the art and science of facilitating adult learning, has evolved into a pivotal framework within adult education. Unlike pedagogy, which focuses on teaching children, andragogy recognizes that adults have different learning needs, motivations, and constraints. Adult learners often bring a wealth of experience to the learning process, which can be a valuable resource for both the learner and the educator. Andragogy emphasizes the importance of self-directed learning, where adults take responsibility for their learning journey, set their own goals, and choose the best methods for them. Knowledge has profoundly influenced contemporary educational practices. Malcolm Knowles's interpretation of andragogy emphasizes self-directed learning and the importance of experiential learning. Knowles identified six key principles of andragogy: the need to know, the learner's self-concept, the role of the learner's experience, readiness to learn, orientation to learning, and motivation. These principles highlight the importance of designing educational experiences that are relevant, practical, and aligned with the learner's life goals.

While Knowles's contributions are widely recognized, it is equally important to explore the historical roots and alternative interpretations of andragogy before his work, particularly those offering different insights into adult learning processes (Loeng & Omwami, 2018). For example, andragogy has been influenced by various educational theories and philosophies, including constructivism, humanism, and experiential learning. These perspectives emphasize the importance of active learning, critical thinking, and the social context of education. Understanding these different approaches can help educators design more effective and inclusive learning experiences for adult learners. Mandelelize and Sepeng (2024) remind us that, despite the appeal of adult learning, adult learners face various challenges. These challenges can include balancing work, family, and educational responsibilities, overcoming previous negative experiences with education, and navigating complex and often inflexible educational systems. The theory of andragogy explains that external responsibilities can hinder adult learners, negatively impacting their educational progress.

To address these challenges, adult learners require tailored solutions that effectively overcome these barriers while supporting their academic journey. For example, flexible learning options such as online courses, modular learning, and competency-based education can give adult learners the flexibility they need to balance their responsibilities. Scholars agree that the andragogical approach empowers learners to explore their own learning needs, fostering greater independence, active participation, and motivation to learn rather than being passively instructed. Arutmayanti and Hiyanto (2023) systematically reviewed articles on the andragogical approach in educational settings, examining publications from 2018 to 2023.

Their findings underscore the importance of this approach in curriculum and teaching innovation and highlight its broader impact on shifting the learning paradigm. The review also revealed that implementation involves shifting the focus of learning from teachers to students (student-centered learning), applying andragogy in specific subjects and courses, utilizing peer tutors, and introducing innovative teaching methods. The andragogical approach aligns well with the potential of AI in education. AI technologies can support and enhance the principles of andragogy by providing tools that allow adult learners to take control of their learning, access personalized content, and engage in self-assessment and reflection. For instance, AI-driven learning platforms can provide adult learners with real-time feedback, suggest resources based on their progress, and create adaptive learning paths that respond to their individual needs and goals.

This leads to a review of the impact of andragogical implementation, which is overwhelmingly positive. However, to fully appreciate its effect, it is essential first to define and understand the origins of andragogy. 'Andragogy' originates from the Greek word *andragogos*, meaning 'teaching adults.' Knowles (1980) defines andragogy as the art and science of facilitating adult learning. This terminology clarifies the focus on adult learners and underscores the distinction between the practical application of 'adult education' and the more theoretical and scholarly approach of 'andragogy.' This distinction is important because it highlights the need for educational practices and technologies to meet adult learners' needs rather than simply adapting methods initially developed for children.

SECTION THREE: INTEGRATING CHATBOTS IN ONLINE LEARNING ENVIRONMENTS TO INCREASE STUDENT ENGAGEMENT AND COMMUNICATION IN HIGHER EDUCATION

3.1 Online Learning Environments

Online learning in higher education has expanded, and even more so since the COVID-19 pandemic. However, when higher education institutions quickly moved from in-person instruction to online delivery modalities, there wasn't time to fully understand the implications of online pedagogy on student transition and engagement (Brown et al., 2022). Students perform differently within unique and sophisticated learning management systems (LMSs) that universities employ, and they may struggle with the unfamiliarity of online pedagogies and tools that maximize their learning experiences, especially students who are non/low-engaged (Brown et al., 2022).

Although students' experiences within a university's learning management system (LMS) vary, LMSs have proven effective at collecting data about learner behaviors and providing feedback to improve teaching, learning, and decision-making (Brown et al., 2022). However, response to these data is based on the conditions that student's access to resources can be collected as data via learning analytics; professors will have access to data about their students' interactions with the online course, and professors can utilize these data to make decisions about the course curriculum and then communicate these decisions with students (Brown et al., 2022). Learning Analytics (LA) has proven helpful in monitoring online and learner engagement – the level of engagement of a student – whether low/non-engaged (Brown et al., 2022). For example, statistics can be collected about levels of student activity, the frequency of contact with online course content, and the overall assessment of a student's performance – therefore allowing campus agents to make informed decisions about the types of intentional support to provide a student, and what kinds of early interventions to initiate for students (Brown et al., 2022).

3.2 Effective Communication in Online Learning Environments

When designing and utilizing online learning environments, their communication strategies must engage students, especially those who are disengaged (Brown et al., 2022). Brown et al. (2022) identify three concepts of communication that enhance student learning and engagement: 1) Expectation, 2) Engagement, and 3) Nudging. *Expectation* management involves explicit and transparent communication throughout the course to promote a positive learning experience (rules, expectations, course objectives, goals, etc.) (Brown et al., 2022). *Engagement* requires a) Communicating engagement expectations before the term begins, b) promoting resources, c) tracking online engagement, and d) recognizing and reinforcing positive online engagement (Brown et al., 2022). Finally, *Nudges* support online engagement and learning by promoting valuable resources, activities, and engagement opportunities for disengaged students, increasing their motivation (Brown et al., 2022). Nudges are most effective when it is determined what to nudge (items relating to student success like academic performance), who to nudge (a specific group of students like those who are disengaged) when to nudge (when students have not interacted with key success markers and/or during particular times of the term like the add/drop period); and the type of nudge (the intervention or communication) (Brown et al., 2022).

3.3 AI Chatbots in Higher Education

A high student-to-teacher ratio can interfere with students' receiving positive social interaction, timely and consistent communication, and rapport within the classroom, which impacts learning outcomes (Chen et al., 2023). In response to this challenge, some colleges and universities offer a wide variety of self-paced learning options (asynchronous courses) through online learning communities/ platforms, which provide diverse learning experiences and student-teacher interactions. However, this method still needs to solve the limited time challenge for instructors with large course enrollments (Chen et al., 2023). To further enhance online learning experiences and to support professors and student engagement, AI chatbots have been developed to simulate a conversation between the user and a computer, allowing the user to engage in a conversation with an AI robot using natural language rather than a human for support and personalized services (Yang & Evans, 2019; Abbas et al., 2022).

With the main objectives of introducing new services or improving current ones, conversational agents (also known as Chatbots) have been integrated into higher education as tools to answer questions, student queries, and service inquiries due to the increase of AI and natural language processing techniques (Pérez et al., 2020; Chen et al., 2023). In the early 1980s, chatbots were studied and researched. Still, it was not until recently, when AI and language processing developed, that chatbots gained more interest and attention, especially in teaching, learning, pedagogy, and andragogy (Chen et al., 2023). Chatbots in higher education are developing, and they have been utilized in strategic areas of education to engage students and provide timely responses, answers, and support. On some college campuses, chatbots have been used to teach modern languages and computer programming languages and provide interviewing training to generate knowledge like a human being (Yang & Evans, 2019).

In contrast, some chatbots offer answers in a more question-and-answer role on the institution's website, acting more like a service-oriented chatbot (Pérez et al., 2020). High-traffic areas of a university benefit from chatbots that can receive high-volume inquiries from the campus community, address questions and basic requests, and then re-route inquiries to specific regions of human support as needed. For example, utilizing a helpdesk chatbot is advantageous in areas of a university with large workloads and staff shortages (Yang & Evans, 2019).

Chatbots in higher education offer diverse student services, including addressing inquiries, supporting cognition and learning, forming supportive teams, and providing career counseling (Chen et al., 2023). They enhance student engagement by improving motivation, attention, collaborative learning, and communication while fostering a sense of belonging through learning communities (Studente et al., 2020). As intelligent assistants, chatbots provide quick answers, study tips, and support career exploration and mental well-being, making them invaluable for student engagement (Chen et al., 2023). Key strengths of chatbots include their responsiveness, interactivity, and confidentiality. They offer students a faster, tailored learning experience and a safe space for asking questions (Chen et al., 2023). However, limitations exist, such as their inability to fully understand complex inquiries and their lack of emotional connection, which can result in transactional interactions (Chen et al., 2023).

Ethical considerations that higher education institutions must be aware of when implementing chatbots are their ability to understand the needs of students who are marginalized (including international students) and/or those students with limited physical skills in tandem with being transparent about being a computer rather than a human voice (Chen et al., 2023). Furthermore, higher education institutions must be mindful of chatbot spaces that consist of innovative technology, questions of identity, race, and other factors that affect humans' daily lives that are interconnected and often oppose one another (Schlesinger et al., 2018). Other concerns about using AI technology in higher education center around the security and privacy of its users, as well as social risks (Chen et al., 2023).

As the technology for chatbots develops, several areas of strength and technical challenges have been discovered during their development. For example, when students engage with a chatbot, they report being aware that they are not talking to a human, and in some instances, chatbots cannot answer all the questions the student asks (Yang & Evans, 2019). One solution might be utilizing search skills that connect to a series of databases and redirect students' questions to human support (Yang & Evans, 2019). Also, high-level AI programming (i.e., "tone analysis") is being explored to read users' feelings and emotional states, creating a more positive customer service experience (Yang & Evans, 2019). Another technical challenge for chatbots is that they are not fully integrated with the universities' broader systems like websites, mailing systems, and helpdesk systems. Therefore, they're still functioning as standalone applications which aren't always in alignment with the university's policies regarding data privacy (Yang & Evans, 2019).

Some chatbots have been developed to provide more equitable services for rural communities, and parents who do not speak English as their first language, which address equity and accessibility concerns. To advance in these areas, educational leaders must dismantle implicit bias in dataset development and recreate diverse and racially conscious databases (Schlesinger et al., 2018; Chen et al., 2023). Schlesinger et al. (2018) explain that these databases are relatively simple to manage and adapt because they are versatile sites capable of technical and social change that already include conversational text and a variety of race-talk (conversations about history, living as a person of color, living with privilege, talking across languages other than English, and culture, etc.). These cultural references represent the user, so there must be an understanding of whose cultural references are being archived and whose culture is being omitted. If the racial legacy of those databases is not being investigated, then they will continue to archive what has been socially constructed as "normal" - white, cisgender, heterosexual male (Schlesinger et al., 2018).

3.4 The Adult Learner

The increase of adult learners who have entered or returned to higher education is consistent across higher education. Therefore, there is an ongoing need for institutions to provide unique and intentional support through the design of programs specific to adult learners (Renner & Skursha, 2023). Defining an adult learner can be ambiguous, but some scholars define adult learners as undergraduate students over 25 with unique life variables that influence their enrollment outcomes and abilities to meet personal and educational goals (Renner & Skursha, 2023).

Adult learners are among the fastest-growing student demographics in higher education (Abbas et al., 2022; Renner & Skursha, 2023). They may be labeled as "at-risk" or "at promise" due to their unique challenges compared to their traditional student counterparts. Many adult learners enroll part-time, work full-time, and withdraw from the institution after one year due to lack of motivation and participation challenges (Abbas et al., 2022). Many adult learners feel disconnected from the campus community and face the pressure of balancing finances and familial obligations, which interferes with their sense of belonging (Abbas et al., 2022). This is a concern for campus agents because the retention rates of adult learners are negatively impacted by these unique challenges.

To support adult learners and their ability to navigate higher education, their needs (their "existence needs") must be met (Renner & Skursha, 2023). Existence needs involve being informed about expectations and completing various learning activities (Renner & Skursha, 2023). Examples of existence needs include transparency, technical support, and a sense of belonging combined with peer and faculty interaction (Renner & Skursha, 2023).

3.5 Student Engagement for Adult Learners

Student engagement is a critical outcome that most institutions strive for on their campuses. For example, student engagement might involve student employment, tutorial support, peer mentoring, and co-curricular opportunities like student government or study abroad, or it might involve Greek Life, intramural sports, or conducting research with faculty depending on the campus. Student engagement is significant for adult learners who engage in an online learning environment, where the connection with faculty (approachability, genuine interest in students, and enthusiasm) and peers (interaction with one another to provide academic and personal support) is critical to reducing isolation and disconnection (Abbas et al., 2022). When adult learners are engaged, they become active learners, their academic performance improves, and they are more likely to remain at the institution (Abbas et al., 2022).

Student engagement, driven by academic and social interactions, is crucial for retention (Renner & Skursha, 2023). Universities must prioritize retaining adult students, who face challenges like academic preparation, financial concerns, and work-family responsibilities that hinder their campus engagement. Unsupportive policies and past negative experiences further exacerbate these challenges. Institutions must focus on eliminating these obstacles and humanizing the adult learner experience to ensure their success (Renner & Skursha, 2023). Engaging students with their institutions is a persistent challenge in higher education (Studente et al., 2020) so to address this, some institutions focus on interventions like personalized interactions, outreach, student programming, and supportive touchpoints from enrollment to graduation (Renner & Skursha, 2023). With many students enrolled in online courses, support services are offered both virtually and face-to-face. Additionally, chatbots have proven effective in helping students transition to learning communities, mitigating issues of low engagement (Studente et al., 2020).

3.6 Improving Student Engagement with Chatbots

Technology has been a strategy to improve student engagement, especially within online learning environments, by building community. High-impact practices like Peer Mentors and Peer Tutors foster student engagement and motivation, increasing a sense of belonging and reducing feelings of disconnection (Abbas et al., 2022). Furthermore, in online learning environments, timely feedback and responses to students can increase the sense of belonging while lessening feelings of isolation and disconnection (Abbas et al., 2022). In online learning communities, the use of chatbots, peer support, and mobile instant messaging (MIM) like WhatsApp, promote student engagement, enhance social interaction, and encourage interpersonal communication, collaboration, and learning (Abbas et al., 2022; Hwang & Chang, 2023).

Higher education has utilized chatbots to enhance student engagement and lower costs of services by providing teaching-oriented services (reinforce learning as teaching assistants or tutors) or service-oriented services (those assigned to answer frequently asked questions about grades, clubs, and important dates) (Abbas et al., 2022). These AI services aim to promote student engagement and decrease or eliminate feelings of loneliness and isolation (Abbas et al., 2022).

Many mature/adult learners reported feeling more comfortable asking questions within online communities anytime and anywhere without being judged. They found these online learning communities a valuable environment to connect with peers, increasing their sense of belonging (Abbas et al., 2022). Students who can easily access AI chatbots as part of their online learning experience feel more engaged with the university (Abbas et al., 2022). Furthermore, coupling these experiences with thorough technology training that explains how the application's unique features benefit students, can create a positive user experience (Abbas et al., 2022).

SECTION FOUR: ARTIFICIAL INTELLIGENCE FOR 21ST-CENTURY EDUCATION: TRANSFORMING ADULT LEARNING IN URBAN SETTINGS

AI has swiftly become a transformative educational force, particularly in urban environments. As AI technologies evolve, they present unique opportunities for enhancing teaching and learning processes, especially for adult learners. Scholars and practitioners alike are increasingly focused on understanding and leveraging the potential of AI to optimize adult education, or andragogy, in the 21st century. This section explores the exponential growth of AI-generated technology, its origin and evolution, the rapid expansion of AI's influence in education, and the multifaceted impact of AI on the cognitive, behavioral, and emotional aspects of adult learning. Additionally, the section will critically analyze the ethical implications of AI's integration into educational systems and explore the potential future role of AI in shaping adult education in urban settings.

4.1 Origin and Evolution of AI in Education

The journey of AI in education can be traced back to the mid-20th century, with the advent of early computer-based learning systems. One of the pioneering systems, PLATO (Programmed Logic for Automated Teaching Operations), laid the foundation for what would eventually evolve into the sophisticated AI-driven educational platforms we see today (Woolf, 2010). Initially, AI in education was limited to simple algorithmic tutoring systems designed to provide essential feedback and guidance to learners. However, with the advancement of AI technologies, particularly the rapid development of Large Language Models (LLMs) and robust computer systems, its application has become ubiquitous, especially in the education sector.

The evolution of AI in education has been marked by significant milestones, beginning with artificial narrow intelligence (ANI), which focuses on specific tasks like language translation and game playing. As AI technology progressed, Generative Artificial Intelligence (GAI) emerged, characterized by its ability to generate text, audio, and video content in response to prompts. This advancement developed tools like ChatGPT, Gemini, and DALL-E, which have since become integral to modern educational environments (Holmes et al., 2019). The current trajectory of AI suggests that we are on the brink of achieving Artificial General Intelligence (AGI), which could perform tasks at a level comparable to or even exceeding human capabilities. This evolution has profound implications for education, particularly in urban settings where AI tools are utilized to provide personalized instruction, adaptive assessments, and real-time feedback tailored to the specific needs of individual learners (Woolf, 2010).

4.2 Exponential Growth of AI-Generated Technology in Education

Over the past two decades, AI-generated technology has advanced at an unprecedented rate, bringing about a diverse array of tools and applications that are revolutionizing the landscape of adult education, particularly in urban settings. Innovations such as ChatGPT, Gemini, Alexa, Siri, and Copilot have become ubiquitous in educational environments, offering novel avenues for learners to engage with content, access information, and seek assistance in real time (Wooldridge, 2021). These technologies provide scalable solutions that support learners' varied and complex needs, significantly enhancing the learning experience by making education more accessible and personalized (Luckin & Holmes, 2016). The number of peer-reviewed articles, textbook publications, conferences, seminars, and webinars dedicated to AI within the last two years after the launch of ChatGPT 3.5 should be an unambiguous clue for anyone to imply the future of AI-humanity marriage.

For example, AI-generated live translation has scattered a significant traditional barrier in education for non-English speaking learners. Moreover, AI-driven virtual assistants like Alexa and Siri have become invaluable tools for adult learners, helping them to navigate educational resources, manage their schedules, and receive real-time feedback on their progress. The ability of these virtual assistants to process and respond to voice commands allows learners to interact with educational content more naturally and intuitively, thus breaking down barriers to learning that may have existed previously (Heffernan & Heffernan, 2014). Additionally, AI-powered writing assistants such as ChatGPT have emerged as crucial resources for adult learners, aiding them in refining their writing skills by providing instant feedback, personalized learning opportunities, and suggestions for improvement. These tools enhance the quality of learners' work and foster a deeper engagement with the learning process, as learners can iteratively improve their output based on the AI's guidance (Woolf, 2010). AI could break the barriers between economic class differences by opening various employment opportunities for people from every ground.

Moreover, the economic potential of these AI technologies must be recognized. For example, it has been predicted that with the deployment of ChatGPT 4.0, the third industrial revolution could generate up to $13-$22 trillion of value annually by 2033 (Ng, 2024). This projection highlights AI technologies' transformative economic impact in education and across various sectors, further amplifying the importance of integrating AI into educational systems.

4.3 The Rapid Growth of AI Use and Influence in Education

The past two decades have witnessed explosive growth in the application and influence of AI in education, driven by rapid advancements in machine learning, natural language processing, and data analytics (ElAtia et al., 2016). These technological advancements have enabled the creation of AI-driven educational tools capable of processing vast amounts of data in real time, analyzing learner behavior, recognizing patterns, and offering personalized learning experiences tailored to individual needs and preferences (Popenici & Kerr, 2017). In urban educational settings, AI has become an essential tool for enhancing educational access, fairness, and quality, particularly for diverse groups of learners who may face barriers to traditional educational methods (Wooldridge, 2021). The proliferation of digital devices, the increasing availability of big data, and its contribution to LLMs have further facilitated the widespread adoption of AI technologies in education, enabling more efficient and effective learning processes.

One of the most significant contributions of AI to urban adult education is its ability to provide personalized learning experiences that cater to the unique needs of each learner. AI-powered career counseling systems, for example, offer tailored recommendations for educational pathways based on an individual's skills, interests, and current labor market trends (Brynjolfsson & McAfee, 2014). These systems help learners navigate the complex landscape of adult education, allowing them to make informed decisions about their educational and career trajectories. Similarly, AI-driven adaptive learning platforms dynamically adjust the difficulty of learning materials to ensure that adult learners remain engaged and motivated, regardless of their prior knowledge or learning preferences (Heffernan & Heffernan, 2014).

4.4 Impact of AI on Cognitive, Behavioral, and Emotional Aspects of Adult Education

Integrating AI into adult education profoundly influences learning's cognitive, behavioral, and emotional aspects. Cognitively, AI enhances learning by delivering personalized instruction that adapts to each learner's strengths and weaknesses, facilitating deeper understanding and retention, particularly in complex subjects (Holmes et al., 2019). This approach especially benefits adult learners with diverse knowledge levels and learning styles. Behaviorally, AI increases engagement and motivation through gamification techniques like rewards and challenges, encouraging positive learning behaviors such as time management and self-regulation (Popenici & Kerr, 2017). Emotionally, AI can reduce anxiety and boost confidence by offering immediate feedback and personalized support, though it may also increase feelings of isolation and stress due to over-reliance and pressure in AI-driven assessments (Luckin & Holmes, 2016; Seldon et al., 2020; Holmes & Porayska-Pomsta, 2023). These effects emphasize the need for well-designed AI tools that promote a balanced, holistic learning experience for adult learners.

4.5 AI: A Great Servant but a Bad Master

As AI becomes increasingly integrated into education, it is essential to consider the ethical implications of its use, misuse, and abuse. A central concern is the balance between using AI to enhance education and the risk of over-reliance on these systems, potentially eroding human agency and critical thinking (University of Arizona, 2024). While AI can potentially empower learners and educators by providing advanced tools for learning, there is also a risk that dependence on AI could diminish human agency, making learners passive recipients of information rather than active participants in their education. Furthermore, experts recommend utilizing AI as an aid to human needs rather than as an all-knowing authority. The latest version of Chat GPT 4.0 received its most recent update in October 2023. Hence, users should understand the system's functionality and limitations to prevent excessive reliance on fabricated or hallucinated information. Applying critical and humane skills to assess and process AI-generated output is crucial. In simpler terms, humans should act as diligent and mindful drivers of this sophisticated and highly efficient vehicle of AI to navigate and reach their intended destination.

To address these concerns, educators are encouraged to set clear guidelines on AI usage, foster open dialogue about its role in coursework, and help students critically evaluate AI-generated content to ensure academic integrity (University of Arizona, 2024). It is also important to address ethical issues such as data privacy, access inequities, and the potential biases inherent in AI tools. By promoting transparency and accountability in AI use, educators can ensure that these technologies enhance learning without compromising the values of education (University of Arizona, 2024).

In urban adult education, where learners are expected to develop critical thinking and self-directed learning skills, the ethical use of AI is vital. AI systems should be designed to support and enhance human judgment and creativity rather than replace them (Seo et al., 2024). By doing so, AI can empower learners, helping them become more autonomous and capable of making informed decisions about their education and careers (Brynjolfsson & McAfee, 2014). Case studies from urban education settings provide valuable insights into how AI can be used ethically and effectively to empower learners. For example, AI-powered platforms that offer personalized learning paths can be designed with built-in mechanisms for learner reflection and choice, ensuring that learners remain active participants in their educational journey (Popenici & Kerr, 2017).

4.6 Growing with AI in the 21st Century and the Future of Adult Education

As we move further into the 21st century, integrating AI into adult education will continue to expand, bringing opportunities and challenges. AI has the potential to revolutionize urban education by providing personalized, scalable, and accessible learning solutions that meet the diverse needs of adult learners (ElAtia et al., 2016). However, the future of AI in education will also require careful consideration of ethical issues, such as data privacy, equity, and the potential for AI to exacerbate existing inequalities (Nguyen et al., 2023). To ensure that AI is used effectively and ethically in urban adult education, educators, policymakers, and technology developers must work together to create AI systems that are inclusive, transparent, and supportive of human agency (Holmes & Porayska-Pomsta, 2023). This collaboration is crucial to harnessing AI's full potential to enhance education and create a future where all learners can thrive in a rapidly changing world (Wooldridge, 2021). By embracing

AI's capabilities while remaining mindful of its limitations, educators can ensure that AI is used to complement and enhance human learning rather than replace it.

The future of adult education in urban areas will rely on our ability to integrate AI reasonably and inclusively and support lifelong learning. As AI advances, like the arising of any form of technology, it will be crucial to balance the benefits of AI and the need to maintain human agency, ensuring that education remains a fundamental human pursuit (Nguyen et al., 2023). By doing so, we can create a future where AI is a powerful tool for enhancing education while preserving the essential human elements of learning and personal growth (Holmes et al., 2019).

CONCLUSION

Integrating AI in urban education is an emerging trend and a pivotal advancement in addressing urban schools' complex challenges. As highlighted by Welsh and Swain (2020), urban education is intricately connected to demographic composition, socioeconomic context, and educational disparities. AI offers the potential to mitigate these challenges through data-driven solutions that enhance decision-making, personalize learning, optimize resource allocation, and ultimately foster more equitable and effective educational environments. However, the successful implementation of AI in education hinges on thoughtful and ethical strategies that ensure these technologies fulfill their promise of transforming urban education, promoting more significant equity, and driving academic success across diverse student populations.

Despite AI's promise, deploying these systems across various sectors—including education—often occurs without meaningful input from the communities they are intended to benefit. This oversight can lead to poorly designed applications that fail to account for the complexities of human behavior and social systems, reinforcing existing inequalities rather than addressing them (Black et al., 2020). Thus, the intersection of AI and social justice is critical, emphasizing the need for technological advancements to be carefully aligned with efforts to rectify deep-seated inequities. In education, AI technologies such as chatbots have shown considerable potential in enhancing student engagement and learning experiences. Students respond positively to these interactive tools, appreciating their ability to provide diverse resources, real-time feedback, and personalized interactions (Chen et al., 2023; Liu et al., 2022). However, there remains a significant gap in understanding the ethical implications of AI, particularly regarding privacy concerns and the nuanced understanding required for effective AI interactions in educational settings (Hwang & Chang, 2023). As the use of AI in education continues to evolve, there is a critical need for ongoing research to refine these technologies and ensure they are used ethically and effectively.

Looking ahead, AI presents unprecedented opportunities for enhancing adult education, especially in urban settings. However, these opportunities come with complex challenges that require careful navigation. By examining the origins and evolution of AI in education, understanding its rapid growth and impact, and considering the ethical implications of its use, educators and administrators can strategically harness AI to improve teaching and learning in urban environments. The future of adult education will be shaped by how AI is integrated into educational systems, ensuring that it serves as a valuable tool for educators rather than an authoritative force. The balance between leveraging AI's capabilities and preserving the human elements crucial to meaningful education will ultimately determine the success of AI's role in shaping the future of urban education.

REFERENCES

Abbas, N., Whitfield, J., Atwell, E., Bowman, H., Pickard, T., & Walker, A. (2022). Online chat and chatbots to enhance mature student engagement in higher education. *International Journal of Lifelong Education*, 41(3), 308–326. DOI: 10.1080/02601370.2022.2066213

Arutmayanti, N., & Hiryanto, H. (2023). Implementation of the andragogy approach in educational settings: A systematic literature review. *International Journal of Multicultural and Multireligious Understanding*, 10(8), 335–346.

Ayeni, O. O., Al Hamad, N. M., Chisom, O. N., Osawaru, B., & Adewusi, O. E. (2024). AI in education: A review of personalized learning and educational technology. *GSC Advanced Research and Reviews*, 18(2), 261–271. DOI: 10.30574/gscarr.2024.18.2.0062

Biloslavo, R., Edgar, D., Aydin, E., & Bulut, C. (2024). Artificial intelligence (AI) and strategic planning process within VUCA environments: A research agenda and guidelines. *Management Decision*. Advance online publication. DOI: 10.1108/MD-10-2023-1944

Black, E., Williams, J., Madaio, M. A., & Donti, P. L. (2020, April). A call for universities to develop requirements for community engagement in ai research. In *The Fair and Responsible AI Workshop at the 2020 CHI Conference on Human Factors in Computing Systems.*

Brown, A., Lawrence, J., Basson, M., & Redmond, P. (2022). A conceptual framework to enhance student online learning and engagement in higher education. *Higher Education Research & Development*, 41(2), 284–299. DOI: 10.1080/07294360.2020.1860912

Brynjolfsson, E., & McAfee, A. (2014). *The second Machine Age: Work, progress, and prosperity in a time of brilliant technologies*. WW Norton & Company.

Buccella, A. (2022). “AI for all” is a matter of social justice. *AI and Ethics*, 3(4), 1143–1152. DOI: 10.1007/s43681-022-00222-z PMID: 36189174

Chen, Y., Jensen, S., Albert, L. J., Gupta, S., & Lee, T. (2023). Artificial Intelligence (AI) student assistants in the classroom: Designing chatbots to support student success. *Information Systems Frontiers*, 25(1), 161–182. DOI: 10.1007/s10796-022-10291-4

Chklovski, T., Jung, R., Anderson, R., & Young, K. (2021). Comparing 2 years of empowering families to solve real-world problems with AI. *Kunstliche Intelligenz*, 35(2), 207–219. DOI: 10.1007/s13218-021-00738-2 PMID: 34316096

Dhar, S., Shyam, H. S., Tomar, S., & Rani, M. (2023). Digital Disparity in The Technological Era of Big Data and Artificial Intelligence. *2023 9th International Conference on Advanced Computing and Communication Systems (ICACCS), 1*, 2475–2478. https://doi.org/DOI: 10.1109/ICACCS57279.2023.10113094

Ekoto, C. E., & Gaikwad, P. (2015). The impact of andragogy on learning satisfaction of graduate students. *American Journal of Educational Research*, 3(11), 1378–1386.

ElAtia, S., Ipperciel, D., & Zaïane, O. R. (Eds.). (2016). *Data mining and learning analytics: Applications in educational research*. John Wiley & Sons. DOI: 10.1002/9781118998205

Eubanks, V. (2018). *Automating inequality: How high-tech tools profile, police, and punish the poor*. St. Martin's Press.

Gruetzemacher, R., & Whittlestone, J. (2022). The transformative potential of artificial intelligence. *Futures, 135*, 102884-. https://doi.org/DOI: 10.1016/j.futures.2021.102884

Hadzi, A. (2019). Social Justice and Artificial Intelligence by Dr. Adnan Hadzi (University of Malta). *Body, Space & Technology Journal, 18*(1), 145-. https://doi.org/DOI: 10.16995/bst.318

Heffernan, N. T., & Heffernan, C. L. (2014). The ASSISTments ecosystem: Building a platform that brings scientists and teachers together for minimally invasive research on human learning and teaching. *International Journal of Artificial Intelligence in Education*, 24(4), 470–497. DOI: 10.1007/s40593-014-0024-x

Holmes, W., Bialik, M., & Fadel, C. (2019). *Artificial Intelligence in Education: Promises and Implications for Teaching and Learning*. Center for Curriculum Redesign.

Holmes, W., & Porayska-Pomsta, K. (2023). *The ethics of artificial intelligence in education*. Routledge Taylor.

Hwang, G. J., & Chang, C. Y. (2023). A review of opportunities and challenges of chatbots in education. *Interactive Learning Environments*, 31(7), 4099–4112. DOI: 10.1080/10494820.2021.1952615

Hwang, G. J., & Tu, Y. F. (2021). Roles and research trends of artificial intelligence in mathematics education: *A bibliometric mapping analysis and systematic review. Mathematics*, 9(6), 584. DOI: 10.3390/math9060584

Knowles, M. S. (1970). *The modern practice of adult education: Andragogy versus pedagogy*. Cambridge Book Company.

Knowles, M. S., Holton, E. F., III, Swanson, R. A., & Robinson, P. A. (2020). Andragogy: History, meaning, context, and function. In *The adult learner* (9th ed., pp. 284–292). Routledge. https://doi.org/DOI: 10.4324/9780429299612-16

Kukulska-Hulme, A. (2012). How should the higher education workforce adapt to advancements in technology for teaching and learning? *The Internet and Higher Education*, 15(4), 247–254. DOI: 10.1016/j.iheduc.2011.12.002

Li, F., Ruijs, N., & Lu, Y. (2022). Ethics & AI: A systematic review on ethical concerns and related strategies for designing with AI in healthcare. *AI*, 4(1), 28–53. DOI: 10.3390/ai4010003

Liu, L., Subbareddy, R., & Raghavendra, C. G. (2022). AI intelligence chatbot to improve students learning in the higher education platform. *Journal of Interconnection Networks*, 22(Supp02), 1–17. DOI: 10.1142/S0219265921430325

Loeng, S. (2018). Various ways of understanding the concept of andragogy. *Cogent Education, 5*(1), 1496643-. https://doi.org/DOI: 10.1080/2331186X.2018.1496643

Luckin, R., & Holmes, W. (2016). *Intelligence Unleashed: An Argument for AI in Education*. Pearson Education.

Madaio, M., Blodgett, S. L., Mayfield, E., & Dixon-Román, E. (2021). Confronting structural inequities in AI for education. *arXiv preprint arXiv:2105.08847*.

Mandelelize, N., & Sepeng, M. (2024). Exploring challenges of adult learners in selected adult education and training centers in South Africa: An analysis of Knowles' theory of andragogy. *Social Sciences and Education Research Review*, 2(1), 152–160.

Müller, M. S. M., & Reggelin, I. T. (2021, June). Handling of Logistic Deadlocks with Machine Learning. In *14th International Doctoral Students Workshop on Logistics* (p. 77).

Nallaluthan, K., Masran, M. N., Thurasingam, V., & Kanapathy, K. (2023). Malcolm Knowles' Theory of Andragogy at Research Management and Innovation Centre Universiti Pendidikan Sultan Idris (RMIC-UPSI): Work-Based Learning Model. *Evaluation Studies in Social Sciences*, 4(2), 30–50.

Nguyen, A., Ngo, H. N., Hong, Y., Dang, B., & Nguyen, B. P. T. (2023). Ethical principles for artificial intelligence in education. *Education and Information Technologies*, 28(4), 4221–4241. DOI: 10.1007/s10639-022-11316-w PMID: 36254344

O'Neil, C. (2016). *Weapons of math destruction: How big data increases inequality and threatens democracy*. Crown Publishing Group.

Onesi-Ozigagun, O., Ololade, Y. J., Eyo-Udo, N. L., & Ogundipe, D. O. (2024). Revolutionizing education through AI: A comprehensive review of enhancing learning experiences. *International Journal of Applied Research in Social Sciences*, 6(4), 589–607. DOI: 10.51594/ijarss.v6i4.1011

Pérez, J. Q., Daradoumis, T., & Puig, J. M. M. (2020). Rediscovering the use of chatbots in education: A systematic literature review. *Computer Applications in Engineering Education*, 28(6), 1549–1565. DOI: 10.1002/cae.22326

Popenici, S. A., & Kerr, S. (2017). Exploring the impact of artificial intelligence on teaching and learning in higher education. [AI Now Institute.]. *Research and Practice in Technology Enhanced Learning*, 12(1), 22. DOI: 10.1186/s41039-017-0062-8 PMID: 30595727

Renner, B. J., & Skursha, E. (2023). Support for adult students to overcome barriers and improve persistence. *The Journal of Continuing Higher Education*, 71(3), 332–341. DOI: 10.1080/07377363.2022.2065435

Schlesinger, A., O'Hara, K. P., & Taylor, A. S. (2018). Let's talk about race: Identity, chatbots, and AI. In *Proceedings of the 2018 Chi Conference of Human Factors in Computing* (pp. 1-14). DOI: 10.1145/3173574.3173889

Seldon, A., Abidoye, O., & Metcalf, T. (2020). *The Fourth Education Revolution Reconsidered: Will Artificial Intelligence Enrich Or Diminish Humanity?* Legend Press Ltd.

Selwyn, N. (2019). *Should robots replace teachers?: AI and the future of education*. Polity Press.

Seo, K., Yoo, M., Dodson, S., & Jin, S.-H. (2024). Augmented teachers: K-12 teachers' needs for artificial intelligence's complementary role in personalized learning. *Journal of Research on Technology in Education*, •••, 1–18. DOI: 10.1080/15391523.2024.2330525

Shahvaroughi Farahani, M., & Ghasemi, G. (2024). *Artificial Intelligence and Inequality: Challenges and Opportunities*. Qeios., DOI: 10.32388/7HWUZ2

Shrungare, J. (2024). Tech and Social Justice. [Association for Computing Machinery]. *Crossroads*, 30(4), 67–69. DOI: 10.1145/3665606

Siemens, G., & Long, P. (2011). Penetrating the fog: Analytics in learning and education. *EDUCAUSE Review*, 46(5), 30.

Studente, S., Ellis, S., & Garivaldis, S. F. (2020). Exploring the potential of chatbots in higher education: A preliminary study. *International Journal of Educational and Pedagogical Sciences*, 14(9), 768–771.

Tatineni, S., & Chakilam, N. V. (2024). Integrating Artificial Intelligence with DevOps for Intelligent Infrastructure Management: Optimizing Resource Allocation and Performance in Cloud-Native Applications. *Journal of Bioinformatics and Artificial Intelligence*, 4(1), 109–142.

Tegmark, M. (2017). LIFE 3.0: Being human in the age of artificial intelligence. In A. Knopf (Ed.), *Humanist perspectives* (Number 202, pp. 39-81). Canadian Humanist Publications.

Torre, F., Teigland, R., & Engstam, L. (2019). 7 AI leadership and the future of corporate governance. *The digital transformation of labor, 116.*

Welsh, R. O., & Swain, W. A. (2020). (Re) defining urban education: A conceptual review and empirical exploration of the definition of urban education. *Educational Researcher*, 49(2), 90–100. DOI: 10.3102/0013189X20902822

West, S. M., Whittaker, M., & Crawford, K. (2019). *Discriminating Systems: Gender, Race and Power in AI.* AI Now Institute. https://ainowinstitute.org/ discriminatingsystems.html

Wooldridge, M. (2021). *A brief history of artificial intelligence: what it is, where we are, and where we are going*. Flatiron Books.

Woolf, B. P. (2010). *Building intelligent interactive tutors: Student-centered strategies for revolutionizing e-learning*. Morgan Kaufmann.

Yang, S., & Evans, C. (2019). Opportunities and challenges in using AI chatbots in higher education. In *Proceedings of the 2019 3rd International Conference on Education and E-Learning* (pp. 79-83). DOI: 10.1145/3371647.3371659

Zawacki-Richter, O., Marín, V. I., Bond, M., & Gouverneur, F. (2019). Systematic review of research on artificial intelligence applications in higher education–where are the educators? *International Journal of Educational Technology in Higher Education*, 16(1), 1–27. DOI: 10.1186/s41239-019-0171-0

Chapter 12
AI in Education: Reflections and Future Directions for Pedagogical and Andragogical Integration

Graig Kaiser
Azusa Pacific University, USA

Sue Kaiser
California State University, San Bernardino, USA

ABSTRACT

This chapter serves as a culmination of our exploration into the integration of artificial intelligence (AI) in both pedagogical and andragogical education. It synthesizes the comprehensive analysis presented throughout the book on how AI is reshaping teaching and learning for children and adults. The chapter underscores the transformative potential of AI in creating personalized, engaging, and effective educational environments while addressing the critical challenges of data privacy, algorithmic bias, and the digital divide. Through a review of key findings, ethical considerations, and practical implications, the chapter provides a forward-looking perspective on the future of AI in education. It emphasizes the need for a collaborative effort among educators, technologists, and policymakers to harness AI's potential effectively, supported by case studies that illustrate successful implementations. The insights offered aim to inspire and guide educators, researchers, and decision-makers as they navigate the evolving landscape of AI in education.

DOI: 10.4018/979-8-3373-0502-8.ch012

INTRODUCTION

As we conclude our exploration of integrating artificial intelligence (AI) into pedagogical and andragogical education, it is essential to reflect on the journey we have undertaken. This book has comprehensively analyzed the multifaceted ways AI is transforming teaching and learning for children and adults. The synthesis of these insights not only underscores the potential of AI, but also highlights the challenges and considerations that educators must address to harness this potential effectively.

Throughout this book, we have delved into various dimensions of AI in education, exploring its implications for teaching methods, learning processes, and educational outcomes. We have examined how AI technologies can be leveraged to create more personalized, engaging, and effective learning environments. By integrating AI into educational practices, we can better meet the needs of diverse learners, provide real-time feedback, and foster a more inclusive and equitable educational landscape.

We have discussed the ethical and practical considerations that come with the adoption of AI in education. Ensuring data privacy, addressing algorithmic biases, and bridging the digital divide are crucial aspects that educators and policymakers must tackle. The successful integration of AI into education requires a collaborative effort from all stakeholders, including teachers, administrators, technologists, and policymakers. We have also examined a variety of case studies and success stories that highlight the transformative potential of AI in education, offering concrete examples of how these technologies can be implemented effectively.

This chapter examines the key findings and provides a forward-looking perspective on the future of AI in education. We will reflect on the evolution of AI technologies, their impacts on pedagogical and andragogical practices, and the ethical and practical challenges that must be addressed. By synthesizing these insights, we hope to offer a comprehensive conclusion that will inform and inspire educators, policymakers, and researchers in their work to integrate AI into education.

THE EVOLUTION OF AI IN EDUCATION

The integration of AI into education is not a new phenomenon, but its rapid evolution and increasing sophistication have made it a central topic in contemporary educational discourse. From early implementations of adaptive learning systems to the sophisticated AI-driven personalized learning environments we see today, the trajectory of AI in education has been marked by continuous innovation and improvement (Luckin et al., 2016).

AI's initial foray into education involved simple automation tasks and rudimentary adaptive learning systems. These early systems, although limited, laid the groundwork for more advanced applications. Over time, AI technologies have evolved to include complex algorithms capable of deep learning, natural language processing, and real-time data analysis, significantly enhancing their educational utility (Holmes et al., 2019).

One of the earliest examples of AI in education was the development of intelligent tutoring systems (ITS). These systems used rule-based algorithms to provide personalized instruction and feedback to students. Early ITS, such as SCHOLAR and PLATO, demonstrated the potential of AI to support individualized learning. However, these systems were constrained by their dependence on pre-programmed rules and lacked the capacity to adapt to each learner's specific needs (Wenger, 1987). For instance, SCHOLAR, developed in the 1960s, was an early ITS that provided geography instruction by responding to student queries using a large knowledge base of facts. As AI technologies advanced, so did the capabilities of educational applications. Machine learning and data mining techniques has enabled more advanced analysis of student data. Adaptive learning platforms, such as Knewton and DreamBox, emerged, leveraging AI to tailor instructional content to each student's specific needs and preferences. These platforms analyze extensive datasets to detect patterns and trends, allowing them to make real-time adjustments to the learning experience. (Pane et al., 2015). For example, Knewton's adaptive learning platform uses predictive analytics to recommend personalized learning paths, improving student outcomes in various subjects.

The development of natural language processing (NLP) technologies further expanded the possibilities for AI in education. NLP enables AI systems to understand and generate human language, providing more interactive and intuitive educational tools. For example, AI-powered chatbots can answer student queries instantly, simulate conversations, and offer personalized guidance. AI-powered content creation tools can produce personalized learning materials, such as quizzes, summaries, and flashcards, thereby enhancing the efficiency and effectiveness of teaching and learning. (Chen et al., 2020). An example is the AI-driven platform Cognii, which uses NLP to provide real-time feedback on students' written responses, promoting deeper understanding and critical thinking skills.

AI has progressed to encompass more advanced applications, including predictive analytics and machine learning. Predictive analytics can forecast student outcomes and identify at-risk students who may need additional support. This proactive approach enables educators to intervene early and provide targeted assistance, potentially improving student retention and success rates. Machine learning algorithms, conversely, can continuously learn from new data, enhancing their accuracy and effectiveness over time. This capability allows AI systems to evolve alongside educational needs and trends, ensuring they remain relevant and impactful (Aguilar, 2018).

Another significant development in AI's evolution in education is the integration of AI with other emerging technologies, such as virtual reality (VR) and augmented reality (AR). These technologies, when combined with AI, can create immersive learning environments that offer experiential learning opportunities. For instance, VR can transport students to historical events or scientific phenomena, allowing them to interact with content in ways that traditional instructional methods cannot match. AI can enhance these experiences by personalizing the content and providing real-time feedback, making the learning process more engaging and effective (Freina & Ott, 2015).

The future of AI in education is poised to bring even more innovative solutions. Developments in AI technologies, such as deep learning and neural networks, are anticipated to enhance the capabilities of educational applications further These technologies can improve the accuracy of predictive models, enable more sophisticated data analysis, and support the development of advanced educational tools that can address complex learning needs. As AI continues to evolve, it will undoubtedly play an increasingly important role in shaping the future of education (Russell & Norvig, 2016).

Recent advancements in AI, such as the development of transformer models like GPT-4, have shown the potential to create more sophisticated educational tools. These models can generate human-like text, answer complex questions, and assist with language translation, providing new avenues for educational content creation and personalized learning experiences. For instance, AI-driven writing assistants can aid students in enhancing their writing skills by offering real-time feedback on grammar, style, and coherence, while language translation tools can support multilingual education by making content accessible in various languages (Brown et al., 2020).

Integrating AI in education also opens up new possibilities for lifelong learning and professional development. With AI-powered platforms, learners can access personalized learning resources, receive targeted recommendations, and engage in self-paced learning activities. This is particularly valuable in today's rapidly changing job market, where individuals must continuously update their skills and knowledge to stay competitive. By leveraging AI, educational institutions and employers can provide tailored learning opportunities that meet each learner's specific needs and goals, fostering a culture of continuous learning and adaptability (Baker & Inventado, 2014).

PEDAGOGICAL IMPACTS

In the realm of pedagogy, AI has demonstrated significant potential in enhancing student engagement, personalization, and outcomes. AI-powered tools can provide real-time feedback, adapt learning pathways based on individual student performance, and identify areas where students may need additional support. These capabilities enable a more personalized and responsive educational experience, fostering deeper engagement and understanding (Hwang et al., 2020).

One of the key benefits of AI in pedagogy is its ability to provide personalized learning experiences. Conventional teaching methods often employ a one-size-fits-all approach, which may not address individual students' diverse needs and learning styles. AI-powered adaptive learning platforms, such as ALEKS and Smart Sparrow, use algorithms to analyze student performance data and customize the content and pace of instruction accordingly. This tailored approach permits students to learn at their own pace., reinforcing concepts they find challenging and progressing quicker through material they easily grasp. (Pane et al., 2015).

AI can enhance student engagement by providing interactive and immersive learning experiences. Virtual reality (VR) and augmented reality (AR) technologies, powered by AI, can create realistic simulations and environments that make learning more engaging and enjoyable. For example, students can explore historical sites, conduct virtual science experiments, or practice language skills through immersive simulations. These experiences make learning more fun and encourages participation and deeper learning of the subject matter (Bacca et al., 2014). For instance, the use of VR in a history class can allow students to virtually visit ancient civilizations, making the subject matter more tangible and memorable.

AI-powered tools also provide timely and actionable feedback to students. In traditional classroom settings, feedback is often delayed due to the workload of teachers and the time required to grade assignments. AI-driven assessment tools, such as Gradescope and Turnitin, can automate the grading process, providing instant feedback on assignments, quizzes, and exams. AI-powered tools also provide timely and actionable feedback to students. (Gehringer, 2017). This immediate feedback loop not only enhances the learning process but also alleviates the administrative burden on teachers, enabling them to devote more time to personalized instruction and student support.

AI can facilitate differentiated instruction, a pedagogical approach that involves tailoring teaching methods and resources to meet the diverse needs of students. For example, AI-powered platforms like DreamBox Learning use adaptive algorithms to adjust the difficulty of tasks based on a student's performance in real-time. This adaptability ensures that each student is appropriately challenged, promoting growth and preventing frustration or boredom. Studies have shown that such adaptive learning technologies can significantly improve student achievement and engagement, particularly in mathematics and reading (Kulik & Fletcher, 2016).

Another significant impact of AI in pedagogy is the enhancement of collaborative learning. AI-driven tools can enhance group work by pairing students according to their skills and learning styles, promoting diverse and effective collaboration. Tools like Piazza and Slack, augmented with AI, can manage discussions, answer frequently asked questions, and provide resources, thus enhancing the collaborative learning experience. This fosters a sense of community and improves critical thinking and communication skills among students (Rosé et al., 2015).

However, the integration of AI in pedagogical settings also raises critical issues related to data privacy, equity, and the role of human teachers. Ensuring that AI tools are used ethically and inclusively is paramount. Teachers must remain central to the educational process, with AI serving as a supportive tool rather than a replacement (Williamson, 2017). Concerns about data privacy emerge from the extensive collection and analysis of student information by AI systems. It is vital to implement strong data protection measures and ensure that students' personal information is managed securely and transparently. (West, 2019).

Equity is another significant concern in the integration of AI in education. While AI has the potential to close educational gaps and offer personalized learning opportunities, it can also worsen existing inequalities if not implemented thoughtfully. AI-powered tools and resources access may be limited for students from disadvantaged backgrounds, widening the digital divide. To ensure equitable access, policymakers and educators must work together to provide the necessary infrastructure, training, and support for all students (Selwyn, 2019). For instance, initiatives such as providing free or subsidized internet access and devices to underserved communities can help bridge this gap.

The role of human teachers remains crucial in the AI-integrated classroom. While AI can offer personalized and efficient support, the importance of human interaction, empathy, and mentorship cannot be understated. Teachers bring a unique human element to education, fostering relationships, understanding individual student needs, and providing emotional and social support that AI cannot replicate. The integration of AI should enhance the teacher's role, allowing them to focus on these critical aspects rather than replace them (Darling-Hammond, 2020).

For successful implementation of AI, teachers must acquire the knowledge and skills to seamlessly integrate AI tools into their educational practices. This includes how to appropriately interpret data provided by AI systems, adapting teaching strategies based on AI-generated insights, and addressing ethical and privacy concerns. Continuous professional development programs provide the opportunity for teachers stay current with the latest advancements in AI technology and pedagogical best practices, ensuring they can apply AI to enhance their teaching and support their students (Holmes et al., 2019).

ANDRAGOGICAL IMPACTS

AI can support the principles of andragogy, which emphasize self-directed learning, experiential learning, and the application of knowledge to real-world contexts. Adult learners typically bring a wealth of prior knowledge and experience to their learning, and AI can help leverage this background to create more relevant and meaningful learning experiences. For example, AI-powered learning management systems (LMS) can analyze learners' profiles, including their work history, skills, and learning preferences, to recommend personalized learning paths and resources (Knowles et al., 2020). An example is the AI-driven platform LinkedIn Learning, which suggests courses based on users' professional backgrounds and career aspirations.

AI-driven platforms can offer flexible learning opportunities that accommodate the demanding schedules of adult learners. Online learning platforms, such as Coursera, edX, and Udacity, offer various courses and programs that learners can access anytime, anywhere. These platforms use AI to personalize the learning experience, recommend courses based on learners' interests and goals, and provide real-time feedback and support. This flexibility allows adult learners to pursue educational goals without compromising their work or personal responsibilities (Kumar et al., 2019). AI can also facilitate lifelong learning by providing continuous and adaptive learning opportunities. In today's rapidly changing world, the need for upskilling and reskilling has become increasingly important.

AI-powered platforms can assist adult learners in staying updated with the latest industry developments, acquiring new skills, and advancing their careers. For example, AI-driven recommendation engines can suggest relevant courses, articles, and resources based on learners' career goals and interests, enabling them to continuously expand their knowledge and skills (Chen et al., 2020). AI can support andragogical principles by fostering self-directed learning and critical thinking. AI-driven tools, including intelligent tutoring systems and virtual mentors, can offer personalized guidance and support, helping learners set goals, plan their learning journeys, and monitor their progress. These tools can also encourage learners to engage in reflective practice, critical thinking, and problem-solving, essential skills for lifelong learning and professional development (Gikandi et al., 2011). For instance, the AI-powered platform Replika offers a virtual mentor that helps users practice self-reflection and develop emotional intelligence.

In corporate training environments, AI-driven platforms are being used to deliver personalized and scalable training programs. IBM's Watson, for instance, is utilized to create customized learning paths for employees, providing them with tailored content that aligns with their career development goals. This has significantly improved employee engagement and skill acquisition (Marr, 2018). Such applications highlight the potential of AI to support continuous professional development and ensure that adult learners can keep pace with industry advancements.

However, similar to pedagogical contexts, there are challenges to address in the integration of AI in andragogical education. Providing access to AI tools are accessible for all adult learners, regardless of their technological proficiency, is essential. Many adult learners may have limited experience with digital technologies, and providing adequate training and support is vital to ensure effective use of AI-powered tools. It is important to ensure that AI tools support rather than hinder the development of critical thinking and self-directed learning skills. AI should be used as a supportive tool that enhances learners' autonomy and critical thinking, rather than as a substitute for these essential skills (Williamson, 2017).

There is a need for continuous assessment and improvement of AI-driven educational tools to ensure they meet the evolving needs of adult learners. Regular feedback from users can help developers refine these tools, making them more effective and user-friendly. Collaborative efforts between educators, technologists, and learners are essential to create AI solutions that truly enhance the learning experience (Holmes et al., 2019).

The integration of AI in andragogical education must consider the diverse backgrounds and experiences of adult learners. AI tools should be designed to be culturally responsive and inclusive, recognizing the unique challenges faced by learners from different socio-economic, cultural, and professional backgrounds. This requires a concerted effort from developers and educators to ensure that AI systems are not only technically proficient but also socially aware and sensitive to the needs of all learners (Brookfield, 2013).

The use of AI in andragogical education can support the development of essential soft skills, such as communication, collaboration, and emotional intelligence. AI-powered simulations and virtual reality environments can create realistic scenarios where learners can practice these skills in a safe and controlled setting. For example, AI-driven virtual reality training programs in the healthcare industry allow medical professionals to practice patient interactions, improving their communication and empathy skills. Such applications demonstrate AI's potential to enhance technical skills and interpersonal competencies that are crucial for success in various professional contexts (Zary et al., 2019).

CASE STUDIES AND SUCCESS STORIES

Throughout this book, we have examined a variety of case studies that highlighted the transformative impact of AI in education. These examples demonstrate how AI can enhance learning experiences, improve educational outcomes, and support educators in their teaching practices. From AI-powered tutoring systems to intelligent content creation tools, the possibilities are vast and varied.

One notable case study involved the use of an AI-driven platform in a K-12 setting, where the technology was used to personalize learning paths for students. The results showed significant improvements in student engagement and academic performance, highlighting the potential of AI to revolutionize traditional educational models (Pane et al., 2015). In a middle school in California, the implementation of an AI-powered adaptive learning platform resulted in a 20% increase in math scores and a 15% increase in reading comprehension scores over a single academic year. Teachers reported that the platform helped identify students' learning gaps and provided targeted interventions, significantly enhancing the overall learning experience (Pane et al., 2015).

In higher education, another case study focused on an AI system designed to assist with grading and providing feedback on assignments. The system not only reduced the workload for instructors but also provided timely and detailed feedback to students, enhancing their learning experience (Breslow et al., 2013). At a university in the United Kingdom, the implementation of an AI-driven grading system for essay assignments led to a 30% reduction in grading time for instructors and improved the quality of feedback provided to students. Students reported higher satisfaction with the feedback received, as it was more detailed, specific, and actionable, helping them improve their writing skills (Breslow et al., 2013).

AI-powered tools can support language learning and cultural exchange programs. For example, Duolingo, an AI-driven language learning platform, has successfully helped millions of users worldwide learn new languages through personalized and gamified learning experiences. The platform uses AI algorithms to adapt the difficulty and content of lessons based on users' progress, ensuring a tailored learning experience that keeps learners engaged and motivated (Settles et al., 2018). Duolingo's success story demonstrates how AI can make language learning more accessible and enjoyable, breaking down language barriers and fostering cross-cultural understanding (Settles et al., 2018).

Another success story comes from the corporate training sector, where AI-powered platforms enhance employee training and development programs. For instance, IBM's Watson AI developed personalized learning experiences for employees, providing customized training modules, career recommendations, and real-time support. Implementing Watson AI in IBM's training programs resulted in a 50% increase in employee engagement and a 30% improvement in skill acquisition and retention. This case study highlights the potential of AI to support continuous learning and professional development in the workplace (Marr, 2018).

In addition to these examples, AI has also been used to support special education. Tools like the AI-powered app KidSense use speech recognition technology to help children with speech and language difficulties improve their communication skills. By providing real-time feedback and personalized exercises, KidSense has helped many children make significant progress in their speech development. This application of AI demonstrates its potential to provide targeted support to students with special needs, improving their educational outcomes and overall quality of life (Golonka et al., 2014).

AI has been instrumental in facilitating remote learning, particularly during the COVID-19 pandemic. AI-driven platforms like Google Classroom and Microsoft Teams have enabled schools to transition to online learning seamlessly. These platforms use AI to manage administrative tasks, facilitate communication, and provide personalized learning resources, ensuring that students can continue their education despite disruptions. The success of these platforms during the pandemic underscores the importance of AI in supporting flexible and resilient educational systems (Huang et al., 2020).

AI-powered platforms like Khan Academy have played a crucial role in democratizing education by providing free access to high-quality educational content worldwide. During the COVID-19 pandemic, Khan Academy saw a significant increase in users, with millions of students and teachers relying on the platform for remote learning. The platform uses AI to personalize learning paths, provide instant feedback, and offer resources tailored to individual student needs. This widespread adoption and impact highlight the potential of AI to make education more accessible and equitable on a global scale (Khan, 2020).

AI has been used to develop innovative assessment tools that provide more holistic evaluations of student performance. Platforms like Gradescope use AI to assist in grading complex assignments, such as essays and coding projects. These tools can identify patterns, provide detailed feedback, and ensure consistency and fairness in grading. By automating repetitive tasks, AI frees up educators' time, allowing them to focus on more meaningful interactions with students and support their learning more effectively (Piech et al., 2015).

IMPACT ON POLICY DEVELOPMENT

The integration of AI into education has profound implications for policy development at local, national, and international levels. Policymakers must consider the regulatory frameworks, ethical guidelines, and strategic plans necessary to support the effective and responsible use of AI in education. The following subsections discuss key areas where AI impacts policy development and the steps needed to address these issues.

Data Privacy and Security Policies

One of the most critical policy areas impacted by AI in education is data privacy and security. AI systems rely on large datasets, often containing sensitive personal information about students, teachers, and educational institutions. Policymakers must develop robust data privacy and security regulations to protect this information from misuse and breaches. These policies should define clear guidelines for data collection, storage, processing, and sharing practices. (West, 2019). The General Data Protection Regulation (GDPR) in the European Union sets stringent standards for data protection and privacy. Educational institutions using AI must ensure compliance with such regulations to safeguard the personal information of their students and staff. Policymakers should also promote transparency by requiring institutions to inform stakeholders about data usage practices and secure informed consent for data collection and processing (Regan & Jesse, 2019).

Policies must address the ethical use of data in AI systems. This includes ensuring that data is used to promote educational goals and not for commercial exploitation. The Family Educational Rights and Privacy Act (FERPA) in the United States provides guidelines on the use and protection of student data, emphasizing the need for consent and transparency. Policymakers can look to such regulations as models for developing comprehensive data privacy policies that protect students' rights while allowing for the innovative use of AI in education (Schneider, 2020).

Access and Equity

AI has the potential to both bridge and widen educational disparities, depending on how it is implemented. Policymakers must develop strategies to ensure equitable access to AI-powered educational tools and resources, particularly for students from disadvantaged backgrounds. This may involve investing in infrastructure, such as high-speed internet and digital devices, and providing financial support to schools and communities in need (Selwyn, 2019).

Policies should promote digital literacy and competency among students and educators. It is essential to offer training and professional development opportunities to ensure that all stakeholders have the skills and knowledge needed to effectively utilize AI technologies. Policymakers should also encourage the development of AI tools that are accessible and user-friendly for individuals with varying levels of technological proficiency (Holmes et al., 2019). Initiatives like the Digital India campaign aim to enhance digital infrastructure and literacy across the country, ensuring that students in rural and underserved areas have access to digital learning resources. Such policies can serve as models for other countries looking to bridge the digital divide and ensure that AI technologies benefit all students, regardless of their socio-economic background (Pradhan & Dash, 2017).

Policies should address the affordability of AI-powered educational tools and resources. This may involve partnerships between governments, educational institutions, and technology companies to provide subsidized or free access to AI tools for schools and students in need. Policymakers can promote a more equitable educational environment by ensuring that financial constraints do not restrict access to AI technologies, where all students have the opportunity to benefit from personalized and engaging learning experiences (Selwyn, 2019)

Teacher Training and Professional Development

Substantial investment in teacher training and professional development is essential for successfully integrating of AI in education. Policymakers should endorse initiatives that equip educators with the skills and knowledge to successfully incorporate AI tools into their teaching practices. This may involve funding for training programs, workshops, and online courses that focus on AI literacy and its applications in education (Popenici & Kerr, 2017).

Policies should also encourage the incorporation of AI-related content into teacher education programs. By embedding AI literacy into the curriculum, future educators can be better prepared to leverage AI technologies in their classrooms. Ongoing professional development training should be provided to ensure educators remain current with the latest advancements and best practices in AI integration. (Luckin et al., 2016). The Future of Learning Fund in the UK provides grants to schools and educational institutions for the professional development of teachers in AI and digital technologies. These initiatives can act as exemplars for other countries aiming to enhance the digital skills of their educators and ensure that they can effectively integrate AI into their teaching practices (BESA, 2019).

Teacher training programs should focus on developing critical thinking and ethical decision-making skills in the context of AI. Educators must recognize the potential biases and ethical implications of AI technologies and be equipped to address these issues in their classrooms. Encouraging a culture of ethical awareness and responsibility, teacher training programs can ensure that educators are prepared to use AI tools in ways that promote fairness, equity, and student well-being (Holmes et al., 2019).

Research and Innovation

Promoting research and innovation in AI for education is essential for driving progress and addressing the challenges associated with its integration. Policymakers should support funding for research initiatives that explore the development and impact of AI technologies in educational settings. Collaborative partnerships between educational institutions, technology companies, and research organizations can foster innovation and ensure that AI solutions are evidence-based and effective (Holmes et al., 2019).

Policies should also encourage the dissemination of research findings and best practices to inform policy development and educational practice. By creating platforms for knowledge exchange and collaboration, policymakers can help build a robust evidence base that supports the responsible and effective use of AI in education (Chen et al., 2020). The US National Science Foundation (NSF) funds research projects that explore the integration of AI in education, supporting studies on the effectiveness of AI-driven learning tools and the development of ethical guidelines for AI use. Such initiatives not only advance the understanding of AI's impact on education but also provide valuable insights for policymakers and educators seeking to implement AI technologies in their institutions (National Science Foundation, 2018).

Innovation hubs and incubators can play a crucial role in fostering the development of new AI technologies for education. These hubs can bring together researchers, educators, and technology developers to collaborate on innovative solutions that address the specific needs and challenges of educational settings. By supporting these collaborative environments, policymakers can help drive the creation of cutting-edge AI tools that enhance teaching and learning (Luckin et al., 2016).

INTERNATIONAL COLLABORATION

The global nature of AI development and its applications in education necessitates international collaboration and cooperation. Policymakers should collaborate internationally to establish shared standards and guidelines for the ethical and responsible implementation of AI in education. International organizations, such as UNESCO and the OECD, can be instrumental in fostering dialogue and coordination among countries. (UNESCO, 2019).

Collaborative efforts can ensure that AI technologies are developed and implemented in ways that advance global educational goals, including equity, inclusion, and quality education for all. By sharing resources, knowledge, and best practices, countries can collectively address the challenges and opportunities associated with AI in education (OECD, 2019). The AI for Education initiative by UNESCO aims to promote the ethical use of AI in education and foster international collaboration on AI-related research and policy development. The initiative brings together experts from various countries to share insights, develop guidelines, and support the implementation of AI technologies in educational systems worldwide. Such collaborative efforts can help ensure that AI technologies align with global educational objectives and promote equity and inclusion. (UNESCO, 2019).

THE FUTURE OF AI IN EDUCATION

Looking ahead, the future of AI in education is both exciting and challenging. Developments in AI technologies, including natural language processing, machine learning, and cognitive computing, will continue to create new opportunities for personalized and adaptive learning. However, the effective integration of AI into education will rely on our ability to tackle the associated challenges and ensure that these technologies are employed in ways that are ethical, inclusive, and aligned with educational objectives. (Chen et al., 2020).

Natural language processing (NLP) is one of the most promising areas of AI in education. NLP enables AI systems to understand, interpret, and generate human language, facilitating more interactive and intuitive learning experiences. For example, AI-powered chatbots can answer student queries instantly, simulate conversations, and offer personalized guidance. These chatbots can be used to support language learning, provide tutoring in various subjects, and assist with administrative tasks. As NLP technologies advance, more sophisticated and human-like interactions between students and AI systems will occur, thereby enhancing the overall learning experience. (Chen et al., 2020).

Machine learning, a branch of AI that analyzes large data sets and make predictions or decisions, holds substantial potential in the educational sector. Machine learning can analyze student performance data, identify learning patterns, and predict future outcomes. For example, predictive analytics can identify students at risk and provide timely interventions to support their learning. Machine learning can be employed to develop adaptive learning platforms that continuously adjusts the pacing of instruction based on individual student performance, providing a truly personalized learning experience (Luckin et al., 2016).

Cognitive computing, which involves simulating human thought processes in AI systems, offers exciting possibilities for enhancing critical thinking and problem-solving skills. Cognitive computing systems can analyze vast amounts of data, generate insights, and provide recommendations to support decision-making. In education, cognitive computing can be used to develop intelligent tutoring systems that provide personalized guidance and feedback, fostering deeper understanding and critical thinking. For example, an AI-powered tutoring system can guide students through complex problem-solving tasks, encouraging critical thinking and apply their knowledge in new ways (Holmes et al., 2019).

However, successfully integrating these advanced AI technologies in education requires careful consideration of ethical, practical, and pedagogical issues. Ensuring data privacy, addressing algorithmic bias, and bridging the digital divide remain critical challenges that must be addressed. It is essential to provide adequate training and support to educators and students to ensure they can effectively use AI-powered tools. Policymakers and educational leaders must work together to develop guidelines and policies that promote the ethical and inclusive use of AI in education (Selwyn, 2019).

The future of AI in education also hinges on developing a culture of innovation and collaboration. Educational institutions, technology companies, researchers, and policymakers must work together to explore new possibilities, share best practices, and address common challenges. Collaborative initiatives, such as research partnerships, pilot programs, and professional development networks, can help accelerate the adoption and integration of AI in education. By nurturing a collaborative and innovative mindset, the potential of AI to revolutionize teaching and learning can be fully leveraged. (Holmes et al., 2019).

One promising area for future research is the development of AI systems understands and adapts to the emotional and social needs of learners. Affective computing, a field of study that explores the development of systems that can recognize and respond to human emotions, has the potential to create more empathetic and supportive educational environments. For example, AI systems could use facial recognition and voice analysis to detect when a student is frustrated or confused and provide appropriate support and encouragement. This could enhance the overall learning experience and improve student outcomes (Picard, 1997).

The future of AI in education may involve the integration of AI with other emerging technologies, such as blockchain and the Internet of Things (IoT). Blockchain technology can provide secure and transparent record-keeping for educational credentials and achievements, while IoT devices can create smart learning environments that adapt to the needs of students in real-time. These technologies, when combined with

AI, have the potential to create more efficient, secure, and personalized educational systems (Grech & Camilleri, 2017).

The future of AI in education could see the rise of AI-driven virtual classrooms that provide immersive and interactive learning experiences. These virtual classrooms can recreate real-world settings and scenarios, enabling students to participate in hands-on learning activities and collaborate with peers globally. simulated environment, offering a safe and cost-effective alternative to traditional lab setups. Such innovations can revolutionize the way we approach education, making learning more accessible, engaging, and effective (Freina & Ott, 2015).

The future of AI in education may involve the development of AI systems that can support personalized learning plans for students with special needs. By evaluating individual learning profiles and tailoring instructional strategies accordingly, AI can facilitate the creation of more inclusive learning environments that address the diverse needs of all students. AI-powered assistive technologies, such as speech recognition and text-to-speech tools, can provide personalized support to students with disabilities, enhancing their learning experiences and promoting their academic success (Holmes et al., 2019).

FINAL THOUGHTS

In conclusion, the integration of AI into pedagogical and andragogical education offers tremendous potential to enhance and transform teaching and learning. By harnessing AI's capabilities, educators can develop effective learning experiences for students of all ages. However, realizing AI's potential requires careful consideration of ethical, practical, and pedagogical issues. As AI continues to evolve, it is essential to understand its educational potential, promoting a collaborative and informed approach to its integration. By doing so, we can ensure that AI serves as an increasingly powerful tool to support and enhance education, empowering learners and educators alike.

Thank you for joining us on this journey. We hope that this book has provided valuable insights and inspired new ideas for integrating AI into pedagogical and andragogical education. The future of education is bright, and with thoughtful and responsible integration of AI, we can create a more equitable, effective, and engaging educational landscape for all.

REFERENCES

Aguilar, S. J. (2018). Learning analytics: At the nexus of big data, digital innovation, and social justice in education. *TechTrends*, 62(1), 37–45. DOI: 10.1007/s11528-017-0226-9

Bacca, J., Baldiris, S., Fabregat, R., & Graf, S., & Kinshuk. (2014). Augmented reality trends in education: A systematic review of research and applications. *Journal of Educational Technology & Society*, 17(4), 133–149.

Binns, R. (2018). Fairness in machine learning: Lessons from political philosophy. In *Proceedings of the 2018 Conference on Fairness, Accountability, and Transparency* (pp. 149-159).

Breslow, L., Pritchard, D. E., DeBoer, J., Stump, G. S., Ho, A. D., & Seaton, D. T. (2013). Studying learning in the worldwide classroom: Research into edX's first MOOC. *Research & Practice in Assessment*, 8, 13–25.

Chen, X., Zou, D., Cheng, G., & Xie, H. (2020). Detecting and addressing students' problematic learning behaviors in MOOCs: A neural network-based approach. *Computers in Human Behavior*, 104, 106159.

Floridi, L., Cowls, J., Beltrametti, M., Chatila, R., Chazerand, P., Dignum, V., Luetge, C., Madelin, R., Pagallo, U., Rossi, F., Schafer, B., Valcke, P., & Vayena, E. (2018). AI4People—An ethical framework for a good AI society: Opportunities, risks, principles, and recommendations. *Minds and Machines*, 28(4), 689–707. DOI: 10.1007/s11023-018-9482-5 PMID: 30930541

Freina, L., & Ott, M. (2015). A literature review on immersive virtual reality in education: State of the art and perspectives. In *The International Scientific Conference eLearning and Software for Education* (pp. 133-141). DOI: 10.12753/2066-026X-15-020

Gikandi, J. W., Morrow, D., & Davis, N. E. (2011). Online formative assessment in higher education: A review of the literature. *Computers & Education*, 57(4), 2333–2351. DOI: 10.1016/j.compedu.2011.06.004

Golonka, E. M., Bowles, A. R., Frank, V. M., Richardson, D. L., & Freynik, S. (2014). Technologies for foreign language learning: A review of technology types and their effectiveness. *Computer Assisted Language Learning*, 27(1), 70–105. DOI: 10.1080/09588221.2012.700315

Grech, A., & Camilleri, A. F. (2017). *Blockchain in education*. Publications Office of the European Union.

Holmes, W., Bialik, M., & Fadel, C. (2019). *Artificial intelligence in education: Promises and implications for teaching and learning*. Center for Curriculum Redesign.

Huang, R. H., Liu, D. J., Tlili, A., Yang, J. F., & Wang, H. H. (2020). *Handbook on facilitating flexible learning during educational disruption: The Chinese experience in maintaining undisrupted learning in COVID-19 outbreak*. Smart Learning Institute of Beijing Normal University.

Hwang, G. J., Xie, H., Wah, B. W., & Gasevic, D. (2020). Vision, challenges, roles, and research issues of artificial intelligence in education. *Computers & Education: Artificial Intelligence*, 1, 100001.

Knowles, M. S., Holton, E. F.III, & Swanson, R. A. (2020). *The adult learner: The definitive classic in adult education and human resource development* (9th ed.). Routledge. DOI: 10.4324/9780429299612

Kulik, J. A., & Fletcher, J. D. (2016). Effectiveness of intelligent tutoring systems: A meta-analytic review. *Review of Educational Research*, 86(1), 42–78. DOI: 10.3102/0034654315581420

Luckin, R., Holmes, W., Griffiths, M., & Forcier, L. B. (2016). *Intelligence unleashed: An argument for AI in education*. Pearson Education.

Marr, B. (2018). How IBM is using AI, IoT, and blockchain to transform the food industry. *Forbes*.

OECD. (2019). *AI in education: Challenges and opportunities for sustainable development*. OECD Publishing.

Pane, J. F., Steiner, E. D., Baird, M. D., & Hamilton, L. S. (2015). *Continued progress: Promising evidence on personalized learning*. RAND Corporation. DOI: 10.7249/RR1365

Picard, R. W. (1997). *Affective computing*. MIT Press. DOI: 10.7551/mitpress/1140.001.0001

Popenici, S. A., & Kerr, S. (2017). Exploring the impact of artificial intelligence on teaching and learning in higher education. *Research and Practice in Technology Enhanced Learning*, 12(1), 22. DOI: 10.1186/s41039-017-0062-8 PMID: 30595727

Regan, P. M., & Jesse, J. (2019). Ethical challenges of edtech, big data and personalized learning: Twenty-first century student sorting and tracking. *Ethics and Information Technology*, 21(3), 167–179. DOI: 10.1007/s10676-018-9492-2

Rosé, C. P., Wang, Y. C., Cui, Y., Arguello, J., Stegmann, K., Weinberger, A., & Fischer, F. (2015). Analyzing collaborative learning processes automatically: Exploiting the advances of computational linguistics in computer-supported collaborative learning. *International Journal of Computer-Supported Collaborative Learning*, 3(3), 237–271. DOI: 10.1007/s11412-007-9034-0

Russell, S. J., & Norvig, P. (2021). *Artificial intelligence: A modern approach* (4th ed.). Pearson.

Selwyn, N. (2019). Should robots replace teachers? AI and the future of education. *British Journal of Educational Technology*, 50(6), 1263–1272.

Settles, B., Brust, C., Gustafson, E., Hagiwara, M., & Madnani, N. (2018). Second language acquisition modeling. In *Proceedings of the Thirteenth Workshop on Innovative Use of NLP for Building Educational Applications* (pp. 56-65). DOI: 10.18653/v1/W18-0506

UNESCO. (2019). *Artificial intelligence in education: Challenges and opportunities for sustainable development*. UNESCO Publishing.

Wenger, E. (1987). *Artificial intelligence and tutoring systems: Computational and cognitive approaches to the communication of knowledge*. Morgan Kaufmann Publishers.

West, S. M. (2019). Data capitalism: Redefining the logics of surveillance and privacy. *Business & Society*, 58(1), 20–41. DOI: 10.1177/0007650317718185

Williamson, B. (2017). Decoding ClassDojo: Psycho-policy, social-emotional learning and persuasive educational technologies. *Learning, Media and Technology*, 42(4), 440–453. DOI: 10.1080/17439884.2017.1278020

Compilation of References

Abbas, N., Whitfield, J., Atwell, E., Bowman, H., Pickard, T., & Walker, A. (2022). Online chat and chatbots to enhance mature student engagement in higher education. *International Journal of Lifelong Education*, 41(3), 308–326. DOI: 10.1080/02601370.2022.2066213

Acikkar, M., & Akay, M. F. (2009). Support vector machines for predicting the admission decision of a candidate to the School of Physical Education and Sports at Cukurova University. *Expert Systems with Applications*, 36(3), 7228–7233. DOI: 10.1016/j.eswa.2008.09.007

Adelakun, N. O. (2024, May 14). Exploring the impact of artificial intelligence on information retrieval systems. *Information Matters, 4*(5). https://informationmatters.org/2024/05/exploring-the-impact-of-artificial-intelligence-on-information-retrieval-systems/

Aguilar, S. J. (2018). Learning analytics: At the nexus of big data, digital innovation, and social justice in education. *TechTrends*, 62(1), 37–45. DOI: 10.1007/s11528-017-0226-9

Ainscow, M. (2020). Inclusion and equity in education: Making sense of global challenges. *Prospects*, 49(3), 123–134. DOI: 10.1007/s11125-020-09506-w

Akcayir, M., & Akcayir, G. (2017). Advantages and challenges associated with augmented reality for education: A systematic literature review. *Educational Research Review*, 20, 1–11. DOI: 10.1016/j.edurev.2016.11.002

Akgun, S., & Greenhow, C. (2022). Artificial intelligence in education: Addressing ethical challenges in K-12 settings. *AI and Ethics*, 2(3), 431–440. DOI: 10.1007/s43681-021-00096-7 PMID: 34790956

AlAli, R., & Wardat, Y. (2024). Opportunities and challenges of integrating generative artificial intelligence in education. *International Journal of Religion*, 5(7), 784–793. DOI: 10.61707/8y29gv34

Alamri, H. A., Watson, S., & Watson, W. (2020). Learning technology models that support personalization within blended learning environments in higher education. *TechTrends*, 65(1), 62–78. DOI: 10.1007/s11528-020-00530-3

Alasadi, E. A., & Baiz, C. R. (2023). Generative AI in education and research: Opportunities, concerns, and solutions. *Journal of Chemical Education*, 100(8), 2965–2971. DOI: 10.1021/acs.jchemed.3c00323

Alfredo, V., Echeverria, V., Jin, Y., Yan, L., Swiecki, A., Gasevic, D., & Martinez-Maldonado, R. (2024). Human-centred learning analytics and AI in education: A systematic literature review. *Computers and education. Artificial Intelligence*, 6, 1–23.

Al-khresheh, M. H. (2024). Bridging technology and pedagogy from a global lens: Teachers' perspectives on integrating ChatGPT in English language teaching. Computers & Education. *Artificial Intelligence*, 100218, 100218. Advance online publication. DOI: 10.1016/j.caeai.2024.100218

Al-Mughairi, H., & Bhaskar, P. (2024). Exploring the factors affecting the adoption AI techniques in higher education: Insights from teachers' perspectives on ChatGPT. *Journal of Research in Innovative Teaching & Learning*. DOI: 10.1108/JRIT-09-2023-0129

Almusaed, A., Almssad, A., Yitmen, I., & Homod, R. Z. (2023). Enhancing student engagement: Harnessing "AIED"'s power in hybrid education—A Review analysis. *Education Sciences*, 13(7), 632. DOI: 10.3390/educsci13070632

Alqahtani, T., Badreldin, H. A., Alrashed, M., Alshaya, A. I., Alghamdi, S. S., Bin Saleh, K., Alowais, S. A., Alshaya, O. A., Rahman, I., Al Yami, M. S., & Albekairy, A. M. (2023). The emergent role of artificial intelligence, natural learning processing, and large language models in higher education and research. *Research in Social & Administrative Pharmacy*, 19(8), 1236–1242. DOI: 10.1016/j.sapharm.2023.05.016 PMID: 37321925

Alshater, M. (2023). Exploring the role of artificial intelligence in enhancing academic performance: a case study of ChatGPT. *SSRN*, (January 2023). DOI: 10.2139/ssrn.4312358

Altbach, P. G., & Peterson, P. M. (Eds.). (1999). *Higher education in the 21st Century: Global challenge and national response*. Institute of International Education.

al-Zyoud, H. M. M. (2020). The role of artificial intelligence in teacher professional development. *Universal Journal of Educational Research*, 8(11B), 6263–6272. DOI: 10.13189/ujer.2020.082265

Amaratunga, D., & Baldry, D. (2000). Assessment of facilities management performance in higher education properties. *Facilities*, 18(7/8), 293–301. DOI: 10.1108/02632770010340681

American Council on Education. (2011). *Strength through global leadership and engagement: U.S. higher education in the 21st Century*. Report of the Blue Ribbon Panel on Global Engagement. Author. https://www.acenet.edu/Documents/2011-CIGE-BRPReport.pdf

Andris, C., Cowen, D., & Wittenbach, J. (2013). Support vector machine for spatial variation. *Transactions in GIS*, 17(1), 41–61. DOI: 10.1111/j.1467-9671.2012.01354.x

Arogundade, O. (2023). Structuring Knowledge Bases with AI and Machine Learning. *Information and Knowledge Management*, 13(1), 27–35. DOI: 10.7176/IKM/13-1-03

Arutmayanti, N., & Hiryanto, H. (2023). Implementation of the andragogy approach in educational settings: A systematic literature review. *International Journal of Multicultural and Multireligious Understanding*, 10(8), 335–346.

Association for Career and Technical Education. (2022, January 10). Leveraging VR, AR & AI for CTE student success. https://www.acteonline.org/tech-changes-how-we-learn/

Association of College and University Educators. (2024). *Teaching with AI: Inclusive and AI-resistant learning experiences*. Association of College and University Educators.

Atlas, S. (2023). *ChatGPT for higher education and professional development: A guide to conversational AI*. https://digitalcommons.uri.edu/cgi/viewcontent.cgi?article=1547&context=cba_facpubs

Atlas, S. (2023). *ChatGPT for higher education and professional development: A guide to conversational AI*. University of Rhode Island. https://digitalcommons.uri.edu/cba_facpubs/548

Australian Government - Tertiary Education quality and Standards Agency. (2023). *Assessment reform for the age of artificial intelligence*. Retrieved from TESQA: https://www.teqsa.gov.au/sites/default/files/2023-09/assessment-reform-age-artificial-intelligence-discussion-paper.pdf

Ayeni, O. O., Al Hamad, N. M., Chisom, O. N., Osawaru, B., & Adewusi, O. E. (2024). AI in education: A review of personalized learning and educational technology. *GSC Advanced Research and Reviews*, 18(2), 261–271. DOI: 10.30574/gscarr.2024.18.2.0062

Azevedo, R., & Aleven, V. (Eds.). (2013). *International handbook of metacognition and learning technologies*. Springer. DOI: 10.1007/978-1-4419-5546-3

Bacca, J., Baldiris, S., Fabregat, R., & Graf, S., & Kinshuk. (2014). Augmented reality trends in education: A systematic review of research and applications. *Journal of Educational Technology & Society*, 17(4), 133–149.

Bada, J. K., Laamanen, M., & Miiro, E. (2013). A project-based learning approach for teaching robotics to undergraduates. *Makerere Journal of Higher Education*, 5(1), 35–47. DOI: 10.4314/majohe.v5i1.3

Bahadır, E. (2016). Using Neural Network and Logistic Regression Analysis to Predict Prospective Mathematics Teachers' Academic Success upon Entering Graduate Education. *Educational Sciences: Theory & Practice*. Advance online publication. DOI: 10.12738/estp.2016.3.0214

Baïdoo-Anu, D., & Owusu Ansah, L. (2023). Education in the era of generative artificial intelligence (AI): Understanding the potential benefits of chatgpt in promoting teaching and learning. *Journal of AI*, 7(1), 52–62. DOI: 10.61969/jai.1337500

Baker, R. S., & Inventado, P. S. (2014). Educational data mining and learning analytics. In J, Larusson, J., & B. White (Eds.,) *Learning analytics* (pp. 61-75). Springer. DOI: 10.1007/978-1-4614-3305-7_4

Baker, T., Smith, L., & Anissa, N. (2019). Educ-AI-tion rebooted? Exploring the future of artificial intelligence in schools and colleges. https://media.nesta.org.uk/documents/Future_of_AI_and_education_v5_WEB.pdf

Baker, T., Smith, L., & Anissa, N. (2019). Educ-AI-tion rebooted? Exploring the future of artificial intelligence in schools and colleges. https://www.nesta.org. UK/report/education-rebooted/

Banaji, M., & Dobbin, F. (2023, September 18). Why DEI Training Doesn't Work -- And How to Fix It -- WSJ. *Dow Jones Institutional News*https://link.ezproxy.neu.edu/login?url=https://www.proquest.com/wire-feeds/why-dei-training-doesnt-work-how-fix-wsj/docview/2865953838/se-2

Banihashem, S. K., Taghizadeh Kerman, N., Noroozi, O., Moon, J., & Drachsler, H. (2024). Feedback sources in essay writing: Peer-generated or AI-generated feedback? *International Journal of Educational Technology in Higher Education*, 21(1), 23. DOI: 10.1186/s41239-024-00455-4

Barrett, A., & Pack, A. (2023). Not quite eye to A.I.: Student and teacher perspectives on the use of generative artificial intelligence in the writing process. *International Journal of Educational Technology in Higher Education*, 20(1), 59. DOI: 10.1186/s41239-023-00427-0

Bates, T. (2022). Teaching in a digital age (3rd ed.). BCcampus.

Bates, T., Cobo, C., Mariño, O., & Wheeler, S. (2020). Can artificial intelligence transform higher education? *International Journal of Educational Technology in Higher Education*, 17(42), 42. Advance online publication. DOI: 10.1186/s41239-020-00218-x

Baykasoğlu, A., Özbel, B. K., Dudaklı, N., Subulan, K., & Şenol, M. E. (2018). Process mining based approach to performance evaluation in computer-aided examinations. *Computer Applications in Engineering Education*, 26(5), 1841–1861. DOI: 10.1002/cae.21971

Benjamin, L. T. (1988). A history of teaching machines. *The American Psychologist*, 43(9), 703–712. DOI: 10.1037/0003-066X.43.9.703

Berendt, B., Littlejohn, A., & Blakemore, M. (2020). AI in education: Learner choice and fundamental rights. *Learning, Media and Technology*, 45(3), 312–324. DOI: 10.1080/17439884.2020.1786399

Bhimdiwala, A., Neri, R. C., & Gomez, L. M. (2022). Advancing the design and implementation of artificial intelligence in education through continuous improvement. *International Journal of Artificial Intelligence in Education*, 32(3), 1–27. DOI: 10.1007/s40593-021-00278-8

Bhutoria, A. (2022). Personalized education and artificial intelligence in United States, China, and India: A systematic Review using a Human-In-The-Loop model. *Computers and Education: Artificial Intelligence*, 3, 100068. DOI: 10.1016/j.caeai.2022.100068

Biloslavo, R., Edgar, D., Aydin, E., & Bulut, C. (2024). Artificial intelligence (AI) and strategic planning process within VUCA environments: A research agenda and guidelines. *Management Decision*. Advance online publication. DOI: 10.1108/MD-10-2023-1944

Binns, R. (2018). Fairness in machine learning: Lessons from political philosophy. In *Proceedings of the 2018 Conference on Fairness, Accountability, and Transparency* (pp. 149-159).

Black, E., Williams, J., Madaio, M. A., & Donti, P. L. (2020, April). A call for universities to develop requirements for community engagement in ai research. In *The Fair and Responsible AI Workshop at the 2020 CHI Conference on Human Factors in Computing Systems*.

Boettcher, J. V., & Conrad, R. M. (2016). *The online teaching survival guide: Simple and practical pedagogical tips*. John Wiley & Sons.

Bond, M., Khosravi, H., De Laat, M., Bergdahl, N., Negrea, V., Oxley, E., Pham, P., Chong, S. W., & Siemen, G. (2024). A meta systematic review of artificial intelligence in higher education: A call for increased ethics, collaboration, and rigour. *International Journal of Educational Technology in Higher Education*, 21(4), 1–41. DOI: 10.1186/s41239-023-00436-z

Borenstein, J., & Howard, A. (2021). Emerging challenges in AI and the need for AI ethics education. *AI and Ethics*, 1(1), 61–65. DOI: 10.1007/s43681-020-00002-7 PMID: 38624388

Bower, M. (2019). Technology-mediated learning theory. *British Journal of Educational Technology*, 50(3), 1035–1048. DOI: 10.1111/bjet.12771

Bozhurt, A., & Bae, H. (2024). May the force be with you JedAI: Balancing the light and dark sides of Generative AI in the educational Landscape. *Online Learning : the Official Journal of the Online Learning Consortium*, 28(2), 1–6. https://www.doi.org/10.24059/olj.v28i2.4563

Bozkurt, A., Karadeniz, A., Baneres, D., Guerrero-Roldán, A. E., & Rodríguez, M. E. (2021). Artificial intelligence and reflections from educational landscape: A review of AI studies in half a century. *Sustainability (Basel)*, 13(2), 800. DOI: 10.3390/su13020800

Brandon, E., Eaton, L., Gavin, D., & Papini, A. (2023), December 12). Cross-Campus approaches to building a Generative AI policy. *EDUCAUSE Review*. https://er.educause.edu/articles/2023/12/cross-campus-approaches-to-building-a-generative-ai-policy

Bravo, M. C. M., Chalezquer, C. S., & Serrano-Puche, J. (2021). Meta-framework of digital literacy: A comparative analysis of 21st-century skills frameworks. *Revista Latina de Comunicacion Social*, (79), 76–109.

Breines, M., & Gallagher, M. (2020). A return to Teacherbot: Rethinking the development of educational technology at the University of Edinburgh. *Teaching in Higher Education*, 28(3), 517–531. DOI: 10.1080/13562517.2020.1825373

Breslow, L., Pritchard, D. E., DeBoer, J., Stump, G. S., Ho, A. D., & Seaton, D. T. (2013). Studying learning in the worldwide classroom: Research into edX's first MOOC. *Research & Practice in Assessment*, 8, 13–25.

Brookfield, S. (1995, 2017). *Becoming a critically reflective teacher*. John Wiley & Sons.

Brookfield, S. D. (2005). *The power of critical theory*. Jossey-Bass.

Brown, H., Crawford, S., Miffitt, K., Mendolia-Moore, T., Nevins, D., & Weiss, J. (2023, December 6). 7 things you should know about Generative AI. *EDUCAUSE Review*.https://er.educause.edu/articles/2023/12/7-things-you-should-know-about-generative-ai

Brown, A., Lawrence, J., Basson, M., & Redmond, P. (2022). A conceptual framework to enhance student online learning and engagement in higher education. *Higher Education Research & Development*, 41(2), 284–299. DOI: 10.1080/07294360.2020.1860912

Brynjolfsson, E., & McAfee, A. (2014). *The second Machine Age: Work, progress, and prosperity in a time of brilliant technologies*. WW Norton & Company.

Buccella, A. (2022). "AI for all" is a matter of social justice. *AI and Ethics*, 3(4), 1143–1152. DOI: 10.1007/s43681-022-00222-z PMID: 36189174

Buckingham Shum, S., Lim, L., Boud, D., Bearman, M., & Dawson, P. (2023). A comparative analysis of the skilled use of automated feedback tools through the lens of teacher feedback literacy. *International Journal of Educational Technology in Higher Education*, 20(1), 40. Advance online publication. DOI: 10.1186/s41239-023-00410-9

Bulathwela, S., Perez-Ortiz, M., Holloway, C., & Shawe-Taylor, J. (2021). Could AI democratize education? *Socio-Technical Imaginaries of an EdTech Revolution.*

Çağataylı, M., & Çelebi, E. (2022). Estimating academic success in higher education using big five personality traits, a machine learning approach. *Arabian Journal for Science and Engineering*, 47(2), 1289–1298. DOI: 10.1007/s13369-021-05873-4

Cao, Y., Zhou, L., Lee, S., Cabello, L., Chen, M., & Hershcovich, D. (2023). Assessing cross-cultural alignment between ChatGPT and human societies: An empirical study. Proceedings of the First Workshop on Cross-Cultural Considerations in NLP. https://aclanthology.org/2023.c3nlp-1.7.pdf

Carbonell, J. (1970). AI in CAI: an artificial intelligence approach to computer aided instruction. *Science, 167*, 190e202.

Carbonell, J. R. (1970). AI in CAI: An artifical-intelligence approach to computer-assisted instruction. *IEEE transactions on Man-Mahine Systems, MMS-11*(4), 190-202.

Cassidy, C. (2023, January 17). Lecturer detects bot-use in one fifth of assessments as concerns mount over AI in exams. *The Guardian.* https://www.theguardian.com/australianews/2023/jan/17/lecturer-detects-bot-use-in-one-fifth-of-assessments-as-concerns-mount-over-ai-in-exams

Celik, I., Dindar, M., Muukkonen, H., & Järvelä, S. (2022). The promises and challenges of artificial intelligence for teachers: A systematic review of research. *TechTrends*, 66(4), 616–630. Advance online publication. DOI: 10.1007/s11528-022-00715-y

Centre for Innovation. Design and Digital Learning. (2024). *CIDDL.* The Impact of AI on Education: https://ciddl.org/wp-content/uploads/2024/04/InclusiveIntelligence_a11y_navadded.pdf

Chan, C. K. Y. (2023). A comprehensive AI policy education framework for university teaching and learning. *International Journal of Educational Technology in Higher Education*, 20(1), 38. DOI: 10.1186/s41239-023-00408-3

Chan, C. K. Y., & Hu, W. (2023). Students' voices on generative AI: Perceptions, benefits, and challenges in higher education. *International Journal of Educational Technology in Higher Education*, 20(1), 43. DOI: 10.1186/s41239-023-00411-8

Chan, K. S., & Zary, N. (2019). Applications and challenges of implementing artificial intelligence in medical education: Integrative review. *JMIR Medical Education*, 5(1), e13930. DOI: 10.2196/13930 PMID: 31199295

Chen, X., Xie, H., & Hwang, G. J. (2020). A multi-perspective study on artificial intelligence in education: Grants, conferences, journals, software tools, institutions, and researchers. *Computer & Education: Artificial Intelligence 1.*https://www.sciencedirect.com/science/article/pii/S2666920X20300059

Chen, J.-F., & Do, Q. H. (2014). Training neural networks to predict student academic performance: A comparison of cuckoo search and gravitational search algorithms. *International Journal of Computational Intelligence and Applications*, 13(01), 1450005. DOI: 10.1142/S1469026814500059

Chen, L., Chen, P., & Lin, Z. (2020). Artificial intelligence in education: A review. *IEEE Access : Practical Innovations, Open Solutions*, 8, 75264–75278. DOI: 10.1109/ACCESS.2020.2988510

Chen, X., Zou, D., Cheng, G., & Xie, H. (2020). Detecting and addressing students' problematic learning behaviors in MOOCs: A neural network-based approach. *Computers in Human Behavior*, 104, 106159.

Chen, Y., Jensen, S., Albert, L. J., Gupta, S., & Lee, T. (2023). Artificial intelligence (AI) student assistants in the classroom: Designing chatbots to support student success. *Information Systems Frontiers*, 25(1), 161–182. DOI: 10.1007/s10796-022-10291-4

Chern, O. S., & Cheeb, L. C. (2022). Examining the Use of Scaffolding Approach in Teaching Case Study: An Approach Towards Enhancing Students' Critical Thinking and Problem-Solving Skills. In *Proceeding of the 7th Inspirational Scholar Symposium* (pp. 180-192).

Chetry, K. (2024). Transforming Education: How AI is Revolutionizing the Learning Experience. *International Journal of Research Publication and Reviews*, 5(5), 6352–6356. DOI: 10.55248/gengpi.5.0524.1277

Chklovski, T., Jung, R., Anderson, R., & Young, K. (2021). Comparing 2 years of empowering families to solve real-world problems with AI. *Kunstliche Intelligenz*, 35(2), 207–219. DOI: 10.1007/s13218-021-00738-2 PMID: 34316096

Ciampa, K., Wolfe, Z. M., & Bronstein, B. (2023). ChatGPT in education. Transforming digital literacy practices. *Journal of Adolescent & Adult Literacy*, 67(3), 186–195. DOI: 10.1002/jaal.1310

Ciechanowski, L., Przegalinska, A., Magnuski, M., & Gloor, P. (2019). In the shades of the uncanny valley: An experimental study of human–chatbot interaction. *Future Generation Computer Systems*, 92, 539–548. DOI: 10.1016/j.future.2018.01.055

CIPD. (2024). *AI generated content: Considerations for course design*. Center for Integrated Professional Development, Illinois State. https://prodev.illinoisstate.edu/pedagogy/ai/

Cipriano, B. P., Fachada, N., & Alves, P. (2022). Drop project: An automatic assessment tool for programming assignments. *SoftwareX*, 18, 101079. DOI: 10.1016/j.softx.2022.101079

College Board. (2024, March 12). *Digital SAT launches across the country, completing the transition to digital and providing a simpler testing experience for students and educators*. College Board. https://newsroom.collegeboard.org/digital-sat-launches-across-country-completing-transition-digital-and-providing-simpler-testing

Cope, B., Kalantzis, M., & Searsmith, D. (2021) Artificial intelligence for education: Knowledge and its assessment in AI-enabled learning ecologies, *Educational Philosophy and Theory, 53*(12), 1229-1245. DOI: https://doi.org/DOI: 10.1080/00131857.2020.1728732

Cotton, D. R. E., Cotton, P. A., & Shipway, J. R. (2023). Chatting and cheating: Ensuring academic integrity in the era of ChatGPT. *Innovations in Education and Teaching International*, 61(2), 228–239. DOI: 10.1080/14703297.2023.2190148

Cox, A. (2023). How artificial intelligence might change academic library work: Applying the competencies literature and the theory of the professions. *Journal of the Association for Information Science and Technology*, 74(3), 367–380. DOI: 10.1002/asi.24635

Cox, A. M. (2021). Exploring the impact of Artificial Intelligence and robots on higher education through literature-based design fiction. *International Journal of Educational Technology in Higher Education*, 18(1), 3. DOI: 10.1186/s41239-020-00237-8

Craig, S. D., Hu, X., Graesser, A. C., Bargagliotti, A. E., Sterbinsky, A., Cheney, K. R., & Okwumabua, T. (2013). The impact of a technology-based mathematics after-school program using ALEKS on student's knowledge and behaviors. *Computers & Education*, 68, 495–504. DOI: 10.1016/j.compedu.2013.06.010

Cranton, P. (2006). *Understanding and promoting transformative learning: A guide for educators of adults*. Jossey-Bass.

Cranton, P., & Hoggan, C. (2012). We are evaluating transformative learning. In Taylor, E. W., & Cranton, P. (Eds.), *Handbook of transformative learning: Theory, research, and practice*. Jossey-Bass.

Crawford, J., Cowling, M., & Allen, K.-A. (2023). Leadership is needed for ethical ChatGPT: Character, assessment, and learning using artificial intelligence (AI). *Journal of University Teaching & Learning Practice*, 20(3). Advance online publication. DOI: 10.53761/1.20.3.02

Crompton, H., & Burke, D. (2023). Artificial intelligence in higher education: The state of the field. *International Journal of Educational Technology in Higher Education*, 20(22), 1–22. DOI: 10.1186/s41239-023-00392-8

Crompton, H., & Song, D. (2021). The potential of artificial intelligence in higher education. *Revista Virtual Universidad Católica del Norte*, 62(62), 1–4. DOI: 10.35575/rvucn.n62a1

Cross, K. P., Major, C. H., & Barkley, E. F. (2014). *Collaborative learning techniques: A handbook for college faculty* (2nd ed.). John Wiley & Sons.

Darling-Hammond, L., Hyler, M. E., & Gardner, M. (2017). *Effective teacher professional development.* Learning Policy Institute., DOI: 10.54300/122.311

Davison, R. M., Chughtai, H., Nielsen, P., Marabelli, M., Iannacci, F., van Offenbeek, M., Tarafdar, M., Trenz, M., Techatassanasoontorn, A. A., Díaz Andrade, A., & Panteli, N. (2024, January). The ethics of using generative AI for qualitative data analysis. *Information Systems Journal*, 34(5), 1433–1439. Advance online publication. DOI: 10.1111/isj.12504

Deeva, G., Bogdanova, D., Serral, E., Snoeck, M., & De Weerdt, J. (2021). A review of automated feedback systems for learners: Classification framework, challenges and opportunities. *Computers & Education*, 162, 104094. DOI: 10.1016/j.compedu.2020.104094

Demszky, D., Liu, J., Hill, H. C., Jurafsky, D., & Piech, C. (2024). Can Automated Feedback Improve Teachers' Uptake of Student Ideas? Evidence From a Randomized Controlled Trial in a Large-Scale Online Course. *Educational Evaluation and Policy Analysis*, 46(3), 483–505. DOI: 10.3102/01623737231169270

Devedžić, V., Jovanović, J., Delić, V., Ševarac, Z., & Medenica, M. (2021). A framework for evaluating AIEd solutions' pedagogical, ethical, and privacy aspects. *Education Sciences*, 11(12), 840.

Dever, D. A., Azevedo, R., Cloude, E. B., & Wiedbusch, M. (2020). The impact of autonomy and types of informational text presentations in game-based environments on learning: Converging multi-channel processes data and learning outcomes. *International Journal of Artificial Intelligence in Education*, 30(4), 581–615. DOI: 10.1007/s40593-020-00215-1

Dewey, J. (1938). *Education and experience.* Collier Books.

Dhar, S., Shyam, H. S., Tomar, S., & Rani, M. (2023). Digital Disparity in The Technological Era of Big Data and Artificial Intelligence. *2023 9th International Conference on Advanced Computing and Communication Systems (ICACCS), 1*, 2475–2478. https://doi.org/DOI: 10.1109/ICACCS57279.2023.10113094

Dianova, V. G., & Shultz, M. D. (2023). Discussing ChatGPT's implications for industry and higher education: The case for transdisciplinarity and digital humanities. *Industry and Higher Education*, 37(5), 593–600. DOI: 10.1177/09504222231199989

Dignum, V. (2021). The role and challenges of education for responsible AI. *London Review of Education*, 19(1), 1–11. DOI: 10.14324/LRE.19.1.01

Dillenbourg, P., & Jermann, P. (2010). Technology for classroom orchestration. In Khine, M., & Saleh, I. (Eds.), *New Science of Learning* (pp. 525–552). Springer., DOI: 10.1007/978-1-4419-5716-0_26

Dimitriadou, E., & Lanitis, A. (2023). A critical evaluation, challenges, and future perspectives of using artificial intelligence and emerging technologies in smart classrooms. *Smart Learning Environments*, 10(1), 12. Advance online publication. DOI: 10.1186/s40561-023-00231-3

Dirette, D. P. (2024). Artificial intelligence: Analysis and guidelines for scholarly writing. *The Open Journal of Occupational Therapy*, 12(2), 1–5. DOI: 10.15453/2168-6408.2331

Dobbin, F., & Kalev, A. (2018). Why doesn't diversity training work?: The challenge for industry and academia. *Anthropology Now*, 10(2), 48–55. DOI: 10.1080/19428200.2018.1493182

Doerr, M., & Meeder, S. (2022). Big health data research and group harm: The scope of IRB review. *Ethics & Human Research*, 44(4), 34–38. DOI: 10.1002/eahr.500130 PMID: 35802789

Dogan, M. E., Goru Dogan, T., & Bozkurt, A. (2023). The use of artificial intelligence (AI) in online learning and distance education processes: A systematic review of empirical studies. *Applied Sciences (Basel, Switzerland)*, 13(5), 3056. DOI: 10.3390/app13053056

du Boulay, B. (2019). Can we learn from ITSs*? In International conference on intelligent tutoring systems,* 9-17. Springer.

Dumont, H., & Ready, D. D. (2023). On the promise of personalized learning for educational equity. *NPJ Science of Learning*, 8(1), 26. Advance online publication. DOI: 10.1038/s41539-023-00174-x PMID: 37542046

Duong, L. (2017). *Natural language processing for resource-poor languages*. University of Melbourne.

Eke, O. D. (2023). ChatGPT and the rise of generative AI: Threat to academic integrity? *Journal of Responsible Technology*, 13, 100060. DOI: 10.1016/j.jrt.2023.100060

Ekoto, C. E., & Gaikwad, P. (2015). The impact of andragogy on learning satisfaction of graduate students. *American Journal of Educational Research*, 3(11), 1378–1386.

ElAtia, S., Ipperciel, D., & Zaïane, O. R. (Eds.). (2016). *Data mining and learning analytics: Applications in educational research*. John Wiley & Sons. DOI: 10.1002/9781118998205

Elias, J. L., & Merriam, S. B. (2004). *Philosophical foundations of adult education* (3rd ed.). Krieger Publishing Company.

Elias, J. L., & Merriam, S. B. (1995). *Philosophical foundations of adult education.* Krieger Publishing Company.

Engage (2024). *The future of learning.* https://engagevr.io/school-of-ai/

Escalante, J., Pack, A., & Barrett, A. (2023). AI-generated feedback on writing: Insights into efficacy and ENL student preference. *International Journal of Educational Technology in Higher Education*, 20(1), 57. DOI: 10.1186/s41239-023-00425-2

Eubanks, V. (2018). *Automating inequality: How high-tech tools profile, police, and punish the poor.* St. Martin's Press.

European Commission, Directorate-General for Education, Youth, Sport and Culture. (2022). *Ethical guidelines on the use of artificial intelligence (AI) and data in teaching and learning for educators*, Publications Office of the European Union. https://data.europa.eu/doi/10.2766/153756

Fabiano, N., Gupta, A., Bhambra, N., Luu, B., Wong, S., Maaz, M., Fiedorowicz, J. G., Smith, A. L., & Solmi, M. (2024). How to optimize the systematic review process using AI tools. *JCPP Advances*, 4(2), e12234. DOI: 10.1002/jcv2.12234 PMID: 38827982

Farhi, F., Jeljeli, R., Aburezeq, I., Dweikat, F. F., Al-Shami, S. A., & Slamene, R. (2023). Analyzing the students' views, concerns, and perceived ethics about chat GPT usage. *Computers and Education.Artificial Intelligence*, 5, 100180. DOI: 10.1016/j.caeai.2023.100180

Fariani, R. I., Junus, K., & Santoso, H. B. (2022). A systematic literature review on personalised learning in the higher education context. *Technology. Knowledge and Learning*, 28(2), 449–476. DOI: 10.1007/s10758-022-09628-4

Farrelly, T., & Baker, N. (2023). Generative Artificial Intelligence: Implications and Considerations for Higher Education Practice. *Education Sciences*, 13(11), 1109. https://www.mdpi.com/2227-7102/13/11/1109. DOI: 10.3390/educsci13111109

Federer, L. (2018). Defining data librarianship: A survey of competencies, skills, and training. *Journal of the Medical Library Association: JMLA*, 106(3). Advance online publication. DOI: 10.5195/jmla.2018.306 PMID: 29962907

Feng, S., Zhou, S., & Liu, Y. (2011). Research on data mining in university admissions decision-making. *International Journal of Advancements in Computing Technology*, 3(6), 176–186. DOI: 10.4156/ijact.vol3.issue6.21

Feng, Y., Zhan, G., & Li, Z. (2019). Research on the co-construction of sharing of teaching resources under the "Internet Plus" environment. *10th International Conference on Information Technology in Medicine and Education,* Qingdao, China, pp. 498–502. DOI: 10.1109/ITME.2019.00117

Ferretti, A., Ienca, M., Hurst, S., & Vayena, E. (2020). Big data, biomedical research, and ethics review: New challenges for IRBs. *Ethics & Human Research*, 42(5), 17–28. DOI: 10.1002/eahr.500065 PMID: 32937036

Filippucci, F., Gal, P., Jona-Lasinio, C., Leandro, A., & Nicoletti, G. (2024, April 16). The impact of Artificial Intelligence on productivity, distribution and growth: Key mechanisms, initial evidence and policy challenges. OECD iLibrary. https://www.oecd-ilibrary.org/docserver/8d900037-en.pdf

Floridi, L., Cowls, J., Beltrametti, M., Chatila, R., Chazerand, P., Dignum, V., Luetge, C., Madelin, R., Pagallo, U., Rossi, F., Schafer, B., Valcke, P., & Vayena, E. (2018). AI4People—An ethical framework for a good AI society: Opportunities, risks, principles, and recommendations. *Minds and Machines*, 28(4), 689–707. DOI: 10.1007/s11023-018-9482-5 PMID: 30930541

Fornaciari, C. J., & Dean, K. L. (2014). The 21st-century syllabus: From pedagogy to andragogy. *Journal of Management Education*, 38(5), 701–723. DOI: 10.1177/1052562913504763

Franklin University. (2024). Office of Community Standards Academic Misconduct Process. https://www.franklin.edu/sites/default/files/fr/documents/Academic-Misconduct-Process-rev-Sep2023.pdf

Freina, L., & Ott, M. (2015). A literature review on immersive virtual reality in education: State of the art and perspectives. In *The International Scientific Conference eLearning and Software for Education* (pp. 133-141). DOI: 10.12753/2066-026X-15-020

Freire, P. (1970). *Pedagogy of the oppressed.* Seabury Press.

Friesen, P., Douglas-Jones, R., Marks, M., Pierce, R., Fletcher, K., Mishra, A., Lorimer, J., Véliz, C., Hallowell, N., Graham, M., Chan, M. S., Davies, H., & Sallamuddin, T. (2021). Governing AI-Driven health research: Are IRBs up to the task? *Ethics & Human Research*, 43(2), 35–42. DOI: 10.1002/eahr.500085 PMID: 33683015

Frontiers. (2023). *Educational transformation: 21st Century skills and challenges for higher education*. Frontiers Research Topics.

Fuchs, K. (2023). Exploring the opportunities and challenges of NLP models in higher education: Is chat GPT a blessing or a curse? *Frontiers in Education*, 8, 1166682. Advance online publication. DOI: 10.3389/feduc.2023.1166682

Gabriele, L., Marocco, D., Bertacchini, F., Pantano, P., & Bilotta, E. (2017). An educational robotics lab to investigate cognitive strategies and to foster learning in an arts and humanities course degree. *International Journal of Online Engineering*, 13(4), 7–19. DOI: 10.3991/ijoe.v13i04.6962

Gallegos, I. O., Rossi, R. A., Barrow, J., Tanjim, M. M., Kim, S., Dernoncourt, F., Yu, T., Zhang, R., & Ahmed, N. K. (2024). Bias and fairness in large language models: A survey. *Computational Linguistics*, 50(3), 1–79. DOI: 10.1162/coli_a_00524

Garg, R. (2024). The impact of generative artificial intelligence on higher education: Disruption or seamless integration? *Social Science Research Network*.https://ssrn.com/abstract=4762814

Gasser, U., & Almeida, V. A. (2017). A layered model for AI governance. *IEEE Internet Computing*, 21(6), 58–62. DOI: 10.1109/MIC.2017.4180835

Gattupalli, S., & Maloy, R. (2024, August 10). *On human centered AI in education.* https://scholarworks.umass.edu/items/5cdf7696-2916-444c-bb4c-e237755ec6b6

George, B., & Wooden, O. (2023). Managing the strategic transformation of higher education through artificial intelligence. *Administrative Sciences*, 13(9), 196. DOI: 10.3390/admsci13090196

Gerecke, U., & Wagner, B. (2007). The Challenges and Benefits of Using Robots in Higher Education. *Intelligent Automation & Soft Computing*, 13(1), 29–43. DOI: 10.1080/10798587.2007.10642948

Gergen, K. (2009). Foreword. In G. Strohschen *The handbook of Blended Shore education: Adult Education Program Development and Delivery*. Springer Verlag International.

Ghotbi, N., Ho, M. T., & Mantello, P. (2022). Attitude of college students towards ethical issues of artificial intelligence in an international university in Japan. *AI & Society*, 37(1), 283–290. DOI: 10.1007/s00146-021-01168-2

Gikandi, J. W., Morrow, D., & Davis, N. E. (2011). Online formative assessment in higher education: A review of the literature. *Computers & Education*, 57(4), 2333–2351. DOI: 10.1016/j.compedu.2011.06.004

Goel, A. K., & Polepeddi, L. (2016). *Jill Watson: A virtual teaching assistant for online education.* Georgia Institute of Technology. http://hdl.handle.net/1853/59104

Gökoğlu, S. (2024). Challenges and limitations of Generative AI in education. In Sharma, R., & Bozkurt, A. (Eds.), *Transforming Education with Generative AI: Prompt Engineering and Synthetic Content Creation* (pp. 158–181). IGI Global., DOI: 10.4018/979-8-3693-1351-0.ch008

Golan, R., Reddy, R., Muthigi, A., & Ramasamy, R. (2023). Artificial intelligence in academic writing: A paradigm-shifting technological advance. *Nature Reviews. Urology*, 20(6), 327–328. DOI: 10.1038/s41585-023-00746-x PMID: 36829078

Goldman, S. R., Taylor, J., Carreon, A., & Smith, S. J. (2024). Using ai to support special education teacher workload. *Journal of Special Education Technology*, 39(3), 434–447. DOI: 10.1177/01626434241257240

Golonka, E. M., Bowles, A. R., Frank, V. M., Richardson, D. L., & Freynik, S. (2014). Technologies for foreign language learning: A review of technology types and their effectiveness. *Computer Assisted Language Learning*, 27(1), 70–105. DOI: 10.1080/09588221.2012.700315

Graesser, A. C., VanLehn, K., Rosé, C. P., Jordan, P. W., & Harter, D. (2001). Intelligent tutoring systems with conversational dialogue. *AI Magazine*, 22(4), 39–39.

Grech, A., & Camilleri, A. F. (2017). *Blockchain in education*. Publications Office of the European Union.

Grosso, D., Bowling, M., Chun, S., & Delaney, B. (2024). Protecting student data privacy in light of artificial intelligence. *National Law Review*. https://www.natlawreview.com/article/development-ai-and-protecting-student-data-privacy

Gruetzemacher, R., & Whittlestone, J. (2022). The transformative potential of artificial intelligence. *Futures, 135*, 102884-. https://doi.org/DOI: 10.1016/j.futures.2021.102884

Guan, C., Mou, J., & Jiang, Z. (2020). Artificial intelligence innovation in education: A twenty-year data-driven historical analysis. *International Journal of Innovation Studies*, 4(4), 134–147. DOI: 10.1016/j.ijis.2020.09.001

Gupta, G. (2023, September 18). The AI advantage: Boosting student engagement in self-paced learning through AI. Faculty Focus. https://www.facultyfocus.com/articles/teaching-with-technology-articles/the-ai-advantage-boosting-student-engagement-in-self-paced-learning-through-ai/

Habermas, J. (1971). *Knowledge and human interests*. Beacon Press.

Hadzi, A. (2019). Social Justice and Artificial Intelligence by Dr. Adnan Hadzi (University of Malta). *Body, Space & Technology Journal, 18*(1), 145-. https://doi.org/DOI: 10.16995/bst.318

Haenlein, M., & Kaplan, A. (2019). A Brief History of Artificial Intelligence: On the Past, Present, and Future of Artificial Intelligence. *California Management Review*, 61(4), 1–10. DOI: 10.1177/0008125619864925

Halaweh, M. (2023). ChatGPT in education: Strategies for responsible implementation. *Contemporary Educational Technology*, 15(2), 15. DOI: 10.30935/cedtech/13036

Haleem, A., Javaid, M., Qadri, M. A., & Suman, R. (2022). Understanding the role of digital technologies in education: A review. *Sustainable Operations and Computers, 3*(3), 275–285. https://www.sciencedirect.com/science/article/pii/S2666412722000137

Han, B., Nawaz, S., Buchanan, G., & McKay, D. (2023). Ethical and pedagogical impacts of AI in education. In N. Wang, N., G. Rebolledo-Mendez, N. Matsuda, O. C. Santos, & Dimitrova, V. (Eds.) *Artificial Intelligence in Education*. AIED 2023. *Lecture Notes in Computer Science, 13916*. Springer. DOI: 10.1007/978-3-031-36272-9_54

Han, P.-C. (2022). Creating a developmental pathway for developing intercultural effectiveness competencies. *International Forum of Teaching and Studies, 18*(1), 27-60).

Han, K. (2021). Fostering students' autonomy and engagement in efl classroom through proximal classroom factors: Autonomy-supportive behaviors and student-teacher relationships. *Frontiers in Psychology*, 12, 767079. DOI: 10.3389/fpsyg.2021.767079 PMID: 34744946

Harris, J., Wihak, C., & Van Kleef, J. (2014). *Handbook of the recognition of prior learning: Research into practice*. National Institute of Adult Continuing Education.

Harry, A. (2023). Role of AI in Education. [INJURITY]. *Interdiciplinary Journal and Hummanity*, 2(3), 260–268.

Hartel, R. (2022). ReX Submission Platform. *Journal of Food Science*, 87(8), 3333–3334. DOI: 10.1111/1750-3841.15279 PMID: 35962979

Hase, S., & Kenyon, C. (2000). From Andragogy to Heutagogy. *Ultibase Articles*, 5, 1–10.

Health, T. L. D.The Lancet Digital Health. (2023). ChatGPT: Friend or foe? *The Lancet. Digital Health*, 5(3), e102. DOI: 10.1016/S2589-7500(23)00023-7 PMID: 36754723

Heaven, W. (2020, July 20). OpenAI's new language generator GPT-3 is shockingly good—and completely mindless. *MIT Technology Review*. https://www.technologyreview.com/2020/07/20/1005454/openai-machine-learning-language-generator-gpt-3-nlp/

Heffernan, N. T., & Heffernan, C. L. (2014). The ASSISTments ecosystem: Building a platform that brings scientists and teachers together for minimally invasive research on human learning and teaching. *International Journal of Artificial Intelligence in Education*, 24(4), 470–497. DOI: 10.1007/s40593-014-0024-x

Henschke, J. A. (2011). Considerations regarding the future of andragogy. *Adult Learning*, 22(1), 34–37. DOI: 10.1177/104515951102200109

Highland, S. (2023, January 17). Designing modern CTE classrooms: Four keys to success. *Essentials Magazine*. https://essentials.edmarket.org/2023/01/designing-modern-cte-classrooms-four-keys-to-success/

Hoffer, E. R. (2020). Case-based teaching: Using stories for engagement and inclusion. *International Journal on Social and Education Sciences*, 2(2), 75–80.

Holian, J. (1971). Alienation and social awareness among college students. *The Sociological Quarterly*, 13(1), 114–125. DOI: 10.1111/j.1533-8525.1971.tb01835.x

Holmes, W., Bialik, M., & Fadel, C. (2019). *Artificial intelligence in education: Promises and implications for teaching and learning*. Center for Curriculum Redesign. https://curriculumredesign.org/our-work/artificial-intelligence-in-education/

Holmes, K., & Preston, G. (2020). Concept of pedagogy and andragogy education. *Community Medicine and Education Journal*, 1(1), 12–18. DOI: 10.37275/cmej.v1i1.166

Holmes, W., Anastopoulou, S., Schaumburg, H., & Mavrikis, M. (2018). *Technology-enhanced personalized learning: Untangling the evidence*. Rob Bosch Stiftung.

Holmes, W., Bialik, M., & Fadel, C. (2019). *Artificial intelligence in education: Promises and implications for teaching and learning*. Center for Curriculum Redesign.

Holmes, W., Bialik, M., & Fadel, C. (2019). *Artificial Intelligence in Education: Promises and Implications for Teaching and Learning*. Center for Curriculum Redesign.

Holmes, W., & Porayska-Pomsta, K. (2023). *The ethics of artificial intelligence in education*. Routledge Taylor.

Huang, J., & Chen, Z. (2016). The research and design of a web-based intelligent tutoring system. *International Journal of Multimedia and Ubiquitous Engineering*, 11(6), 337–348. DOI: 10.14257/ijmue.2016.11.6.30

Huang, R. H., Liu, D. J., Tlili, A., Yang, J. F., & Wang, H. H. (2020). *Handbook on facilitating flexible learning during educational disruption: The Chinese experience in maintaining undisrupted learning in COVID-19 outbreak*. Smart Learning Institute of Beijing Normal University.

Huong, X. V. (2024). The Implications of artificial intelligence for educational systems: Challenges, opportunities, and transformative potential. *The American Journal of Social Science and Education Innovations*, 6(03), 101–111. DOI: 10.37547/tajssei/Volume06Issue03-17

Hwang, G. J., & Chang, C. Y. (2023). A review of opportunities and challenges of chatbots in education. *Interactive Learning Environments*, 31(7), 4099–4112. DOI: 10.1080/10494820.2021.1952615

Hwang, G. J., Sung, H. Y., Chang, S. C., & Huang, X. C. (2020). A fuzzy expert system-based adaptive learning approach to improving students' learning performances by considering affective and cognitive factors. *Computers and Education: Artificial Intelligence*, 1, 100003. DOI: 10.1016/j.caeai.2020.100003

Hwang, G. J., & Tu, Y. F. (2021). Roles and research trends of artificial intelligence in mathematics education: *A bibliometric mapping analysis and systematic review. Mathematics*, 9(6), 584. DOI: 10.3390/math9060584

Hwang, G. J., Xie, H., Wah, B. W., & Gasevic, D. (2020). Vision, challenges, roles and research issues of artificial intelligence in education. *Computers & Education*, •••, 1.

Hwang, G. J., Xie, H., Wah, B. W., & Gašević, D. (2020). Vision, challenges, roles and research issues of artificial intelligence in education. *Computers and Education: Artificial Intelligence*, 1, 100001. DOI: 10.1016/j.caeai.2020.100001

Hwang, G. J., Xie, H., Wah, B. W., & Gasevic, D. (2020). Vision, challenges, roles, and research issues of artificial intelligence in education. *Computers & Education: Artificial Intelligence*, 1, 100001.

Ismail, H., Hussein, N., Harous, S., & Khalil, A. (2023). Survey of personalized learning software systems: A taxonomy of environments, learning content, and user models. *Education Sciences*, 13(7), 741. DOI: 10.3390/educsci13070741

ISTE. (2024). A guide on ethics and AI for the classroom hands-on. https://iste.org/ai

Jackson, E. A. (2024). The evolution of artificial intelligence: A theoretical review of its impact on teaching and learning in the digital age. EconStor *Preprints*. https://ideas.repec.org/p/zbw/esprep/280893.html

Jarrah, A. M., Wardat, Y., & Fidalgo, P. (2023). Using ChatGPT in academic writing is (not) a form of plagiarism: What does the literature say? *Online Journal of Communication and Media Technologies*, 13(4), e202346. DOI: 10.30935/ojcmt/13572

Jerry, T., & Aaron, C. (2010). The impact of augmented reality software with inquiry-based learning on students' learning. *International Conference on Educational Technology and Computer, 2*(1). DOI: 10.1109/ICETC.2010.5529447

Jewitt, C. (2013). Multimodal methods for researching digital technologies. In *The SAGE handbook of digital technology research* (pp. 250–265). SAGE Publications., DOI: 10.4135/9781446282229.n18

Johnson, S. (2022). *The Turing test: AI still hasn't passed the "imitation game."*https://bigthink.com/the-future/turing-test-imitation-game/

Kabudi, T., Pappas, I., & Olsen, D. H. (2021). AI-enabled adaptive learning systems: A systematic mapping of the literature. *Computers and Education: Artificial Intelligence*, 2, 100017.

Kalota, F. (2024). A primer on artificial intelligence. *Education Sciences*, 172(14), 172. DOI: 10.3390/educsci14020172

Kang, Y., Cai, Z., Tan, C. W., Huang, Q., & Liu, H. (2020). Natural language processing (NLP) in management research: A literature review. J. Manag. *Analyt.*, 7(2), 139–172. DOI: 10.1080/23270012.2020.1756939

Kaplan-Rakowski, R., Grotewold, K., Hartwick, P., & Papin, K. (2023). Generative AI and teachers' perspectives on its implementation in education. *Journal of Interactive Learning Research*, 34(2), 313–338.

Kardan, A. A., Sadeghi, H., Ghidary, S. S., & Sani, M. R. F. (2013). Prediction of student course selection in online higher education institutes using neural network. *Computers & Education*, 65, 1–11. DOI: 10.1016/j.compedu.2013.01.015

Karim, R. (2024, June 25). *Is an AI winter coming?: Navigating the cycles of AI hype and just regulation.* https://lens.monash.edu/@business-economy/2024/06/25/1386756/is-an-ai-winter-coming-navigating-the-cycles-of-ai-hype-and-just-regulation

Kasneci, E., Seßler, K., Küchemann, S., Bannert, M., Dementieva, D., Fischer, F., Gasser, U., Groh, G., Günnemann, S., Hüllermeier, E., Krusche, S., Kutyniok, G., Michaeli, T., Nerdel, C., Pfeffer, J., Poquet, O., Sailer, M., Schmidt, A., Seidel, T., & Kasneci, G. (2023). ChatGPT for good? On opportunities and challenges of large language models for education. *Learning and Individual Differences*, 103, 102274. DOI: 10.1016/j.lindif.2023.102274

Kassorla, M. (2023, December 14). Teaching with GAI in mind. *EDUCAUSE Review*. https://er.educause.edu/articles/2023/12/teaching-with-gai-in-mind

Kay, R. H., & Lauricella, S. (2011). Exploring the benefits and challenges of using laptop computers in higher education classrooms: A formative analysis. *Canadian Journal of Learning and Technology / La revue canadienne de l'apprentissage et de la technologie, 37*(1). DOI: 10.21432/T2S598

Kay, J. (2012). AI and education: Grand challenges. *IEEE Intelligent Systems*, 27(5), 66–69. DOI: 10.1109/MIS.2012.92

Kelkar, S. (2022). Between AI and learning science: The evolution and commercialization of intelligent tutoring systems. *IEEE Annals of the History of Computing*, 44(1), 20–30. DOI: 10.1109/MAHC.2022.3143816

Kew, S. N., & Tasir, Z. (2022). Learning analytics in online learning environment: A systematic review on the focuses and the types of student-related analytics data. *Technology. Knowledge and Learning*, 27(2), 405–427. DOI: 10.1007/s10758-021-09541-2

Khalifa, M., & Albadawy, M. (2024). Using artificial intelligence in academic writing and research: An essential productivity tool. *Computer Methods and Programs in Biomedicine Update*, 5, 100145. Advance online publication. DOI: 10.1016/j.cmpbup.2024.100145

Kidd, J. R. (1973). *How adults learn* (revised). Association Press.

Kidd, T. T., & Keengwe, J. (Eds.). (2010). *Adult learning in the digital age: Perspectives on online technologies and outcomes*. IGI Global., DOI: 10.4018/978-1-60566-828-4

Kim, J. H. (2023). Leading teachers' perspective on teacher-AI collaboration in education. *Education and Information Technologies*. Advance online publication. DOI: 10.1007/s10639-023-12109-5

Kim, N. J., & Kim, M. K. (2022). Teacher's perceptions of using an artificial intelligence-based educational tool for scientific writing. *Frontiers in Education*, 7, 7. DOI: 10.3389/feduc.2022.755914

Kinney, L. B. (1953). *The measure of a good teacher*. Teachers Association.

Kirschner, P. A., Sweller, J., Kirschner, F., & Zambrano, R. J. (2018). From cognitive load theory to collaborative cognitive load theory. *International Journal of Computer-Supported Collaborative Learning*, 13(2), 213–233. DOI: 10.1007/s11412-018-9277-y PMID: 30996713

Knowles, M. S., Holton, E. F., III, Swanson, R. A., & Robinson, P. A. (2020). Andragogy: History, meaning, context, and function. In *The adult learner* (9th ed., pp. 284–292). Routledge. https://doi.org/DOI: 10.4324/9780429299612-16

Knowles, M. S., Holton, E. F., III, Swanson, R. A., & Robinson, P. A. (2020). *The adult learner: The definitive classic in adult education and human resource development* (9th ed.). Routledge/Taylor & Francis Group. DOI: 10.4324/9780429299612

Knowles, M. S., Holton, E., & Swanson, A. (2011). *The adult learner: The definitive classic in adult education and human resource development* (7th ed.). Taylor & Francis.

Knowles, M. (1980). *The modern practice of adult education: From andragogy to pedagogy*. Associated.

Knowles, M. S. (1970). *The modern practice of adult education: Andragogy versus pedagogy*. Cambridge Book Company.

Knowles, M. S. (1975). *Self-directed learning*. Association Press.

Knowles, M. S. (1980). *The modern practice of adult education: From pedagogy to andragogy*. Association Press.

Knowles, M. S. (1980). *The modern practice of adult education: from pedagogy to andragogy*. Prentice Hall., https://bigthink.com/the-future/turing-test-imitation-game/

Knowles, M. S., Holton, E., & Swanson, A. (1998). *The adult learner: The definitive classic in adult education and human resource development*. Gulf Publishing Company.

Kolb, D. A. (2014). *Experiential learning: Experience as the source of learning and development*. FT press.

Kolodner, J. L., Cox, M. T., & González-Calero, P. A. (2005). Case-based reasoning-inspired approaches to education. *The Knowledge Engineering Review*, 20(3), 299–303. DOI: 10.1017/S0269888906000634

Koltay, T. (2019). Accepted and emerging roles of academic libraries in supporting research 2.0. *Journal of Academic Librarianship*, 45(2), 75–80. DOI: 10.1016/j.acalib.2019.01.001

Korzynski, P., Mazurek, G., Krzypkowska, P., & Kurasinski, A. (2023). Artificial intelligence prompt engineering as a new digital competence: Analysis of generative AI technologies such as ChatGPT. *Entrepreneurial Business and Economics Review*, 11(3), 25–37. DOI: 10.15678/EBER.2023.110302

Kostka, I., & Toncelli, R. (2023). Exploring applications of ChatGPT to English language teaching: Opportunities, challenges, and recommendations. *TESL-EJ*, 27(3), n3. DOI: 10.55593/ej.27107int

Koumpouros, Y. (2024). Revealing the true potential and prospects of augmented reality in education. *Smart Learning Environ*, 11(2), 2. DOI: 10.1186/s40561-023-00288-0

Kroeper, K. (2022). Identifying teaching behaviors that foster growth mindset classroom cultures. *American Psychological Association*. https://www.apa.org/ed/precollege/psychology-teacher-network/introductory-psychology/growth-mindset-classroom-cultures

Kukulska-Hulme, A. (2012). How should the higher education workforce adapt to advancements in technology for teaching and learning? *The Internet and Higher Education*, 15(4), 247–254. DOI: 10.1016/j.iheduc.2011.12.002

Kulik, J. A., & Fletcher, J. D. (2016). Effectiveness of intelligent tutoring systems: A meta-analytic review. *Review of Educational Research*, 86(1), 42–78. DOI: 10.3102/0034654315581420

Kumar, D. (2023). How emerging technologies are transforming education and research: Trends, opportunities, and challenges. *Infinite Horizons: Exploring the Unknown*, 89-117.

Kurtz, G., Amzalag, M., Shaked, N., Zaguri, Y., Kohen-Vacs, D., Gal, E., Zailer, G., & Barak-Medina, E. (2024). Strategies for integrating generative AI into higher education: Navigating challenges and leveraging opportunities. *Education Sciences*, 14(5), 503. DOI: 10.3390/educsci14050503

Labadze, L., Grigolia, M., & Machaidze, L. (2023). Role of AI chatbots in education: Systematic literature review. *International Journal of Educational Technology in Higher Education*, 20(1), 56. DOI: 10.1186/s41239-023-00426-1

Laupichler, M. C., Aster, A., Schirch, J., & Raupach, T. (2022). Artificial intelligence literacy in higher and adult education: A scoping literature review. In *Computers and Education* (Vol. 3, p. 100101). Artificial Intelligence., DOI: 10.1016/j.caeai.2022.100101

Lavy, S. (2008). Facility management practices in higher education buildings: A case study. *Journal of Facilities Management*, 6(4), 303–315. DOI: 10.1108/14725960810908163

Lee, S. J., & Kwon, K. (2024). A systematic review of AI education in K-12 classrooms from 2018 to 2023: Topics, strategies, and learning outcomes. *Computers and Education: Artificial Intelligence*, 6, 100211. DOI: 10.1016/j.caeai.2024.100211

Leiker, D., Finnigan, S., Gyllen, R., & Cukurova, M. (2023). Prototyping the use of Large Language Models (LLMs) for adult learning content creation at scale. CEUR Workshop proceedings. https://doi.org//arXiv.2306.01815DOI: 10.48550

Leung, K.-H. (2019). *The picture of artificial intelligence and the secularization of thought*. Political Theology. DOI: 10.1080/1462317X.2019.1605725

Levy, A. (2020, April 8). While parents Zoom, their kids are flocking to an app called Roblox to hang out and play 3D games. CNBC. https://www.cnbc.com/2020/04/08/roblox-is-seeing-a-surge-during-coronavirus-shelter-in-place.html

Li, F., He, Y., & Xue, Q. (2021). Progress, Challenges and Countermeasures of Adaptive Learning: A Systematic Review. *Educational Technology and Society, 24*(3), 238–255. https:// eric. ed. gov/? id= EJ130 5781

Liang, Zhang., Xiaomei, Zeng., & Ping, Lv. (2022). Higher Education-Oriented Recommendation Algorithm for Personalized Learning Resource. *International Journal of Emerging Technologies in Learning*.

Li, F., Ruijs, N., & Lu, Y. (2022). Ethics & AI: A systematic review on ethical concerns and related strategies for designing with AI in healthcare. *AI*, 4(1), 28–53. DOI: 10.3390/ai4010003

Li, J., Peng, Y., & Su, J. (2023). Analysis of the impact of artificial intelligence on college students and countermeasures based on the perspective of comprehensive development. The *Frontiers of Society. Science, and Technology*, 5(9), 24–33.

Lim, W. M., Gunasekara, A., Pallant, J. L., Pallant, J. I., & Pechenkina, E. (2023). Generative AI and the future of education: Ragnarök or reformation? A paradoxical perspective from management educators. *International Journal of Management Education*, 21(2), 100790. Advance online publication. DOI: 10.1016/j.ijme.2023.100790

Lin, C., Cheng, E. S., Huang, A. Y., & Yang, S. J. (2024). DNA of learning behaviors: A novel approach of learning performance prediction by NLP. *Computers and Education: Artificial Intelligence*, 6, 100227. DOI: 10.1016/j.caeai.2024.100227

Lindeman, E. C. (1926). *The meaning of adult education.* Research Center for Continuing Professional and Higher Education.

Liu, L., Subbareddy, R., & Raghavendra, C. G. (2022). AI intelligence chatbot to improve students learning in the higher education platform. *Journal of Interconnection Networks*, 22(Supp02), 1–17. DOI: 10.1142/S0219265921430325

Lixandru, I. D. (2024). The use of artificial intelligence for qualitative data analysis: ChatGPT. *Informatică Economică, 28*(1/2024), 57–67. DOI: 10.24818/issn14531305/28.1.2024.05

Ljujić, B., Miljković, J., & Grozdić, V. (2023). ChatGPT and academic writing in higher education. In Radulović, M., & Trajković, M. (Eds.), *Towards a more equitable education: From research to change: Book of proceedings, 29th International Scientific Conference "Educational Research and School Practice"* (pp. 104–109). Institute for Educational Research., https://www.ipisr.org.rs/images/pdf/towards-a-more-equitable-education.pdf

Loeng, S. (2018). Various ways of understanding the concept of andragogy. *Cogent Education, 5*(1), 1496643-. https://doi.org/DOI: 10.1080/2331186X.2018.1496643

Luan, H., Geczy, P., Lai, H., Gobert, J., Yang, S. J., Ogata, H., Baltes, J., Guerra, R., Li, P., & Tsai, C. C. (2020). Challenges and future directions of big data and artificial intelligence in education. *Frontiers in Psychology*, 11, 580820. DOI: 10.3389/fpsyg.2020.580820 PMID: 33192896

Luan, H., & Tsai, C. C. (2021). A review of using machine learning approaches for precision education. *Journal of Educational Technology & Society*, 24(1), 250–266.

Luan, L., Liang, J. C., Chai, C. S., Lin, T. B., & Dong, Y. (2020). Development of the new media literacy scale for EFL learners in China: A validation study. *Interactive Learning Environments*, 31(1), 244–257. DOI: 10.1080/10494820.2020.1774396

Lubart, T., Zenasni, F., & Barbot, B. (2013). Creative potential and its measurement. *International Journal for Talent Development and Creativity*, 1(2), 41–50.

Luckin, R. (2018). *Machine learning and human intelligence: The future of education for the 21st century*. UCL IOE Press.

Luckin, R., & Cukurova, M. (2019). Designing educational technologies in the age of AI: A learning sciences-driven approach. *British Journal of Educational Technology*, 50(6), 2824–2838. DOI: 10.1111/bjet.12861

Luckin, R., Cukurova, M., Kent, C., & Du Boulay, B. (2022). Empowering educators to be AI-ready. *Computers and Education: Artificial Intelligence*, 3, 100076. DOI: 10.1016/j.caeai.2022.100076

Luckin, R., & Holmes, W. (2016). *Intelligence Unleashed: An Argument for AI in Education*. Pearson Education.

Luckin, R., Holmes, W., Griffiths, M., & Forcier, L. B. (2016). *Intelligence unleashed. An argument for AI in education*. Pearson.

Luckin, R., Holmes, W., Griffiths, M., & Forcier, L. B. (2016). *Intelligence unleashed: An argument for AI in education*. Pearson Education.

Luckin, R., Holmes, W., Griffiths, M., & Forcier, L. B. (2016). *Intelligence Unleashed: An argument for AI in Education*. Pearson.

Lu, J., Zheng, R., Gong, Z., & Xu, H. (2024). Supporting teachers' professional development with generative AI: The effects on higher order thinking and self-efficacy. *IEEE Transactions on Learning Technologies*, 17, 1279–1289. DOI: 10.1109/TLT.2024.3369690

Lu, Y. (2019). Artificial intelligence: A survey on evolution, models, applications and future trends. *Journal of Management Analytics*, 6(1), 1–29. DOI: 10.1080/23270012.2019.1570365

Madaio, M., Blodgett, S. L., Mayfield, E., & Dixon-Román, E. (2021). Confronting structural inequities in AI for education. *arXiv preprint arXiv:2105.08847*.

Mahoney, J. M., & Quick, B. G. (2000). Personality correlates of alienation in a university sample. *Psychological Reports*, 87(3_suppl), 1094–1100. DOI: 10.2466/pr0.2000.87.3f.1094 PMID: 11272749

Mandelelize, N., & Sepeng, M. (2024). Exploring challenges of adult learners in selected adult education and training centers in South Africa: An analysis of Knowles' theory of andragogy. *Social Sciences and Education Research Review*, 2(1), 152–160.

Maphoto, K. B., Sevnarayan, K., Mohale, N. E., Suliman, Z., Ntsopi, T. J., & Mokoena, D. (2024). Advancing students' academic excellence in distance education: Exploring the potential of Generative AI integration to improve academic writing skills. *Open Praxis, 2–2*, 142–159. DOI: 10.55982/openpraxis.16.2.649

Marr, B. (2018). How IBM is using AI, IoT, and blockchain to transform the food industry. *Forbes*.

Martin, J., & Armstrong, M. (2024, April 12). *Tips and trends: AI developments and resources for academic librarians*. Association of College & Research Libraries https://acrl.ala.org/IS/tips-and-trends-ai-developments-and-resources-for-academic-librarians/

Masleg, N., Fattorini, L., Brynjolfsson, E., Etchemendy, J., Ligett, K., Lyons, T., Manyika, J., Ngo, H., Niebles, J. C., Parli, V., Shoham, Y., Wald, R., Clark, J., & Perrault, R. (2023). *The AI Index 2023 Annual Report*. AI Index Steering Committee, Stanford Institute for Human-Centered AI, Stanford University.

Maslow, A. H. (1970). *Motivation and personality* (2nd ed.). Harper Collins.

Ma, Y., & Siau, K. (2019). Intelligent tutoring systems and learning outcomes: A meta-analysis. *Journal of Educational Psychology*, 106(4), 901–918. DOI: 10.1037/a0037123

Mazurkiewicz, G., & Kołodziejczyk, J. (2017). Management and education during the times of interregnum. ruj.uj.edu.pl, 149-158.

Mazurkiewicz, G., & Fischer, J. M. (2021). *The power of responsive educational leadership: Building schools for global challenges*. Routledge. DOI: 10.4324/9781003130277

McCormack, M. (2023). EDUCAUSE QuickPoll results: Adopting and adapting to Generative AI in higher ed tech. *EDUCAUSE Review – EDUCAUSE Research Notes*. https://er.educause.edu/articles/2023/4/educause-quickpoll-results-adopting-and-adapting-to-generative-ai-in-higher-ed-tech

McDonald, N., & Pan, S. (2020). Intersectional AI: A study of how information science students think about ethics and their Impact. *PACM on Human-Computer Interaction, 4*, (Issue CSCW2). *Proceedings of the ACM on Human-Computer Interaction*, 147(CSCW2), 1–19. Advance online publication. DOI: 10.1145/3415218

McKinsey Global Institute. (2023). *The economic potential of generative AI: The next productivity frontier*. McKinsey & Company. https://www.mckinsey.com/capabilities/mckinsey-digital/our-insights/the-economic-potential-of-generative-ai-the-next-productivity-frontier

McNulty, N. (2024, January 24). AI for inclusive education: Enhancing learning opportunities for all. https://www.niallmcnulty.com/2024/01/ai-for-inclusive-education/

Memarian, B., & Doleck, T. (2023). Fairness, accountability, transparency, and ethics (FATE) in artificial intelligence (AI) and higher education: A systematic review. *Computers and Education: Artificial Intelligence*, 5, 100152. DOI: 10.1016/j.caeai.2023.100152

Merchant, Z., Goetz, E. T., Cifuentes, L., Keeney-Kennicutt, W., & Davis, T. J. (2014). Effectiveness of virtual reality-based instruction on students' learning outcomes in K-12 and higher education: A meta-analysis. *Computers & Education*, 70, 29–40. DOI: 10.1016/j.compedu.2013.07.033

Merriam, S. B., & Baumgartner, L. M. (2020). *Learning in adulthood: A comprehensive guide* (4th ed.). Jossey-Bass.

Merriam, S. B., & Bierema, L. L. (2014). *Adult learning: Linking theory and practice*. Jossey-Bass.

Merriam, S. B., & Brockett, R. G. (1997). *The profession and practice of adult education: An introduction*. Jossey-Bass.

Messer, M., Brown, N. C., Kölling, M., & Shi, M. (2024). Automated grading and feedback tools for programming education: A systematic review. *ACM Transactions on Computing Education*, 24(1), 1–43. DOI: 10.1145/3636515

Meyer, J., Jansen, T., Schiller, R., Liebenow, L., Steinbach, M., Horbach, A., & Fleckenstein, J. (2024). Using LLMs to bring evidence-based feedback into the classroom: AI-generated feedback increases secondary students' text revision, motivation, and positive emotions. *Computers & Education: Artificial Intelligence*, 6, 100199. DOI: 10.1016/j.caeai.2023.100199

Mezirow, J. (1975). *Education for perspective transformation: Women's reentry programs in community colleges*. Center for Adult Education, Teachers College, Columbia University.

Mezirow, J. (1991). *Transformative dimension of adult learning*. Jossey-Bass.

Mezirow, J. (1991). *Transformative dimensions of adult learning*. Jossey-Bass.

Mezirow, J. (2000). Learning to think like an adult. In Mezirow, J. (Eds.), *Learning as transformation: Critical perspectives on a theory in progress* (pp. 3–31). Jossey-Bass.

Miao, Y., & Yao, Y. (2021). Professional development of college teachers in the era of artificial intelligence: Role rebuilding and development path. In Sugumaran, V., Xu, Z., & Zhou, H. (Eds.), *Application of intelligent systems in multi-modal information analytics* (Vol. 1233, pp. 618–626). Springer International Publishing., DOI: 10.1007/978-3-030-51431-0_89

Mickunas, A., & Pilotta, J. (2023). *A critical understanding of artificial intelligence: A phenomenological foundation*. Bentham Books. DOI: 10.2174/97898151234011230101

Milana, M., Brandi, U., Hodge, S., & Hoggan-Kloubert, T. (2024). Artificial intelligence (AI), conversational agents, and generative AI: Implications for adult education practice and research. *International Journal of Lifelong Education*, 43(1), 1–7. DOI: 10.1080/02601370.2024.2310448

Mohanty, S., & Parida, A. K. (2022). Intelligent learning using artificial intelligence: Applications, challenges, and adaptation. *Education and Information Technologies*.

Mollick, E. R., & Mollick, L. (2023). Assigning AI: Seven Approaches for Students, with Prompts. *SSRN*. DOI: 10.2139/ssrn.4475995

Moorhouse, B. J., & Wong, K. M. (2021). Blending asynchronous and synchronous digital technologies and instructional approaches to facilitate remote learning. *Journal of Computers in Education*, 9(1), 51–70. DOI: 10.1007/s40692-021-00195-8

Moronianu, N., Iacob, S., & Constantin, A. (2023). Artificial intelligence in education: a systematic review. *Proceedings of the 6th International Conference on Economics and Social Sciences*, (pp. 906-921). Romania.

Mote, A. P. (2024). Role of AI in personalized education. *International Journal of Advanced Research in Science. Tongxin Jishu*, 4(4). https://ijarsct.co.in/Paper15919.pdf

Moustaghfir, S., & Brigui, H. (2023). Exploring Moroccan English teacher's perception towards the use of interactive tools in teaching English as a foreign language on the development of critical thinking skills in young students. *International Journal of Linguistics, Literature, and Translation*, 6(8), 236–249. DOI: 10.32996/ijllt.2023.6.8.24

Müller, M. S. M., & Reggelin, I. T. (2021, June). Handling of Logistic Deadlocks with Machine Learning. In *14th International Doctoral Students Workshop on Logistics* (p. 77).

Nagar, N. (2024). Importance of artificial intelligence in education. [IJSREM]. *International Journal of Scientific Research in Engineering and Management*, 8(4).

Nallaluthan, K., Masran, M. N., Thurasingam, V., & Kanapathy, K. (2023). Malcolm Knowles' Theory of Andragogy at Research Management and Innovation Centre Universiti Pendidikan Sultan Idris (RMIC-UPSI): Work-Based Learning Model. *Evaluation Studies in Social Sciences*, 4(2), 30–50.

Nandigam, D., Tavva, V., & Reddy, N. V. S. (2022). Applications of artificial intelligence in education for visually impaired people: A review. *Assistive Technology*, 1, 11.

Naous, T., Ryan, M. J., Ritter, A., & Xu, W. (2024). Having Beer after Prayer? Measuring Cultural Bias in Large Language Models. *arXiv.Org*. https://doi.org// arxiv.2305.14456DOI: 10.18653/v1/2024.acl-long.862

Nazaretsky, T., Ariely, M., Cukurova, M., & Alexandron, G. (2022). Teachers' trust in AI-powered educational technology and a professional development program to improve it. *British Journal of Educational Technology*, 53(4), 914–931. DOI: 10.1111/bjet.13232

NEA. (2021, March 25). *Rethinking the classroom for blended learning*. National Education Association. https://www.nea.org/professional-excellence/student -engagement/tools-tips/rethinking-classroom-blended-learning

Neubert, M., Rams, W., & Utikal, H. (2020). Experiential learning with live case studies. *International Journal of Teaching and Case Studies*, 11(2), 173–190. DOI: 10.1504/IJTCS.2020.109726

Ng, D. T. K., Leung, J. K. L., Su, J., Ng, R. C. W., & Chu, S. K. W. (2023). Teachers' AI digital competencies and twenty-first century skills in the post-pandemic world. *Educational Technology Research and Development*, 71(1), 137–161. Advance online publication. DOI: 10.1007/s11423-023-10203-6 PMID: 36844361

Nguyen, H. (2021, March 26). How to use gameplay to enhance classroom learning. Edutopia. https://www.edutopia.org/article/how-use-gameplay-enhance-classroom -learning

Nguyen, A., Ngo, H. N., Hong, Y., Dang, B., & Nguyen, B. P. T. (2023). Ethical principles for artificial intelligence in education. *Education and Information Technologies*, 28(4), 4221–4241. DOI: 10.1007/s10639-022-11316-w PMID: 36254344

Nicolaides, A., & Marsick, V. (2016). Understanding adult learning in the midst of complex social "liquid modernity.". *New Directions for Adult and Continuing Education*, 149(Spring), 9–20. DOI: 10.1002/ace.20172

Niewint-Gori, J. (2023). *A snapshot of the evolving landscape of artificial intelligence in education*. Ital-IA. https://www.semanticscholar.org/paper/A-snapshot-of -the-evolving landscape-of-artificial-Niewint-Gori/cc5410f5cd3dc0fd230e31182d-cff204468b6dbf

Nilsson, N. J. (1998). *Artificial intelligence: A new synthesis*. Morgan Kaufmann Publishers, Inc.

Niyozov, N., Bijanov, A., Ganiyev, S., & Kurbonova, R. (2023). The pedagogical principles and effectiveness of utilizing ChatGPT for language learning. *E3S Web of Conferences, 461*, 01093. DOI: 10.1051/e3sconf/202346101093

Noetel, M., Griffith, S., Delaney, O., Harris, N. R., Sanders, T., Parker, P., del Pozo Cruz, B., & Lonsdale, C. (2022). Multimedia design for learning: An overview of reviews with meta-meta-analysis. *Review of Educational Research*, 92(3), 413–454. https://doi-org.ezproxy.neu.edu/10.3102/00346543211052329. DOI: 10.3102/00346543211052329

Nohria, N. (2021). What the case study method really teaches. *Harvard Business Review*, •••, 21.

Nurjanah, I. N. Salsabilla, A. Azzahra, Rahayu, R., & Marlina, N. (2024). Artificial intelligence (AI) usage in today's teaching and learning process. *Ridwan Institute*, 6.

O'Neil, C. (2016). *Weapons of math destruction: How big data increases inequality and threatens democracy*. Crown Publishing Group.

OECD. (2019). *AI in education: Challenges and opportunities for sustainable development*. OECD Publishing.

Office of Educational Technology. (2023). *Artificial intelligence and the future of teaching and learning: insights and recommendations*. U.S. Department of Education.

Onesi-Ozigagun, O., Ololade, Y. J., Eyo-Udo, N. L., & Ogundipe, D. O. (2024). Revolutionizing education through AI: A comprehensive review of enhancing learning experiences. *International Journal of Applied Research in Social Sciences*, 6(4), 589–607. DOI: 10.51594/ijarss.v6i4.1011

Open, A. I. (2023, March). *GPT-4 Developer livestream* [Video]. YouTube. https://www.youtube.com/watch?v=outcGtbnMuQ

Open, A. I. (n.d.). GPT-3 powers the next generation of apps. https://openai.com/blog/gpt-3-apps?ref=digitvibe

Osakwe, I., Chen, G., Whitelock-Wainwright, A., Gašević, D., Pinheiro Cavalcanti, A., & Ferreira Mello, R. (2022). Towards automated content analysis of educational feedback: A multi-language study. *Computers and Education: Artificial Intelligence*, 3, 100059. DOI: 10.1016/j.caeai.2022.100059

Otto, S., Bertel, L. B., Ruan, E., Markman, A. O., Andersen, T. F., & Ryberg, T. (2023). Emerging digital practices supporting student-centered learning environments in higher education: A review of literature and lessons learned from the Covid-19 Pandemic. *Education and Information Technologies*. Advance online publication. DOI: 10.1007/s10639-023-11789-3 PMID: 37361841

Ouyang, F., & Jiao, P. (2021). Artificial intelligence in education: The three paradigms. *Computers & Education*, 2, •••. https://www.sciencedirect.com/science/article/pii/S2666920X2100014X

Ouyang, F., & Jiao, P. (2021). Artificial intelligence in education: The three paradigms. *Computers & Education: Artificial Intelligence*, 100020, 100020. Advance online publication. DOI: 10.1016/j.caeai.2021.100020

Ouyang, F., Zheng, L., & Jiao, P. (2022). Artificial intelligence in online higher education: A systematic review of empirical research from 2011 to 2020. *Education and Information Technologies*, 27(6), 7893–7925. DOI: 10.1007/s10639-022-10925-9

Ozmen Gariby, O., Winslow, B., Andolina, S., Antona, M., Bodenschatz, A., & Coursaris, C.. (2023). Six Human centered Artificial Intelligence Grand Challenges. *International Journal of Human-Computer Interaction*, 39(3), 391–347. DOI: 10.1080/10447318.2022.2153320

Pampana, A. K., Jeon, J., Yoon, S., Weidner, T. J., & Hastak, M. (2022). Data-driven analysis for facility management in higher education institution. *Buildings (Basel, Switzerland)*, 12(12), 2094. DOI: 10.3390/buildings12122094

Pane, J. F., Griffin, B. A., McCaffrey, D. F., & Karam, R. (2014). Effectiveness of cognitive tutor algebra I at scale. *Educational Evaluation and Policy Analysis*, 36(2), 127–144. DOI: 10.3102/0162373713507480

Pane, J. F., Steiner, E. D., Baird, M. D., & Hamilton, L. S. (2015). *Continued progress: Promising evidence on personalized learning*. RAND Corporation. DOI: 10.7249/RR1365

Papadima, G. (2021, July). Is there a split between adult educator's educational philosophy in learning and teaching process? *International Journal of Instruction*, 14(3), 583–596. DOI: 10.29333/iji.2021.14334a

Pappas, C. (2014). *Nine tips to apply adult learning theory to eLearning*. eLearning Industry.

Pavlik, J. V. (2023). Collaborating with ChatGPT: Considering the implications of generative artificial intelligence for journalism and media education. *Journalism and Mass Communication Educator*, 8(1), 84–93. DOI: 10.1177/10776958221149577

Pawar, P. (2023). AI-enhanced education: Personalized learning and educational technology. https://doi.org/DOI: 10.25215/9358791152.01

Perez Vallejos, E., Dowthwaite, L., Creswich, H., Portillo, V., Koene, A., Jirotka, M., McCarthy, A., & McAuley, D. (2021). The impact of algorithmic decision-making processes on young people's well-being. *Health Informatics Journal*, 27(1), 146045822097275. DOI: 10.1177/1460458220972750 PMID: 33446031

Pérez, J. Q., Daradoumis, T., & Puig, J. M. M. (2020). Rediscovering the use of chatbots in education: A systematic literature review. *Computer Applications in Engineering Education*, 28(6), 1549–1565. DOI: 10.1002/cae.22326

Perrigo, B. (2023). OpenAI Used Kenyan Workers on Less Than $2 Per Hour to Make ChatGPT Less Toxic. *Time*.

Picard, R. W. (1997). *Affective computing*. MIT Press. DOI: 10.7551/mit-press/1140.001.0001

Picciano, A. G. (2024). Graduate teacher education students use and evaluate ChatGPT as an essay-writing tool. *Online Learning : the Official Journal of the Online Learning Consortium*, 28(2). Advance online publication. DOI: 10.24059/olj.v28i2.4373

Placani, A. (2024). Anthropomorphism in AI: Hype and fallacy. *AI and Ethics*, 4(3), 1–6. DOI: 10.1007/s43681-024-00419-4

Popenici, S., & Kerr, S. (2017). Exploring the impact of artificial intelligence on teaching and learning in higher education. *Research and Practice in Technology Enhanced Learning*, 12(1), 22. Advance online publication. DOI: 10.1186/s41039-017-0062-8 PMID: 30595727

Pranav, S. S. Nausheen Noor Zaidi, & Rana, S. (2024). Application of AI in education: Dynamic course generation, International Journal for Research in Applied Science & Engineering Technology, 12(5). https://discovery.researcher.life/article/application-of-ai-in-the-field-of-education-dynamic-course-generation/26f15f04b11636a2b810554b7a617c7f

Prinsloo, P., Khalil, M., & Slade, S. (2024). Vulnerable student digital well-being in AI-powered educational decision support systems in higher education. *British Journal of Educational Technology*, 55(5), 2075–2092. DOI: 10.1111/bjet.13508

Ramesh, D., & Sanampudi, S. K. (2022). An automated essay scoring systems: A systematic literature review. *Artificial Intelligence Review*, 55(3), 2495–2527. DOI: 10.1007/s10462-021-10068-2 PMID: 34584325

Rawan, G., Adnan, S., Abrar, M., & Al, S. (2022). Higher Education Transformation for Artificial Intelligence Revolution: Transformation Framework. *International Journal of Emerging Technologies in Learning*, 17(19). https://online-journals.org/index.php/i-jet/article/view/33309

Regan, P. M., & Jesse, J. (2019). Ethical challenges of edtech, big data and personalized learning: Twenty-first century student sorting and tracking. *Ethics and Information Technology*, 21(3), 167–179. DOI: 10.1007/s10676-018-9492-2

Renner, B. J., & Skursha, E. (2023). Support for adult students to overcome barriers and improve persistence. *The Journal of Continuing Higher Education*, 71(3), 332–341. DOI: 10.1080/07377363.2022.2065435

Renz, A., & Hilbig, R. (2020). Prerequisites for artificial intelligence in further education: Identification of drivers, barriers, and business models of educational technology companies. *International Journal of Educational Technology in Higher Education*, 17(1), 14. DOI: 10.1186/s41239-020-00193-3

Ribeiro de Oliveira, T., Biancardi Rodrigues, B., Moura da Silva, M., Spinassé, R. A. N., Ludke, G. G., Gaudio, M. R. S., Rocha Gomes, I. R., Guio Cotini, L., da Silva Vargens, D., Queiroz Schimidt, M., Varejão Andreão, R., & Mestria, M. (2023). Virtual reality solutions employing artificial intelligence methods: A systematic literature review. *Association for Computing Machinery*, 55(10), 1–29. DOI: 10.1145/3565020

Riedl, M. O. (2019). Human-centered artificial intelligence and machine learning. *Human Behavior and Emerging Technologies*, 1(1), 33–36. DOI: 10.1002/hbe2.117

Rogers, C. R. (1969). *Freedom to learn*. Merrill.

Rojas-Contreras, M., & Ruiz-Bautista, L. E. (2020, December). Online laboratories are supported with virtual reality for higher education. In *Journal of Physics: Conference Series, 1708* (Vol. 1). IOP Publishing. DOI: 10.1088/1742-6596/1708/1/012036

Römer, K. (2021, February 9). *It's time to embrace not just the lifelong but the life-wide dimension of learning*. [Blog]. https://thelifelonglearningblog.uil.unesco.org/2021/02/09/its-time-to-embrace-not-just-the-lifelong-but-the-life-wide-dimension-of-learning/

Roose, K. (2023, March 30). How should I use A.I. chatbots like ChatGPT? *The New York Times*.https://www.nytimes.com/2023/03/30/technology/ai-chatbot-chatgpt-uses-work-life.html

Rose, C. P., McLaughlin, E. A., Liu, R., & Koedinger, K. R. (2019). Explanatory learner models: Why machine learning (alone) is not the answer. *British Journal of Educational Technology*, 50(6), 2943–2958. DOI: 10.1111/bjet.12858

Rosé, C. P., Wang, Y. C., Cui, Y., Arguello, J., Stegmann, K., Weinberger, A., & Fischer, F. (2015). Analyzing collaborative learning processes automatically: Exploiting the advances of computational linguistics in computer-supported collaborative learning. *International Journal of Computer-Supported Collaborative Learning*, 3(3), 237–271. DOI: 10.1007/s11412-007-9034-0

Roski, M., Sebastian, R., Ewerth, R., Hoppe, A., & Nehring, A. (2024). Learning analytics and the Universal Design for Learning (UDL): A clustering approach. *Computers & Education*, 214, 105028. DOI: 10.1016/j.compedu.2024.105028

Russell, S., & Norvig, P. (2021). *Artificial intelligence: A modern approach* (4th ed.). Pearson.

Ryan, R. M., & Deci, E. L. (2000). Self-determination theory and the facilitation of intrinsic motivation, social development, and well-being. *The American Psychologist*, 55(1), 68–78. DOI: 10.1037/0003-066X.55.1.68 PMID: 11392867

Sales, A., Portera, A., & Milani, M. (2023). Developing intercultural competences through participatory strategies: A multiple case study. *Intercultural Education*, 34(4), 426–445. https://doi-org.ezproxy.neu.edu/10.1080/14675986.2023.2211854. DOI: 10.1080/14675986.2023.2211854

Salmi, J. (2001). Tertiary education in the Twenty-First Century: Challenges and opportunities. *Higher Education Management*, 3(2), 105–130.

Sánchez, H., Martínez, L. S., & González, J. D. (2019). Educational robotics as a teaching tool in higher education institutions: A bibliographical analysis. *Journal of Physics: Conference Series*, 1391(1), 012128. DOI: 10.1088/1742-6596/1391/1/012128

Satya, R., & Mohammed, L. A. (2024). Interdisciplinary Insights: The Convergence of AI and Educational Leadership. *International Journal of Research and Innovation in Social Science*. https://rsisinternational.org/journals/ijriss/articles/interdisciplinary-insights-the-convergence-of-ai-and-educational-leadership/

Savery, J. R. (2006). Overview of problem-based learning: Definitions and distinctions. *The Interdisciplinary Journal of Problem-Based Learning*, 1(1). Advance online publication. DOI: 10.7771/1541-5015.1002

Sawyer, K. (2008). Optimising learning: Implications of learning sciences research. OECD/CERI International Conference "Learning in the 21st Century: Research, Innovation and Policy". OECD Publishing.

Schiff, D. (2022). Education for AI, not AI for education: The role of education and ethics in national AI policy strategies. *International Journal of Artificial Intelligence in Education*, 32(3), 527–563. DOI: 10.1007/s40593-021-00270-2

Schlesinger, A., O'Hara, K. P., & Taylor, A. S. (2018). Let's talk about race: Identity, chatbots, and AI. In *Proceedings of the 2018 Chi Conference of Human Factors in Computing* (pp. 1-14). DOI: 10.1145/3173574.3173889

Schmager, S., Pappas, I., & Vassilakopoulou, P. (2023). Defining human centered AI: A comprehensive review of HCAI literature. *The 15th Mediterranean Conference on Information Systems (MCIS) and the 6th Middle East & North Africa Conference on Digital Information Systems (MENACIS), Madrid 2023*, (pp. 1-12). Retrieved from Easycha.

Schön, D. A. (1992). *The reflective practitioner: How professionals think in action.* Routledge Imprint of Taylor & Francis., DOI: 10.4324/9781315237473

Schwab, K. (2016). *The fourth industrial revolution.* World Economic Forum.

Sedlbauer, J., Cin, J., Slavík, M., Hartlová, A., & Sedlbauer, J. (2024). Students' reflections on their experience with ChatGPT. *Journal of Computer Assisted Learning*, 40(4), 1–9. DOI: 10.1111/jcal.12967

Sedlmeier, P. (2001). Intelligent tutoring systems. In Neil. J. Smelser, & Paul. B. Baltes (Eds.), International Encyclopedia of the Social & Behavioral Sciences (pp. 7674e7678). Pergamon. https://doi.org/DOI: 10.1016/B0-08-043076-7/01618-1

Seldon, A., Abidoye, O., & Metcalf, T. (2020). *The Fourth Education Revolution Reconsidered: Will Artificial Intelligence Enrich Or Diminish Humanity?* Legend Press Ltd.

Selman, G. (1989). The enemies of adult education. *Canadian Journal of University Continuing Education*, 15, 68–81.

Selwyn, N. (2019). Should robots replace teachers? AI and the future of education. *British Journal of Educational Technology*, 50(6), 1263–1272.

Selwyn, N. (2019). *Should robots replace teachers?: AI and the future of education.* Polity Press.

Selwyn, N. (2022). The future of AI and education: Some cautionary notes. *European Journal of Education*, 57(4), 620–631. DOI: 10.1111/ejed.12532

Seo, K., Yoo, M., Dodson, S., & Jin, S.-H. (2024). Augmented teachers: K-12 teachers' needs for artificial intelligence's complementary role in personalized learning. *Journal of Research on Technology in Education*, •••, 1–18. DOI: 10.1080/15391523.2024.2330525

Settles, B., Brust, C., Gustafson, E., Hagiwara, M., & Madnani, N. (2018). Second language acquisition modeling. In *Proceedings of the Thirteenth Workshop on Innovative Use of NLP for Building Educational Applications* (pp. 56-65). DOI: 10.18653/v1/W18-0506

Shahvaroughi Farahani, M., & Ghasemi, G. (2024). *Artificial Intelligence and Inequality: Challenges and Opportunities*. Qeios., DOI: 10.32388/7HWUZ2

Shaw, C., Yuan, L., Brennan, D., Martin, S., Janson, N., Fox, K., & Bryant, G. (2023, October 23). Tyton Partners' *Generative AI in higher education: Fall update 2023*. https://www.tytonpartners.com/time-for-class-2023/GenAI-Update

Shelle, G., Earnesty, D., Pilkenton, A., & Powell, E. (2018). Adaptive Learning: An Innovative Method for Online Teaching and Learning. *Journal of Extension*, 56(5). Advance online publication. DOI: 10.34068/joe.56.05.17

Shemshack, A., & Spector, J. M. (2020). A systematic literature review of personalized learning terms. *Smart Learning Environments*, 7(1), 33. Advance online publication. DOI: 10.1186/s40561-020-00140-9

Shneiderman, B. (2021). Human centered AI. *Issues in Science and Technology*, (Winter), 56–61.

Shoaib, M., Sayed, N., Singh, J., Shafi, J., Khan, S., & Ali, F. (2024). AI student success predictor: Enhancing personalized learning in campus management systems. *Computers in Human Behavior*, 158, 108301. DOI: 10.1016/j.chb.2024.108301

Shrungare, J. (2024). Tech and Social Justice. [Association for Computing Machinery]. *Crossroads*, 30(4), 67–69. DOI: 10.1145/3665606

Shu, X., & Ye, Y. (2023). Knowledge discovery: Methods from data mining and machine learning. *Social Science Research*, 110, 102817. DOI: 10.1016/j.ssresearch.2022.102817 PMID: 36796993

Shwartz, V. (2024, Feb 13). Artificial intelligence needs to be trained on culturally diverse datasets to avoid bias. *The Conversation*.https://theconversation.com/artificial-intelligence-needs-to-be-trained-on-culturally-diverse-datasets-to-avoid-bias-222811

Siemens, G. (2005). Connectivism: A learning theory for the digital age. *International Journal of Instructional Technology and Distance Learning*, 2(1), 3–10.

Siemens, G., & Long, P. (2011). Penetrating the fog: Analytics in learning and education. *EDUCAUSE Review*, 46(5), 30.

Silverman, J. A., Ali, S. A., Rybak, A., van Goudoever, J. B., & Leleiko, N. S. (2023). Generative AI: Potential and pitfalls in academic publishing. *JPGN Reports*, 4(4), e387. DOI: 10.1097/PG9.0000000000000387 PMID: 38034432

Skinner, B. F. (1974). *About behaviorism*. Knopf.

Slimi, Z. (2023). The impact of artificial intelligence on higher education: An empirical study. Deusto University-Spain. *National University of Sciences and Technology*. https://files.eric.ed.gov/fulltext/EJ1384682.pdf

Slimi, Z., & Carballido, B. V. (2023). Navigating the ethical challenges of artificial intelligence in higher education: An analysis of seven global AI ethics policies. *TEM Journal, 12*(2). https://doi.org/DOI: 10.18421/TEM122-02

Smolansky, A., Cram, A., Raduescu, C., Zeivots, S., Huber, E., & Kizilcec, R. F. (2023). Educator and student perspectives on the impact of Generative AI on assessments in higher education. *Proceedings of the Tenth ACM Conference on Learning @ Scale*, 378–382. DOI: 10.1145/3573051.3596191

Soccorsi, L. (2013). Instilling a personal teaching philosophy in preservice teachers: Vitally important but not always easy to achieve. *Journal of Student Engagement: Education Matters*, 3(1), 21–28.

Sommerhoff, D., Szameitat, A., Vogel, F., Loderer, O., & Fischer, F. (2018). What do we teach when we teach the learning sciences? A document analysis of 75 graduate programs. *Journal of the Learning Sciences*, 27(2), 319–351. DOI: 10.1080/10508406.2018.1440353

Spolaôr, N., & Benitti, F. B. V. (2017). Robotics applications grounded in learning theories on tertiary education: A systematic review. *Computers & Education*, 112, 97–107. DOI: 10.1016/j.compedu.2017.05.001

Stallbaumer, C. (2023, March 16). *Introducing Microsoft 365 Copilot – _A whole new way to work. Microsoft* 365. https://www.microsoft.com/en-us/microsoft-365/blog/2023/03/16/introducing-microsoft-365-copilot-a-whole-new-way-to-work/

Starcic, A. I. (2019). Human learning and learning analytics in the age of artificial intelligence. *British Journal of Educational Technology*, 50(6), 2974–2976. DOI: 10.1111/bjet.12879

Steenbergen-Hu, S., & Cooper, H. (2014). A meta-analysis of the effectiveness of intelligent tutoring systems on college students' academic learning. *J. Educ.Psychol., 106*(2), 331e347. https://psycnet.apa.org/doi/10.1037/a0034752

Steenbergen-Hu, S., & Cooper, H. (2014). A meta-analysis of the effectiveness of intelligent tutoring systems on college students' academic learning. *Journal of Educational Psychology*, 106(2), 331–347. DOI: 10.1037/a0034752

Storey, V. A. (2023). AI technology and academic writing: Knowing and mastering the "craft skills.". *International Journal of Adult Education and Technology*, 14(1), 1–15. DOI: 10.4018/IJAET.325795

Storey, V., & Wagner, A. (2024). Integrating artificial intelligence (AI) into adult education: Opportunities, challenges, and future directions. *International Journal of Adult Education and Technology*, 15(1), 1–15. DOI: 10.4018/IJAET.345921

Strohschen, G., & Elazier, K. (2019, November 25-26). The Metagogy Theorem: A Framework for Educating Adults. *International Forum of Teaching and Studies, 15*(1), 3-15.American Scholars Press.

Strohschen, G. (2011). Teaching Adults across Cultures, Distance, and Learning Preferences: Universal Tools for the 21st Century. In Wang, V. X. (Ed.), *Encyclopedia of Information Communication and Adult Education Integration* (pp. 469–484). IGI Global. DOI: 10.4018/978-1-61692-906-0.ch028

Strohschen, G. (2014). Education Collaboration Development: A Blended Shore Education Approach to Sustainable Development. In Wang, V. X. (Ed.), *Handbook of Research on Transnational Higher Education* (pp. 512–525). IGI Global. DOI: 10.4018/978-1-4666-4458-8.ch026

Strohschen, G., & Elazier, K. (2020). Metagogy: Toward a Contemporary Adult Education Praxis. In Pushpanadham, K. (Ed.), *Teacher Education in the Global Era, Perspectives and Practices* (pp. C1–C2). Springer. DOI: 10.1007/978-981-15-4008-0_19

Studente, S., Ellis, S., & Garivaldis, S. F. (2020). Exploring the potential of chatbots in higher education: A preliminary study. *International Journal of Educational and Pedagogical Sciences*, 14(9), 768–771.

Successful Real-World Use Cases for LLMs and Lessons They Teach. (Mar 8, 2024). Forbes Tech Council. https://www.forbes.com/sites/forbestechcouncil/2024/03/07/successful-real-world-use-cases-for-llms-and-lessons-they-teach/

Sullivan, M., Kelly, A., & McLaughlan, P. (2023). ChatGPT in higher education: Considerations for academic integrity and student learning. *Journal of Applied Learning and Teaching*, 6(1). Advance online publication. DOI: 10.37074/jalt.2023.6.1.17

Susanto, S., Andrianingsih, A., Sutawan, K., Marwintaria, V. A., & Astika, R. (2023). Transformation of learner learning: Improving reasoning skills through artificial intelligence (AI). [JoERI]. *Journal of Education, Religious, and Instructions*, 1(2), 37–46. DOI: 10.60046/joeri.v1i2.74

Sutton, K. S., & DeSantis, J. (2017). Beyond change blindness: Embracing the technology revolution in higher education. *Innovations in Education and Teaching International*, 54(3), 223–228. DOI: 10.1080/14703297.2016.1174592

Swindell, A., Greeley, L., Farag, A., & Verdone, B. (2024). Against Artificial Education: Towards an ethical framework for Generative Artificial Intelligence (GAI) use in education. *Online Learning : the Official Journal of the Online Learning Consortium*, 28(2). Advance online publication. DOI: 10.24059/olj.v28i2.4438

Tahiru, F. (2021). AI in education: A systematic literature review. *Journal of Cases on Information Technology*, 23(1), 1–20. DOI: 10.4018/JCIT.2021010101

Tarisayi, K. S. (2024). Strategic leadership for responsible artificial intelligence adoption in higher education. *CTE Workshop Proceedings, 11*, 4-14. DOI: 10.55056/cte.616

Tatineni, S., & Chakilam, N. V. (2024). Integrating Artificial Intelligence with DevOps for Intelligent Infrastructure Management: Optimizing Resource Allocation and Performance in Cloud-Native Applications. *Journal of Bioinformatics and Artificial Intelligence*, 4(1), 109–142.

Tawfik, A. A. (2015). Essential readings in problem-based learning: Exploring and extending the legacy of Howard S. Barrows. *The Interdisciplinary Journal of Problem-Based Learning*, 9(2). Advance online publication. DOI: 10.7771/1541-5015.1593

Taylor, D. C., & Hamdy, H. (2013). Adult learning theories: Implications for learning and teaching in medical education: AMEE Guide No. 83. *Medical Teacher*, 35(11), e1561–e1572. DOI: 10.3109/0142159X.2013.828153 PMID: 24004029

Taylor, E. W., & Cranton, P. (2012). *The handbook of transformative learning: Theory, research, and practice*. Jossey-Bass.

Taylor, R. D. (2020). Quantum artificial intelligence: A "precautionary" U.S. approach? *Telecommunications Policy*, 44(6), 101909. DOI: 10.1016/j.telpol.2020.101909

Tegmark, M. (2017). LIFE 3.0: Being human in the age of artificial intelligence. In A. Knopf (Ed.), *Humanist perspectives* (Number 202, pp. 39-81). Canadian Humanist Publications.

The Future of Jobs Report. (2023). World Economic Forum https://www.weforum.org/reports/future-of-jobs-report-2023

Thorndike, E. L., Bregman, E. O., Tilton, J. W., & Woodyard, E. (1928). *Adult learning*. Macmillan.

Tiffin University Online Resources. (2023). *Design statements*. Tiffin University website. https://tuonlineresources.com/design-statement

Tisdell, E. J., & Taylor, E. W. (2000). Adult education philosophy informs practice. *Adult Learning*, 11(2), 6–10. DOI: 10.1177/104515959901100203

Torre, F., Teigland, R., & Engstam, L. (2019). 7 AI leadership and the future of corporate governance. *The digital transformation of labor, 116*.

Torrisi-Steele, G., & Carim, G.Jr. (2019). An adult-learner approach to the learning design of safety management system training in aviation. *International Journal of Adult Vocational Education and Technology*, 10(3), 39–53. DOI: 10.4018/IJAVET.2019070103

Tsai, M. J., Hsu, C. Y., & Tsai, C. C. (2012). Investigation of high school students' online science information searching performance: The role of implicit and explicit strategies. *Journal of Science Education and Technology*, 21(2), 246–254. DOI: 10.1007/s10956-011-9307-2

Tsai, Y. S., Poquet, O., Gasevic, D., Dawson, S., & Pardo, A. (2019). Complexity leadership in learning analytics: Drivers, challenges, and opportunities. *British Journal of Educational Technology*, 50(6), 2839–2854. DOI: 10.1111/bjet.12846

Tuomi, I. (2018). *The impact of artificial intelligence on learning, teaching, and education policies for the future*. JRC Science for Policy Report., DOI: 10.2760/12297

U.S. Department of Education, Office of Educational Technology. (2023). *Artificial intelligence and future of teaching and learning: insights and recommendations.* Washington._https://tech.ed.gov

UNESCO. (2019). *Artificial intelligence in education: Challenges and opportunities for sustainable development*. UNESCO Publishing.

UNESCO. (2023). Global education monitoring report, 2023: technology in education: A tool on whose terms? https://unesdoc.unesco.org/ark:/48223/pf0000385723

United Nations Educational, Scientific and Cultural Organization, & Organization, C. (2021). *Recommendation on the Ethics of Artificial Intelligence*. United Nations Educational._https://unesdoc.unesco.org/ark:/48223/pf0000379920.page=14

VanLehn, K. (2011). The relative effectiveness of human tutoring, intelligent tutoring systems, and other tutoring systems. *Educational Psychologist*, 46(4), 197–221. DOI: 10.1080/00461520.2011.611369

Verdú, E., Regueras, L. M., Gal, E., De Castro, J. P., Verdú, M. J., & Kohen-Vacs, D. (2017). Integration of an intelligent tutoring system in a course of computer network design. *Educational Technology Research and Development*, 65(3), 653–677. DOI: 10.1007/s11423-016-9503-0

Vinuesa, R., Azizpour, H., Leite, I., Olsson, C., Boeva, V., Smith, D. M., Jamone, L., & Lourenco, A., Edsinger, & Brachmond, F. (2022). The role of artificial intelligence in achieving the Sustainable Development Goals. *Nature Communications*, 13(1), 1–13. PMID: 34983933

von Krogh, G., Roberson, Q., & Gruber, M. (2023). We recognize and utilize novel research opportunities with artificial intelligence. *Academy of Management Journal*, 66(2), 367–373. DOI: 10.5465/amj.2023.4002

Walter, Y. (2024). Embracing the future of artificial intelligence in the classroom: The relevance of AI literacy, prompt engineering, and critical thinking in modern education. *International Journal of Educational Technology in Higher Education*, 21(15), 15. Advance online publication. DOI: 10.1186/s41239-024-00448-3

Wang, T., Brady, D., Lund, D., Marengo, A., Pagano, A., Zoe, T., Pange, J., & Pange, W. (2023). Exploring the potential impact of artificial intelligence (AI) on international students in higher education: Generative AI, Chatbots, analytics, and international student success. Applied Sciences. https://www.mdpi.com/2076-3417/13/11/6716

Wang, C., Cai, J., Gao, C., & Ye, X. (2023). History, status, and development of AI-based learning science. *SN Computer Science*, 4(3), 316. DOI: 10.1007/s42979-023-01778-1

Wang, T., Lund, B. D., Marengo, A., Pagano, A., Mannuru, N. R., Teel, Z. A., & Pange, J. (2023). Exploring the potential impact of artificial intelligence (AI) on international students in higher education: Generative AI, chatbots, analytics, and international student success. *Applied Sciences (Basel, Switzerland)*, 13(11), 6716. DOI: 10.3390/app13116716

Wang, V. (2003). *Principles of adult education*. Pearson.

Wang, W., & Siau, K. (2019). Artificial intelligence, machine learning, automation, robotics, future of work and future of humanity. *Journal of Database Management*, 30(1), 61–79. DOI: 10.4018/JDM.2019010104

Wang, X., Li, L., Tan, S. C., Yang, L., & Lei, J. (2023). Preparing for AI-enhanced education: Conceptualizing and empirically examining teachers' AI readiness. *Computers in Human Behavior*, 146, 107798. DOI: 10.1016/j.chb.2023.107798

Wass, R., & Golding, C. (2014). Sharpening a tool for teaching: The zone of proximal development. *Teaching in Higher Education*, 19(6), 671–684. DOI: 10.1080/13562517.2014.901958

Webber, K. L., & Zheng, H. Y. (2024). Artificial intelligence and advanced data analytics. Implications for higher education. *New Directions for Higher Education*, 2024(207), 1–9. DOI: 10.1002/he.20508

Weizenbaum, J. (1966). ELIZA d a computer program for the study of natural language communication between man and machine. *Commun. ACM, 26*(1), 23e28. https://doi.org/. January 1983.DOI: 10.1145/357980.357991

Welham, D. (2008). AI in training (1980–2000): Foundation for the future or misplaced optimism? *British Journal of Educational Technology*, 39(2), 287–303. DOI: 10.1111/j.1467-8535.2008.00818.x

Welsh, R. O., & Swain, W. A. (2020). (Re) defining urban education: A conceptual review and empirical exploration of the definition of urban education. *Educational Researcher*, 49(2), 90–100. DOI: 10.3102/0013189X20902822

Wenger, E. (1987). *Artificial intelligence and tutoring systems: Computational and cognitive approaches to the communication of knowledge*. Morgan Kaufmann Publishers.

West, S. M., Whittaker, M., & Crawford, K. (2019). *Discriminating Systems: Gender, Race and Power in AI.* AI Now Institute. https://ainowinstitute.org/ discriminatingsystems.html

West, S. M. (2019). Data capitalism: Redefining the logics of surveillance and privacy. *Business & Society*, 58(1), 20–41. DOI: 10.1177/0007650317718185

Wigmore, I. (2020). *Fourth Industrial Revolution. TechTarget.*https://www.techtarget .com/whatis/definition/fourth-industrial-revolution

Williamson, B. (2017). Decoding ClassDojo: Psycho-policy, social-emotional learning and persuasive educational technologies. *Learning, Media and Technology*, 42(4), 440–453. DOI: 10.1080/17439884.2017.1278020

Wise, B., Emerson, L., Van Luyn, A., Dyson, B., Bjork, C., & Thomas, S. E. (2024). A scholarly dialogue: Writing scholarship, authorship, academic integrity and the challenges of AI. *Higher Education Research & Development*, 43(3), 578–590. DOI: 10.1080/07294360.2023.2280195

Wolf, M. J., Miller, K. W., & Grodzinsky, F. S. (2017). Why we should have seen that coming: Comments on Microsoft's Tay experience and broader implications. *The ORBIT Journal*, 1(2), 1–12. DOI: 10.29297/orbit.v1i2.49

Wooldridge, M. (2021). *A brief history of artificial intelligence: what it is, where we are, and where we are going*. Flatiron Books.

Woolf, B. P. (2010). *Building intelligent interactive tutors: Student-centered strategies for revolutionizing e-learning*. Morgan Kaufmann.

Wright, T. S. A., & Wilton, H. (2012). Facilities management directors' conceptualizations of sustainability in higher education. *Journal of Cleaner Production*, 31, 118–125. DOI: 10.1016/j.jclepro.2012.02.030

Xia, Q., Chiu, T., Lee, M., Temitayo Sanusi, I., Dai, Y., & Sing Chai, C. (2022). A self-determination theory (SDT) design approach for inclusive and diverse artificial intelligence (AI) education. *Computers & Education*, 189, 189. DOI: 10.1016/j.compedu.2022.104582

Xu, E., Wang, W., & Wang, Q. (2023). The effectiveness of collaborative problem solving in promoting students' critical thinking: A meta-analysis based on empirical literature. *Humanities & Social Sciences Communications*, 10(1), 1–11. DOI: 10.1057/s41599-023-01508-1 PMID: 37192950

Xu, W. (2024). The correction strategy of artificial intelligence embedding into the negative social mentality of the marginal group of college students in the new era. *Journal of Electrical Systems*, 20(2). https://journal.esrgroups.org/jes/article/view/1222

Yang, E., & Beil, C. (2024). Ensuring data privacy in AI/ML implementation. *New Directions for Higher Education*, 2024(207), 63–78. DOI: 10.1002/he.20509

Yang, H., & Kyun, S. (2022). The current research trend of artificial intelligence in language learning: A systematic empirical literature review from an activity theory perspective. *Australasian Journal of Educational Technology*, •••, 180–210. DOI: 10.14742/ajet.7492

Yang, S., & Evans, C. (2019). Opportunities and challenges in using AI chatbots in higher education. In *Proceedings of the 2019 3rd International Conference on Education and E-Learning* (pp. 79-83). DOI: 10.1145/3371647.3371659

Yang, S., Ogata, H., Matsui, T., & Chen, N. (2021). Human centered artificial intelligence in education: Seeing the invisible through the visible. *Computers and Education: Artificial Intelligence*, 2, 1–5. DOI: 10.1016/j.caeai.2021.100008

Yan, L., Sha, L., Zhao, L., Li, Y., Martinez-Maldonado, R., Chen, G., Li, X., Jin, Y., & Gašević, D. (2024). Practical and ethical challenges of large language models in education: A systematic scoping review. *British Journal of Educational Technology*, 55(1), 90–112. DOI: 10.1111/bjet.13370

Yin, W. J. (2024, January 24). Will our educational system keep pace with AI? A student's perspective on AI and learning. *EDUCAUSE Review*.https://er.educause.edu/articles/2024/1/will-our-educational-system-keep-pace-with-ai-a-students-perspective-on-ai-and-learning

Yoon, S., Weidner, T., & Hastak, M. (2021). Total-package-prioritization mitigation strategy for deferred maintenance of a campus-sized institution. *Journal of Construction Engineering and Management*, 147(3), 04020185. DOI: 10.1061/(ASCE)CO.1943-7862.0001956

Yue, M., Jong, M. S.-Y., & Ng, K. (2024). Understanding K–12 teachers' technological pedagogical content knowledge readiness and attitudes toward artificial intelligence education. *Education and Information Technologies*, 29(15), 19505–19536. Advance online publication. DOI: 10.1007/s10639-024-12621-2

Yusuf, A., Pervin, N., & Román-González, M. (2024). Generative AI and the future of higher education: A threat to academic integrity or reformation? Evidence from multicultural perspectives. *International Journal of Educational Technology in Higher Education*, 21(1), 21. DOI: 10.1186/s41239-024-00453-6

Zadorina, O., Kurskaya, V., Sobolyeva, S., Grekova, L., & Vasylyuk-Zaitseva, S. (2024). The role of artificial intelligence in the creation of future education: Possibilities and challenges. *Futurity Education*, 4(2), 163–185.

Zaman, B. (2023). Transforming education through AI, benefits, risks, and ethical considerations. *Education, Computer Science*. https://www.techrxiv.org/users/691638/articles/683292-transforming-education-through-ai-benefits-risks-and-ethical-considerations

Zawacki-Richter, O., Marin, V. I., Bond, M., & Gouverneur, F. (2019). Systematic review of research on artificial intelligence applications in higher education – where are the educators? *International Journal of Educational Technology in Higher Education*, 16(39), 39. https://educationaltechnologyjournal.springeropen.com/articles/10.1186/s41239-019-0171-0. DOI: 10.1186/s41239-019-0171-0

Zhai, X., Chu, X., Chai, C., Jong, M., Istenic, A., Spector, M., & Li, Y. (2021). A review of artificial intelligence (AI) in education from 2010 to 2020. *Complexity*, 2021(1), 1–18. DOI: 10.1155/2021/8812542

Zhang, K., & Aslan, A. B. (2021). AI technologies for education: Recent research & future directions. *Computers and Education: Artificial Intelligence*, 2, 100025. DOI: 10.1016/j.caeai.2021.100025

Zheng, L., Niu, J., Zhong, L., & Gyasi, J. F. (2021). The effectiveness of artificial intelligence on learning achievement and learning perception: A meta-analysis. *Interactive Learning Environments*. Advance online publication. DOI: 10.1080/10494820.2021.2015693

Zhou, Y. (2022). Beliefs and practice evaluation based on artificial intelligence models under the IP environment. *Journal of Environmental and Public Health*, 2022(1), 1415142. DOI: 10.1155/2022/1415142 PMID: 36203503

About the Contributors

Viktor Wang has brought leadership to the study of Education. Alongside the production of 240 + Refereed Publications, Dr. Wang has provided many opportunities for his peers and students to develop their scholarly capabilities and stimulated the research agendas of numerous colleagues. To date, colleagues and doctoral students have contributed 200+ articles to his journals and 1500+ chapters to his books. Please check out articles and book chapters by the world's leading scholars in Dr. Wang's journals and books cataloged by Stanford University Libraries and other leading university libraries around the globe. He received the 2016 Presidential Award for Exceptional and Innovative Leadership from American Association For Adult and Continuing Education in addition to multiple institutional awards. Thus far, he has graduated more than 80 dissertation candidates.

Lucy Bunning is an Assistant Teaching Professor in NU Global at Northeastern University. She develops a curriculum and teaches English language, communication, and service-learning courses for international students. She was a Faculty Scholar with Northeastern's Center for Advancing Teaching and Learning Through Research in 2016-2017 and 2017-2018. Her classroom-based research focuses on students' language development during service-learning, class participation, on increasing students' engagement and language development in classroom and community settings. She develops and teaches speaking, listening, and service-learning courses. Dr. Bunning earned her PhD in Educational Studies, with a concentration in adult second language education, from Lesley University. Dr. Bunning has taught English for speakers of other languages in university, private, and community-based language programs in the United States, Kenya, and Rwanda. Contact at l.bunning@northeastern.edu or https://www.linkedin.com/in/lucy-bunning-0b42563a.

Angela Crevar serves as an assistant professor at Mercer University. She received her Ph.D. in Educational Leadership and Policy from Texas Tech University. Angela served as a postdoctoral researcher at Texas Tech University, and she served as a high school principal for ten years. Her research is focused on the nexus of high school to college and career readiness with a focus on pathways through education to student success. These pathways include career technical education, hybrid education, and non-traditional pathways. Her work has been published in the Journal of Higher Education and Policy and Leadership Studies and Early Education and Development. Her work has also been presented at the Association for Public Policy Analysis and Management, American Educational Research Association, Association for Education Finance and Policy, University Council for Educational Administration, and the Society for Research on Educational Effectiveness national conferences.

Ashley L. Dockens, PhD, AuD, CCC-A, is a dynamic academic leader serving at Lamar University as the Assistant Provost of Academic Innovation & Quality Assurance, Office of Academic Affairs and the Associate Dean of Policy and Procedure, College of Graduate Studies. In these roles, she shapes and implements policies to drive academic excellence and compliance. Having previously served as the Director of the Center for Teaching and Learning Enhancement, Dr. Dockens is dedicated to promoting innovative teaching practices and leading all university AI initiatives, ensuring ethical and effective integration into academic programs. As an Associate Professor of Audiology, she shares her passion for the field, having previously directed the Doctor of Audiology program. In higher education, she serves as a regular speaker on the topic of generative AI at state, national, and international venues. Beginning March 2024, Dr. Dockens committed to serve as Chair of the AI Taskforce for the Council of Academic Programs in Communication Sciences and Disorders, an international accreditor for the field. Dr. Dockens' diverse roles reflect her commitment to higher education through leadership, contributing to the overall success of the academic community.

Praveen Dubey is an assistant professor of education and director of clinical experiences and partnerships at Montana State University Northern. His research interest focuses in the areas of Multicultural Education, Diversity, Equity, & Inclusivity, Leadership and Change, Technology in Education (Digital Equity & AI), STEM education, Immigrant Education, Comparative and International Education, Teacher Quality, and Teacher Choice for diverse classrooms. In his research, he uses the statistical tools of Structural Education Modelling (SEM), Mediation & Moderation, and R programming to address the issues that intersect in improving the learning experiences of diverse student population, immigrant/refugee students, and minority students. He has presented research papers at several national research conferences such as AERA, UCIE, AEFP, SREE, etc. and is currently working on different projects and grants.

Linda Ellington, after working in IBM for 23 years, Linda is a Professor of Business at Southern New Hampshire University, where she has taught since 2010. She conducted her doctoral research at the University of Oxford and the University of Warwick, United Kingdom. Her research focus is on the intersection of leadership and organizational change, uncovering strategies that explore how effective leaders navigate complex challenges to make impactful strategic choices. Dr. Ellington has published extensively in top-tier journals, scholarly books, and is a member of several university doctoral dissertations, such as at the University of Johannesburg, South Africa. Beyond academia, she has published eight children's books in the genre of bullying and taking care of the planet. She collaborates with community leaders to read stories to local children, fostering a love of literacy and inspiring the next generation of readers. She lives with her two coolest four-legged friends, Max and Riley.

Marvin Espinoza, M.Ed., is a seasoned educational leader and community advocate with over 25 years of experience in program management and leadership across the nonprofit sector and higher education. Currently a doctoral candidate at California State University, San Bernardino, he has dedicated his career to advancing educational outcomes and expanding services for underserved communities. His expertise spans teaching, strategic planning, youth development, community engagement, grant writing, program development, and quality assurance. As the Chief Operating Officer at the Girls Club of Los Angeles, Mr. Espinoza ensures that the organization's mission aligns with its operations, driving significant community impact. His leadership extends to higher education, where he has been an adjunct faculty member at East Los Angeles College for 18 years, contributing to in-person and online learning. Mr. Espinoza holds a Master of Arts in Education and a Bachelor of Arts in Liberal Studies and Child Development from California State University, Dominguez Hills, and an Associate of Arts in Child Development from Los Angeles Southwest College. His professional development includes certifications such as a Leadership Certificate from the Executive Directors Leadership Institute and a Project Grantsmanship Certificate from The Grantsmanship Center. His work has been recognized with several awards, including the City of Los Angeles Commendation Award, LAUSD Outstanding Director, and County of Los Angeles Commendation. Marvin Espinoza remains committed to empowering children and families through innovative programs and strategic partnerships, contributing significantly to educational leadership and community development.

Patricia Goodman Hayward As an educator, I am honored to be in the role of Program Lead for the Bachelor's of Science Digital Communications and Media program, along with an Associate Teaching Professor for the Northeastern

University College of Professional Studies Master of Science in Corporate and Organizational Communication. My career has been filled with various leadership and communication roles within the social service field from correction and judicial services, mental health, secondary education, higher education, and executive education. I can draw on my experiences to highlight the importance of transferring theory into practice. As a consultant at the Harvard School of Public Health and Harvard University Office of Sustainability, I developed stakeholder communication systems to enhance internal and external relations. As HR Director for a community mental health center, I instituted internal and external communication strategies to improve employee relations, Board of Director recruitment and orientation process, along with community engagement. I was particularly proud to be a leading member of a team to develop and advocate for the Marion County Diversion of Non-violent Mentally Ill Offenders to Treatment. I was part of a small partnership to present this program to the State of Florida congressional committee. Ultimately, this program was adopted and funded by the state. More recently, my research and travels have supported my curiosity and drive. With my previous students, now alumnus, we co-edited a multi-case book, Women Community Leaders and Their Impact as Global Changemakers (2022) published through IGI Global. Recently was an invited speaker on Leaders Exploring Cultural Transformation, at the 11th World Women's University Presidents Forum in Zhengzhou, China. As for my formal education, I have a Doctorate in Education from George Washington University through the Executive Leadership Program with a concentration in adult learning. My Master of Liberal Arts is from Harvard University with a concentration in information management systems. In addition, I have a MA in Personnel Management through the University of Phoenix from Arizona. My undergraduate degree was from University of Florida with a BS in Business Management with a major in management and minor in marketing. In addition to the joy of teaching, I consider myself a social scientist. My research focus has been in adult learning and communications, specifically: intercultural communication, cultural intelligence, cross-generational communication, cultural transformation, self-directed learning, team learning, and transformative learning

Greg Kaiser, PhD, is a distinguished Professor of Education at Azusa Pacific University, where he has dedicated 29 years to advancing the field of educational leadership. Earning his doctorate from Claremont Graduate University, Dr. Kaiser is recognized for his expertise in systems and school leadership, as well as his deep understanding of organizational structures in schools and the translation of theory into practice. An innovative and creative educator, Dr. Kaiser is known for being at the cutting edge of educational strategies, continually pushing the boundaries of traditional teaching and leadership methodologies to inspire and equip the next generation of educational leaders.

Sue Kaiser, EdD, is a respected faculty member at California State University, San Bernardino, with a doctorate in Educational Administration from the University of Southern California. With over 40 years of experience in education, Dr. Kaiser has held numerous leadership roles, including teacher, administrator, and consultant. Her expertise lies in leadership development, organizational change, and educational equity, making her a sought-after authority in the field. Dr. Kaiser is deeply committed to mentoring future educational leaders, contributing significantly to both the academic and practical aspects of educational leadership through her teaching, research, and extensive consulting work.

Wallace Lages is an Assistant Professor with a joint appointment in the Department of Art + Design and the Khoury College of Computer Sciences. His research focuses on user experience of Augmented and Virtual Reality applications, leveraging methods from disciplines such as design, engineering, and psychology. His artistic practice has been part of inaugural exhibitions and has been displayed in Brazil, the United States, Italy, and Singapore. He was also a co-founder of the game studio Ilusis Interactive Graphics. Prior to joining Northeastern University, Lages was an Assistant Professor at Virginia Tech and Universidade Federal de Minas Gerais. Lages holds a PhD degree in Computer Science from Virginia Tech, and a MS and BS degrees in Computer Science from Universidade Federal de Minas Gerais. Contact at w.lages@northeastern.edu or https://www.linkedin.com/in/wallacelages/.

Sailesh Maharjan has been an adjunct professor at California State University, San Bernardino (CSUSB) since 2017. He is experienced in mindfulness meditation and delivers talks on Buddhist Philosophy focused on applying Buddhism in everyday life. Sailesh is a doctoral candidate at CSUSB focusing on Higher Education Leadership and has been selected as one of two Holmes Scholars from Cohort 16. Sailesh was a Theravadin Buddhist monk for 16 years, including 12 years in Sri Lanka. He earned one bachelor's degree in Buddhism and Pali Studies and one in Psychology from the University of Peradeniya. In 2012, he received the Royal Pandit (Rājakīya Pandita) Degree in Pali, Sanskrit, and Sinhala from the Oriental Studies Society of Sri Lanka. In 2012, he came to the United States as a religious worker to serve at Sambuddhaloka Buddhist Vihara Inc. in Moreno Valley, California. He traveled across California, Las Vegas, Texas, Arizona, Chicago, and Virginia as a spiritual guide and Buddhist speaker for several years before pursuing a master's in Clinical Psychology at CSUSB. As a professor, Sailesh incorporates modern technology and novel evidence-based tools, such as Generative AI, into his classes. He intends to use technology and research findings to address student mental health challenges, equitable assessment tools, student readiness, resource accessibility, and inclusiveness in higher education. He also focuses on incorporating mindfulness in higher education to develop programs to bolster faculty success in delivering quality education. Sailesh plans to use his doctoral training to identify problems and implement solutions within and beyond the college, county, and state education system. Sailesh Maharjan loves woodwork, painting, cooking, and gardening with his wife and daughter.

James Martinez, EdD, MPH, is an assistant clinical professor with the School of Public Health at Loma Linda University in Loma Linda, California. He teaches courses and workshops on database design, cartography, and Geographic Information Systems (GIS) applications in public health. He is also the Chief Data Officer at McCune Law Group, an environmental justice firm, where he spearheads efforts to enhance decision-making through meaningful data analysis, strategically utilizing data to achieve desired business outcomes. Prior to this he served as an epidemiologist at the Los Angeles County Department of Public Health. James holds a master's degree in epidemiology and a doctorate in health education from Columbia University, NY. His research interests include integrating technology and mobile solutions to enhance education and for improving patient health outcomes.

Thomas Robles, a first-generation Latino from the Inland Empire, embodies resilience in his relentless commitment to expanding opportunities for California college students and their families. His journey, marked by the challenges of higher education, multiple jobs, and caring for his terminally ill parents, is a testament to his determination and unwavering pursuit of academic excellence. These personal experiences have given him a profound understanding of the barriers that first-generation students, particularly those from underrepresented backgrounds, face in accessing and succeeding in higher education. With 17 years of dedicated public service, Thomas has consistently sought to empower underrepresented communities and dismantle systemic barriers to success. His commitment to social justice is unwavering. Currently pursuing an EdD at California State University, San Bernardino, his research focuses on the experiences of first-generation Latino college students, specifically exploring the concept of Family Achievement Guilt. Thomas's scholarly work is deeply informed by his own experiences, allowing him to contribute valuable insights into the challenges students from similar backgrounds face. In addition to his academic pursuits, Thomas is an Adjunct Faculty member at the University of Redlands, where he teaches Internet and Social Media Marketing. He blends practical expertise with academic theory to prepare the next generation of marketers. He also holds key positions at Long Beach City College as an EOPS Program Specialist and at San Bernardino Valley College as a Social Media Coordinator, where he leverages his expertise to enhance student support services and promote inclusive practices. As a board president of the UC Riverside Alumni Network—Orange County Branch and a leader within the San Bernardino Valley College Foundation, Thomas is deeply committed to fostering alumni connections, advocating for the needs of marginalized communities, and driving meaningful change within higher education. His dedication to social justice is not just a part of his work but a reflection of his core values. This commitment is evident in his ongoing work on his dissertation, which examines the impact of Family Achievement Guilt among Latino males at the community college level. Thomas's passion for social justice fuels his desire to continue his career in higher education, where he aims to be a steadfast advocate for students and a catalyst for systemic change.

Kaye Shelton is a Professor of Educational Leadership at Lamar University in the Center for Doctoral Studies. In this role, she teaches doctoral courses for educational technology leadership and research writing and chairs dissertation studies. Since 2011, she has chaired over 100 completed dissertation studies. Previously as Dean of Online Education for Dallas Baptist University, she led the development and ongoing operations of online programs with over 55 majors and degrees offered fully online. She is a certified online instructor and has taught online since 1999. In addition, Dr. Shelton works nationally and internationally with the OLC Quality Scorecard for the Administration of Online Programs. She is also an Online Learning Consortium Quality Scorecard program evaluator and teaches workshops regarding its implementation. Dr. Shelton has been involved with research in online education since 1997 and has advised peer institutions regarding the creation of online learning programs and best practices for teaching online and faculty support. An inductee of the Texas Distance Learning Hall of Fame, an Online Learning Consortium Fellow, and winner of the both the Blackboard and eLearning exemplary online course awards, she has published articles and book chapters along with An Administrator's Guide to Online Education. Dr. Shelton was awarded a Sloan-C Effective Practice award for her research regarding the Quality Scorecard for the Administration of Online Education Programs and the John R. Bourne award for Outstanding Achievement in Online Education.

Valerie A. Storey retired from the University of Central Florida in the School of Teaching, Learning, and Leadership /Educational Leadership Programs as Associate Professor Emerita. She is currently an adjunct professor in the Professional Practice Doctorate at Franklin University, Ohio. She earned her doctoral degree in Educational Leadership and Policy from Peabody College, Vanderbilt University, master's from Manchester University (UK) and her Bachelor's from Leeds University (UK). In the public schools she has served as an administrator at the school and district level. Dr. Storey's primary research interests include: leadership preparation, innovative andragogy, EdD program design, and dissertation models. She is Chair of the American Education Research Association (AERA), Division A: Educational Leadership Outstanding Dissertation Award, and President of the Florida Association of Professors of Educational Leadership. Dr. Storey has over 50 scholarly works in refereed and/or peer-reviewed dissemination outlets.

Leon P. Strayer grew up on an island west of Seattle, Washington, and attended Washington State University. He earned degrees in Psychology and Education to become an elementary school teacher. After teaching first grade for several years, he continued his education at Florida State University and earned his master's degree in Higher Education. Leon has worked in higher education for over 24years where he has gained valuable experiences at large public universities, private institutions, and the California State University system (CSU). He is a doctoral candidate in Educational Leadership at California State University, San Bernardino Currently, and serves as the Assistant Coordinator of Educational Opportunity Program (EOP) Advising Services at Cal Poly Pomona where he serves and supports First-Generation and low-income college students. In addition, Leon will be entering his eighth year of volunteering as a staff mentor for the Male Success Initiative at Cal Poly Pomona. For Leon, one of the most rewarding parts of working in higher education is witnessing the tremendous growth his students make each year and how proud this makes him feel. Leon truly values the relationships that he develops with his students, and he continues to be amazed and encouraged by them every day. When Leon's not assisting students, he enjoys spending time with family and their three pups, going for long runs, drinking strong coffee, watching a good movie, or reading a book in the hammock in their backyard.

Geraldine Torrisi-Steele is an associate professor in the school of Information and Communication Technology at Griffith University, Australia. She is a Senior Fellow of the Higher Education Academy (UK). Her interest in learning and teaching, learning theory, technology for learning, human computer interaction, and leadership distils from her 'pre-academia' experiences in secondary school mathematics and physics teaching, and the design, development, and project management of digital interactive media for learning in higher education. Cutting across her interests is a belief in design with 'the human at the centre'

Amiee Wagner earned a Bachelor of Arts from Otterbein College with a double major in Life Sciences and Physics, a minor in Chemistry, a Master of Science in

Biophysics from Ohio State University, and a Doctor of Education in Organizational Leadership from Franklin University. Her love of science and its applications has not only influenced her teaching style but also deepened her interest in the use of technology to engage learners. Work on several grant-funded, large-scale course redesigns led to Dr. Wagner's nomination as a Redesign Scholar by the National Center of Academic Transformation as part of their Colleagues Committed to Course Redesign (C2R) program. This program gave her the opportunity to meet and work with faculty from more than 50 institutions to support their efforts in improving learning through innovative educational technologies. Dr. Wagner continues to champion the integration of emerging technologies in her current position as a Lead Faculty in Doctoral Studies and IRB Administrator at Franklin University.

Index

A

B

C

D

E

F

G

H

I

L

M

N

P

www.ingramcontent.com/pod-product-compliance
Ingram Content Group UK Ltd.
Pitfield, Milton Keynes, MK11 3LW, UK
UKHW050948290926
15470UKWH00005B/1704

9 798337 305028